THE EXISTENTIALIST READER:
AN ANTHOLOGY OF KEY TEXTS

Edited by

Paul S. MacDonald

ROUTLEDGE
NEW YORK

Published in the U.S.A. and Canada in 2001 by
Routledge
29 West 35th Street
New York, NY 10001
www.routledge-ny.com

By arrangement with
Edinburgh University Press

Typeset in Sabon and Gill Sans
by Bibliocraft Ltd, Dundee, and
printed and bound in Great Britain
by The Cromwell Press, Trowbridge,
Wilts

Cataloging-in-Publication Data is available
from the Library of Congress

ISBN 0 415 93670 5 (hardback)
ISBN 0 415 93663 2 (paperback)

CONTENTS

ACKNOWLEDGEMENTS

I would like to take this opportunity to publicly acknowledge those teachers who decisively influenced my long-standing interest in Phenomenology and Existentialism. My respectful thanks then to the following individuals: to Prof. Arthur Newgarden, State University of New York at Plattsburgh, for awakening my initial curiosity in Husserl's Cartesian Meditations; to Dr Pina Moneta, then at the University of Vermont in Burlington, for her unforgettable seminar on Heidegger's Being and Time; to Prof. Leonard Ehrlich, the University of Massachusetts at Amherst, for making Jaspers' philosophy a living presence in my postgraduate studies; and to Dr Charles Gordon Sanderson, who for more than twenty-five years has shared with me a deep and abiding pursuit of philosophical understanding.

My special thanks to Prof. David Cooper, at the University of Durham, whose own work on Existentialist issues has always been an inspiration to me, and who was the first one to suggest this alternative anthology of major existentialist texts. Jackie Jones and her colleagues at Edinburgh University Press have done an excellent job of sorting out the original outline, making numerous suggestions and following through on many time-consuming tasks.

As with the published work which I have done, and with the work which I hope to do someday, this book is dedicated to my wife Fiona, for her sense of humour and patience, but most of all for kindness and good faith.

My thanks to the following publishers for their permission to reprint copyright material:

HarperCollins, for Martin Heidegger, 'Letter on Humanism', from Basic Writings. English translation © 1977 by Harper & Row, Publishers, Inc. General Introduction and Introductions to Each Selection © 1977 by David Farrell Krell. Reprinted by permission of HarperCollins Publishers, Inc.

The University of Chicago Press, for Jean-Paul Sartre, 'A new, authentic way of being oneself', from Notebooks for an Ethics, translated by David Pellauer. Chicago: University of Chicago Press, 1992.

The University of Chicago Press, for Karl Jaspers, 'Philosophizing Starts with our Situation', from Philosophy, vol. 1, translated by E. B. Ashton. Chicago: University of Chicago Press, 1969.

Penguin Books, for Albert Camus, 'An Absurd Reasoning', from The Myth of Sisyphus, translated by Justin O'Brien. English translation © Justin O'Brien, 1955.

Alfred A. Knopf, for The Myth of Sisyphus and Other Essays by Albert Camus, translated by Justin O'Brien. © 1955 by Alfred A. Knopf, Inc. Reprinted by permission of Alfred A. Knopf, a Division of Random House, Inc.

Taylor & Francis, for Maurice Merleau-Ponty, 'The Cogito', from The Phenomenology of Perception, translated by Colin Smith. London: Routledge and Kegan Paul, 1962.

Citadel Press, for Simone de Beauvoir, 'Ambiguity and Freedom', from The Ethics of Ambiguity, translated by Bernard Frechtman. New York: Philosophical Library, 1948; Citadel Press, 1962.

Citadel Press, for Gabriel Marcel, 'On the Ontological Mystery', from The Philosophy of Existentialism, translated by Manya Harari. New York: Philosophical Library, 1949; Citadel Press, 1961.

Oxford University Press, for José Ortega y Gasset, 'History as a System', translated by William C. Atkinson, from Philosophy and History, edited by R. Klibansky and H. J. Paton. Oxford: The Clarendon Press, 1936.

A NOTE ON THE SELECTION OF TEXTS

There have been several edited volumes of Existential writings in the past forty years; some of them have recently been reissued. Most of these anthologies draw from a wide variety of novelists, essayists, dramatists, and thinkers who fall under a very broad notion of Existential orientation or concern. All of them present their authors' texts in an abbreviated, condensed or even (sometimes) crudely synopsised format. This current reader presents the work of eight philosophers, where each selection is intact as the author intended (the de Beauvoir extract is slightly edited). Although Kierkegaard and Nietzsche are rightly considered to be important contributors to Existential thought, selections from their writings have not been included; pertinent texts have been heavily anthologised and are readily available in many other formats.

INTRODUCTION:
BACKGROUND AND THEMES

THE HORROR AND CHARM OF THINGS

In the spring of 1933, Jean-Paul Sartre and Simone de Beauvoir were sitting together in a small Paris café, drinking aperitifs, smoking strong cigarettes and arguing passionately with their friends about everything, much as French intellectuals have been doing for centuries and still do today. Perhaps at the time they were absorbed in the writings of Hegel and Kant, in preparation for the *aggregation* at the École Normale Supérieure, but their philosophical world was about to be turned upside down. In later life, de Beauvoir recalled this curious, even amusing, incident:

> Raymond Aron was spending a year at the French Institute in Berlin and studying Husserl at the same time as he was preparing his historical thesis. When he came to Paris, he spoke of Husserl to Sartre. We spent an evening together at the Bec de Gaz ... [and] ordered the specialty of the house, apricot cocktails. Aron said, pointing to his glass: 'You see, my dear fellow, if you are a phenomenologist, you can talk about this cocktail and make philosophy out of it!' Sartre turned pale with emotion at this. Here was just the thing he had been longing to achieve for years – to describe objects just as he saw and touched them, and extract philosophy from the process. Aron convinced him that phenomenology exactly fitted in with his special preoccupations: bypassing the antithesis of idealism and realism, affirming simultaneously both the supremacy of reason and the reality of the visible world as it appears to our senses. On the Boulevard Saint-Michel, Sartre purchased Levinas' book on Husserl, and was so

eager to inform himself on the subject that he leafed through the volume as he walked along, without ever having cut the pages.[1]

One may well wonder how accurate her characterisation of Husserl's phenomenology may be, or at least her characterisation of what Sartre *took to be* important in it; in any case, we will sort that out as we go along. It's strange to reflect, with the benefit of hindsight, that if Sartre had been in the right place at the right time, he could have attended in person Husserl's lectures at the Sorbonne in 1929. These lectures, the *Cartesian Meditations*, were published two years later in a French translation by Emmanuel Levinas, who then published a short work on *The Concept of Intuition in Husserl's Philosophy*, the very book which Sartre read on his walk home. Within the next two years, Sartre had gone on leave to Germany where he studied the writings of Husserl, Max Scheler and Martin Heidegger, and returned to Paris virtually 'converted' to the strange and beautiful discipline of Phenomenology. He was so provoked by his reading of Heidegger, to whose works he turned again and again over the next thirty years, that as a prisoner of the Germans during the Occupation, he conducted a seminar on Heidegger's *Being and Time* in the prison camp. In the January 1939 issue of *Nouvelle Revue Française*, not long before the outbreak of hostilities towards France and her allies, he published a very brief article, only four pages long, which concludes with these words:

> Husserl has restored to things their horror and their charm. He has restored to us the world of artists and prophets – frightening, hostile and dangerous, with its havens of mercy and love. He has cleared the way for a new treatise on the passions which would be inspired by this simple truth, so utterly ignored by the refined among us: if we love a woman, it is because she is lovable ... We are delivered from the 'internal life': in vain would we seek the caresses and fondlings of our intimate selves ... like a child who kisses his own shoulder, since everything is finally outside, everything, even ourselves. Outside, in the world, among others. It is not in some hiding-place that we will discover ourselves; it is on the road, in the town, in the midst of the crowd, a thing among things, a man among men.[2]

The imminent passage of the European world will indeed be 'frightening, hostile and dangerous', and the 'havens of mercy and love' will become more and more difficult to find. In the early 1930s, the European nations were in a political, economic and cultural tumult which was to reach a catastrophic culmination in the Second World War. As leader of the Nazi Party, Adolf Hitler was elected Chancellor of Germany, books by Jewish and anti-Nazi writers were publicly burned, the labour unions were suppressed, and the first wave of intellectuals and artists began an exodus from Germany. In the Soviet Union, Stalin's autocratic regime had imposed the Second Five-Year Plan for collectivisation of farms and industry; ethnic pogroms and mass starvation swept through Russia and the Ukraine – within a few years, millions had died. In the United

States, unemployment had reached disastrous levels, financial markets were seriously unstable, drought and famine devastated the Midwest, and President Roosevelt introduced the New Deal to provide federal assistance to farmers, communities and businesses. France went through a delayed reaction to the Great Depression and much of its political energies were devoted to helping its East European allies. Between 1932 and 1935, there were eleven governments and fourteen grand economic plans, an exchange of incoherent power plays which contributed to an increased sense of unease and instability. Existentialism found an especially strong foothold in France just before the war, perhaps due to circumstances of the sort that Paul Guerin remarked on in the spring of 1939: 'The political regime is paradoxical, conservative in purpose, revolutionary at heart, extremist and idealist in its programmes, opportunist and moderate in its actions.'[3]

In those extraordinary years of upheaval and danger, threat and promise, several publications by a number of mostly unknown philosophers would dramatically reshape the central topics of immediate philosophical concern. They were not so much influenced in a thoughtful, meditative way by the events unfolding about them as provoked and threatened by a challenge to the dominant worldview; thus, one could say that these writers became *engaged* in articulating a new vision. For the first time, in these essays and lectures, they will seek to define the philosopher's own intellectual and moral responsibility, a task which could only have been conceived as the consequence of their radically new understanding of the unique status of human being. For the Existentialist thinker, a human being is not the subject of his or her circumstances, nor an instance of a timeless essence, but a unique manner of *existence*. The few years from 1932 to 1935 witnessed the first attempts to spell out this new understanding: Gabriel Marcel's 'Ontological Mystery', Karl Jaspers' three-volume *Philosophy*, Levinas' translation and introduction to Husserl's *Cartesian Meditations*, Ortega y Gasset's *Man and Crisis* and *History as a System*, Martin Heidegger's rise to pre-eminence through his post-*Being and Time* lectures, and Merleau-Ponty's first proposals for studies in the Phenomenology of Perception.

These philosophical statements were in large measure an indication of a profound crisis in philosophy itself, as well as in the European cultural milieu. They were responses, in one way or another, to a complex situation which artists, architects, novelists, film-makers and others were addressing, often in a subversive fashion. Some of the intellectual and cultural issues which were expressed by these cultural agents were also driving forces behind the Existentialist philosophers: the failure of the Enlightenment Project for Reason, the anonymity of bureaucracy in the modern state, the alienation of human beings through oppression, the collapse of an elitist ethics, and the falling away of Christian beliefs, at least among the intellectuals. Until the 1970s (perhaps) and the advent of structuralism, hermeneutics and deconstruction, arguments for and against Existentialism dominated philosophy debates on the Continent. But more than that, the Existentialists' emphasis on alienation, absurdity and anxiety offered an antidote to the complacency, self-satisfaction and every-dayness which became commonplace *after* the Second World War. On the one hand, it is a curious irony to observe that there are few (if any) philosophers who would now consider themselves to be Existentialists. On the other hand, much of our current popular psychological vocabulary, the very way in which we describe ourselves and our relationships with others, is the verbal precipitate of key Existentialist terminology. Sunday newspapers, popular magazines, television chat shows and many others routinely employ phrases such as genuine commitment, personal relationship, realising one's potential, being your own person, significant other and so forth. This comment is *not* a claim that the current usage of clichés like 'being your own person' or 'being honest with yourself' can be traced back to Nietzsche or Sartre's understanding of authentic human existence. Rather the point here is that Existentialist pronouncements from the 1930s onwards decisively shaped the way we think about ourselves now – whether for good or ill.

Existentialism as a philosophical orientation can be difficult to define; in fact, numerous attempts by commentators to proffer a comprehensive definition often fall foul of one or another Existentialist writer who *denies* or in some other way contradicts some component of the definition. It looks like a grand name for a philosophical orientation or discipline that focuses on 'existence'. It doesn't seem to help the reader or student at all when he or she learns that Jean-Paul Sartre, perhaps the most famous Existentialist, rejected this appellation. Simone de Beauvoir, his lifelong collaborator and intimate friend, described their reaction to this label.

> During a discussion organized during the summer [of 1945] . . . Sartre had refused to allow Gabriel Marcel to apply this adjective to him. 'My philosophy is a philosophy of existence; I don't even know what Existentialism is.' I shared his irritation. I had written my novel [*The Blood of Others*] before I had even encountered the term Existentialism; my inspiration came from my own experience, not from a system. But our protests were in vain. In the end, we took the epithet that everyone used for us and used it for our own purposes.[4]

In the years immediately after the war, French philosophers such as Merleau-Ponty, Gabriel Marcel and Emmanuel Levinas, as well as the writer and critic Albert Camus, were grouped under the label Existentialism by journalists hungry for provocative stories about the European intellectual scene, long suppressed during the occupation. The German philosophers, such as Martin Heidegger and Karl Jaspers, had already written extensively about the unique character and structure of human existence and Jaspers anyway was not adverse to being described in these new terms; Heidegger instantly disowned any association with this 'school'.

Lectures and heated debates which took place in the university seminar rooms and especially the Paris cafés were heavily attended; they brought out a number of concerns shared by various writers who began to construct an ancestry or genealogy for Existentialist Philosophy. Two thinkers prior to the turn of the century were generally recognised as foreseeing or even exerting an influence on core Existentialist doctrines, Søren Kierkegaard and Friedrich Nietzsche. Jaspers, Heidegger and Martin Buber explicitly proclaimed their intellectual debt to the precocious Danish philosopher who wrote a hundred years earlier about the leap of faith, the inwardness of subjective truth and the strength to love one thing above all else. Nietzsche's devastating, many faceted critique of the assumptions of traditional western metaphysics and the poverty of Christian morality and the herd instinct paved the way for a new insight on human being, a new concept of human freedom and the triumph of the strong-willed individual. It is important, then, to understand that Kierkegaard and Nietzsche were adopted into the standard 'canon' of Existentialist thinkers *in light of* the concerns of the principal figures from the 1930s. We will later look to the one immensely influential philosopher who came after Nietzsche and who inspired or provoked all of these Existentialist writers – Edmund Husserl and his project for Pure Phenomenology.

It is also important to distinguish Existentialist Philosophy in its many guises from an existentialist fashion that swept through western Europe and the United States in the 1950s. Ever since Descartes complained about the vogue for neo-scepticism and libertine depravity in the early seventeenth century, France (or Paris anyway) has often been the milieu in which its intellectuals' more colorful pronouncements are transformed into both a diagnosis of cultural malaise and its flamboyant exibition. The counter-cultural vogue for existentialist *poseurs* gave rise to the world-weary pseud, brooding on anxiety, absurdity and alienation, reading Kafka and Beckett, and dressed all in black. Simone de Beauvoir observed all of this as early as the autumn of 1947:

> The Existentialist label had been applied to all of our books ... also to a certain style of painting and certain sort of music. Anne-Marie Cazalis had the idea of profiting by this vogue ... While talking to some journalists, she baptized the clique of which she was the center, and the young people who prowled between the Tabou and the Pergola [cafés] as Existentialists ... [They] wore the new 'Existentialist' uniform – black sweaters, black shirts and black pants.[5]

But the counter-cultural appropriation of style, posture and slogan should not distract us from the significance of what the Existentialists were proclaiming – a radical shift in how human beings should think about themselves and their responsibility towards others. Perhaps it would be wise at this point to outline with broad strokes those issues which all of these writers, at one time or another, made into philosophical themes.

To denominate this philosophical orientation as Existentialist means that *existence*, properly speaking, *belongs only to human beings*; in a famous phrase, human being is the only Being for whom Being is an issue. Second, there are various modes in which or through which humans live their existence, various ways in which they comport themselves toward the radical contingency at the root of their existence. Third, in Sartre's famous phrase, 'human existence precedes essence', that is an individual's essence, his 'real' nature, is not fixed in advance, at least not completely fixed beyond his genetic makeup. Rather, in the most significant sense, an individual's essence is determined through his or her own choices. Fourth, an individual can 'fall away' from the difficult task of choosing him or herself and become lost in the public, the herd, or the 'they' (as in, '*they* say that you should always say "thank you" to your host'). If you live your life within this public mentality, with the public's beliefs and values, knowing you haven't really faced your task in making a choice, you are in 'bad faith'. And finally, only human beings are always in the process of becoming, they are always ahead of themselves and oriented toward the future. David Cooper summarises this core Existentialist point of view in the following manner, with the proviso that each of the key terms will need to elucidated:

> Existence ... is a constant *striving*, a perpetual *choice*; it is marked by a radical *freedom* and *responsibility*; and it is always prey to a sense of *Angst* which reveals that, for the most part, it is lived *inauthentically* and in *bad faith*. And because the character of a human life is never *given*, existence is *without foundation*; hence it is *abandoned* or even *absurd*.[6]

FROM THINKING THING TO DIALECTICAL CONSCIOUSNESS

In order to appreciate the details beneath these broad brush strokes, we have to have a better grasp of why these key tenets are taken to be a *rejection* of previous thinking. Existentialism took its point of departure from a profound dissatisfaction with a core doctrine of most modern philosophical considerations of human *nature*. In a crude picture, to be refined as we proceed, the Existentialists discerned a previously undisclosed problem in the presupposition that humans had a nature (or essence) in the same way that worldly things had natures, that is things had invariant natures as entities in the natural world. Subjectivity was conceived in opposition to objectivity, and a subject was characterised in terms of the *essential* feature of thought. Perhaps the earliest and clearest statement of this position is to be found in the writings of Descartes (1596–1650), usually accorded the accolade of 'Father of Modern Philosophy'. In the *Discourse on the Method* (1637) and the *Meditations* (1641), Descartes laid out both the method and principles for a well-grounded investigation of the kind of knowledge which can be gained regarding the world and humans' place in it.

In the famous argument presented in the First and Second Meditation, the meditator examines his belief that everything he knows has been acquired either from or through the senses. But his next thought is that our sensory faculties sometimes deceive us; in fact when we are dreaming, all appearances are deceptive. Should we trust a source of information which we know is sometimes faulty, at least until we have some criterion for discriminating veracious from dubious occasions? Even granted this, can we not be certain of mathematics or logical truths? Surely nothing can impugn the knowledge that two and two equal four or that the angles of a triangle equal the sum of two right angles. But, he asks, what reason do we have for not thinking that some power (an evil demon) may deceive us about the connections a thinker makes between a series of mathematical or logical propositions? His response to this is that, although he may have no body, although the world as he knows it may not in fact exist, it is still true that he *seems* to be warmed, to see light, to hear noises, and so on. No matter how powerful the source of pervasive deception may be, that is no matter how strong the grounds for doubt about sensory knowledge of worldly things are alleged to be, it cannot be the case that he who thinks does not exist. And since he can *conceive* himself as existent without his body, he concludes that his *essence* or true 'nature' is a thinking thing, whose modes are affirming, doubting, willing and believing. In the Fifth Meditation, he reaches the further conclusion that the essence or true 'nature' of body is extension in space and its modes are size, shape and motion/rest. In sum, he claims that human 'nature' is the substantial union of two things, the mind and its body; the reason why such a union obtains is beyond his or anyone's comprehension – it exists by the grace of God.

Descartes' vision of a new philosophy was designed as a universal science which encompassed all the particular sciences; his scientific explanation of human 'nature' was through a combination of rational faculties and mechanical movements. A human was composed of two things, mind and body, each of which could exist independently of the other. His dualistic picture of human 'nature' meant that he had to reconcile the principles that governed mental events or thoughts with physical events. One of his metaphysical principles was that inquiries should first be directed toward the essence of the thing in question and then only later toward its existence. One cannot establish *whether* some thing exists until one has determined *what* the thing is – *essence precedes existence for all things*. The laws of nature in general were ordained by God, whose continuous agency preserves or maintains everything in its being. One's human 'nature' is the union of mind and body maintained by living in accordance with physical laws which teach us about pain and pleasure, hunger and thirst. Human freedom, for Descartes and other rationalists like Spinoza and Leibniz, consists in the voluntary capacity to affirm or deny what one has clearly and distinctly perceived. One is free to the extent that one *understands* the causes of one's beliefs and actions. In ignorance, one may feel some licence to do whatever one chooses, but this notion shows that one is deceived about the real constraints on action which are explicable on mechanical principles. Moral laws are also ordained by God and living according to the 'light of grace' means opening your eyes to what God commands of you in terms of your status as one of His creatures.

For more than a hundred and fifty years an intractable, stubborn debate smouldered between the Cartesian-inspired Rationalists and the Empirical

Philosophy of Hobbes, Locke and Hume. Among the many points of dispute were the priority accorded to rational principles over experience through the senses and the inborn nature of human beings versus the acquisition of contingent, accidental characteristics. The Critical Philosophy of Kant (1724–1804) was seen by its author as a Copernican revolution; in the *Critique of Pure Reason* (first edition 1781, second 1787) and other texts he argued that there was a third way between the extreme positions of Rationalist and Empiricist metaphysics. Copernicus, Kant said, had explained celestial phenomena by appeal to the *movement* of human observers, i.e. on a planet in orbit about the Sun, thus going against the commonsense view that earth-bound observers were stationary and the heavens moved around them. In an analogous fashion, Kant claimed that there were a priori structures of human consciousness, the categories of the understanding, under which cognition of objects was possible. These structures were not given with any empirical content, like Descartes' primary truths, nor were they directives about the actual constraints of natural laws, but were the necessary conditions for any experience at all to occur. The a priori elements in cognition as a whole are the conditions that make representations of objects possible for human beings; the a priori features of objects are those by virtue of which objects conform to these enabling structures. In contrast with both Descartes' substantial thinking thing and Hume's empirical self as 'a bundle of perceptions', Kant postulated the transcendental ego, the necessary ground for the unification of all given experiences in one conscious being. For even the simplest cognition to take place, the mind must have a synthetic unity, i.e. a connection among its states brought about by cognitive operations which coherently combine aspects of an object over time. Kant's transcendental idealism takes the position that the order and regularity humans observe in nature are our own since what we consider to be aspects of the natural world are reflections of our own internal standards.

Moreover, it does seem that, for Kant, the transcendental categories, the understanding's principles and the ego are timeless, universal and ideal concepts. The great German philosopher G. W. F. Hegel (1770–1831) agreed with Kant that human experience presupposes forms of understanding through which humans interpret everything. The fundamental concepts through which what humans perceive is taken to form an objective world comprise what Hegel called our underlying metaphysics, which means 'nothing other than the range of general determinations of thought, the diamond lattice, as it were, into which we bring all material and thereby first make it intelligible.'[7] One of Hegel's points of departure from the Kantian system is his central claim that these higher-order categories, such as being, nothing, substance, causality and so forth, are not timeless, immutable concepts of human understanding, but are conceived in different shapes in different cultures and in different historical periods. Hegel argued that the Kantian categories are *implicit* (folded-into) the fundamental structure of human consciousness, but become *explicit* (folded-out) over time; the cultural education of the human species is the process of becoming conscious of these very concepts. The development of the human species, which varies in its rate over different cultures, involves the discovery of more complex categories and more sophisticated models of natural regularities and human institutions. Since the concepts in terms of which humans think about things are not imposed by outside forces but are inherent in human 'nature', and since we humans are self-moving beings whose force for action lies within, we are able to determine ourselves through our own understanding – and for Hegel such self-determination is *freedom*.

The Hegelian framework for the investigation of the manifold, culture-specific forms in which historical consciousness unfolds had a profound influence on some of the Existentialists, especially in France between the wars. The first six chapters of Hegel's *Phenomenology of Mind (or Spirit)* from 1807 are devoted to an exposition of the structural dialectics of consciousness, dialectic in the Hegelian sense of temporal, oppositional 'moments' in the process of becoming explicit. Hegel's distinctive analyses were transmitted to an eager attentive crowd of French thinkers in a series of lectures by the brilliant Russian emigrée scholar Alexandre Kojève (1902–68). For six years, from 1933 to 1939, Kojève's lectures at the École des Hautes Études provided an exhaustive commentary on Hegel's text, adroitly syncretising the Russian's intimate knowledge of Hegel, Karl Marx and Heidegger, with whom he had recently studied. Along with Sartre's friend and colleague, Jean Wahl, whose new book *The Unhappy Consciousness in the Philosophy of Hegel* had appeared in 1929, it was Kojève who brought Hegel's thought into the arena of Existentialist concerns. His lectures were attended by Merleau-Ponty, Raymond Aron, Jacques Lacan, Georges Bataille, Pierre Klossowski, André Breton and Raymond Queneau, among other later famous French thinkers; there is some doubt whether Sartre attended these lectures in person or read the transcripts. In any case, Raymond Queneau, an innovative novelist, essayist and surrealist-collaborator, later became editor at Gallimard and arranged for the publication of Kojève's lectures on Hegel in 1947.

Stanley Rosen, who knew Kojève in the early 1960s, remarks that Kojève was 'not only a philosopher of extraordinary gifts, but a self-taught economist of world-stature ... He was perhaps the most respected, and in many ways feared, philosopher in France during his mature years.'[8] In his lectures Kojève begins with Hegel's typification of human being as self-conscious; unlike an animal which has only feeling-of-self, a human is conscious of himself, that is self-conscious through the fact of being aware of things. A human becomes absorbed in objects in the natural world, some of which he desires – food to eat, water to drink, and so forth. In contrast with knowledge that keeps him in passive quiet, desire disquiets him and moves him to action. The action taken to satisfy a desire negates or destroys the object as it was on its own (so speak); the action of consumption transforms an object into something else. The desiring ego is an emptiness that receives a positive content by a negating action that assimilates and internalizes some thing that is foreign or alien to the ego. The ego created by the active satisfaction of desire will have the same 'nature' as the things toward which that desire is directed; it will be a thing-like ego, a merely animal ego. For there to be a self-conscious being, desire must be directed toward a non-natural object, toward some thing that goes beyond the given reality. Now, according to Hegel's ingenious dialectic, the only thing that goes beyond the given reality is desire itself. Desire on its own is only 'a revealed nothingness, an unreal emptiness', it is 'the presence of the absence of a reality', and thus entirely distinct from the thing desired, which is 'a static and given real being that stays eternally identical with itself'. But the desire of a self-conscious being can be directed toward another desire, or another being's desire, and thus create by the negating and assimilating action an ego that is basically distinct from the animal ego. Since desire, on the above definition, is realised through actions that negate the given, the very being of this new, emergent ego will be an action within or *for* itself. The self-conscious human ego is negating-negativity, a being with nothing at its core that makes nothing of other beings.

> Therefore, its continuation in existence will signify for this ego: not to be what it is (as static and given being, as natural being, as 'innate character') and to be (that is, to become) what it is not. Thus this [ego] will be its own product: it will be (in the future) what it has become by negation (in the present) of what it was (in the past), this negation being accomplished with a view to what it will become.[9]

This statement is made in almost exactly the same words as one of Sartre's most famous declarations: I am not what I am and I am what I am not; that is, I *am not* my past in the mode of being it; and I *am* my future in the mode of not yet being it.

> I do not know what I shall be, but I do know that it will not be what I now am, and also that nothing I now am or can know will *determine* what I shall be. My anguished being, therefore, is the freedom to become what I am not, to be it already under the mode of not being it.[10]

Hegel goes on to argue that in order for this animal desire to become human desire there must be other human desires that can become its 'objects'. Thus, human beings appear in herds or crowds, multiplicities of desires each directed toward other members of the herd; desire is only human if the ego desires, not just the body, but the *desire* of the other. The self-conscious ego does not want to merely consume the other self-conscious being, like it consumes animal beings, but to possess or assimilate the other's desiring power, that is the *for-itself* wants to be desired, to be loved and, most of all, to be *recognised* in his or her human value. The human being is realised by the active satisfaction of its self-conscious desires, especially for recognition, through the satisfaction of that which it assimilates in much the same way as its animal body is satisfied with other beings' bodies as food. It's not feasible for us to continue our synopsis of Kojève's exemplary exposition except to remark that, in the following chapters,

Hegel builds into his dialectical account several other key features of Existential thought: anxiety as self-conscious awareness of one's own potential non-being, alienation of the for-itself from both itself and its world, the transcendent character of human being which overcomes its own facticity through time, and the concept of freedom as human beings' ownmost (authentic) essence to realise what it can become.

FROM LIGHTNESS AND WEIGHT TO THE LEAP OF FAITH

Kierkegaard is generally regarded as the first thinker to explicitly make his philosophical concerns into what we now understand to be central Existentialist themes. Kierkegaard enters our story through his appropriation of the Hegelian dialectic of the in-itself and the for-itself and his rejection of Hegel's universal 'spirit' of Reason, the telos of which is to bring about all that which is Real. Kierkegaard also rejects Hegel's endorsement of conventional morality and the subjugation of the individual in the realisation of the political good of the state. Instead, he promotes a logic and a truth which is found within the individual conscience, a morality where the individual is higher than the universal, and the incitement to make a leap of faith on the strength of the absurd. For Kierkegaard, the absurd is found within the human situation that unites the finite with the infinite; the only true realisation of this was through Christ's incarnation as a human being. His deeply personal reflections on these issues provide important insights into Existentialist doctrines such as the common 'falling away' from one's calling in the crowd or public mentality, anguish in the face of the ineradicable contingency of one's existence, and the crucial notion that personal faith requires not that one choose among possible courses of action, but that one choose the kind of person one wants to become.

Kierkegaard has a unique place in the western philosophical 'canon'; many of his works defy any sort of category, both because of their literary style, which is often aphoristic, lyrical and elliptical, and also because of his openly religious and polemical message. In one of his later works (*The Point of View of my Work as an Author*), he declares that his entire literary *oeuvre* has been conducted under divine guidance. He thought that he had to adopt the guise of a poet and a philosopher in order to become a true Christian and philosophy was the best method for clarifying his interest in Christ's personal message and its hidden meaning. In order to achieve this purpose, for which he felt philosophical argumentation was decidedly ill-suited, he published many of his titles under pseudonyms, such as Johannes de Silentio, Constantine Constantius or Johannes Climacus. There seem to be several reasons why he would have engaged in such 'indirect discourse' with his readers: to conceal his identity (at least in his early writings); to put himself at one remove from the character's speech; or to draw the reader into a story made more credible by the character's persona. The author's many voices often make it difficult to identify a specific point of view as Kierkegaard's own. To some extent, this issue is made less confusing by his comments on his own works in *Concluding Unscientific Postscript* (itself published under a pseudonym). Nevertheless, it would be wrong to attempt to remove entirely the ambiguity in his authorial voice, because each of these works expresses the 'subjective truth' of one stage on life's way.

The first two stages are best illustrated in his early work *Either-Or* whose text is presented in two volumes, the first written by 'A', the aesthete, the second by 'B', the ethicist. Kierkegaard invites the reader to enter as deeply as possible into the situation of each character and to arrive at his or her own conclusions as the result of the story that unfolds. Hegel's dialectical system forms the backdrop for the two interlinked stories: one position (the thesis) juxtaposed with or gives way to its opposite (the antithesis) and this leads to an emergent third position (the synthesis). One should not jump to conclusions, however, since it would be wrong, though not surprising, to think that the choice was between one or the other; instead one needs the synthesis of these opposing stages in an unforeseen new stage. The aesthete is a person devoted to pleasure; although sometimes melancholic, he is also given to sudden impulsive interests in the fine arts and music, erotic passion and elaborate charades. Perhaps the most famous section of *Either-Or* is 'The Diary of a Seducer', an account of the aesthete's careful plotting of a complex web of situations around a young woman in order to savour each mood, each moment of his intimate intrigue. His greatest concern is to obviate boredom, not to permit the gravity or weight of responsibility to drag him down from his light-hearted and poetic detachment. This Don Juan character would be familiar to many readers today in the character of Tomas in the Czech novelist Milan Kundera's *The Unbearable Lightness of Being*, or Valmont the French seducer in the film *Dangerous Liaisons* (itself based on an eighteenth-century Romantic novel in letters).

The ethicist 'B' responds to the aesthete's rhapsodies on lack of seriousness and the pursuit of transient passions by holding out the inescapable force of the weight which attaches to one's basic choices. Where the aesthete has an unswerving passion toward beauty, pleasure and self-amusement, the ethicist has an unswerving attachment to the ideals of the moral life, ideals such as fidelity, integrity and seriousness. 'B' endorses a conventional bourgeois morality where the moral telos of love between a man and a woman is found in the institution of marriage. Kierkegaard, the true author of these two pictures of alternate ways of living, does not want the reader to assume that it is an arbitrary choice between *either* an aesthetic point of view *or* an ethical point of view, since this would reduce the choice of one's beliefs and the capacity for other choices to the aesthete's criterion of whatever interests one most. Any choice makes sense only in light of a certain goal; having these goals is the consequence of having certain *final* or *deep values*. But these values cannot themselves be the result of a further arbitrary choice, or else an endless regress of choices sets in. It seems to be the case for human agents that these deep values are unjustified or even unjustifiable – one must make *a leap of faith*, but in what direction? The important Existentialist theme here is Kierkegaard's insistence that it is a certain kind of *self* that one chooses through this leap and this self has the choices (or the capacity for choices) which one would want to have. One must be serious then, not as a matter of philosophical detachment, but as a matter of *passion* which is expressed through the self that one chooses *to be*. Kierkegaard shows us through this conflict of alternative ways of life that one must be prepared to consider one's choices as valid subjects for *anxiety*, to understand that one really *cares* about the life guided by those choices, since one can *lose* those things (and persons) one cares for most. With regard to marriage, the seducer cannot choose to be married for a while, to find out what it 'feels like', since this is to completely falsify the sense of marriage as the loving union with another *for the rest of one's life*. The terrible fear (which the author himself had known) for anyone truly in love with another is the awareness of future life without the loved one.[11]

In his next work, *Fear and Trembling*, Kierkegaard turns to a careful scrutiny of this leap of faith and presents the next 'stage' on life's way, that of religious faith. His starting point is the Genesis story of Abraham, commanded by his God to sacrifice his beloved son Isaac. The 'author', Johannes de Silentio, begins his meditation with the remark that either Abraham should be condemned as a murderer or he should be an 'object' of the utmost admiration. According to any ethical standard, whether it endorses Christian morality or the philosophical morality of Kant or Hegel, Abraham should be condemned – there is no possible ethical ground upon which his (attempted) action could be construed as morally right. But ethical standards, such as those presented above by 'B', have universal application, that is they apply to everyone irrespective of their circumstance or station in life. Abraham chooses to *suspend the ethical* for a higher purpose, he chooses to consider the individual (himself) as higher than the universal. He does this on the *strength of the absurd*, the absurd belief that, through his murder of Isaac, he will *both* follow God's command (which cannot be a bad thing) *and* retain his son (which is a good thing).

The central point of Kierkegaard's insight into the leap of faith is that the ethical universal ignores the deeply private, the unique character of the individual. There are some beliefs and values which are a matter of such deep conviction that, unless one acted in accordance with them, one could not be *true to oneself*. In acting in a conventional moral sense, a person becomes anonymous or falls back into the public way of behaving; *anyone* could have or should have behaved in the way that you did. But this would be to give up one's identity, the self one had chosen for the purpose of realising certain deeply held beliefs. Personal faith stands above the claims of conventional morality, since there are occasions when competing claims for moral action cannot resolve the question of how one should behave. However, Kierkegaard does think that most of the time, as a general rule, one should follow moral guidelines; the significance of his analysis of Abraham's unusual dilemma is to bring to the surface what factors allow one to *make an exception* of oneself. These cannot be factors about one's other interests and purposes because then these would be the basis for one's deepest values. Kierkegaard's distinctively Existentialist treatment of these issues makes a theme of the *subjective truth of inwardness*, a passionate attachment to the truthfulness or authenticity of one's being. This is disclosed through a uniquely human comportment towards the absurdity that lies at the heart of one's existence – one is not responsible for the *fact* that one exists, but one is responsible for the person one becomes.[12]

THE INWARD DEPTH OF TRUTH

In his final great work, the *Concluding Unscientific Postscript*, Kierkegaard criticises the concepts of subject and object as they are used to support the doctrine of objectivity as publicly available and historically unfolding, in accord with an inner necessity, and the related notion that subjectivity is the special characteristic of conscious thought, the hidden faculty of abstract thinking and contemplation. He argues that the way in which an object exists is nothing like the way in which a human being exists; 'the existing subject, on the other hand, is *engaged in existing*, which is indeed the case with every human being.' He returns to the issue of subjective truth several sections later:

> Whether truth is defined more empirically, as the conformity of thought and being, or more idealistically, as the conformity of being with thought, it is in either case important to carefully note what is meant by being ... Take heed lest the knowing spirit be tricked into *losing itself* in the indeterminate, so that it fantastically becomes a something that no existing human being ever was or can be, a sort of phantom with which the individual occupies himself upon occasion ... That the knowing spirit is an existing individual spirit, and that every human being is such an entity *existing for himself* is a truth which I cannot too often repeat.[13]

The lesson here is that abstract thought, in its contemplation of the essence of human being, its efforts to grasp in rational insight the invariant within the variant, only ever discovers human being *in general*, in its biological or social or economic character. But this will never avail a person who asks questions of his or her own life; this perspective adopts the view of conventional, publicly agreed upon value standards, whether moral or non-moral values. Conventional value codes, such as ethical precepts, can only ever treat each agent as *an example of the type*, i.e. as an instance of the universal, human being. One should bear in mind that this universal, absolute feature of Kantian ethics is usually considered to be one of its strongest points. But the example of Abraham confronted with the demand to murder his son Isaac is a perfect illustration of the utter failure of such moral principles to make sense of his actions (or projected actions). This failure occurs for the simple reason that Kierkegaard emphasises again and again – Abraham is addressed through God's injunction as a unique individual. No one can replace Abraham, no one can stand in his place, just as no one can stand in *my* place in terms of some of the direct duties that I have to others and they have to me.

The unique individual, addressed through a summons to carry out its very own duty, has a special relation to the truth.

> For an existing spirit *qua* existing spirit, the question of the truth will
> again exist. The abstract answer has significance only for the abstraction
> into which an existing spirit is transformed when he abstracts *qua* existing
> individual ... It is therefore an existing spirit who is now conceived as
> raising the question of truth, presumably in order *that he may exist in it.*[14]

In this formulation, Kierkegaard clearly differentiates the human being as an
instance of human in general from the human as *this one here*, this one who
questions or who is *in question*. To abstract literally means 'to pull out of' (as in
'tractor' or 'traction'), so his point is that in abstraction from one's uniqueness,
one's ownmost being, something is lost, some factor which cannot be compen-
sated for by building in a reference which could be made an index for some
other person. It was through the process of 'abstraction' in the Second Meditation that Descartes arrived at the essence of the meditating self as a 'thinking
thing'; in another connected passage he claims that one must know *what* some
thing is before one can know *that* some thing is (or exists). Thus Kierkegaard
rejects both of these claims, since on his view these assertions transform the
human into another kind of object, one which is privileged by being conscious
and aware of itself. In addition, the reader might also want to bear in mind that
when we come to Heidegger's exposition of Dasein as the being for whom being
is an issue and who lives in the 'clearing' of truth, Kierkegaard had already
expressed similar Existentialist sentiments.

The pseudonymous editor Climacus continues:

> Existence itself, namely, existence as it is in the individual who raises the
> question and himself exists, keeps the two moments of thought and being
> apart, so that reflection presents him with two alternatives. For an
> objective reflection the truth becomes an object, something objective,
> and thought must be pointed away from the subject. For a subjective
> reflection the truth becomes a matter of appropriation, of inwardness, of
> subjectivity, and thought must probe more and more deeply into the
> subject and his subjectivity.[15]

The truth which the subject lives within must somehow bear the mark of its
diremption from the concept of truth as conformity of thought with its object,
for the subject is more than any thought could summarise, more than any
concept could contain, and the 'thing' towards which this thought (if one could
have one) is directed is not an 'object' for the self, though, of course, it can be
an 'object' for others' thoughts. Kierkegaard's definition of this new existentialist truth is: 'An objective uncertainty held fast in an appropriation process of
the most passionate inwardness, [it is] the highest truth attainable for an
existing individual.'[16] This is a difficult statement to understand, to say the
least, but then he once remarked that, since so many people thought that so
much worth knowing was easy, he set himself the task of making difficulties
everywhere.

The task which is set for every human being engages him in existence, but it is not a task which can be completed *within* one's life, like sailing round the world, or publishing a great book, it is the task of living one's life as one's own. 'The task of becoming subjective furnishes a human being with enough to do to suffice him for his entire life; so that it is not the zealous individual but only the restless one who manages to get through with life before life gets through with him.'[17] The task of becoming subjective leads the individual to the insight that there are four, not just three, spheres of existence: the aesthetic, the ethical, religious 'A' and religious 'B'. An individual in the aesthetic sphere is committed to enjoyment, in the ethical sphere to absolute choice, and in the first sphere of the religious attitude, after the leap of faith, to self-annihilation before God. Where before he had thought that faith was self-contained and oriented toward a personalised duty to God, in the *Postscript* he asserts that there is a second higher sphere of faith, religious 'B', in which an individual can be committed to a personalized cause or grand project. In the first religious attitude, the contradictions in the aesthetic and ethical spheres become apparent and demonstrate that the attempt to become a self will necessarily result in failure. In this state of faith he says that the individual arrives at 'the highest pitch of perfection when he becomes suited to God through becoming absolutely nothing in himself.'

But this surrender or self-annihilation before God does not mean that one returns in despair to the levelling of the present age, the average everyday being of humankind. Rather faith brings with it the promise that only once the individual gives up trying to be a self can it overcome this levelling. Religious 'A' defines the finite in terms of a person's desires and the infinite in terms of a person's absolute indifference to the satisfaction of those desires. To maintain an absolute relation to the absolute goal and a relative relation to relative goals is to be absolutely indifferent to the satisfaction of one's desires and thus to allow all of these desires to have only relative significance. The point of this religious attitude is to attempt to satisfy one's needs and desires in the present while remaining absolutely indifferent to their being satisfied in the future. But now another contradiction becomes apparent, since how could anyone be said to have specific, personal needs and desires if one is indeed absolutely *indifferent* to their satisfaction? In this case, a person can neither overcome the levelling of the everyday nor can he or she become invulnerable to his or her needs and desires not being satisfied. Kierkegaard proposes a second faithful attitude, religious 'B', in which a person comes to understand that only a personalised commitment to something concrete and specific, something that is intrinsically one's own, can overcome both levelling and immunity to the hazards of fortune. But one must never forget that even this more advanced and enlightened state of faith is maintained only through the leap in the face of the absurd. The person who avows the religious 'B' attitude can learn 'to live joyfully and happily ... every moment on the strength of the absurd, every moment ... to find, not repose in the pain of resignation, but joy on the strength of the absurd.'[18]

HOW TO BECOME WHAT ONE IS

Nietzsche's place here follows some of the themes set forth in the section above on Kierkegaard. Here we will explore some of Nietzsche's most distinctive 'teachings', especially as they relate to the later Existentialists' appropriation of this great 'philosopher of the future'. These 'teachings' include: his utter contempt for 'herd' morality, whether secular or organised Christian; the notion of the 'free spirit' who stands above 'the tablets of good and bad'; the message about the 'death of god' without whose assurance all things are permissible; the key concept of the bad conscience which is closely aligned with the Existentialist notion of 'bad faith' and inauthenticity; the assertion that all claims to knowledge can be collapsed into their constituent perspectives, that 'truth is an army of metaphors on the march'; and the strange, *non-Existentialist* doctrine of the eternal recurrence of the same.

Nietzsche's begins his exposé of the real 'nature' of moral beliefs with an experimental history about the origins of values in terms of a society's customs. He imagines a prehistoric community whose energies are taken up with defence against aggressors; this community has no morality or moral code, merely rules for survival. The persons who are most admired are warriors and leaders who are called 'good', i.e. 'noble' or *aristos*, in a non-moral sense. When the safety of the community has been assured these strong persons become a threat because of their power; the fear is that they might turn their power against their fellows. From fear of this projected threat, the weak join together and make a system of rules that will constrain the behaviour of everyone, weak as well as strong. According to Nietzsche, fear is thus the mother of morality, and the values codified through this basic insecurity will be those of pity, charity and humility, since these are the values that disempower the strong. Some kind of slave or herd morality has always been a success in history, for various reasons: there are more weak than strong persons, they are more cunning and they have constructed myths to support their story. The weak construct religious beliefs and rituals devoted to the worship of vengeful gods who side with the meek. In this sense, a moral code is a device used by the weak majority to assert and maintain their power against others. The priestly leaders and elders of the weak majority attempt to indirectly legitimate their version of a moral code by exploiting the idea of free will so that the weak can then claim that they have chosen *not* to exercise their own strength; thus, there is no need for anyone to display power in order to be right.

Nietzsche does not hold that such crucial beliefs are false *because* they serve the values of the weak. If a moral belief is mistaken this has nothing to do with its historical origin; perhaps one might argue that its correctness or incorrectness is not tied into its importance in social evolution. The basic belief in free-choice, that there are actions which can be praised or blamed, rests on a mistaken folk psychology which posits a mythical subject (the self) which is distinct from its overt forms of behaviour. In contrast with this, Nietzsche's doctrine of will to power says that all actions (in some sense) are selfish, since their purpose is to maintain or increase the agent's power; but there is no other thing, the self, which is singled out as being the locus of selfishness. The 'bad' conscience, which many of the weak experience, is the directing inwards of aggressive instincts (or drives) that no longer have an external outlet. The belief in equality among humans is absurd because there is always a rank order of importance among members of any society, a ranking in terms of skills, character and actual resources. And finally, suffering is the precondition of an individual's achievement of goals and realisation of values; the sentiment of pity is to be deplored because it is another kind of suffering that helps neither the pitier nor the pitied.

Nietzsche's relation to Existentialist thought has often been recorded, though the details of this relation are usually little discussed; his alleged 'preview' of many central Existentialist themes is ambiguous and sometimes misleading. In his own eccentric 'destruction' of traditional metaphysics he often exaggerated what had been downplayed, rejected the most prevalent assumptions and turned common sense upside-down – but these extremist views alone would hardly differentiate him from other philosophers, such as Berkeley or Leibniz or Wittgenstein. Since Existentialist thinkers such as Heidegger, Jaspers and Sartre were resolved to expunge the metaphysical predilections for detached theory, neutral objectivity, the diremption of fact from value and so forth, it would not be difficult to uncover somewhere one of Nietzsche's aphorisms which supported their own view. Nietzsche himself characterised his hypercritical reflection as turning the false into the true, the improbable into the probable, reality into an illusion, and other gymnastic inversions. Nietzsche's writing style and his general critical posture go hand in hand; short, pithy micro-essays, sometimes only two or three lines long, are ideally suited to a form of communication which is perspectival, multifaceted, puzzle-setting and designed to shock. Alex Nehamas has claimed that Nietzsche's aphorisms are often hyperbolic; an exaggerated statement 'attracts attention, and in its startlingness reveals quite unexpected connections. But the aphorism is an essentially isolated sentence or short text, and precisely because of its isolation it disarms the hyperbole as, at the very same time, it highlights it.'[19]

On the other hand, his positive, forward-looking challenges to dumbstruck everyday thinking follow from his critical rejection of some of the standard distinctions made in traditional metaphysics. He repudiates the alleged dichotomies between mind and matter, human and world, intellect and passion (or drive), cause and effect, and subject versus object. The world is not some thing which lies over against human being: 'the whole pose of "man against the world", of man as a "world-negating" principle, of man as the measure of the value of things . . . the monstrous insipidity of this pose has finally come home to us and we are sick of it.'[20] In the First Essay in *The Genealogy of Morals*, he debunks the notion of an independent, self-contained subject, the possessor of a soul or spirit; the 'subject' is nothing more than a highly concealed fiction with which the weak deceive themselves.[21] And against the Cartesian and Kantian privilege accorded to the intellect, the faculty or innate power of rational insight, Nietzsche proposes instead the cumulative outcome of contending drives. In *The Gay Science*, he ridicules Spinoza's assertion that intellectual understanding subsumes the passions; one is wrong to think that the intellect 'must be something conciliatory, just and good – something that stands essentially opposed to the drives, while it is actually nothing but a certain behavior of the drives toward one another.'[22]

These vigorous repudiations of categorical distinctions are entirely compatible with Nietzsche's strange ontology of the will to power; more than that, it helps to make sense of his comments about cause and effect, the fiction of the soul, and so forth. A careful analysis of his ontological schema does show that many of his distinctively Existential claims are the precipitates of a stormy new vision of the constitution of the world, worldly things and humans' place in the world. In conjunction with his 'prehistory' about the genesis of moral values and the consequent repression of drives, his ontological framework provides the setting for an appreciation of his most distinctive Existential-psychological statements. The doctrine of the will to power is perhaps Nietzsche's most misunderstood 'teaching'. The will to power is not the egocentric pursuit of pleasure, nor is it the constant struggle for mastery, though some of its manifestations appear as mastery over others. Every single thing, not just a sentient and conscious being, really *is* a composite or collective of wills to power. This doctrine is an ontological commitment at the most basic level, in terms of which an individual thing's ordinary, observable properties are true of that thing only relative to some perspective. It may seem a strange teaching indeed to claim that *every* thing is a will to power, or collective of wills to power, as though an insensate object could ever *will* anything. The closest version of Nietzsche's postulate familiar to some readers is Spinoza's concept of *conatus*, the drive to maintain oneself in being. But our difficulty in understanding this doctrine is due to our ineradicable presumption that there are distinct, isolable and independent objects – and Nietzsche denies this also. His use of the concept of will to power is applied not to agents, such as animals and humans, but to force (*Kraft*) or drive (*Trieb*, which is often misleadingly translated as 'instinct'); the simplest units of these drives are energy points or quanta.[23] Nietzsche claims that it is precisely because humans are constituted out of drives or forces that we do not *will* anything in the ordinary sense of the word.

An individual thing is a collective or composite of power points or energy quanta, each with its own internal ends, the whole organised according to a higher-order or dominant power which strives to reach an optimal balance between its competing drives. However, this striving within the individual is not itself an end, but a continuous process of becoming. Animals and humans are not different in kind from other things, they are only different in the degree of variety, intensity and complexity of their drives; this teaching strongly segregates Nietzsche from Existentialists who claim that humans have (or are) a special mode of existence. Despite this, some humans do indeed aim at end-states, such as comfort, security, tranquillity and so forth, but these are deficient modes of being, they have 'fallen away from' their essences as wills to power.[24] In this regard, Nietzsche's trenchant comments on herd mentality, the poor bastards who only want a bit of peace and quiet, are strongly resonant with the Existentialist analysis of the unaware person's lostness in the 'they'-self, the crowd, the everyday manner of existing.

On Nietzsche's view the will to power comes in one of two basic forms, either active or reactive. The contrast between wills to power which strive for optimal growth and those which are directed towards rest and quietude is crucially important for Nietzsche's constructive philosophy as a whole; it shows up on many different levels and through many different topics. The reactive or deficient human will to power is one which is, more often than not, obedient to another will to power, not through some external compulsion, but through the internalisation of the stronger will's beliefs and values, and its adoption of those in preference to its own beliefs and values. A reactive will to power is one which has a tendency, perhaps ingrained through habit, to obey another by being persuaded into willing and valuing goals or end-states which are alien to its original goals. Moreover, a reactive will can do so not only by obeying the stronger through slavish allegiance, but also by taking over the other's goals and values as something to struggle *against*. The negative version of the reactive will is one which has internalised the guiding principles of the stronger in order to guide itself away; it does so through negation and denial.[25]

In contrast with the slave as member of the herd who adopts the master's values in a positive manner, the *resentful* individual holds these values close to his heart, so to speak, in order to repudiate them. On the other hand, the active will to power is more rare, it keeps allegiance with itself and to the values which favour its own personalised balance of internal drives. The active will commands others from an internal perspective through the appropriation of their perspective and the incorporation of their own first-order end-states. These are the 'free spirits', those who are able to overcome their own limitations, to make others' reactive wills subordinate to their own. They are confident in the worth of the values they are directed towards, confident in the strength to bring about a world which exemplifies those values. For Nietzsche, the value of a will to power lies in its specific, personal form or style, that is a style which confers commitment on its own original goals and values. Nietzsche's position on the issue of genuine commitment to one's own values has a strong resonance with the Existentialist notion of an authentic mode of human existence, and in particular to Merleau-Ponty's description of an agent's bodily-affective style.

Nietzsche's doctrine of energy points or power quanta and their basis in drives helps to explain two of his other distinctive theses: that human beings do not have any real freedom, except in the case of 'free spirits' or hopeful monsters, as he calls himself at one point; and that an individual's directedness towards his or her own thoughts, actions and goals is best described in terms of corporeal intentionality, what Heidegger would later call 'comportment'. Nietzsche's denial of the unity of the self in the Kantian or Hegelian sense is the logical result of his construal of the individual as the team effort of competing drives; his denial of the unity of the self is also coupled with his derogation of consciousness as the seat or locus of thinking.

> [The] ridiculous overestimation and misunderstanding of consciousness [is that] one thinks that it constitutes the kernel of man; what is abiding, eternal, ultimate, and most original in him. One takes consciousness for a determinate magnitude. One denies its growth and its intermittences. One takes it for the 'unity of the organism'.[26]

Nietzsche proposes that consciousness is a functional state in the evolutionary development of human being.[27] In addition he argues that contemplation or abstract reflection, which philosophers have elevated to a pre-eminent status via the exemplification of theoretical insight, is a strategy by the weak-willed to turn detachment and dispassion into an intellectual virtue. What we take to be the 'object' of conscious intentions and our cognitive directedness towards that 'object' are rather a total involvement at all levels in a sort of corporeal intentionality in which conscious thought plays a derivative role. Much of what we take to be an overt steering toward thoughts and goals takes place at an unconscious level. 'By far the greatest part of our spirit's activity remains unconscious and unfelt ... conscious thinking, especially that of the philosopher, is the least vigorous and therefore also the relatively mildest and calmest form of thinking.'[28] And further:

> We could think, feel, will, and remember, and we could also 'act' in every sense of that word, and yet none of this would have to 'enter our consciousness' ... The whole of life would be possible without, as it were, seeing itself in a mirror. *For what purpose*, then, any consciousness at all when it is in the main superfluous?[29]

Nietzsche's dismissal of consciousness as a glorified fiction leads to his notion of the levelling down of average human understanding and humans' place in the world. It is hardly the case that abstract contemplation provides the thinking person with an avenue to genuine rational insights; instead, contemplation places too great a weight on the thin membrane which separates 'inside' from 'outside', subject from object.

> Whatever becomes conscious becomes by the same token shallow, thin, relatively stupid, general sign, herd signal; all becoming conscious involves a great and thorough corruption, falsification, reduction to superficialities and generalizations. Ultimately the growth of consciousness becomes a danger; and anyone who lives among the most conscious Europeans even knows that it is a disease.[30]

This thesis brings our exposition back to his story about the genesis of conventional morality: disease indicates a reactive will to power, the condition of the weak-willed who incorporate others' goals and values. The weak-willed are members of the herd or mass who have only the thinnest, most pedestrian experiences. But more than that, they are afflicted with a *bad conscience*, 'bad' in the sense of spoiled or diseased as befits their deficient mode of existence. Nietzsche devotes the Second Essay in *The Genealogy of Morals* to a *tour de force* exposition of the bad conscience. It is a 'serious illness' which emerges when humans have found security and peace; a 'dreadful heaviness', something like Kierkegaard's gravity and weight, crushes them, repressing or pushing under the drives which had been deflected from strong goals and values, and impressing them with the burden of guilt, an awareness of living in falseness. Nietzsche says that it is the inward human suffering, or under-going, of humans' own nature: humans suffer *from* being human. As such, this is a striking precursor of Sartre's notion of *bad faith*, living out a false existence, that is carrying forward a grand project which is not one's own. The weak-willed are alienated from themselves, from a genuine understanding of their own true natures, that is their nature or essence whose basic units are wills to power. But although these essential (in the sense of necessary) power units are given in advance to each individual, it is within each person's scope to optimise his or her dominant drives in order to realise self-chosen goals and values.

The subtitle of Nietzsche's last book *Ecce Homo* is 'How One Becomes What One Is', and here he affirms one of the most powerful Existentialist themes. Those philosophers of the future whom he often addresses, the free spirits who sail on open seas, look toward an exemplary individual who will show them that a true human being is 'a way, an episode, a bridge, a great promise'.[31] As early as in the Third of the *Untimely Meditations* Nietzsche had already formulated his thoughts on the central idea that a person with a *good* conscience creates his or her own goals and values, or at least aligns their strongest pregiven drives toward a future project of their own design. 'Those who do not wish to belong to the mass need only to cease taking themselves easily; let them follow their conscience, which *calls* to them: "Be your self! All that you are now doing, thinking, desiring, is not you yourself."'[32] Thus Nietzsche provides the attentive reader with a clear expression of the Existentialist thesis of authenticity, the clear-headed apprehension of one's own limitations, the projection of personal goals and values, and the resolution to follow through this project. An aphorism in *The Gay Science* succinctly states this view: 'What does your conscience say? You shall become the person your are.'[33] This may seem an incoherent, even impossible, precept given his later advocacy of the doctrine of the Eternal Recurrence of the Same, the hypothesis that everything that has happened in your life, in anyone's life, will happen again and again, in the same sequence, without end. In conjunction with his denial of any real basis for human freedom, in what way could anyone *not* become who they already are?

THE HEAVIEST THOUGHT

This *becoming who one is* pertains not to the selection of various options in the future, but to an *affirmative attitude* towards everything that one has done in the past and will do in the future; in his famous phrase, it means that you are willing to say 'yes' to every moment, to make that moment your own. Becoming is a continual process of integration of one's ownmost (i.e. authentic) features, habits and beliefs within one whole whose overall 'profile' is a matter of style. One can attain a level of self-understanding sufficient to realise that even older, discarded features, ones that have been *disowned are* one's own, in the sense that they were necessary for one's subsequent development. One can discern or learn the lesson of this difficult injunction by reviewing some of the salient points that lead to Nietzsche's paradoxical position. First, every individual is made up of a collective of will to power units that are expressed through drives. Second, the drives themselves are not chosen by a mature person, but are given to every infant at birth; they are a biological-genetic inheritance. Third, an individual's drives are either partly disaggregated in a weak or reactive will, or they are organised under 'a single predominant impulse' in a strong or active will. Fourth, the weak-willed, either of the placid or resentful sort, subordinate their goals and values to the strong-willed, and the strong-willed harmonise their drives in order to attain their self-chosen goals and values. Fifth, although the strong person or 'free spirit' can no more choose options and traits than he or she could choose his or her drives, the free spirit has the *flexibility* to make use of all the contributive elements within his or her character in a never finally completed whole. And last, the flexible or plastic way in which one expresses this personalised integration is a form of artistic creation, and the 'profile' this integration process assumes over time is an artistic style.[34] Nietzsche's remark that for a person to exist as a concrete individual is an art should remind the reader of Kierkegaard's claim that 'the subjective thinker is not a man of science, but an artist; existing is an art', and further, that 'the subjective thinker has a form … and this form constitutes his style.'[35]

The nightmare scenario which Nietzsche's haunted imagination constructed is first famously expressed in *The Gay Science* (section 341) and becomes one of the dominant motifs in Book Three of *Thus Spoke Zarathustra*. What if a demon were to come to you 'in your loneliest loneliness' and inform you of 'the greatest weight' – 'this life as you now live it and have lived it, you will have to live once more and innumerable times more' – how would you respond? It is vitally important to bear in mind that here (and elsewhere), Nietzsche expresses this claim as a hypothesis: *what if* your life were to recur again and again, what *would* you do, what would *you* do? Nietzsche answers on behalf of all free spirits that there are two possible attitudes, joy and despair, though some commentators have also suggested a third attitude, indifference. The weak-willed, the poor in 'spirit', would react with despair, because the becoming of their lives was the unfolding of others' goals and values, their lives were tainted with guilt, disgust and resentment – their life was not their *own* life. On the other hand the strong-willed would react with joy because the becoming of their life was itself the exercise of affirmation and integration, the unfolding of their own goals and values.

The hardest thought is an Existentialist challenge, a test of one's resolve:

> The question therefore is not whether I would or would not do the same things again; in this matter there is no room for choice. The question is only whether I would *want* to do the same things all over again. This is simply the question whether I am glad to have done whatever I have done already, and therefore the question whether I would be willing to acknowledge all my doings as my own.[36]

On first glance one might think that life in its recurrence is a replay of a videotape, a tape which reaches STOP, then rewinds to the START and plays again. But this interpretation does not take account of the Nietzschean distinction between the real world of energy quanta and the apparent world, accessible only through diverse perspectives, of things, persons and events which are simply the 'sum of their effects'. One plausible construal of his existential test of courage is that the *elements* or components of one's life are the 'things' that will recur again and again; the strong-willed person exercises flexible control over the adumbration of these elements. On this latter reading, two metaphors for understanding one's life have been stricken out: your life is *not* a narrative that you invent, episode by episode, driving it ahead with an authorial intention or purpose; *nor* is your life a role in a play written by a supreme author, where each scene is permanently blocked out in advance. Perhaps, as Milan Kundera suggests in his novel *Immortality*, a person's life is more like a musical theme with variations: the theme is the basic melodic line which recurs again and again, but each time new friends, new lovers, emergent events and so on confer another variation on the basic theme.[37] To some degree, a strong-willed person can exercise an influence on these variations: he or she can conduct the musical unfolding in a manner which is concordant or discordant, harmonious or not harmonious. In Nietzsche's terms, the basic elements of the theme are given through the preselected wills to power, and artistic control of the variated episodes imparts one's distinctive style. It is thus indeed within *your power* that your theme sounds out like a dull drone, or a lament, or a joyous hymn.

TO THE THINGS THEMSELVES

Edmund Husserl (1859–1938), perhaps more than any other thinker after Nietzsche, had a profound and wide-ranging influence on some of the decisive features of Existentialist philosophy. His phenomenological project was pursued with relentless tenacity from *The Logical Investigations* (1900) through the transcendental idealist stage of the *Ideas* (1913) to his final epoch-making work *The Crisis of European Sciences* (1937). Phenomenological analyses of the intentional, temporal and horizontal structures of consciousness provided thinkers as diverse as Heidegger, Sartre and Merleau-Ponty with the framework and conceptual tools to articulate the unique ontological status of human beings and the constitution of a meaningful world. Husserl conceived of phenomenology as a universal, a priori 'science' (*Wissenschaft*, 'form of knowing') which is a self-founding first philosophy articulated through rigorous descriptive investigations of conscious phenomena, exactly as *and only as* the phenomena are given to consciousness. This stricture means that there can be no legitimate recourse to any other framework of explanation, such as the natural-scientific model, which itself would be constructed on the basis of such achieved knowledge. In addition, the descriptive analyses are strictly the consequence of a specific methodological procedure that 'brackets' or suspends the presumed thesis of the world's being; this is the phenomenological reduction or *epochē*.

In the twentieth century, Existentialist thinkers were well known for the radical position they took on consciousness and human subjectivity; this new philosophical position was made possible by Husserl's devastating critique of naturalist explanation in empirical psychology. In the Prolegomena to the *Logical Investigations* (1900) and his lengthy article, 'Philosophy as Rigorous Science' (1911), Husserl step by step worked through the intractable difficulties of a naturalist attitude in the human sciences, whose concept of 'scientific' knowledge is to render philosophy in its own image. This rendering takes place on at least two fronts: the attempt to make a natural phenomenon of consciousness, including intentionally immanent data; and the attempt to naturalise ideas and all other absolute ideals and norms. This new naturalised philosophy believes that it has already attained the status of an exact science, and looks down with disdain on all other philosophical enterprises. But all natural science, said Husserl, is naïve in one pre-eminent respect – the nature that it seeks to investigate is simply there: every scientific judgement participates in the tacit existential positing of the world's being, in its acceptance of the world as already given. But it is inappropriate to treat consciousness in this manner. Consciousness is not itself given as just another part of the natural world; it is the being who *gives sense* to its experiences of the world and of other subjects. The *naïveté* of the empirical psychologists, in their attempt to ground logical laws on the factual character of mental processes, consists in their acceptance of, first, the *correspondence* of immanent conscious contents with the 'objects' of its experiences, and second, that conscious contents are causally related to their 'objects'.

Unlike physical nature, the 'nature' of the mind is in principle not a unity that could be experienced in a number of separate perceptions as individually identical, not even in perceptions of the same subject. Here there is no distinction between appearance and being: 'If nature is a being that appears in appearances, still appearances themselves ... do not constitute a being which itself appears by means of appearances lying behind it.'[38] From the phenomenological point of view, there is, strictly speaking, only one nature, the one that appears in the appearance of things and that includes the appearance or phenomena of nature in the first sense. A phenomenon is not a substantial unity and has no real properties; it knows of no real parts, no real changes and no causality. Nor does a psychical phenomenon have a temporal unity; it comes and goes, and does not retain an enduring identical being. It is simply not experienced as something that appears, rather it is a 'vital experience' or what he later calls 'living through'. Here Husserl's German apparatus allows him to distinguish *Erlebnis* (lived experience) from *Erfahrung* (outer experience), terms which retain their original roots, *Leben* or 'life' and *Fahrt* or 'path'.

In *Ideas First Book* (1913) Husserl says that no real being is necessary to the being of consciousness itself. Consciousness and real being are not two coordinate *kinds* of being which, under the right circumstances, are related to or connected with one another. Only things which are of the same kind, whose proper essences have a similar sense, can become connected in a legitimate manner, that is can be considered as proper parts of a whole. Mental processes which are immanent to consciousness comprise absolute being, whereas the causal processes of worldly things pertain to transcendent being – thus a 'veritable abyss' yawns between consciousness and reality. Consciousness considered in its pure sense must be thought of as a 'self-contained complex of being', that is an ordered arrangement of absolute being into which nothing can penetrate and out of which nothing can escape. On the other hand, the whole world of spatio-temporal things, from the phenomenological perspective, is a merely intentional being, in the derivative sense that it has being only *for* consciousness. The world then is an acceptance phenomenon in that it is already tacitly posited in all experiences; to make any claim for the world having being beyond that is nonsense.

Descartes' project had been to establish the foundations for an entirely new realm of being, whereas Husserl's project will be to disclose an entirely new sense of the world; these outward and return movements will have parallel trajectories but divergent destinations. It is specifically with reference to the *epoché* that Husserl's rhetorical terminology incorporates this metaphor. The *epoché* suspends or brackets all acts of belief-positing in the natural attitude so that one is able to seize upon what could have effected this alteration.

> That then is what is left as the sought for phenomenological residuum; though we have excluded the whole world with all physical things, living beings and humans, ourselves included. Strictly speaking, we have *not lost* anything but rather *have gained* the whole of absolute being which, rightly understood, contains within itself, constitutes within itself, all worldly transcendencies.[39]

The bracketing of the world leaves intact what is in the brackets, but makes its situation or placement, and hence its *meaning*, stand out. This is the significance of Husserl's remark that where Descartes discovered an entirely new world of being, Husserl himself was concerned to uncover an entirely new sense of the same world.

The significance of a *purified* sense of the world as an 'acceptance phenomenon', one which is subtended by the general thesis of the world's being, can perhaps be made more clear by dramatically rephrasing the question: what does the *epochē* accomplish? What does it mean to say that the whole world is gained *in a new way* once it has been lost? For the phenomenologist, philosophical inquiry is not a matter of *apprising* oneself of the facts in the case, as though the source of knowledge of the world were a puzzle whose answer was hidden somewhere. Rather, it is a matter of *surprise* that the world appears just this way and not otherwise, a radical contingency signified by Husserl's reference to 'the irrational fact of the rationality of the world'. In so far as the philosopher considers the mind's empirical, circumstantial connection with the world, it will always be the case that the world looks just like the philosopher's terms describe it to be. What is it then about the world and the mind such that this fulfilment or correspondence would always take place? One way to answer this question would be to study the various frameworks in which thinkers articulate their vocabularies, for example an archaeology of philosophical discourse. Since it is not possible to ask what the world would be like disengaged from consciousness, another approach to this question would be: what would consciousness be like disengaged from the world? This disengagement is the task of the phenomenological reduction and the domain uncovered thereby is the proper subject-matter of a transcendental phenomenology.

One who begins to philosophise finds him or herself already living in a natural world, surrounded by things, persons, values, traditions, customs and a corpus of received opinions about all of these things. What underscores their appearance is an unexamined belief, a naive acceptance, in the being of the world just as it is given in one's natural living. For those who are motivated to philosophise, that is for those who have already stepped back from this living and made of it a possible theme of inquiry, the sceptical challenge transforms the inquiry into a problematic. It specifically disassociates any query about the world in itself being answered by an appeal to the ways in which worldly things appear to the questioner. It is then my decision, as the philosopher engaged in this activity, to no longer acquiesce in the tacit presupposition that the world exists as an absolute datum. The philosopher does so in the complete freedom to withhold his assent: the attempt to doubt universally belongs to the realm of our perfect freedom.' This is the meaning of the phenomenological *epochē* or reduction:

> The positing undergoes a modification: while it in itself remains what it is, we so to speak, 'put it out of action', we 'exclude it', we 'parenthesize it'. It is *still there*, like the parenthesized in the parentheses, like the excluded outside the context of inclusion. We can also say: the positing is a mental process, but we make no use of it ... [it is] a specifically peculiar mode of consciousness.[40]

The root meaning of parenthesis is 'place beside with': the thesis of the world's being remains 'beside with' the alteration which it undergoes in the *epochē*. The being of the world precisely as it is given to consciousness and thus all those appearances which are or could be illusory, doubtful, etc., are considered as indicative of just those manners of givenness in which appearing things appear.

For Husserl, the universal depriving of acceptance of this general thesis does not leave us confronting nothing. On the contrary, we gain possession of something through the *epochē*: 'my pure living' and the subjective processes which comprise this, i.e. the universe of phenomena and the pure ego for whom these exist. This purified or reduced ego is not a piece (independent part) of the world, nor is the world or any worldly thing a piece of my ego, found in my consciousness as a really inherent part of it, as a complex of data of sensations or a complex of acts. The proper task of reflection is to explicate what can be found in the original subjective process, now altered in such a manner that it exposes the intentional structure of all such pre-reflective processes. In all phenomena, strictly as 'showing-forth', some thing is given to consciousness and always given in some determinate manner, i.e. in the 'how' of its givenness. The exact delineation of the intentional structure of consciousness allows one to discriminate the psychical act from its 'object' in so far as its 'object' is immanent to consciousness, irrespective of course as to whether or not there is some actual object 'out there'.

The way in which an 'object' is included in consciousness is not the way in which an object is a real part of the world. Nor on the other hand, is it included in the way in which psychical acts are moments of a unitary consciousness, which are not only unable to exist without the mind's existence, but are immanent to the ongoing stream of my conscious living. Transcendence consists in the 'object' being non-really included in consciousness, inasmuch as any worldly object participates only in the *reduced* sense of the world as acceptance-phenomenon and the purified ego bears within itself the world as an accepted sense. The way in which an intentional 'object' exists is 'a being-in of a completely unique kind: not a being in consciousness as a really intrinsic component part, but rather a being in it *ideally* as something intentional, something appearing ... a being-in-it as its immanent *objective sense*.'[41] In summary, Husserl took an intentional act to be directed towards its object *by virtue of* its intentional content. Despite some changes in Husserl's views between 1900 and 1913, he remains consistent on one consequence that is crucial for our understanding of his notion of intentionality – the intentional content of a psychical act is a *meaning* (*Bedeutung*) or *sense* (Sinn). It may be helpful to think of the content of an act as the sense that the object has for the subject whose act it is, or the sense of the object *as conceived* under a certain aspect by the subject.[42]

The later Husserl in *Ideas First Book* (1913) introduced a more complex schema of components and structure of intentionality. *Noesis* is Husserl's mature version of an act's *real content* and *noema* is his mature version of *intentional or ideal content*. Husserl's view is that the intentionality of an act is determined by the act's own intrinsic character and for this reason it does not depend on what is actually true of the intended object or even whether it exists or not. One purpose of the phenomenological *epochē* is to turn one's philoso-phical inquiry away from the 'objects' of our mental acts and towards the acts themselves, so that we can discover the inner structures or contents by means of which these acts achieve intentional directedness. The question then is *not* 'what sort of object is intended in an act in order to account for its intentionality?' *but rather* 'what is the phenomenological structure of an act by virtue of which it is an intentional experience, directed towards a given object in a certain way? Husserl rejected the object-oriented approach to intentionality and required a distinction whose lack these approaches suffer from, that is the distinction between the *intended object* of an act, that which it is directed toward, and the act's *content*, that which gives the act its directedness and thus makes it *about* some object. The core doctrine of intentionality and the technique of bracketing will be extensively modified by various Existentialist critics.

ABOVE THIS WORLD, ABOVE THIS LIFE

Existentialist thinkers since the 1930s owe a great deal to Husserl's pheno-menology; Heidegger, Jaspers, Sartre, Merleau-Ponty and Ortega repeatedly acknowledged in print that their point of departure was in Husserl's phenom-enological approach. The central elements of Husserl's thought that these Existentialists adopted are as follows. First, the rejection of Cartesian substance dualism, i.e. the doctrine that the mind and body are distinct things with determinate essences, causally and hence contingently connected. Second, the core doctrine of intentionality according to which the distinctive feature of consciousness is that it is mentally directed towards its 'objects'. Third, the discursive prohibition not to employ traditional philosophical vocabulary and instead to describe the phenomena exactly as and only as they appear to conscious being. Fourth, Husserl's repeated summons to make philosophical understanding one's own through a process of self-discovery and self-libera-tion.[43] And fifth, an insistence on the priority of the lifeworld over the theoretical world of the natural sciences. Equal to the Existentialists' acknowl-edgment of their debt to Husserl was their vigorous declaration of his mistakes, dead ends and failures. It seems to have been vitally important to thinkers in the 1920s and 1930s to claim as much distance as possible between themselves and their former 'master'. Less well remarked perhaps is the discrepancy between the Existentialists' complaints about Husserl's aborted achievements and what Husserl actually delivered.

Some of the specific criticisms of Husserl's assumptions and approach are as follows. First, for Husserl, the dominant dimension of intentional directedness is cognitive, that is, analysis of the total unity of intentional act-and-object is calculative and componential. Second, he places the emphasis in human under-standing on insight or intuition, specifically the ability to *reflect* on one's experiences. Third, the transcendental ego as uncovered through the reduction is a detached spectator, unengaged with the commonsense world and its everyday things. Fourth, consciousness is conceived as a monadic unity through which, or into which, nothing can penetrate; this conception leads to an irretrievable solipsism. Fifth, the final stage of the reduction is meant to bring about an exact science of essences, i.e. material and spiritual essences, correlative to the categories of a formal ontology; but one thing, human being, resists such categorisation since it does not *have* an essence. Sixth, and most damning, the absolutely necessary technique of phenomenological epoché that brackets the world's being cannot be fully performed, that is at least not without seriously damaging the actual relation that conscious beings have with their world.

This capsulised critique, however, does not take adequate account of Husserl's own answers to some of these charges, though, of course, like any thought-capsule it's handy for didactic purposes. Over and over again, for more than twelve years between 1912 and 1925 Husserl worked on clean copies of the Second and Third Books of the *Ideas*. One after the other, his personal assistants prepared new drafts, only to have them returned later revised and corrected; they despaired that the other parts of his great work would ever reach publication. But Heidegger read the manuscript version two years before the publication of his *Being and Time* in 1927, and Merleau-Ponty read them in 'a near rhapsody of excitement'[44] just before the outbreak of war in 1939. Many of the charges levelled against Husserl have responses in these texts, and more than just responses, they *further* Husserl's project into an emergent existential and intersubjective phenomenology. What Husserl in *The Crisis of European Sciences* (1936) calls the lifeworld (*Lebenswelt*) in *Ideas Book Two* he calls the surround-world (*umwelt*), an idea conveyed very nicely by the word *environment*. The *Umwelt* is one's immediate environment; the world which surrounds a person is already structured in determinate ways, i.e. things and persons and events already have value *before* predicative judgements are made about them.

> The surround-world is in a certain way always in the process of becoming ... To begin with, the world is, in its core, a world appearing to the senses and characterized as *on hand*, a world given in straightforward empirical intuitions and perhaps grasped actively.[45]

This should remind the attentive reader of Heidegger's discussion of the variety of items found in one's environment: they are either 'at' or 'to' hand (*zuhanden*) or they are 'for' hand (*vorhanden*), for example the hammer that is perceived circumspectively as an item imbued with use or service. This notion of originary value-perception is hardly surprising since Husserl goes on to illustrate the notion of an object 'apprehendable as in the service of the satisfaction of such needs' as hunger and warmth with 'heating materials, choppers, hammers, etc.' He then goes on to say that such items-on-hand are directly grasped as use-objects, in contrast with those that do not have use-value, objects just lying about. This is not an operation of explicit awareness, no judgement is formed by means of which one could *infer* or derive value; it is thus a *prepredicative* awareness, or as Sartre puts it, prereflective consciousness. These useful items are associated in the surround-world through 'a web of intentions', interlinked by way of meaningful indications, much in the same fashion that Heidegger describes the environing world of the ready-to-hand as 'a referential totality'. One's experience of the manifold connections of all use-objects, artifacts and cultural products, says Husserl, is an experience of *motivated* relations.

The use which an item has for its user motivates (not causes) one to take it up, as well as inspiring other motivations tied in with other use-objects.

> They now engage [the ego's] interest in their being and attributes, in their beauty, agreeableness, and usefulness; they stimulate its desire to delight in them, play with them, use them as a means, transform them according to its purposes, etc. ... In a very broad sense, we can also denote the personal or motivational attitude as the *practical attitude*.[46]

Husserl's endorsement of the importance of practice, moreover the *background* of shared practices (much discussed recently by John Searle), leads us to an answer to one of the other charges against Husserl, his alleged emphasis on theory at the expense of practice, and of reflection to the detriment of lived action. But to denigrate Husserl's supposed reliance on theoretical insight in his elaboration of the intentional structures of consciousness is to ignore his explicit subordination of theory in the transition to consideration of the human being in its psychical constitution.

> What we are seeking does not lie in the consequences of theoretical, mediate thinking but in its beginnings; we are looking for its most originary presuppositions ... Legitimate theory cannot accomplish anything other than the predicative determination, in mediate thinking, of that which was first posited by originary presenting intuition (in our case experience) ... It is the norm which must be presupposed and to which all possible theoretical cognition is rationally bound.[47]

Husserl himself was aware of the possible slippage between a theoretical attitude *about* the origins and structures of the lifeworld into a belief that a theoretical attitude can be found *within* the lifeworld. The danger here is that one might be tempted to unwittingly insert backward into one's lifeworld analysis an observer's point of view which is then 'discovered' to be in place *after* reflection. Perhaps the Cartesian meditative ego, contingently connected to its body, could become detached enough from its surroundings, and could indeed 'float above this world, above this life', but Husserl's human being is intimately bound together with its body.

Husserl rejects the false dilemma that an explanation of mind–body union must be either an interactive account or some version of parallelism. He radically recasts the terms of the standard debate by introducing two terms for body, the object or inert-body (*Korper*) and the lived-body (*Leben*). The first is the subject-matter of physical sciences such as medicine and biology; the second is the subject's matter *through* which the human being lives in the world. In this context, Husserl's key concept of intentionality undergoes a transformation into *comportment*, the same term that Heidegger uses in his critique or overcoming of Husserl's 'pure' phenomenology. The notion of comportment in *Ideas Book Two* refers to the most pervasive, most general manner in which embodied conscious beings orient themselves in the surround-world.[48] In addition, the originary apprehension of other conscious beings in an intersubjective community allows for *empathy* 'accomplished as one with the originary experience of the [lived] body as indeed a kind of presentification, one that nevertheless serves to ground the character of *co*-existence in the flesh.'[49] The internal states of embodied beings who are the source of their own motivation are basic moods or affective adjustments to the surround-world, in a sense similar to Heidegger's concept of attunement (*Befindlichkeit*). Husserl says that there are two layers to the personal ego. One is the intellectual agent, the free ego of its free acts, but also there is the personal underlying basis, constituted from associations, drives, feelings and tendencies that are played out by an embodied being. These are *habitual modes of behaviour*, properties of the person as an individual, and this individuality is '*the total style and habitus of the subject*, pervading as a concordant unity all his modes of behavior, all his activities and passivities, and to which the entire psychic basis constantly contributes.'[50] Husserl's thought here reaches back to Nietzsche's assertion that a free spirit's optimal control of its drives appears as a personal style, and reaches forward to Merleau-Ponty's famous claim that an individual's movements through the lifeworld are characterised by a personal style.

Given the Existentialists' claim that Husserl's vision of phenomenology as an exact science of essences constrains him to an interpretation of everything under the heading of timeless, fixed essences, the following statement from the final section of *Ideas Second Book* may come as a shock. According to an objective assessment of the thing-like qualities of things, is it not the case that how some thing can behave, and further, how it will behave, is predelineated by its own essence?

> But does each thing ... *have such an essence of its own in the first place?* Or is the thing, as it were, *always underway*, not at all graspable therefore in pure Objectivity, but rather in virtue of its relation to subjectivity, in principle only a relatively identical something, which does not have its essence in advance or graspable once and for all, but instead has *an open essence*, one that can always take on new properties according to the constitutive circumstances of givenness? But this is precisely the problem, to determine more exactly the *sense of this openness*, as regards, specifically the 'Objectivity' of natural science.[51]

He goes on to state clearly that consciousness is the universal characteristic of the spiritual (or psychical) dimension of human being and that, as such, *it* has an essence, an essence that eidetic analysis is designed to reveal. But human being also has an underlying basis in its lived body and habitus; it is this basic stratum that individuates each person in his or her individuality, and, as such, the human person does *not* have an essence in advance, but instead is underway, a being open to its future. From my standpoint, this statement is a clear precursor to Existentialist claims made by Heidegger, Sartre and Jaspers that Dasein is underway, ahead of itself and open to the future. In the Fourth Appendix to the *Crisis of European Sciences*, Husserl clearly links his concept of the individual not having an essence in advance, an embodied being that is underway and always becoming, to the core concept of an internal, self-realised freedom and, in doing so, clearly captures the existential concept of freedom

> This life, as personal life, is a constant becoming through a constant intentionality of development. What becomes, in this life, is the person himself. His being is forever becoming ... Human personal life proceeds in stages ... up to the point of seizing in consciousness the idea of autonomy, the idea of a resolve of the will to shape one's whole personal life into the synthetic unity of a life of universal self-responsibility and, correlatively, to shape oneself into the true 'I', the free, autonomous 'I' which seeks to realize his innate reason, the striving to be true to himself, to be able to remain identical with himself as a reasonable 'I'.[52]

PRINCIPAL THEMES AND VARIATIONS

Thus far we have traced the stages in the history (or prehistory) of the philosophical points of departure for Existential thinking, a sequence of steps that now becomes a dance as several connected but distinct thinkers enter the stage. The image of a dance is not so strange when one remembers that Nietzsche likened the thinking of a free spirit to a dance. As our initial scene setting illustrated, the 1920s and 1930s were a watershed for Western European philosophy: Nietzsche's hypercritical reflections were brought to public attention (alas, sometimes, by third-rate Nazi ideologues), new French translations of Kierkegaard's works were in the bookshops, Kojève's lectures on Hegel radiated through the heart of the Parisian intellectual community and Husserl's phenomenology was promoted at every available opportunity. All these factors, and others, provoked angry, young philosophers like Heidegger, Jaspers, Sartre, Marcel and Ortega into addressing some of the perennial philosophical questions in an entirely novel manner. These factors also provoked them into creating an intellectual need to answer questions that had never been posed before, or, in Heidegger's case, towards questions like the meaning of being that had been posed by the ancient Greeks, but whose significance had been lost and buried over.

In order to properly gauge the character and concerns of Existential philosophy, we need to move away from a historical exposition and instead focus our attention on the *central themes* that run through their writings and lectures.

Let's carry forward into a larger framework Milan Kundera's image of an individual human life as a musical theme with variations, where several themes wind in and out of at least a hundred novels, lectures, plays and treatises, each writer glossing these themes with his or her own variations. There are, at the most basic level, six central themes that run through the line of thought from Kierkegaard and Nietzsche to Sartre: existence, embodiment, absurdity, alienation (or lostness), anxiety (or dread or *angst*) and freedom. We will approach these topics in an order that roughly approximates the existential analysis of Dasein in Heidegger's *Being and Time*. This approach has the advantage of avoiding an arbitrary order of topics and endorses the way in which a phenomenological investigation, having eschewed conceptual presuppositions, uncovers the successive layers or dimensions in the constitution of human being.

The Existentialists claim that human beings have (or are) a unique manner of existence – a compact slogan, to be sure, but what is the sense of this claim? It is not the case, they argue, that humans are a unique *kind* of being, unlike, for example, an animal, vegetable or mineral. Sometimes Existentialists seem to argue that there are no natural kinds at all, though it is true that humans have some properties not shared by any other thing or group of things. Instead, they propose that humans have a unique manner or way of being, namely a being for whom being is an issue, and further that the specific individual being that one becomes is not given in advance. It is this way of being that is marked out by the term 'existence'. Heidegger derives a great deal of insight from the root sense of the Greek word 'ex-sisto' which literally means 'to stand out from'. As conscious, sentient and self-moved beings, humans stand out from everything else; moreover, their attention to and interest in things makes these things 'stand out' from the background. Kierkegaard, Heidegger and Sartre insist that each human being has the capacity to become an individual that does not yet fully exist, and this doctrine underlines the significance of time for human being. Only through the passage of time, experienced as the horizon of one's projects, can possible options become one's own actualities. An inanimate thing has no choices at all, an animate thing is constrained by its biological nature and instincts, but a conscious being is aware of its ability to bring about that which would not even be otherwise, that is it can also bring about what it would not itself be otherwise.

In 'History as a System', Ortega says that

> 'Existence itself is not presented to [humans] ready made, as it is to the stone; rather . . . all that happens to him is the realization that he has no choice but to do something in order not to cease existing. This shows that the mode of being of [human] life, even as simple existing, is not *a being already*, since the only thing that is given us and that is when there is human life is the having to make it, each one for himself.[53]

Heidegger carefully links the temporal dimension with this originary sense of existence through his analysis of the three temporal 'ek-stases' (from which the word 'ecstasy') which also means 'stand out from'. He draws his time imagery in one context from an ancient Greek metaphor for time: like a rower in a boat, a person fixes his or her position by looking backward, while his or her actions move the boat forward.

In Sartre's famous formula, for human beings alone 'existence precedes essence'; this formula explicitly reverses the maxim that Descartes proffered in the *Meditations*. One of Descartes' prime concerns was to construct a stable and lasting universal science, which would take as its principal procedure rational insight (or intuition) into essences. His model for this foundational knowledge was a mathematical reconfiguration of the natural world in terms of continuous quantities, a model that reached fruition in Newton's classical mechanics. Thus the essence of any thing can be specified by way of the precise fixing of determinate variables; the essence of a thing was what remained invariable through all conceivable variations. Now, on one hand, this seems to be true of the Existentialists' notion of human being. It *is* indeed the being for whom being is an issue, the being who can become what it is not at the present, but will be in the future if it so chooses, and so forth. Only on the level of individual being, as Husserl argued, does each human not have its own essence in advance. Thus the focus of an existential analysis of the being of human *being* has to be as close to each person as the person is to him or herself. This is one crucial lesson that Kierkegaard draws form his scrutiny of Abraham's dilemma, that the truth of his subjective relation to an absolute duty is found within his own conscience. An ordinary, unreflective thinking about human being stumbles due to a confusion that arises from the use of phrases such as human 'nature' or nurture versus 'nature', or when someone says 'it's not in his "nature" to do such and such'. This makes one think that, since 'nature' is from *natus* (birth), the individuality of an individual is 'inborn', prior to any actions which the person undertakes.

There is a tension in the 'natural' attitude between two extreme versions of explanation about human 'nature' and human behaviour. On one hand, there is the seemingly obvious predilection for scientific explanations of human traits, for example in terms of genetic inheritance, adaptive mechanisms, neurochemical imbalances and so forth, which many (if not all) persons want to believe. Such a reductive account provides an easy grasp, and hence resigned acceptance, of organic disease, birth defects, mental disorders, addictive behaviour and so forth. On the other hand, the credo of self-help, affirmative pseudo-psychology and other related trends, coupled with a watered-down Existentialism, conspire to inculcate the notion that your life is within your power, that you alone give it value and that you are one of a kind (just like everyone else). The basic insight needed to dispel the cloud of obscurity and ambiguity stretched over these two extremes is to understand the relation between essence and necessity. Thus on the Existentialist account it is characteristic of human beings alone that they are *bound* to make choices, or as Kierkegaard expressed this insight, one cannot choose *not* to choose. If each choice brings with it some belief or value or property, and the motivation to achieve the 'object' of each choice lies within, not without, the self, then the one who chooses assumes the beliefs and values of the person who will have these properties. As Ortega stated it:

> I am free by compulsion, whether I wish to be or not. To be free means to be lacking in constitutive identity, not to have subscribed to a determined being, to be able to be other than what one was, to be unable to install oneself once and for all in any given being. The only attribute of the fixed, stable being in the free being is this constitutive instability.[54]

Another reason why the Existentialists reject the interpretation of human being as a special *kind* of being is that division into kinds plays into the hands of the dualism between subject and object. Human beings cannot adequately be described by saying that they are the *subjects* of their own experience, as though the term 'subject' already started your interrogation on the right track; between subject and object lies 'a veritable abyss of being'. Having shut himself up within the realm of his own thoughts (or so the story goes), Descartes struggled in vain to bring the natural world back into being; all the lines that linked him to things and other beings had been cut and thus had to be restored. Kant remarked that it was a scandal that philosophy had never offered a conclusive proof of the existence of the external world, but Heidegger responded that the real scandal was that such a proof should have ever been sought. Husserl clearly stated his repudiation of the dualisms of subject and object, mental and physical, and inner and outer in an unpublished manuscript from 1910: 'Consciousness ... is not a psychical experience, not a network of psychical experiences, not a thing, not an appendage (state or action) to a natural object. Who will save us from the reification of consciousness? He would be the savior of philosophy, indeed the creator of philosophy.'[55] Heidegger certainly saw himself as the saviour of western philosophy, the redeemer of the early Greek promise; he described his later poetic thinking as 'a waiting for god'.

However, from the Existential point of view it is not God who is responsible for a person's life, nor is it God who bestows on each person certain innate qualities that make him that person. An alcoholic, a drug addict, a petty thief, even a terrorist can decide to change their lives, to no longer be the person they are. In this context when one speaks of personal reform or renewal or rehabilitation, notice that one speaks of a formation *again*, a new start *again*, a new habitat *again*. This assuming a position again is possible because each person already finds him or herself with a form of life, a start, a home. Of course, the person who reflects on his or her past and says, 'not again', does not decide to annul the past, to make it nothing, as though it never happened; instead, this person denies that the past must determine what one becomes. Negation thus appears in the temporal horizon of an existent being: one's past life is not the essence of one's life and one's life in the future is not yet. The Existential concept of time as the horizon of human existence is closely tied to the concept of negation through the experience of anxiety.

One of Sartre's best known examples is an excellent illustration of the way in which existence, negation, time, anxiety and absurdity are intimately linked at special moments in a person's life. Someone walking along a narrow path near a steep cliff edge may move confidently forward as long as she keeps in abeyance the direct awareness that from this great height she would fall to her death – that's why *they* say, 'don't look down'. But when she looks over the edge fear can grip her throat; this fear has an 'object', falling to her death, and she is fearful because that event is only inches or seconds away. But then it might occur to her that nothing prevents her from throwing herself over; anxiety is the reflective awareness that there is *nothing* that stands between her and not being. Sartre cleverly places full emphasis on the term *nothing* to show that anxiety is the face-to-face encounter with the abyss between one's being and not being. Struck with existential dread our cliff walker may reflect further: my children at home need me, or the rebels in the mountains, or the wounded people in the next village, and *this* is one reason, my reason, for not killing myself. This little story presents a crucial insight: in that intense moment, the individual can give herself a reason or ground for existence, one that is not given at birth, not given to everyone in general, but to that unique, solitary individual.

The Existentialist thinkers, to one degree or another, were devoted to the 'destruction' of western metaphysics; in some cases, this tearing down left tangled, smoking ruins and not clear ground. But their destruction was an effort to dismantle or collapse every dualist opposition. Perhaps one of the most entrenched, deeply buried oppositions, between inner and outer, between an internal and an external world, is the most difficult for philosophy to dispense with. It seems to run directly against one's basic intuitions to deny any difference between inside and outside one's self; surely, one wants to exclaim, the boundary of my skin separates me from everything else. Even in their own terms, the Existentialists' emphasis on the importance of the lived-body seems to entail the notion that a *lived*-body is lived by someone, in fact *this* one and not *that* one. Perhaps the sense of 'side' in the words 'inside' and 'outside' might help one to see this point, an important statement best expressed by Merleau-Ponty. There isn't anything that can have only one side, every thing is many-sided; but it is *one* thing that has an inside and an outside, not one thing on *this* side and another thing on *that* side. However, my consciousness is not located inside in the way that sand fills the inside of a box; only if one reifies (makes a thing of) consciousness could it be inside in this manner. My skin surface is a membrane through which my encounter with the world takes place. Through my comportment or corporeal intentionality towards things and persons and values, all these items encountered become parts of me, not real object-like parts, but vital moments of my own life. 'Our own body is in the world as the heart is in the organism; it keeps the visible spectacle constantly alive, it breathes life into it and sustains it inwardly, and with it forms a system.' And further: 'The thing and the world are given to me along with the parts of my body, not by any "natural geometry", but in a living connection comparable, or rather identical, with that existing between the parts of my body itself.'[56]

Heidegger coined a new name for this being of human being, its unique manner of existence – Dasein, which literally means 'being-there'. Where? In-the-world, absorbed in things and actions, objects of interest, desire, disgust and so forth. Human being can sever the distance between its desire and the desired thing, bring it closer and make it one's own. In fact, we say of someone who is insane or deeply disturbed that he is 'not all there', and we do not mean that the person is not in the place he stands, that he is not actually at that spot, but that he is not *there* for himself. Ortega's best known statement about this has become almost his epitaph: the human being in its unique mode of existence is the unity of ego and its circumstances. All those things that 'stand around' one's ego are indissolubly parts of one's being, and thus human being 'makes nothing' of the distance that separates self from not-self. Merleau-Ponty's enunciation of this principle is stated with greater exactitude:

> We have the experience of a world ... as an open totality the synthesis of which is inexhaustible. We have the experience of an I not in the sense of an absolute subjectivity, but indivisibly demolished and remade by the course of time ... We must rediscover, as anterior to the ideas of subject and object, the fact of my subjectivity and the nascent object, that primordial layer at which both things and ideas come into being.[57]

Sartre argued in *Being and Nothingness* that 'nothing lies at the heart of human being like a worm'. He tells a story about going to a café to meet his friend Pierre; arriving at the café, he scans the room, looking from face to face – every one of them is *not* Pierre. All the other persons in the café are there, each has his or her own presence, against which Pierre's not-being-there appears as an 'absence' or 'negation'. An important lesson which Sartre draws from this is that the negative *judgement*, 'Pierre is not here', is founded on a more primordial state or condition of nothing *in being*. One should bear in mind that there are three sorts of negation in Sartre's exposition: first, the irruption or seepage of nothingness through the experience of an absence or *negatité*; second, the fact that there is *nothing* which can account for my being conscious of a world, one is suspended over an abyss since the emphasis is on 'nothing' in the statement 'there is nothing which separates my existence from non-existence'; third, the insight that the world is just as it is and *not otherwise*. Sartre refers to the unique being which characterises consciousness as *for-itself* and the inert, passive, non-conscious state of things as *in-itself*.

Human beings alone have the 'power' to generate or bring about a nothing or *negatité*. This does not mean that humans have a power of negation over the beings which actually confront us, rather it is a power which humans have of *changing their relationship* to that kind of being. We can refuse to accept things as they are, we can reject things as having no value, and so forth; in this fashion, we put up some kind of buffer of nothingness between ourselves and the world.

The for-itself can 'secrete a nothingness which isolates it from all other beings'; this isolation is a means of detaching human being from the causal chain of natural events, and this power is what Sartre calls *freedom*. The primary function of freedom on the Existentialist view is to cut off the causal influence of one's own past, to negate all those things which might determine the self one way rather than another. It is within your freedom to *put out of play* all those factors which would have given you good 'cause' to do just this *and not otherwise*.[58]

Now if freedom is the defining mode of being of consciousness, then the structure of consciousness must be such as to take account of this freedom; there must be some 'indication' within consciousness which shows up or illustrates this state of being free. Here Sartre introduces the key term *anxiety* (or anguish) – it describes a spectrum of human feelings which runs from mere unease to outright terror. The main features of existential anxiety are uncertainty, loneliness and responsibility, in Peter Caws' adroit synopsis.[59] You can be said to be afflicted with this form of anxiety when, left to your own devices and without any help, you are still under the necessity of making a choice, making a decision, and moreover committing yourself (and perhaps other persons) to a course of action which may be heavy with consequences. Anxiety must not be confused with fear, for fear has an object; whether it is a danger or a threat, your fear can be dispelled by overcoming or avoiding the object. But anxiety arises in confrontation with oneself and, unless one is in *bad faith*, one cannot attack or run away from oneself. Nevertheless, both fear and anxiety are oriented toward the future: you are afraid because you anticipate some danger to your values, one of which may be the value of being alive. But in anxiety, the threat or danger is toward values which you may not know about, values which you have yet to realise. Thus the uncertainty about the future in this sense attaches not to the being of worldly things but to your own being.

In the ordinary course of events, this absurdity or lack of reason for our existence and our anxiety in the face of this absurdity are concealed or buried by our engagement in the social world in which conventional values are already in place. But when we look more closely, we find that these values don't exist in the objective world the way objects exist in the world; they are created and sustained by other persons whose existential status is no more basic than our own. These values have become our values only through the exercise of our irreducible freedom, though of course if these values have been accepted in an unthinking fashion, it is through our *failure* to exercise a free choice as Camus pointed out. This basic insight does not occur to us as we go about our daily business, where we are constrained by moral and non-moral values which we find all around us, 'sown on our path like thousands of little real demands, like the signs which order us to keep off the grass.'[60] This already-being-in-place only appears upon reflection: 'anguish then is the reflective apprehension of freedom by itself.' The origin of anxiety is the sudden realisation of freedom on the part of a conscious being that naively supposed everything to be ordered and stable, only to discover that this order and stability were its own creation, and thus able to be discarded at will. This insight may cause a feeling of vertigo or *nausea*, another key Sartrean term – the dramatic and vivid sensation of being suspended over an abyss, looking down into great depths, as Nietzsche described so well.

Let us return for a moment to an earlier comment – that good faith consists in keeping a true course with one's life-project. The original sense of the words 'sub-ject', 'ob-ject' and 'pro-ject' is seen in the root notion of *thrownness*: 'iecto' means 'to throw'. Thus subject means 'thrown-under', object means 'thrown-over-against' and project means 'thrown-forward'. The existential significance of 'subject' is that it is the ground under which, or on the basis of which, the world appears at all; the significance of 'object' is that it is inert, unaware of itself, the correlate of conscious awareness; and the significance of 'project' is that a conscious being is future-oriented, a conscious being *throws ahead of itself* the being which it wishes to become. It is through the thrown character of human being that the for-itself can exploit the layer of nothingness which separates it from causal determinism, and hence from any notion that its own future is inevitable. Through the free commitment to a life-project, human being can make actual some (if not all) of its ownmost possibilities.

Heidegger proposes a similar line of thought in *Being and Time*:

> In each case Dasein is mine to be in one way or another. Dasein has always made some sort of decision as to the way in which it is in each case mine. That entity which in its Being has this very Being as an issue, comports itself towards its Being as its ownmost possibility. In each case Dasein *is* its possibility, and it 'has' this possibility . . . It *can*, in its very Being, 'choose' itself and win itself; it can also lose itself and never win itself; or only 'seem' to do so.[61]

Heidegger here introduces his version of one of the key concepts in our discussion, authentic [*eigentlich*], which literally means 'ownmost', in contrast with inauthentic [*uneigentlich*], 'not-ownmost'. Thus, in so far as an individual follows his or her own freely chosen project, he or she is authentic, has 'good faith' (in Sartre's terms), or is an active will to power (in Nietzsche's terms). But if an individual remains lost in the 'they'-world, alienated from her self and her possibilities, then she has or lives in 'bad faith', or is a reactive will to power. In this context Kierkegaard refers to the crowd, Ortega to mass mentality and Jaspers to the tranquillising affect of being an average person.

The true 'nature' of human being then is that it is *not* defined by any essential qualities or features. It is not yet its own future, its future is once more a lack in being. Sartre cleverly plays on an ambiguity in the statement about what one is not. 'Each for-itself is a lack of a certain coincidence with itself'; the in-itself of an object is fully present to itself, or would be if it could ever confront itself after the manner of the for-itself. This presence-to-itself is denied to the for-itself; whose perpetual, ongoing *transcendence* towards the future means that it is, as it were, never fully there to be confronted. But this lack in being is an *object* of self-confrontation; the for-itself of conscious being *is* its lack of presence to itself and is present to itself as this lack, the specific content of which consists precisely in its own possibilities. This synopsis of the dynamics of the for-itself and the in-itself leads to one of Sartre's most important assertions, as formulated by Peter Caws:[62] I am not what I am and I am what I am not; that is, I *am not* my past in the mode of being it; and I *am* my future in the mode of not yet being it. The past has the in-itself status of an object, the in-itself cannot *have* a past, it can only be what the past has determined it to be from the causal perspective; the for-itself does have a past, and *is* its past in so far as it can ever *be* anything. But it cannot *be it now*, since the past is what it *was* and is no longer. For Sartre then, I am the sum of my actions and nothing else; I am responsible for what I have done, and can lay no claim to what I might have done but did not do.

Sartre's *Notebooks for an Ethics* (unpublished in his own lifetime) offers a more mature and complex version of an Existential ethics that recognises not an absolute freedom, but instead a *situated freedom*, circumscribed and affected by the actions of others over whom the individual may have no control. While there are no absolute grounds that justify any particular values or warrant their imposition on others, they nonetheless propose limits for morally acceptable choices. Any choice that denies the basic dimension of freedom is morally unacceptable. Whatever values we choose as individuals, we must always will our own freedom, since our freedom is a necessary precondition for any choice and action. Moreover, a similar recognition holds with respect to the freedom of others; inasmuch as human existence is an ambiguous, embodied existence, human beings are always vulnerable to others. To the extent that their activities take place in a social world, the success of their projects depends at least on the non-interference of others and often on their active assistance. Thus, to recognise this *being-for-others* is to acknowledge the extent to which one's actions are not totally within one's own power. Further, in willing one's own ends, one must will not just the non-interference of others, but also their active assistance, and hence *their* freedom as a precondition of their being able to assist you.[63]

Sartre discusses how, in helping another person, one not only comprehends the other's end but makes it one's own end.

> The other's end [or project] can appear to me as an end only in and through the indication of my adopting that end. In choosing to help someone, I engage myself in action but still recognize the end as not mine. To will this end in 'good faith', I must will the end to be realized by another. To want a value to be realized not because it is mine, not because it is a value, but because it is a value for someone else.[64]

In helping another person, you discover the other's freedom, not as opposed to or a threat to one's own freedom, but *within* your own freedom, namely the freedom you have *to help the other*; 'he unveils it at the heart of his own freedom as a free movement which accompanies him towards his end . . . each freedom is wholly in the other.'[65] Sartre's analyses in this context indicate the possibility of a kind of love that recognises and affirms the freedom of the beloved as well as one's own. On this score he may have been influenced in his thinking by Marcel's and Jaspers' attempt to construct an ethical posture based on unconditional love for the other. Ortega declared that to love someone means to affirm more than one knows about the loved one, to say 'yes' to all the unknown things that lie in the loved one's past and future. For Sartre, to love in good faith is to move beyond the oppressive dialectics of having or owning another person toward 'a deeper recognition and reciprocal comprehension of freedoms'. For this kind of love, Sartre says, 'tension is necessary – to maintain the two faces of ambiguity, to hold them within the unity of one and the same project'.[66]

Sartre's moral position in the *Notebooks*, and de Beauvoir's compatible arguments in *The Ethics of Ambiguity*, argue that each individual stands in his or her own 'concrete singularity'. They develop this position in a dialectical fashion that may remind readers of Kierkegaard's insistence that the leap of faith reveals one's unique relation to others, and establishes a higher, renewed concept of the universal. De Beauvoir's politically situated ethics affirms a way to avoid or overcome some of the processes of *alienation* that have become prevalent in twentieth-century western society. Although some degree of alienation is basic to the human condition, the alienation that results from bad faith or self-deception is not basic and should be expunged. Alienation sometimes occurs on the social level as oppression by dominant groups, but de Beauvoir argues that large-scale alienation is open to the same damning criticisms as those directed at individuals who fail to recognise and affirm their own and others' freedom. In some sections of the *Notebooks* Sartre envisions a utopian future in which such authentic relationships would be possible with 'no strings attached' and with no interference from oppressive social structures. This ideal of reciprocal freedom and genuine cooperation provides a basis for a new understanding of the autonomous individual, one premised on inter-relations and interdependence, and not on complete independence.

Rejection of traditional assumptions about the 'nature' of human being, especially the tacit thesis that humans have essences, the way that objects have invariant properties, creates an abyss or fissure in the monolithic realm of being. Only one thing can make an object of itself, can take what its being is to be an issue about its being, only for human being can failure or success in being defined by its essence matter. It is indeed a consequence of philosophical reflection that such an abyss or fissure opens when one begins to think in this manner. But the challenge, or perhaps the summons, is to not allow this opening to close over – through laziness, habitual thinking or unthinking practices. Keeping the fissure open, however, causes anxiety, for nothing separates you from the being you can become, from those possibilities which the self you choose will realise. The brute fact that the meanings of your future self's acts and beliefs are your own creation imposes both a weight and a levity on your thinking about that self. The weight attaches to the seriousness with which some or most of those meanings must be invested in order for them to be *your* life's goals and values, and not others' goals and values. But at the same time, your present being floats lightly above any constraint to choose a specific set of possible properties to realise. The brute fact that at any moment death could sever your carrying through a projected course of action does not render the course itself empty, but does convert the fact that you *care* about all those things you might not realise into an *absurd* affair. Turning away from the anxiety provoked by this insight into nothing and the absurdity of any efforts to permanently overcome this anxiety may increase the attractions of a tranquil life, one whose fissures have all been paved over, but obviates the truth of the insight with which you were once surprised. The insight that there is no already given *reason* why you should *be* at all, that the ground of your fragile, trembling existence is a gift you make to yourself.

References

1. Simone de Beauvoir (1965) *The Prime of Life*, trans. Peter Green. Harmondsworth: Penguin Books, p. 112.
2. Jean-Paul Sartre (1972) 'Intentionality: A Fundamental Idea of Husserl's Phenomenology, trans. Joseph Fell, *Journal of the British Society for Phenomenology*, vol. 1, no. 2, p. 5.
3. Quoted in Roger price (1997) *A Concise History of France*. Cambridge: Cambridge University Press, p. 246.
4. Simone de Beauvoir (1968) *The Force of Circumstance*, trans. Richard Howard. Harmondsworth: Penguin Books, pp. 45–6.
5. Ibid., pp. 151–2.
6. David Cooper (1999) *Existentialism: A Reconstruction*, 2nd edn. Oxford and New York: Blackwell, p. 3.
7. G. W. Hegel (1970) *Philosophy of Nature*, trans. M. J. Petry. London: Allen & Unwin, section 246.
8. Stanley Rosen (1998) 'Kojève', in Simon Critchley and William Schroeder (eds), *A Companion to Continental Philosophy*. Oxford: Blackwell, pp. 237–8.
9. Kojève (1969) *Introduction to the Reading of Hegel*, trans. James Nichols. Ithaca, NY: Cornell University Press, 1969/80, pp. 4–5; see also p. 38.
10. Sartre (1956) *Being and Nothingness*, trans. Hazel Barnes. London and New York: Routledge, p. 32; on Sartre's appropriation and transformation of Hegel's doctrines, see Pierre Verstraeten (1992) 'Appendix: Hegel and Sartre', in Christina Howells (ed.), *Cambridge Companion to Sartre*. Cambridge: Cambridge University Press, pp. 353–72.
11. The existential theme of love resurfaces in a philosophically significant form in Karl Jaspers' third volume of *Philosophy* (1932), Ortega y Gasset's *Studies on Love* (1939) and Gabriel Marcel's *Creative Fidelity* (1940).
12. There are several excellent commentaries on *Fear and Trembling*; my highest recommendations are for Alistair Hannay (1991) 'The Knight of Faith's Silence', in *Kierkegaard*, Arguments of the Philosophers Series, revised edn. London and New York: Routledge; and Edward Mooney (1991) *Knights of Faith and Resignation*. Albany, NY: State University of New York.
13. Kierkegaard (1961) *Concluding Unscientific Postscript*, trans. David Swenson and Walter Lawrie. Princeton, NJ: Princeton University Press, p. 169; for an excellent commentary on this difficult text, see Merold Westphal (1996) *Becoming a Self*. West Lafayette, IN: Purdue University Press.
14. Kierkegaard, *Concluding Unscientific Postscript*, p. 170.
15. Ibid., p. 171, and again at pp. 267–82.

16. Ibid., p. 182; see Stephen Evans (1998) 'Realism and Antirealism', in Alistair Hannay and Gordon Merino (eds), *Cambridge Companion to Kierkegaard*. Cambridge: Cambridge University Press.
17. Kierkegaard, *Concluding Unscientific Postscript*, p. 146.
18. Kierkegaard (1983) *Fear and Trembling*, trans. H. V. and E. H. Hong. Princeton, NJ: Princeton University Press, p. 79; for this account, see Hubert Dreyfus (1991) 'Appendix' (written with Jane Rubin), in *Being in the World*. Cambridge, MA: MIT Press.
19. Alexander Nehamas (1985) *Nietzsche: Life as Literature*. Cambridge, MA: Harvard University Press, p. 23.
20. Nietzsche (1972) *The Gay Science*, trans. Walter Kaufmann. New York: Vintage Books, section 346.
21. Nietzsche (1967) *The Genealogy of Morals*, trans. Walter Kaufmann. New York: Vintage Books, Book I, section 13.
22. Nietzsche, *The Gay Science*, section 333.
23. Ibid., section 360; see also *Genealogy of Morals*, Book I, section 13.
24. For this account of the will to power ontology, see John Richardson (1996) *Nietzsche's System* (Oxford: Oxford University Press, pp. 16–35.
25. Ibid., pp. 39–44.
26. Nietzsche, *The Gay Science*, section 11; see also section 354.
27. Nietzsche, *The Will to Power*, trans. Walter Kaufmann and R. J. Hollingdale. New York: Vintage Books, no. 477.
28. Nietzsche, *The Gay Science*, section 333.
29. Ibid., section 354.
30. Ibid.
31. Nietzsche, *Genealogy of Morals*, Book II, section 16.
32. Nietzsche (1997) *Untimely Meditations*, ed. Daniel Breazeale, trans. R. J. Hollingdale. Cambridge: Cambridge University Press, Book III, section 1.
33. Nietzsche, *The Gay Science*, section 270.
34. Ibid., section 290.
35. Kierkegaard, *Concluding Unscientific Postscript*, p. 314.
36. Nehamas, *Nietzsche: Life as Literature*, p. 190.
37. Milan Kundera (1991) *Immortality*. London: Faber & Faber, pp. 264–83, 303–11.
38. Husserl (1981) 'Philosophy as a Rigorous Science', in Peter McCormick and Fred Elliston (eds), *Husserl: Shorter Works*. Notre Dame, IN: University of Notre Dame Press, p. 179.
39. Husserl (1982) *Ideas First Book*, trans. Fred Kersten. Dordrecht: Kluwer Academic, p. 113.
40. Ibid., p. 59.
41. Husserl (1965) *Cartesian Meditations*, trans. Dorion Cairns. The Hague: Nijhoff, p. 42.
42. For an excellent exposition of Husserl's concept of intentionality, its many different terms and detailed criticisms, see D. W. Smith and Ronald McIntyre (1982) *Husserl and Intentionality*. Dordrecht: D. Reidel, Chapter III, pp. 87–152.
43. For the points of this critique, see David Cooper, *Existentialism*, pp. 46–7.
44. Heidegger acknowledges his debt to the second part of Husserl's *Ideas* in a footnote to *Being and Time* (New York: Harper & Row, 1962, p. 469, note ii); See also Merleau-Ponty (1996) *Texts and Dialogues*, eds Hugh Silverman and James Barry, Jr, 2nd edn. Atlantic Highlands, NJ: Humanities Press, Appendix by H. L. van Breda.
45. Husserl (1989) *Ideas Second Book*, trans. Richard Rojcewicz and André Schuwer. Dordrecht: Kluwer Academic, p. 196.
46. Ibid., p. 199.
47. Ibid., pp. 96–7.
48. Ibid., pp. 201–2.

49. Ibid., p. 208.
50. Ibid., p. 290; see also p. 341.
51. Ibid., pp. 312–13.
52. Husserl (1970) *The Crisis of European Sciences*, trans. David Carr. Evanston, IL: Northwestern University Press, p. 338.
53. Ortega y Gasset (1936) 'History as a System', trans. William C. Atkinson, in R. Klibansky and H. J. Paton (eds), *Philosophy and History*. Oxford: Clarendon Press, p. 303.
54. Ibid., pp. 304–5.
55. Rudolf Bernet, Iso Kern and Eduard Marbach (1992) *An Introduction to Husserl's Phenomenology*. Evanston, IL: Northwestern University Press, p. 62.
56. Merleau-Ponty (1962) *The Phenomenology of Perception*, trans. Colin Smith. London: Routledge & Kegan Paul, pp. 203, 205.
57. Ibid., p. 219.
58. See Peter Caws (1979) *Sartre*. London: Routledge, pp. 80–3.
59. Sartre, *Being and Nothingness*, p. 32.
60. Ibid., p. 38.
61. Heidegger, *Being and Time*, p. 68, H42.
62. See Peter Caws, *Sartre*, pp. 84–6.
63. See Linda Bell (1999) 'Existential Ethics', in Simon Glendenning (ed.), *Encyclopedia of Continental Philosophy*. Edinburgh: Edinburgh University Press, pp. 165–7.
64. Sartre (1992) *Notebooks for an Ethics*, trans. David Pellauer. Chicago: Chicago University Press, pp. 277–80.
65. Ibid., p. 287.
66. Ibid., p. 415.

RECOMMENDED READING

de Beauvoir, Simone (1965) *The Force of Circumstance*, trans. Richard Howard. Harmondsworth: Penguin Books.

de Beauvoir, Simone (1965) *The Prime of Life*, trans. by Peter Green. Harmondsworth: Penguin Books.

Bernet, Rudolf, Kern, Iso and Marbach, Eduard (1992) *An Introduction to Husserl's Phenomenology*. Evanston, IL: Northwestern University Press.

Cooper, David E. (1999) *Existentialism: A Reconstruction*, 2nd edn. Oxford and New York: Blackwell.

Critchley, Simon and Schroeder, William (eds) (1998) *A Companion to Continental Philosophy*. Oxford and New York: Blackwell.

Dilman, Ilham (1993) *Existentialist Critiques of Cartesianism*. London: Macmillan.

Fell, Joseph (1979) *Heidegger and Sartre: An Essay on Being and Place*. New York: Columbia University Press.

Friedman, Maurice (ed.) (1992) *The Worlds of Existentialism: A Critical Reader*, 2nd edn. New York: Humanities Press.

Glendenning, Simon (ed.) (1999) *Encyclopedia of Continental Philosophy*. Edinburgh: Edinburgh University Press.

Grene, Marjorie (1959) *Introduction to Existentialism*. Chicago: University of Chicago Press.

Grossmann, Reinhardt (1984) *Phenomenology and Existentialism: An Introduction*. London: Routledge, Kegan Paul.

Hammond, Michael, Howarth, Jane and Keat, Russell (1992) *Understanding Phenomenology*. Oxford and New York: Blackwell.

Kaufmann, Walter (ed.) (1975) *Existentialism from Dostoevsky to Sartre*, revised edn. New York: New American Library.

Kearney, Richard (ed.) (1994) *Twentieth-Century Continental Philosophy*. London and New York: Routledge.

Lawrence, Nathaniel and O'Connor, Daniel (eds) (1967) *Readings in Existential Phenomenology*. Englewood Cliffs, NJ Prentice-Hall.

Macann, Christopher (1993) *Four Phenomenological Philosophers*. London and New York: Routledge.

MacDonald, Paul S. (2000) *Descartes and Husserl: The Philosophical Project of Radical Beginnings*. Albany: State University of New York Press.

MacIntyre, Alasdair (1967) 'Existentialism', in Paul Edwards (ed.), *Encyclopedia of Philosophy*. New York: Macmillan.

Macquarrie, John (1973) *Existentialism: An Introduction, Guide and Assessment*. Harmondsworth: Penguin Books.

Moran, Dermot (2000) *Introduction to Phenomenology*. London and New York: Routledge.

Mounier, Emmanuel (1948) *Existentialist Philosophies: An Introduction*, trans. Eric Blow. London.

Olafson, Frederick (1967) *Principles and Persons: An Ethical Interpretation of Existentialism*. Baltimore, MD: Johns Hopkins University Press.

Schnadelbach, Herbert (1984) *Philosophy in Germany 1831–1933*, trans. Eric Matthews. Cambridge: Cambridge University Press.

Sokolowski, Robert (2000) *Introduction to Phenomenology*. Cambridge: Cambridge University Press.

Solomon, Richard C. (1988) *Continental Philosophy Since 1750*. Oxford: Oxford University Press.

Spiegelberg, Herbert (1975) *The Phenomenological Movement*, 3rd edn. The Hague: Nijhoff.

Sprigge, Timothy (1984) *Theories of Existence*. Harmondsworth: Penguin Books.

Wahl, Jean (1969) *Philosophies of Existence*. London: Routledge & Kegan Paul.

Welton, Donn (ed.) (1999) *The Essential Husserl*. Bloomington: Indiana State University Press.

West, David (1996) *An Introduction to Continental Philosophy*. Cambridge: Polity Press.

I

KARL JASPERS
(1883–1969)

Jaspers was born in Oldenburg near the North Sea; his father was a jurist, high constable and director of a bank, and his mother came from a long lineage of farmers. After studying law at his father's request for three semesters, he enrolled as a medical student and received his degree of Doctor of Medicine in 1909. He began an internship as a voluntary assistant in the psychiatric hospital attached to the University of Heidelberg and in 1913 he became Privatdozent in Psychology. On his return to university Jaspers found the standard philosophy courses unfulfilling and his professors' treatment of issues irrelevant to the concerns which already occupied him. Perhaps another factor in his choice of a medical profession was his resolve to overcome his own illness, a serious respiratory ailment and weak heart, a condition which left him with little strength and stamina. At that time the general medical prognosis was bleak; his doctors said that he could not be expected to live beyond his thirties. 'The task', he later said, 'was to treat it correctly, almost without being aware of it, and to work as if the illness did not exist.' Another important factor in his preference for the psychiatric profession was connected with the woman who would become his wife, Gertrud Mayer, and her brother Ernst Mayer, who would become Jaspers' most intimate friend. Gertrud's sister suffered from 'a lingering uncanny mental disease' which saw her constantly confined to an institution. One of Gertrud's close friends had committed suicide and Ernst himself struggled against serious mental problems throughout his life.

During his many years of practice in the Heidelberg psychiatric hospital, Jaspers maintained a studious interest in philosophy, though he later said he did so in an unsystematic and unmethodical fashion. From 1908 to 1915, he was mainly involved in research on the theoretical framework of abnormal psychology, but also conducted and monitored many individual case studies. Jaspers' philosophical orientation drove him to consider the various competing accounts of the origin and meaning of schizophrenia and manic-depressive disorders. His overall impression of the voluminous literature on the subject was that it was 'just so much unfounded chatter'. But he balanced the detached, theoretical approach with the desire to investigate the enormous amount of empirical evidence. 'I felt as if I were living in a world of an unsurveyable variety of ways of looking at things, which were at our disposal in chaotic disorder, yet each one of which individually was of an intolerable simplicity' (1957, p. 17). His great and lasting insight was that all normal and abnormal thoughts, beliefs and behaviour were manifestations, in one way or another, of human consciousness *and* that only a rigorously accurate description of conscious and semi-conscious states would make the relevant evidence available for interpretation. This basic thesis lies at the centre of Jaspers' monumental work, *General Psychopathology*, first published in 1913 and still regarded as one of the great landmark works in the theoretical understanding of psychiatric disorders. (Jaspers continued to revise various editions of this text until the seventh edition of 1959, which was translated into English by Hoenig and Hamilton in 1963.)

Jaspers credited two philosophers with a commendable methodological approach to the study of consciousness, Edmund Husserl and Wilhelm Dilthey. Husserl's phenomenological analyses in the *Logical Investigations* of the intentional structures of consciousness, the constitution of meaning and the elaboration of complex objectivities provided Jaspers with a precise, deductive model for the description of hallucinations, delusions and emotions. Dilthey's descriptive psychology provided him with a model for explaining the genetic connections within mental life, as well as meaningful relations and motives. The significance of Jaspers' work in psychopathology for his later philosophical approach to Existentialism should not be overlooked, as many philosophy reference books are prone to do. 'The totality of [human being] lies way beyond any conceivable objectifiability. He is incompletable both as a being-for-himself and as an object of cognition. He remains, so to speak, "open". Man is always more than what he knows, or can know, about himself' (1957, p. 19). In the 1955 'Epilogue' to the first volume of *Philosophy* (1932), Jaspers reports Husserl's response to the psychiatrist's inquiry about method: 'You are using the method perfectly. Just keep it up. You don't need to know what it is; that is indeed a difficult matter.' Jaspers' appreciation of Husserl's phenomenological approach was, beyond this courteous public statement, strictly limited to issues of descriptive protocol. He later said that he found Husserl's article 'Philosophy as a Rigorous Science' (1911) to be 'another denial' of the genuine philosophical project: 'Husserl seemed to me to have committed the most naïve and pretentious betrayal of philosophy'.

Perhaps as a result of the overtly philosophical approach of his habilitation thesis and partly as a result of his frail health, Jaspers left the hospital and began teaching in the Philosophical Faculty. His previous intensive study of the many divergent accounts of consciousness failed to show him that any one perspective was adequate for an understanding of human being. The two dominant figures in psychiatric explanation of mental disorders at that time, Freud and Hoche, 'accompanied my youth, so to speak, as my enemies', forcing him to combat their quasi-scientific attitude. His next major work, *The Psychology of World-views* (1919), derives some of its philosophical insight from his reading of Hegel, Kierkegaard and Nietzsche, three thinkers whom he later said struck him as revelations. 'They were able to make communicable a universal and at the same time a quite concrete insight into every corner of the human soul and to its very deepest sources' (1957, p. 26). Jaspers later viewed his own book as 'the earliest writing in the later so-called modern Existentialism'. He thought that all of the basic questions which concerned Existentialists after the Second World War were present in that book: the human significance of the world; boundary situations (death, suffering, chance, guilt and struggle) which are inescapable for every person; the multi-dimensional nature of the meaning of time; the movement of freedom in the process of creating one's self; and the concept of Existenz, the uniquely human manner of existence, and its concern with the issue of transcendence.

The other important influence on Jaspers' scholarly orientation was the work of the great German sociologist and historian of religion Max Weber, who died in 1920. In that year, Jaspers said, he stood at the crossroads – whether to continue his 'scientific' inquiries into the large number of psychological studies or to pursue the ultimate philosophical questions. 'My chief concern now became the ascent to the height of philosophy proper [and] that was a slow process ... That meant the decision to make a new start from the beginning' (1957, p. 35). For the next ten years, often in close conjunction with his wife and with occasional suggestions by his friend Ernst Mayer, he worked on the three volumes of *Philosophy*, first published in 1932. That enormous and demanding exposition stands today as his *magnum opus*; in 1955 he remarked that, of all his books, *Philosophy* was closest to his heart. He decided to leave aside all discussion of historical figures in western philosophy, studies which would later be published in two large volumes, *The Great Philosophers*.

> The point is to make our philosophizing a function of our reality itself, to have the thought figures spring from personal life and address themselves to the individual ... [Philosophy] makes no sense as a knowledge of formulae, theses and words ... it does make sense in the inner action which it stirs up or recognizably reflects. (1969–71 [1932], vol. I, p. 13)

In 1921 Jaspers was made full Professor of Philosophy at Heidelberg, after he had declined similar offers from two other universities. In 1937, the National-Socialist regime deprived him of his academic chair and prohibited him from teaching or publishing. Since his wife Gertrud was Jewish, they were under constant threat of either expulsion or arrest. In his 'Autobiography' he reports several near catastrophes during those horrible years, but they never gave up hope. 'We seemed to be miraculously protected as we were spared the worst fate ... Having a sense of shared guilt, we felt increasingly challenged to live right and to work to the very limits of our capacity.' In 1945, Jaspers was reinstated by the American authorities and the next year was made an honorary senator of Heidelberg University. In 1948, he accepted the appointment of Professor of Philosophy at the University of Basel (Switzerland), and in 1958 he was awarded the German Peace Prize at the Frankfurt Book Fair, partly as a result of his book the previous year, *The Atom Bomb and the Future of Mankind*. His 'Autobiography' appeared in 1957 and he continued to write and publish into his eighties before his death in 1969.

The attitude expressed in the Preface to *Philosophy* is one that he shares most closely with Kierkegaard and Nietzsche, the attitude that to engage in philosophy means to make its concerns one's own concerns. His constant challenge throughout this book and many other writings is that philosophising is a forward movement, a journey undertaken in the knowledge that the destination is unknown. His strange and poetic image here is that of a bird in flight – one wing is the movement of his own meditations, the other wing is the harmonious movement of the reader's thinking through these thoughts. Jaspers makes a distinctively personal summons or call to every person to understand the significance of the insight that only human *being* raises the issue of being.

> Awakening to myself, in my situation, I raised the question of being. Finding myself in the situation as an indeterminate possibility, I must *search for being* if I want to find my real self. But it is not till I fail in this search for intrinsic being that I begin to philosophize. This is what we call philosophizing on the ground of possible Existenz, and the method used is transcending.

This statement is highly reminiscent of the opening lines of the first main chapter of Heidegger's *Being and Time*:

> We are ourselves the entities to be analyzed. The Being of any such entity is in each case mine. These entities, in their Being, comport themselves towards their Being. As entities with such Being, they are delivered over to their own Being. Being is that which is an issue for every such entity. (Heidegger, 1962, p. H42)

In any case, although Jaspers' concerns in the three volumes of *Philosophy* (1932) include an existential analysis of human Existenz, he sharply diverges from Heidegger and Sartre in his focus on the nature of the *gift* of Existenz from, and the summons to, Transcendence, the ultimate ground or limit of human concern; in this respect, he is far closer to the theologian Paul Tillich. In the first volume, whose 'Introduction' comprises this selection, Jaspers' attention is focused on 'World Orientation'; my being-in-the-world is the precondition for any questions raised about the meaning of the world and my place in it. But this question and its attendant reflection bring to the fore my experience of disjunction, the disjointness of being, that is the disjunction between the questioner and the rest of the world, between the encompassing and the encompassed. This experience generates the notion that the world as a whole is far greater than what can be known of an object; it is what makes possible the objectiveness of objects lying over against me. This insight may inspire the philosophical attempt to move beyond the concrete circumstances of my situation to a more comprehensive standpoint, but no matter how far these parameters are extended, one is still bounded or limited by the encompassing. Nevertheless, the natural-scientific worldview does achieve positive results, because its success rests on its disciplined ability to suspend or bracket, in the phenomenological sense, all questions which pertain to the worldview, forever inaccessible, which encompasses all other worldviews. In contrast with the scientific limits on knowledge are the existential limits, in *boundary situations*, which reveal or disclose an ineffable dimension of human experience in which the outer and the inner coincide; the language of subject and object is inadequate to communicate the depth of this experience. Since the world-whole escapes one's grasp, these boundary situations point one beyond the known into the unknown. 'Since endlessness delimits both one's orientation and the world, it is this limit … which shows that our being has another source. In the world we comprehend ourselves beyond the world, as Existenz relating to transcendence.'

In the second volume, Jaspers turns to an elucidation of Existenz, the characteristics of the being who asks the question about Being. This movement of thought can function as a constructive 'conversion' to a more intrinsic mode of one's being-in-the-world and a heightened level of transcendent thinking; this can be brought about by the experience of 'the limitedness of limitlessness' in Alan Olson's clever phrase. Jaspers wants to avoid the metaphysical temptation to nullify or render empty the language of objectivity at the expense of subjectivity, or vice versa. His solution is to develop a language of Existenz that mediates between subjectivity and objectivity and elucidates the boundary character of boundary situations. These situations are events that are impossible to consider or articulate apart from the lived situation, such as death, freedom, struggle, guilt and the tragic. As for many Existentialist thinkers, for Jaspers death is the ultimate boundary situation. One knows with utter certainty that one's own death lies ahead, but no one can know anything beyond this. And yet, Jaspers argues, one does not *experience* one's own death, it merely happens as the ending of all experiences. The fact is that in death even appearance disappears, the character of reality as appearance is revealed in its starkness, and all one's speculations about any other reality are at an end.

In the third volume, Jaspers turns his attention to the third dimension of heightened consciousness – transcendence itself and the suppression of subject and object in a form of mystical union. He remarks that all philosophical reflection, especially since Kant, has touched upon this notion, but the reality of transcendence has no way of entering into metaphysical thought. Transcendence has been an issue or a topic in metaphysics, but nothing in metaphysical thinking can motivate one to answer the call which everyone who thinks through the elucidation of Existenz will experience. Traditional metaphysics, he says, lies in an intermediate area where the conceptualization and visualization of truth is not yet the reality of its presence. Since transcendent reality is neither empirical existence nor a supra-mundane world, the experience of transcendence depends on its rupture into immanence – and this occurrence is manifest through *ciphers*. Unlike symbols which have a universal and intelligible meaning, ciphers are known only through one's having lived through their 'event'. These expressions of the transcendental ground must be understood as the cipher-script of transcendence itself, the key to whose decoding is unknown to humans and never achieved with finality or closure; the decoding forever remains an unfinished task and a challenge to human creativity. Jaspers may have acquired this notion from Berkeley's *New Theory of Vision* (1709), Kant's *Critique of Judgment* (1790) or Hofmannsthal's 'Das Gesprach über Gedichte' (1903), but in any case, Jaspers makes this notion uniquely his own. Through the existential encounter with such ciphers as the Holy Trinity, the crucifixion, nature, history, evil, God and the soul, humans can experience a sense of 'hovering', where subject and object are suspended in mysterious indefiniteness. The last moment of Jaspers' great work issues a summons of its own toward philosophical faith:

> Philosophizing is an expression of faith without revelation, an appeal to others traveling the same road ... In a world that has cast doubt on everything, philosophizing is our attempt to hold course without knowing our destination.

PRINCIPAL WORKS

(1913) *General Psychopathology*, trans. J. Hoenig and M. W. Hamilton. Chicago: University of Chicago Press, 1963.
(1919) *Psychology of Worldviews*. Berlin: Springer-Verlag.
(1932) *Philosophy*, 3 vols, trans. E. B. Ashton. Chicago: University of Chicago Press, 1969–71.
(1935) *Reason and Existenz*, trans. William Earle. New York: Noonday Press, 1955.
(1957) 'Autobiography', in Paul Schilpp (ed.), *The Philosophy of Karl Jaspers*. Chicago: Open Court, 1957.
(1962) *Philosophical Faith and Revelation*, trans. E. B. Ashton. Chicago: University of Chicago Press, 1967.

RECOMMENDED READING

Ehrlich, Leonard (1975) *Karl Jaspers: Philosophy as Faith*. Amherst: University of Massachusetts Press.
Ehrlich, Leonard and Wisser, R. (eds) (1988) *Karl Jaspers Today*. Lanham, MA: University Press of America.
Heidegger, Martin (1962) *Being and Time*, trans. John Macquarrie and Edward Robinson. New York: Harper & Row.

Kostenbaum, Peter (1967) 'Karl Jaspers', in Paul Edwards (ed.), *Encyclopedia of Philosophy*. New York: Macmillan, vol. 4, pp. 254–7.

Long, E. E. (1968) *Jaspers and Bultmann: A Dialogue between Philosophy and Theology in the Existentialist Tradition*. Durham, NC: Duke University Press.

Olson, Alan (1979) *Transcendence and Hermeneutics: An Interpretation of Karl Jaspers*. The Hague: Nijhoff.

Salamun, Kurt (1998) 'Jaspers', in Simon Critchley and William Schroeder (eds), *A Companion to Continental Philosophy*. Oxford and New York: Blackwell, pp. 216–22.

Samay, Sebastian (1971) *Reason Revisited: The Philosophy of Karl Jaspers*. Notre Dame, IN: University of Notre Dame Press.

Schrag, Oswald (1971) *Existence, Existenz, and Transcendence*. Pittsburg: Duquesne University Press.

Walraff, Charles (1970) *Karl Jaspers: An Introduction to his Philosophy*. Princeton, NJ: Princeton University Press.

'PHILOSOPHIZING STARTS WITH OUR SITUATION' (1932)[*]

Karl Jaspers

I do not begin at the beginning when I ask questions such as 'What is being?' or 'Why is anything at all? Why not nothing?' or 'Who am I?' or 'What do I really want?' These questions arise from a *situation* in which, coming from a past, I find myself.

When I become aware of myself I see that I am in a world in which I take my bearings. Previously I had taken things up and dropped them again; everything had been a matter of course, unquestioned, and purely present; but now I wonder and ask myself what really is. For all things pass away, and I was not at the beginning, nor am I at the end. Even between beginning and end I ask about the beginning and the end.

I would like an answer that will give me *support*. For though I can neither fully grasp my situation nor see through its origin, the sense of it oppresses me with a vague fear. I can see the situation only as a motion that keeps transforming me along with itself, a motion that carries me from a darkness in which I did not exist to a darkness in which I shall not exist. I concern myself with things and doubt if they matter. The motion takes its course and frightens me with the idea that something will be lost forever if I do not seize it now – yet I do not know what it is. I look for a being that will not just vanish.

---

[*] From *Philosophy*, vol. 1, trans. E. B. Ashton. Chicago: University of Chicago Press, 1969.

I should, it seems, be able to get *generally valid* answers to my questions that will tell me what is and will make me understand how I come to find myself in this situation and what matters in it, to the whole and to me. I am offered such answers. They would make 'being' an object for me and would tell me about it, as about the arrangement of the universe. But any such doctrine is only something that appears to me, along with other objects, in an irresistibly fluid situation. The only way in which I might hold on to some allegedly objective, teachable 'being' would be to forget myself, to turn myself into an object among others. My situation would no longer be the way whose perils are unknown, besetting me, at first, only as fear; it would be something deducible in which I can act correctly because I know whence it comes and whither it goes.

But there is no achieving the self-obliviousness in this deceptive escape from my situation. I might indeed let myself drift awhile, tied to the supposedly known, the supposedly objective, which is and happens without me. But I no sooner start questioning this objectivity than I feel lost again and keep facing myself in the situation along which I change. I remain between beginning and end, fearful of nonexistence, unless I take hold, decide, and thus *dare to be myself*. For in awakening to myself I have a twofold experience: in my situation 'the other' – all that is not I, all that is given and happens without me – is as real and resistant as I myself, in choosing and taking hold, am real and free.

Rather than know the being from which all things come, my objective cognition in this experience is confined to *things in being*, things that occur to me in my situation. The things in the *world* in which I take my bearings can be known and, hopefully, mastered. My orientation in the world proves to be the endlessly advancing illumination of my situation in the direction of an objective being.

But what I know of the world is not to be rounded out into a knowledge of being as such. I may think I grasp the whole situation along with myself, but I never get to the bottom of anything. For the situation is not the beginning of being; it is only the beginning of world orientation and philosophizing. The situation comes out of the past and has historic depth; it is never finished, harboring within itself the possibilities and inevitabilities of the future. There is no other form of reality for me, as I exist in it. It is what I start thinking from and what I return to. Here, at each moment, lies the immediacy of the present, the only thing I am sure of.

When I conceive my situation as such, directly, I am drafting patterns only; as a real situation it is always different. There is always more to it. It *is never something purely immediate*. As something that has come to be, it contains past realities and free decisions. As something that is now, it lets me breathe the possible future. It is never *merely general* – though we can draft general structures of it, as the network of an analysis of existence. In essence, the situation is the historically conveyed, momentarily complete appearance of being.

My chance to see through the situation, to visualize its origins and possible futures, would come only at the end of time. Being, then, would mean a terminated world whose beginning and end I might survey. Until then, however, I still find myself in quest of being. I search for it by my own actions within events outside. From the standpoint of my situation I view other situations, and past situations. But my view always ends in obscurity.

The world, with its knowable premises and historic realities, cannot help me understand my situation; but neither can my situation enable me to understand the world. A philosophizing that begins by casting light on the situation remains in flux because the situation is nothing but a ceaseless flow of mundane events and free choices. For all the determinacy of detail, therefore, philosophizing as a whole remains as *incomplete* as the situation itself. If I take the illumination of the situation for the starting point of philosophizing, I renounce objective explanations that would deduce existence from principles as one whole being. Instead, each objective thought structure merely has its own function. Awakening to myself, in my situation, I raised the question of being. Finding myself in the situation as an indeterminate possibility, I must *search for being* if I want to find my real self. But it is not till I fail in this search for intrinsic being that I begin to philosophize. This is what we call *philosophizing on the ground of possible Existenz*, and the method used is *transcending*.

1 THE SEARCH FOR BEING

General, formal concepts of being:
objective being, subjective being, being-in-itself

To think of being is to make it a distinct being. If we ask what being is, we have many answers to choose from: empirical reality in space and time; dead and living matter; persons and things; tools and material; ideas that apply to reality; cogent constructions of ideal objects, as in mathematics; contents of the imagination – in a word, objectiveness. Whatever being I find in my situation is to me an object.

I am different. I do not confront myself as I confront things. I am the questioner; I know that I do the asking and that those modes of objective being are offered to me as replies. Whichever way I turn, trying to make an object of myself, there is always the 'I' for which my self becomes an object. There remains a being that is I.

Objective being and subjective being are the two modes that strike us first of all, as most different in essence. Objects include persons, of course, who are their own subjects just as I can be their object – and I, as I exist, can even become my own object. But there remains a point where the objective and subjective I are one, despite the dichotomy.

The being of things is unaware of itself; but I, the thinking subject, know about it. When I conceive of this being in the abstract, the way it is independently of its being an object for a subject – that is to say, not as a phenomenon for something else – I call it *being in itself*. This being-in-itself is not accessible to me, however, for the mere thought of it will turn it into an object and thus into something that appears to me as being. It is in myself alone that I know a being that not merely appears to, but is for, itself – one in which being and being known go together. My own being differs radically from any being of things because I can say, 'I am.' But if I objectify my empirical existence, this is not the same as the I-in-itself. I do not know what I am in myself if I am my own object; to find out, I would have to become aware of myself in some way other than cognitive knowledge. And even then the being-in-itself of other things would remain alien to me.

The division of being into objective being, being-in-itself, and subjective being does not give me three kinds of being that exist side by side. It does give me three inseparable poles of the being I find myself in. I may tend to *take one of the three for being as such*. Then I either construe the one and only being as being-in-itself, without noticing that I am making it an object for myself in the process – or I construe it as this object of mine, forgetting in this phenomenal transformation of all being that in objectiveness there must be something which appears, and something it appears to – or I construe it as subjective being, with myself as ultimate reality, without realizing that I can never be otherwise than in a situation, conscious of objects and searching for being-in-itself. Objective being pours out to me in endless variety and infinite abundance; it means the world I can get to know. Subjective being is to me as certain as it is incomprehensible; it can come to be known only to the extent to which it has been objectified as empirical existence and is no longer truly subjective. Being-in-itself defies cognition. It is a boundary concept we cannot help thinking, one that serves to question everything I know objectively – for whenever some objective being should be taken for being proper, in the absolute sense, it will be relativized into a phenomenon by the mere idea of being-in-itself.

Thus we fail to hold fast any being as intrinsic. None of them is being pure and simple, and none can do without the other; each one is a being within being. *The whole eludes us.* There is nothing like a common genus of which the three modes – objective, subjective, and in-itself – might be species; nor is there one source to which they can be traced. They are heterogeneous and repel each other as much as they need each other to be at all – to be, that is, for our consciousness. They almost seem to have dropped out of the unfathomable, three mutual strangers who belong together even though there is no link between them and none of them will help us comprehend another. None may claim precedence, except in some particular perspective. For naïve metaphysics, seeking direct possession of intrinsic being, being-in-itself comes first; but it can only be populated with conceptions from the objective world, which in such metaphysics is supposed to be underlying all existence. Objective being has precedence for all cognition, because objects alone are knowable, and also because in cognition we take being for the sum of knowledge – not including the knower, who is merely added to this being. In illustrative philosophizing, on the other hand, subjective being will come briefly to the fore; from this standpoint of self-comprehension, the questioning and knowing subject tends to accord precedence to itself.

Existence analysis as an analysis of consciousness

We have found being distinctly conceived in objects, directly grasped in self-reflection and evanescently touched – and recognized as inconceivable – in the boundary idea of being-in-itself.

All of these thoughts spring from *the thinker's existence*. From this common ground, to which the search for being takes me, the modes of being appear as perspectives for my thought. The thought itself comprises all perspectives; what it means by being is simply all there is at a time, comprising whatever may occur to me as being. It is my consciousness of temporal existence in the situation I find myself in.

Since existence is consciousness and I exist as consciousness, things are for me only as objects of consciousness. For me, nothing can be without entering into my consciousness. Consciousness as existence is the medium of all things – although we shall see that it is the mere fluid of being.

To analyze existence is to analyze consciousness.

1. Consciousness of objects and of self; existing consciousness

To be conscious is not to be the way a thing is. It is a peculiar kind of being, the essence of which is to *be directed at objects we mean*. This basic phenomenon – as self-evident as it is marvelous – has been called intentionality. Consciousness is intentional consciousness, which means that its relation to its object is not the relation of a thing that strikes another, or is struck by another. There is no causal relation, and indeed no interrelation at all, as between two of a kind or two on one level. In consciousness, rather, I have an object before me. The way I have it does not matter. It may be perception, which is biologically based on causal relations between physical phenomena, though the phenomena as such can never cause intentionality but require intentional acts to animate perception. It may be imagination, or recollection. Or it may be thinking, which can be visual or abstract, aimed at real objects or at imaginary ones. One thing always remains: my consciousness is aimed at what I mean.

Consciousness is self-reflexive. It not only aims at objects, but turns back upon itself – that is to say, it is not only conscious but self-conscious at the same time. The reflexion of consciousness upon itself is as self-evident and marvelous as is its intentionality. I aim at myself; I am both one and twofold. I do not exist as a thing exists, but in an inner split, as my own object, and thus in motion and inner unrest. No consciousness can be understood as stable, as merely extant. Because it is not like the being of spatial and ideal things – things I can walk around, things I can hold fast, things I can visualize so that they stand before me – consciousness evaporates when I would take it for being. While I am conscious of objects as of something else, I am also conscious of myself as an object, but so as to coincide with this object that is myself. It is true that what happens in this confrontation when I observe myself psychologically is that the experience I know and my knowledge of this experience will be so aimed at each other as to make me conscious of two different things at once: what I know, and my knowing it. Yet at the core of the process stands my subjective consciousness, with the one identical 'I' actually doubled by the thought that 'I am conscious of myself.' The coincidence of 'I think' and 'I think that I think' permits neither one to be without the other. A seeming logical absurdity becomes a reality: one is not one but two – and yet it does not become two, but remains precisely this unique one. It is the general, formal concept of the I.

The omnipresent and not otherwise deducible basic phenomenon of consciousness as the split into subject and object means that *self-consciousness and consciousness of objects go together*. True, I become so absorbed in things that I forget myself. But there always remains a last subjective point, an impersonal and purely formal I-point which a thing will confront by existing – that is to say, for which the thing will be an object. Conversely, I cannot so isolate my self-consciousness that I know myself alone: I exist only by confronting other things. There is no subjective consciousness without an objective one, however slight.

Finally there is a consciousness that is neither like the external being of things nor an objectless intentionality. This is the experience of mere inward motion that can light up in sudden intentionality and be known in retrospect, although the lack of any split keeps it dormant and its existence can only be remembered – of experiences had while awakening, for example, and of undefinable sensations. Viewed from the split consciousness, this *merely existing* one is a *limit* that can be empirically illuminated as a start and a transition, and as the encompassing ground; from the viewpoint of things outwardly extant, it is inwardness. Without any splits into subjective and objective consciousness, the merely existing one would be a fulfillment distinguished from an objective, concrete process by the fact that I can recall this experience as existing at a time when I was not myself, and that I can but retrospectively visualize it, that is, make it conscious, objective, and plain.

If existence is consciousness, it is still not just one or all of the definite concepts of consciousness. Opposed to them is *the unconscious*. But if this is to have any being for us, we must either make it conscious or we must be conscious of it as 'the unconscious' – in other words, as a phenomenon, an object of consciousness – and thus, for our consciousness, enable it to be.

The several meanings in which we conceive the unconscious correspond to the concepts of consciousness. The unconscious equivalent of intentional, objective consciousness is nonobjectiveness. The unconscious equivalent of self-consciousness is what we have experienced and objectively sensed but not expressly reflected upon and rated as known. The unconscious equivalent of merely existing consciousness is what we have not inwardly experienced in any sense, what lies entirely outside the realms of our consciousness.

The statement that all existence is consciousness does not mean that consciousness is all. It does mean that for us there is only what enters into the consciousness to which it appears. For us the unconscious is as we become conscious of it.

2. Possibilities of analyzing consciousness

Real consciousness is always the existence of an individual with other things that exist in time; it has a beginning and an end. As such, consciousness is an object of empirical observation and study. It contains the fullness of the world if the world is only the temporal world of real consciousness.

Our *conscious existence as a temporal reality* is a ceaseless urge to satisfy many desires. Raised from a state of nature by knowledge and the faculty of choice, we consciously envision death and seek to avoid it at all costs. The instinct of self-preservation makes us fear perils and distinguish them so as to meet them. We seek pleasure in the enjoyment of existence and in the sense of its expansion, for which we toil each day. In anticipation of things to come we think of distant possibilities and goals and dangers. Worry, born of this reflection on what lies ahead, forces us to provide for the future. To satisfy the boundless will to live and the power drives of existence, we conquer others and delight in seeing our status reflected in our environment; indeed, it is this mirror that seems to give us our real sense of existence. Yet all this will satisfy our consciousness only for moments. It keeps driving us on. Never really bringing content, it achieves no goal and ceases only when we die.

Such are the descriptions of consciousness as the empirically real existence of an instinctual life. It can also be described as formal *consciousness at large*. In self-consciousness, distinct from other selves and from the objects I mean, I know myself as acting, then, and as identical with myself as time passes; I know I remain the one I. In objective consciousness I have the modes of objective being in the categories; I understand what definite being I encounter, and I know that cognition of all mundane existence is possible in generally valid form. My consciousness at large is interchangeable with that of anyone else who is my kind, even though not numerically identical.

Insofar as consciousness with its world – whether existing reality or consciousness at large – is an object and may thus come to be known, it becomes a topic either of psychology, if it is empirical existence, or of logic, if possessed of generally valid knowledge.

But there is a third way to analyze consciousness: not as naturally given the way it is, but as a fulfilled real consciousness which never remains the same, which undergoes transformations and is thus historic. *Historically changing consciousness* not only happens, as does a natural process; it remembers, it affects itself, it engenders itself in its history. Man actively lives the life of his successive generations, instead of merely suffering it in a repetition of the same.

An *objective study* of these metamorphoses constitutes world orientation – as anthropology and analytical psychology and intellectual history. Beginning with the dull mind of primitive man, such study allows us to glimpse the leaps in human history from one form to the other, to see now how germs unfold slowly, and then again the sudden flash of new origins of consciousness. In the individual we trace the inner changes and analyze them up to the limit where the processes defy analysis. We seek to penetrate the worlds and self-illuminations of the personally and historically strangest and most remote forms of consciousness.

The study of changeable consciousness teaches us that we cannot set up any substantial real consciousness as the 'natural consciousness,' or its substance as the 'natural view of the world.' This would be a reduction to the slicked-down form of a distinct phenomenal consciousness – as a society of historically linked individuals will take it for granted – or to the psychological pattern of the drives of living existence in its environment. There is no immediate existence that might be scientifically analyzed, in one exclusively correct way, as the natural one. Objectively, any attempt to construe and characterize such an existence has only relative significance. The man who takes it for a radical cognition of being determines only what his narrow mind will make him think of himself. We can, of course, try to go back beyond all historicity and all concreteness in pursuit of what we might call 'bare existence' – but this will only impoverish us. We may claim that what we know at the end will fit the universal immediacy of existence, but in fact we shall have stated only a very meager and formally empty consciousness of being that will be historically particular and fixed in time. And if we approach the supposedly immediate by construing the seeming genetic priority of primitive tribes as 'natural,' we find that once we know more about their existence it proves to be not at all natural but specifically artificial and strange.

There is no radical departure for the awaking of consciousness. Nobody begins afresh. I do not step into a primal situation. So, as there is no generally determinable, natural, unveiled existence to be discovered by removing fallacies, what really lies at the root of it cannot be sought by abstracting from acquired traits. It can be sought only by questioning what these traits have led to. An understanding of all that has been acquired and evolved remains the ground on which we understand existence. The utmost clarity about existence that we can achieve comes to depend upon what scientific intellectual history has achieved already. I cannot see through existence if I merely know general structures, but only if I take a concrete part in the historic process of factual, active, and cognitive world orientation.

Thus the existence analysis conceived as preceding any research operation in the world – though actually performed only after the completed operation – will be either a schema for consciousness at large, showing the network of the modes of being and the sense of validity, or it will be a diagram of conscious existence in reality, isolating the psychological forces at work as libido, fear, worry, will to power, fear of death, or death wish; or it will be the historic self-understanding of consciousness as it has evolved.

No way of making existence conscious gets me to the bottom of it. Instead, unless I confine myself artificially and try to use a supposed knowledge as an anchor in existence where it cannot take hold, any existence analysis will leave me suspended in my situation. The fact that efforts to get underneath it all – as if there were an existing ground to penetrate – seem to plunge me into a void indicates that existence is not what counts if I want to get at being. What counts is myself. Constructions of existence will not take me to being. They can only help me get there by a leap; and the approach that may enable me to take this leap is not existence analysis any more; it is elucidation of Existenz.

3. Consciousness as a boundary

In analyzing consciousness we work out constructive schemata for logic (the formal visualization of what is valid for consciousness at large), for psychology (the study of empirically existing consciousness), and for the history of consciousness (the reproduction of the mental process).

In part, these objectifying analyses are available in magnificent drafts, but they can never be conclusive. They keep encountering limits that make us feel what is beyond the analyses. Logic, then, will turn about into a formal metaphysical transcending (as in the case of Plotinus); psychology, into elucidation of Existenz (as in Kierkegaard's); and the history of consciousness, into consummate metaphysics (as in Hegel's). Philosophizing cannot be consummated in the self-observation of an empirically existing consciousness, nor in the construction of the ever-present consciousness at large, nor in historical knowledge.

Consciousness is a boundary. It is an object of observation, and yet it already defies objective observation. The statement that in philosophizing we start out from consciousness is untrue insofar as it would seem to confirm that the general – logical, psychological, or historical – analyses of the kind of consciousness that anyone can have at any time amount to philosophical thinking. The statement truly refers to the elucidations that begin and end with *existential consciousness*.

Distinguishing existenz

We saw being as kept in suspension by the inconceivable being-in-itself. We sensed it as a boundary in existence analysis. But while being-in-itself was the utterly other, completely inaccessible to me as nonexistent for thought, I myself, as I exist, am the limit to analyzing existence. Herein lies the next step we must take in our search for being.

1. Empirical existence; consciousness at large; possible existenz

What do I mean when I say 'I'?

The first answer is that in thinking about myself I have made myself an object. I am this body, this individual, with an indefinite self-consciousness reflected in my impact upon my environment – I am *empirical existence*.

Second, I am a subject essentially identical with every other subject. I am interchangeable. This interchangeability is not the identity of average qualities among empirical individuals; it is subjective being as such, the subjectiveness that is the premise of all objectiveness – I am *consciousness at large*.

Third, I experience myself in potential unconditionality. I not only want to know what exists, reasoning pro and con; I want to know from a source beyond reasoning, and there are moments of action when I feel certain that what I want now, what I am now doing, is what I really want myself. I want to be so that this will and this action are mine. My very essence – which I do not know even though I am sure of it – comes over me in the way I want to know and to act. In this potential freedom of knowledge and action I am '*possible Existenz.*'

Thus, instead of an unequivocally determined I, we have several meanings. As consciousness at large I am the subject whose objects are the things of reality and general validity. Every individual shares in this conceptual general consciousness if objectified being appears to him as it does to all men. Next, I am empirical individuality as objectified subjectiveness; as such I am a special and, in this form, singular occurrence in the endless diversity of individuals. Then, again as empirical existence, I am this individual for consciousness at large, which makes me an object for psychology, and an inexhaustible one at that – an object of observation and research, but not of total cognition. Finally, as possible Existenz, I am a being related to its potential and, as such, nonexistent for any consciousness at large. To conceive the meaning of possible Existenz is to break through the circle of all modes of objective and subjective being.

In philosophizing we admit each of the modes of subjective being. We do not lump them together as identical; and in a limited sense we accord a primacy to each one, though reserving the absolute primacy for possible Existenz.

We recognize the primacy of the empirical I as compelled by the needs of existence, but we recognize it relatively, and not for philosophizing itself.

Consciousness at large will be paramount as a requisite of any being for me as the subject. The following two trains of thought may illustrate the meaning of this formal paramountcy that covers all subjectiveness and objectiveness. First, I not only exist like any living thing; I also know that I exist. I can conceive the possibility of my nonexistence. If I try to think of myself as not being at all, however, I notice that in allowing the rest of the world to stand I am involuntarily letting myself stand as well, as a point in consciousness at large for which the world would be. Then I go on to think of the possibility that there were no being at all. But while I can say this, I cannot really think it either, because I still keep thinking as this 'I' – as if I had being even though the world had not. Each time, the questioner remains extant as consciousness at large, while it seems that all other being can really be thought out of existence. The thinker's consciousness at large is entitled to its specific primacy in the limited sense that we can temporarily conceive it as the ultimate being without which there is no other.

In philosophizing, the I of possible Existenz has the decidedly dominant function of breaking through the circle of objective and subjective being, toward the being-in-itself which in that circle can be only negatively defined. Possible Existenz may perhaps open the positive way that is closed to consciousness at large in the world of objects. This kind of philosophizing is as nothing for empirical existence, and a groundless figment of the imagination for consciousness at large. But for possible Existenz it is the way to itself, and to being.

2. Existenz

Existenz is the never objectified source of my thoughts and actions. It is that whereof I speak in trains of thought that involve no cognition. It is what relates to itself, and thus to its transcendence.[1]

Can something be, and yet not be a real object among objects? Obviously it cannot be the 'I am' we conceive as empirical existence or consciousness at large, as comprehensible and deducible. The question is whether all the objective and subjective conceptions of being have brought me to the end, or whether my self can be manifested to me in yet another fashion. We are touching what seems to me the pivotal point of the sense of philosophizing.

To be means to decide about being. It is true that, as I observe myself, I am the way I am; although an individual, I am a case of something general, subject to causality or responding to the valid challenge of objectively fixed commandments. But where I am my own origin, everything has not yet been settled in principle, in accordance with general laws. It is not only due to the infinity of conditions that I do not know how it might be, had it been settled. On quite a different plane it is still my own self that decides what it is.

This thought – impossible to conceive objectively – is the sense of *freedom* of possible Existenz. In this sense I cannot think that, after all, everything takes its course, and that I might therefore do just as I please and vindicate my action by whatever general arguments come to hand. Instead, for all the dependence and determinacy of my existence, I feel sure that ultimately something rests with me alone. What I do or forgo, what I want first and foremost, where I cling to options and where I proceed to realizations – all this results neither from general rules I act upon, as right, nor from psychological laws to which I am subject. It does spring, in the restlessness of my existence and by the certainty of self-being, from freedom. Where I stop observing myself psychologically and still do not act with unconscious naïveté; where I act positively, rather, soaring with a bright assurance that gives me nothing to know but sustains my own being – there I decide what I am.

I know a kind of appeal to which my true self inwardly responds by the realization of my being. But it is not as an isolated being that I come to sense what I am. Against my self-will, against the accident of my empirical existence, I experience myself in *communication*. I am never more sure of being myself than at times of total readiness for another, when I come to myself because the other too comes to himself in our revealing struggle.

As possible Existenz I seize upon the *historicity* of my existence. From the mere diversity of knowable realities it will expand to an existential depth. What is outwardly definite and delimiting is inwardly the appearance of true being.

The man who loves mankind only does not love at all, but one who loves a particular human being does. We are not yet faithful if we are rationally consistent and will keep agreements; we are faithful if we accept as our own, and know ourselves bound to, what we have done and loved. A will to reorganize the world properly and permanently is no will at all; a proper will is to seize as my own whatever chances my historic situation offers.

If I am rooted in historicity, my temporal existence carries no weight in and by itself; but it does carry weight in the sense that *in time I decide for eternity*. What is time, then? As the future, it is possibility; as the past, it is the bond of fidelity; as the present, it is decision. Time, then, is not something that merely passes; it is the *phenomenality of Existenz*. Existenz is gained in time, by our own decisions. Once temporality has this weight and I know it, I have overcome temporality – not by replacing it with an abstract timelessness, not by putting myself outside of time, but by the fact that in time I stand above time. In my conscious life, governed by vital urges and the finite will to be happy, I want time to last as though deliverance from the anxieties of existence were found in blind permanence. I can no more eliminate this will from my living consciousness than I can void the sorrows of mortality. They are part of my existence as such. But if, in time, I act and love absolutely, time is eternal. This is something my intellect cannot grasp, something that will light up only at the moment, and afterwards only in doubtful remembrance. It is no outward possession, to have and to hold.

There is a distinguishing formula, meaningless to intellectual consciousness at large, but an appeal to possible Existenz. It goes as follows: real being loses its reality in all objective cognition, turning into endless duration, into laws of nature, or into the nonbeing of mere transience; but Existenz is realized in choices made in temporal historicity. Thus, despite its objective disappearance, Existenz achieves reality as fulfilled time. Eternity is neither timelessness nor duration for all time; it is the depth of time as the historic appearance of Existenz.

3. World and Existenz

Existenz will find itself with other Existenz in the mundane situation, without coming to be recognizable as mundane being. What is in the world appears as being to my consciousness at large, but only a transcending possible Existenz can be sure of Existenz.

Being that compels recognition exists directly. I can take hold of it, can make something of it, and with it – technically with things, or in arguing with myself and with other consciousness. In it lies the *resistance* of anything given, whether the real resistance of empirical reality or the resistance of logical necessities or impossibilities. It is always objective being, an original object or an adequate objectification like the models or types that serve as research tools, for instance.

Existenz, which in itself does not exist, *appears* to possible Existenz as existence. In our minds, of course, we cannot close the gap between world and Existenz, between things we can know and things we can elucidate, between objective being and the free being of Existenz. In fact, however, the two modes of being are so close together that a consciousness which is also possible Existenz will find the distinction an infinite task whose performance combines the cognition of mundane being with the elucidation of Existenz.

It is only abstractly that we can formulate the distinction of objective being and the free being of Existenz. We can say, for instance, that objective being is given as mechanism, life, and consciousness, while I as Existenz am original – not original being, but my own origin in existence. Measured by the being of things, there is no freedom; measured by freedom, the being of things is not true being. Or we can say that extant being and free being are not two antithetical kinds of being which might be coordinated. They are interrelated but flatly incomparable; being in the sense of objectivity and being in the sense of freedom exclude one another. The one steps from time into timelessness or endless duration; the other steps from time into eternity. What is for all time, or valid, is objectiveness; what is evanescent and yet eternal is Existenz. We can say that one is for a thinking subject only, while the other, though never without an object, is real only for communicating Existenz.

From the point of view of the world, any appearance of Existenz is merely objective being. From that viewpoint we see consciousness and the subjective I, but not Existenz; from there we cannot even understand what is meant by Existenz. *From the point of view of Existenz*, its own being is merely something that appears in existence, an existence that is not an appearance of Existenz, and is not its true self, but is recreant. It is as though originally all existence should be Existenz, and as though whatever part of it is nothing but existence could be understood as depleted, entangled, bereft of Existenz.

There is no pointer to lead us from objective being to another kind of being, unless it be done indirectly, by the disjointness and inconclusiveness of objective being. But Existenz does permeate the forms of that being as media of its realization, and as possibilities of its appearance. Standing *on the borderline of world and Existenz*, possible Existenz views all existence as more than existence. Proceeding from the most remote, from the mechanism, being will approach itself, so to speak, via life and consciousness, seeking to find itself in Existenz as what it is. Or – while consciousness at large conceives existence from this borderline as pure existence – it may be the character of all existence to be potentially relevant for Existenz by providing the impulse for it or serving as its medium.

There can be no Existenz without other Existenz, and yet objectively it makes no sense to speak of it as manifold. For whenever Existenz and Existenz communicate historically in the dark of mundane being, they are one for the other only, invalid for any watching consciousness at large. What is invisible from outside is not surveyable as a being of many.

On the one side, possible Existenz can see the being of the world, split into modes of being, in the medium of consciousness at large; on the other side is every Existenz. *On no side is there a conclusive being*, neither objectively as the one mundane existence nor existentially as a conceivable and surveyable world of all Existenz. If I think of being, it will always be a distinct being, not *the* being. In the ascertainment of possible Existenz I do not have an Existenz for an object, nor do I make sure of an Existenz at all. I only make sure of myself and of the Existenz I communicate with; we are what simply admits of no substitution; we are not cases of a species. Existenz is a sign pointing toward this self-ascertainment of a being that is objectively neither conceivable nor valid – a being that no man knows or can meaningfully claim, either in himself or in others.

Being

We have found no one answer to the question we raised at the start: what is being? An answer to this question satisfies the questioner if it allows him to recognize his own being. But the question of being itself is not unequivocal; it depends upon who asks it. It has no original meaning for our existing consciousness at large, which we can break up into the multiplicity of distinct being. It is only with possible Existenz, in transcending all existence and all objective being, that the impassioned search for being-in-itself begins – only to fall short of the goal of definite knowledge. Whatever exists is phenomenal; it is *appearance*, not being. And yet it is not nothing.

1. Appearance and Being

The sense of "appearance" in such statements has its categorial derivation in a particular, objective relationship: between the way something appears from a standpoint, as a phenomenon, and the way it is in-itself, regardless of the standpoint. In an objectifying sense, then, phenomenality is the aspect of a mental addendum, of something we have to think as objectively underlying but not yet objective itself – something I conceive as an object only because, in principle, I might come to know it as such (as the atom, for instance).

It is in the category of appearance – using it to transcend this definite objectifying relation of phenomenal and underlying elements – that we conceive all being when we seek being as such.

Even so, the being that appears will remain twofold. In temporal existence we cannot overcome the duality of the inaccessible being-in-itself of *transcendence* – which we cannot conceive as the objectively underlying addendum – and the self-being manifest to Existenz, which is not existing consciousness. Existenz and transcendence are heterogeneous, but interrelated. Their relationship appears in existence.

As an object of science, existence is the appearance of something *theoretically* underlying. Science has no access to Existenz, nor to transcendence. But in a philosophical sense the appearance of being-in-itself results from the scientific cognition of a phenomenon *plus* the conception of the underlying addendum. In the scientific study of phenomena we think up the underlying addendum; in philosophizing we use the phenomena to touch being in our interpretation of *ciphers of transcendence*, and in the thinking that *appeals to Existenz*.

Nor is the consciousness we study the same consciousness in which I am sure of self-being and aware of transcendence. There is no unconscious Existenz, but consciousness as an object of scientific cognition is never that existential consciousness. This is why I, the single living individual existing for objective research, can turn, for myself, into the encompassing medium of all being when my consciousness is the psychologically inaccessible absolute assurance of Existenz. For the same reason, the statement that nothing lies outside consciousness is untrue if I understand consciousness as a mere research object. The statement is true in the sense that for me there is only what becomes phenomenal and thus enters into my consciousness. It is in going beyond its own explorable existence that consciousness begins and ends its contact with the unexplorable. For science this is the unconscious with its many meanings; for Existenz, it is transcendence. Yet this supplement to consciousness will of necessity be conscious again – for science as a theory of the unconscious, and for Existenz as the cipher of being in a self-contradictory and thus evanescent form.

The phrase "appearance of being" must be understood as ambiguous if we are to grasp the thesis that *Existenz appears in its own consciousness*. It means neither the appearance of an underlying objectivity nor of a transcendent being-in-itself.

On the one hand, Existenz cannot be psychologically understood as a conscious phenomenon. Only the forms of the existence of consciousness can be objects of psychology – its causally conditioned and intelligibly motivated experiences, but not its existential ground. Instead, in psychological research we think up an underlying unconscious, which we consider the reality of consciousness. In an objectifying sense, consciousness is the phenomenon of this underlying addendum, the way in which it appears. In an existential sense, however, appearance means a way of becoming conscious, a way of having been objectified, in which a simultaneously and wholly present being understands itself. I know eternally what in this way is never known objectively. I am what appears in this way – not as something underlying, but as myself. We group the appearance of consciousness as a research object with the underlying, which to us is outright alien. And we group the appearance of Existenz with what we are originally, what we will answer for. The appearance of the underlying objectivity is generally valid for cognition; the appearance of Existenz is manifest in existential communication.

On the other hand, as the appearance in consciousness of its *subjective* being, Existenz can be sure of itself only in relation to transcendent being-in-itself. This it can feel but cannot be. What manifests itself to Existenz is not plain, straightforward being; it is being that addresses Existenz – itself no more than a subjective appearance – as a possibility.

Appearance is heterogeneous. The underlying objectivity appears in phenomena, transcendent being-in-itself in ciphers, Existenz in the assurance of absolute consciousness. In each direction, this heterogeneousness voids the stability of being. In its entirety it will keep being definitively *disjoint for the questioner as possible Existenz in temporal existence*, even at the root of his search.

2. Being and the many modes of being

In thinking about our question, what is being, we may try to *take one thing for being as such* and all other being for derivative. There are many possible ways to try this, but none to carry it through. Suppose, for instance, I were to equate intrinsic being with objective knowability and to regard myself as derived from the objects, thus making a thing of myself and denying all freedom. Or suppose I were to turn the freedom of the subject into original being, and to derive things from that. Each time, the derivation of one from the other would be a fantastic leap. I can neither comprehend myself by the being of things, nor can I take all things to be myself. Instead, I am in the world; there are things that exist for me; I do make original decisions as a possible Existenz that appears to itself in the world. No rudiment of being enables me to comprehend all the being I find myself in. This is my situation, which I must not forget as I philosophize.

Our search for being started out from manifold being and led back to it, as to the modes of being. If we did not find being, there is still the question *why everything is called being* even though it cannot be brought under one principle or derived from one origin.

The fact we face here is that any statement is made in the form of language. Whatever we may be discussing will take the form of a definite sentence with the predicate 'is' – even if the sentence refers to no being at all, even if it is an indirect suggestion or if it connects a train of thought that may be illustrative as a whole but that does not define an object as the one referred to.

Language is the phenomenal form of all thought. Whether in objective cognition or in nonobjective elucidation – in either case I am thinking. And what I think I have to think in *categories*. These are basic definitions of all thought; there is no superior category of which the rest might be species or derivations; but what they have in common, what defines them, is that they will always state a being. It is thought itself which in some sense is one and will accordingly call heterogeneous being – though no common concept of it is discoverable – by the one name of being.

As we think in categories, the question is whether our thoughts are adequately or inadequately categorized. We have to distinguish between, on the one hand, what is directly what it is, what is to be discovered and then to be straightforwardly discussed in categories – and on the other hand, what is not such an object but will be discussed just the same, in an indirect way, open to misunderstanding, and necessarily also in categories. Schematically we can formulate the distinction as follows: The *discovery of being* is scientific cognition; it gives us our bearings in the world and will always more or less adequately grasp a definite being. The *ascertainment of being* is philosophizing as the transcending of objectivity; in the medium of categories it grasps inadequately, in substituted objectivities, what can never become objective.

Methodologically, therefore, the genuine philosophical steps are to be grasped as modes of transcending. What they express regarding content, from the existential source of an absolute consciousness, is a being that employs such thought for its self-ascertainment as intrinsic being.

As possible Existenz comes to itself by way of philosophizing, it cannot exchange its freedom for the stifling narrowness of a being known as intrinsic. It will always be freedom, not cognition, that lets us experience what proper being is. The impulse behind our dissection of the concepts of being is to loosen our consciousness, to experiment with possibilities so as to get at the root of true philosophizing and there to *search* for the one being, as being proper.

We can approach being either by its *dilution* into everything of which we can indefinitely say it 'is,' or by its *fixation* into a categorially *defined* being that is known, or by the accentuation of *true* being, which is ascertained in thought. We differentiate, accordingly, between definite and indefinite being, between the various definitions, and between the true and the trivial.

True being cannot be found in a sense that we might know. It is to be sought in its *transcendence*, to which only Existenz, not consciousness at large, can ever relate.

One might suppose that any meaningful thinking must indirectly aim at this transcendence if it is not to deteriorate into vacuous intellectual gamesmanship and indifferent factuality. It could be that the designation of all being as being, with no noticeable common denominator save the form of language – that this most tenuous appearance of being in our speech indicates how deeply rooted all of it is in the one being. But these are indefinite thoughts, unless they already signify a transcending. For all categories can be used as means to transcend themselves, to dissolve their particularity in a unity that has neither an existence in the world nor a meaning in logic – namely, in the one being of transcendence which enters only the soul of a historic Existenz, if anything. From there it pervades meaning and existence, seeming to confirm them both, and then again to fracture and dissolve them both.

Ontology as a doctrine of being can achieve only one result nowadays: to make us conscious of being by the modes of being that occur to our thought. In the performance of this task it never touches the one being; it only clears the way for its ascertainment. Today's ontology will not be metaphysics any more; it will be a doctrine of categories. Whatever I may be thinking can only make room for the 'I' as possible Existenz – which is outside my every thought at the same time. To possible Existenz, thoughts mean relative knowabilities, possibilities, appeals, but no more. In the same way, my partner in communicative thinking will stay outside his thoughts, for himself and for me, in order to move with me in possible thoughts and not to be subjected to absolute ones. To meet in communication is to break through the thought that made the breakthrough possible.

2 PHILOSOPHIZING ON THE GROUND OF POSSIBLE EXISTENZ

Our search for being led back to the question of the searcher. He does not merely exist, for existence will not search for being; existence derives its satisfaction from itself. A searcher's being is possible Existenz by the mere fact of his searching, and that search is philosophizing. When Existenz feels the impact of existence, when the urge to reach being by way of thought drives it to philosophize – then, and not until then, does being become a question.

Nor would a philosophizing consciousness at large, bent on a generally valid cognition of being, be the same as philosophizing on the ground of possible Existenz. For consciousness at large knows objects in the world; its sciences constitute orientation in the world; in their sense they find being and have it. They are philosophical if they serve the search for being, but in themselves they are not such a search.

The philosophizing of possible Existenz, sprung from its desire to attain reality in philosophical living, *remains* a search.

The approach to Existenz

Here we must halt in our course of visualizing modes of being and strike out in a new direction. Being was plain to us where it is a matter of objective being, of objects that are nothing but themselves; it would be the comprehensible world. Against that, Existenz and transcendence, as thought figures, are imaginary points. To philosophize is to move around them.

The pivot of this movement, the junction and crossroads of whatever has absolute relevance for us, is Existenz. Without the presence or the possibility of Existenz we lose our way of thinking and our way of life in an endless, senseless waste. If I deny the being of Existenz not just conversationally but really, if I turn objective being into being as such, my existence will be void and dreary throughout the endlessness of things, with the rest an unexistential hustle and bustle impelled by the remaining, pointlike Existenz that leaves me no peace, demanding substance and fulfillment. And those are found nowhere but in the incomprehensible absolute certainty of an Existenz bent upon philosophical self-elucidation.

If I want to look straight at Existenz, however, it will be out of my sight. Things are plain to the extent to which they are objective. What stands visibly before us in space is the sensory archetype of objectiveness; to think objectively means to think in spatial images. The structure of consciousness already lacks this spatial objectivity; it has a derivative, metaphorical one, although still an objectivity that makes it an object we can explore empirically. Not until we approach Existenz do we come close to something absolutely nonobjective – and yet its self-certainty is the center of our existence, the wellspring of the search for being, and the spark that lights the *essentiality* of all objectiveness.

If something cannot become an object at all, we can – so it would seem – not talk about it either; whoever talks about it will turn it into an object anyway. And any supposedly knowable result of such thinking would indeed make

Existenz an object and psychologize it. But objects are not all that we can think and speak of. There are means to become *clear to ourselves* in thought without acquiring insights into anything. To become clear – this is the form in which the nonobjective possible Existenz exists.

We say 'Existenz' and talk of the being of this reality. But Existenz is not a concept; it is a sign that points 'beyond all objectiveness.' Philosophizing on the ground of possible Existenz is the endeavor to use means of thought to get beyond pointing at empty depths and to arrive at a clearer visualization. Not to stop delving into Existenz despite the impossibility of cognition – this is true philosophizing.

It is precisely because we philosophize *on the ground* of possible Existenz that the process cannot make it an object of exploration and cognition. Just as the philosophizing neophyte tends to be lured into taking details for the whole and relatives for absolutes, the real danger in philosophizing is the temptation to objectify Existenz into an absolute. When its consciousness of being comes to seem conclusive in itself, taking Existenz for the absolute may look like the obvious conclusion. But such an absolutizing would doom an Existenz that cannot escape from the process of temporal existence.

Intrinsic being, as the absolute, would have to enable us to comprehend whatever exists at all. But Existenz fails to make existence comprehensible; there is no sense in which we might conceive the world as derived from Existenz. So, Existenz cannot be intrinsic being.

Yet the ultimate test of the question whether or not Existenz is the absolute is not the failure to derive all being from it, nor is it any other logical thought. The ultimate test is our existential consciousness itself. It may reply to the question with fear, being aware of our inconclusiveness and imperfection as well as of our relativity to something dark and strange; or it may reply with defiance, denying the relativity by a self-reliant posture, defensive without the calm of being sheltered in itself. Existenz is quiet and disquiet in one. It can rest neither in existence nor in itself. It will rest only when the sense of freedom in its transcendent dependence puts it in touch with absolute being.

As mere understanding observation of men and things leads to philosophy's dismemberment into phenomenology and psychology, making an absolute of Existenz leads to captivity in an imaginary point which I am, and which I cannot conceive. I go out from this point to think about what I am if I am myself; rather than turn into a being I have, it will approach itself in the world by taking hold of existence. Indirectness is its essence.

Thus the inconclusiveness of Existenz becomes the touchstone of any philosophy of Existenz. The thought of such a philosophy is an incessant loosening, an opening of my mind to the experience of my proper being in the search for my transcendence. If my solipsistic existence is snarled in world-lessness, inimical to things, such thinking will extricate it. If I am uncommunicative, it will free me to be open to other Existenz. If I am godless, it will show me transcendence.

The structure of philosophizing

In essence, the philosophy of Existenz is metaphysics. It believes in its source.

The real will to know originates in Existenz, which is unknowable. When we are thrown back upon it, our philosophical thought has first to split on Existenz, so as to touch indirectly what it cannot reach point-blank. In philosophizing on the ground of possible Existenz we take up everything conceivable and knowable we meet in our search; we want Existenz to come out of this, but Existenz is not the final goal. The philosophizing urge goes beyond it. It wants Existenz to dissolve again, in transcendence. Philosophical thought is a beacon; it means not only the lighted object but the light itself, whose reflection brings us word that Existenz is possible.

The courses of this illustrative philosophizing are not set at random, however. To draft the rudiments of its structure, we start afresh at the point we had reached when three names of diverse being came back to us – names which seem to bespeak the *universality*, the *originality*, and the *unity* of being rather than its isolation and disjunction. Universal existence is the world; we are original as Existenz; and the One is transcendence.

The *world* is what exists, what occurs to me as the being of specific objects, and what I am as empirical existence. My cognition of the world is objective, concerned with things I have before my eyes as objects; but the world itself, the universe, is neither an object nor a whole. Of being – nonobjective as such – I can attempt only an illustrative, inadequately objectified ascertainment. This nonobjective being is *Existenz* if it can originally manifest itself to me in my own being; we call it *transcendence* if it is being in the objective form of a cipher but conceivable for Existenz alone.

That the boundary concept of being-in-itself makes all existence phenomenal; that Existenz cannot equate itself with being; that, rather, it knows of its relation to transcendence – these three facts prepared us for the impulse to search for being. The search has thus three goals resulting one from the other, however undefinable they may remain. We go into the world to find our bearings; we go beyond the world to appeal to our own possible Existenz; and we open ourselves to transcendence. On our way into the world we tackle what can be known and rebound from it into philosophical *world orientation*; stepping out of mere worldly existence, awakened to the activity of self-realization, we *elucidate Existenz*; we conjure being and engage in *metaphysics*.

1. How we think in world orientation

To consciousness at large, being is what can become objectively known. This 'world' is interminable for our cognition. Whatever we come to know in it becomes both *an object* and *objective* in the sense of generally valid. The concept of objectivity covers both meanings.

Our knowledge of existing objects is called world orientation. It is only an *orientation* because it can never be complete and remains an infinite process; it is *world* orientation because it compiles what is known of a distinct being, of being *in* the world.

World orientation as the knowledge of things in the world has to be distinguished from *existence analysis*, in which I try to grasp existence at large as comprising everything, world orientation included. This is an attempted general visualization of the patterns governing not only world orientation but whatever has being for me. World orientation is an activity of scientists; existence analysis is a philosophizing step in the search for being.

In itself, we divide world orientation into a scientific and a philosophical one. Scientific world orientation is the cognition produced by the self-education of thought in pursuit of objectivity. Although this thought is real only among empirical individuals whose factual worlds, at first, are not the same at all, it is capable of producing cognitive results that are held in common with everyone else, as consciousness at large. There are as many worlds as there are consciously thinking individuals; but for world orientation this diversity itself is simply one more object.

World orientation moves in an expanding circle. The empirical individual, initially tied to his subjectivity, would like objectively to comprehend the real world. At first this exists for him in its diversity, and in it he would have to include his own individuality as one of innumerable cases. The result would be a generally valid being detached from individual bonds, since the seemingly included subject would also have to recognize himself as a deceptive factor and to cancel himself in order to achieve the objectivity he seeks. And yet, for himself, he will always exist again in his bondage, as his particular reality. He knows the leap into the universality of the world, the leap that may lift the barriers, just as he knows the return to his own reality. To himself, he remains miraculously able, from his infinitesimal particularity, to grasp the entire world as universal and valid – not in fact, of course, but in intent.

Objective cognition as world orientation is found only in the sciences as they have evolved to date. Without them there can be no philosophical world orientation. Without constant adoption of the scientific world orientation, and without research work of our own, our philosophizing becomes immaterial and empty. We must run up against the hard, cogent ways of existence if we would advance to intrinsic being as a possibility beyond knowledge. No man who has not been passionately engaged in factual world orientation can truthfully find the philosophical one in it.

Philosophical world orientation does not fuse the latest research results into a unified world image. What it does is show that such a valid image of the world as the one and absolute one is an impossibility. It looks for *what is doubtful* in factual world orientation.

To our intellect, for instance, it seems like a self-evident presupposition that the *universe* exists. Whether, transcending all world orientation, the intellect conceives a metaphysical process of the Creation, whether it drafts a positivistic picture of the mechanical course of the world or a sociological one of the necessary course of history – in each case, a whole is supposedly brought into the grasp of a cognition that conquers its objects. It takes specific trains of thought to reverse this fixation in a whole, particularly of a universe in a world image. It takes a reduction to the factual test of the supposed knowledge in my situation; it takes thoughts that will show up fissures, contradictions, and limits in any thinking that deals with the universe. In philosophical world orientation we examine the principles and meanings of the acts of cognition that appear in science.

A second premise of the intellect is that whatever is must be *objective* and *knowable* – that being is identical with objective being, or with conceivability as an object. What casts doubt upon this absolutizing of the intellect is the thought that objective being consists, *not of itself*, but of being for a knowing subject, as it appears to that subject. If the being that appears in world orientation has a tendency to impress itself on us as being as such, philosophical world orientation makes us aware that any being of the world-orientational sciences will be a distinct and particular one, and thus cannot be being as such. Knowing these modes of being, philosophical world orientation takes us from one to the other and beyond all of them. In no form can the objective being of world orientation be isolated and made to appear by itself. Philosophically, I set foot on it only by my original realization that I must break through it.

The third premise of the intellect is that the potent, the intrinsic quality of being is to *last in time* – as demonstrated, first, by matter, to which all life returns; then by biological life, on which mind and soul remain dependent; then by human masses and human averages as well as by the materially conditioned social processes that will leave room for, or make use of, ideas only by accident, at best, and for a while. The intellect puts weight and emphasis upon successes due to visible causes and effects. What Existenz rates most highly seems most feeble to the intellect. The quietude of existential communication is inaccessible to mundane knowledge, except where it has grown superficial. But that the power of ideas is nonobjective – that in the honest view of empirical knowledge they are indeed wholly powerless – is the very sign that they concern being as freedom, not being as duration. A matter of freedom cannot possibly be turned into a knowledge of processes.

All these premises are perfectly correct for the knowledge of empirical world orientation. They would be stating ultimate truths if the world, as knowable objective being, were all there is. The world as being-in-itself would be identical, then, with the body of objectively valid knowledge; and therein, what lasts in time would be what is. Until I break through this conclusive world, by means of philosophical world orientation, I cannot return to myself and open my mind to transcendence.

2. How we think in elucidating Existenz

In reverting from each distinct being *to existence* as the all-encompassing consciousness, the only site of whatever has being for us, philosophy brought to mind the rudiments of an analysis of existence. In reverting from all mundane objective being *to Existenz* it takes up the task of existential elucidation. Existence analysis and the elucidation of Existenz have heterogeneous meanings.

Existence analysis is existentially noncommittal. It is performed in consciousness at large, which also comprehends itself in it. It shows the universal of existence. In existence analysis everyone will recognize himself, not as this individual, but as an I at large. It is unequivocally and directly communicable. Elucidation of Existenz, on the other hand, involves commitment. It speaks from the individual to the individual. Instead of general insights, it conveys possible lucidities, showing the potential of the individual in his unconditional roots and ends. Not everyone will recognize himself in it, but each one does so more or less, both in adoption and in rejection, by translating it into his own reality as this very individual. Its communication has many meanings and may be misunderstood. Its appeal to the man to whom it appeals at all will be to involve his self.

The philosophical relevance of existence analysis lies not so much in itself as in its distinction from the elucidation of Existenz, which presupposes it: the clearer my analysis of existence, the greater the lucidity I can achieve in Existenz. For the clarity of existence analysis will make me feel, at its limits, that consciousness in its immanence flatly excludes myself, the self of which I am conscious. Thus existence analysis becomes a *boundary construction* against the elucidation of Existenz.

In the broadest sense, any philosophizing may be called existential elucidation. No more of it can be found in the thinking to which we specifically give this name than in philosophical world orientation and in metaphysics. Aiming at the universe, I lose my way in its inconclusiveness and am flung back upon myself; in this repulsion the stress is not on existence – I would be sliding down into that from the universe – but on myself in my freedom. And when metaphysics has put me through the experience of finding none of its objectivities valid for everyone, the recoil will again be on myself, and being myself will illuminate my relation to transcendence.

Yet even if no philosophizing can fail to cast light upon Existenz incidentally, we still have to talk of this elucidation in a *special sense*: in the sense of speaking in signs of my own origin and of my own potential, of making me feel unconditionality as against relativity, freedom as against mere generality, the infinity of possible Existenz as against the finiteness of existence. The objectivities produced in the course of such thinking are bound to throw me back upon myself again, but this rebuff differs in character from those administered by the universe or by transcendence. There Existenz related to something else; here it relates to the concept of its own potential. Here the illustrative thought recoils from itself, with the illumination circling round itself.

The thinking that elucidates Existenz can achieve no cognition of being. Instead, if it is active thinking in life, it will *produce a certainty of being*, and it makes this certainty *possible* if its appeal is communicated in philosophical language. It will not flinch at the suspension resulting from philosophical world orientation. Yet the more pervasively clear the freedom of Existenz in the entire attainable scope of philosophizing, the more decisive the manifestation of its transcendence. Every one of its ways leads to metaphysics.

As long as man can rise above his existence, philosophizing will urge him to soar in metaphysics. There lies what really matters to him. There he can abysmally delude himself, but as a thinker he can also find there his most profound self-assurance.

3. How we think in metaphysics

Existenz, acting unconditionally in boundary situations, will get its bearings from the ciphers of transcendence that fill its consciousness as *absolute objectivities*, as objects in the world fill consciousness at large.

But in metaphysics, if we seek a *direct* approach to the absolute objectivity of a cipher of transcendence, it will elude our grasp. We must attempt to touch its existential roots, rather. If we succeed, by illuminating our own boundary situations and unconditional actions, the contact will validate the objectivity of the symbols because their content will have been felt. Philosophical metaphysics is the systematic analysis of absolute objectivity, its adoption, and – if it is not mere observation and history, but a concept formed in thought – its creation.

To questions raised by consciousness at large I can find answers in the world that may be valid for all as a general knowledge. To questions raised by possible Existenz in boundary situations I find no such answers. But if an Existenz understands itself historically in view of being, it will hear answers from transcendent depths in images and concepts which, as finite objects, are *symbols*. Made conscious by questioning its objectivity, the symbol turns into a *cipher*: the generally illegible, existentially deciphered handwriting of something else. If the object is to be held fast as though its objectiveness were transcendence itself, it will prove unstable and will fall apart. But where Existenz beholds in it something absolute, it is incomparably real. In the disappearance of its objectivity it makes true being manifest to Existenz.

This brings up an objectivity not mentioned in our analyses of the concepts of being. The items belonging to it are not realities in the sense that they might somewhere be given to me empirically, as objects. As such, and from the standpoint of mundane existence and scientific realism, they are vague fantasies of consciousness. They are absolute objects in consciousness to Existenz, however, if they serve to make it transparent to itself and certain of its transcendence. Not the intellect, but imagination – and not the random one of consciousness, but an imagination playing with the existential roots – emerges as the organ that lets Existenz make sure of being.

To a substantive, still unquestioning consciousness, absolute objects as transcendent phenomena exist as a matter of course. The symbol has not been made conscious as a cipher, then, and no line has yet been drawn between empirical and transcendent being. What will some day be transcendence stands in unquestionable objectivity before the human eye, existing together with everything else that exists. No reflection is aimed at it, nor is there a sense of subjectivity. As yet, belief and unbelief are not at odds. One of the great crises of existential consciousness is the moment when being ceases to be so self-evident. It is then that the differentiation of empirically real and transcendent objects begins. No individual is spared this crisis, which in the history of the objectifying human mind has occurred several times in the great periods of enlightenment. We cannot reverse it; we cannot even wish that it would not occur. For it is the font of clarity and truth, of question and risk for self-being.

In tradition – the objectified historicity of human Existenz – we meet a vast world of metaphysical objects with no empirical existence adequate to their meaning. Their source is Existenz, reaching out at objectivity so as to touch transcendence. They speak another language, but they do not speak it as the insignificant objects that exist for consciousness at large as well; what they represent in this language is something that can never be objective. This is why they are symbols, not tangible realities or compelling validities. They are ciphers of realities which manifest themselves in the thinking of Existenz, which alone perceives them, reading their language in the medium of consciousness at large.

This philosophizing comes last in the sequence of conscious elucidation, but historically it came first. Long before man arrived at pure world orientation, long before he came to clarify its limits and to elucidate Existenz in self-being, he would use symbolic objects to ascertain the being to which he relates as true.

Because it is historic, metaphysical thinking can neither be completed nor nailed down as the one and only true one. It always remains in a tension, with itself and with alien forms of the time.

Any metaphysics is in danger of going astray; the danger lies in the nature of objectivation. There remains a temptation after the crisis of consciousness, when the original unity was fractured: in spite of critical reflection, we may again take absolute objectivities for existing objects. We may imagine the beyond as if it were another country from whose point of view existence becomes worthless. Existenz will resist this temptation if it regards as true transcendence only one that speaks to it presently, in the world. Only an immanent transcendence can lend weight to Existenz in existence. True transcendence can never be existence for a subject; it can only be a reality for freedom. Hence any objective fixation of an objectified being, whether a distant beyond or a bewitched here and now, must be a slip.

There is no permanence in which we definitely find the absolute. The objectivities will melt. An existential faith, as absolute consciousness, moves dialectically on the borderline of unbelief as a mere sense of existence. Existenz can live a full life of its own with an absolute objectivity that will always be specific, will always dissolve, but will shed light even in disappearing.

The experience of the last boundary makes me wish to get out of the world. It invites world negation and arrangements for a flight from the world that will deliver me from participation in worldly existence even in my lifetime. It is only a possibility that I can truthfully leave the world, however; in practice, any relativization of worldliness promptly becomes *a reentry into the world*. I then face it as a man independent of it, tied to a reality I have brought back from my possible exit from it. In this real world I take my bearings, give myself to it, take up my fate, and believe in it as unconditionality.

As an independent being in the world, I can seek God. The mystic will receive a direct answer; it comes in the extinction of his search when he steps out of time. The believer's only answer comes out of the world. It is the answer he must give to himself by listening to the realities of worldly existence and of his own actions. To be really independent of the world in my relation to transcendence, I have to be active in the world.

A supposed knowledge of transcendence seems to show us *the whole of the one self-contained being*. But this view would be deceptive. The beginning and the end remain obscure. Everything remains in process; everything is still risky and dangerous as a whole, not for myself alone. Existenz keeps feeling a fear it cannot overcome, and a faith that goes with it – not faith in the being-in-itself of a substance, but faith in the being of a transcendence realized in each Existenz, yet veiled from all.

Whatever we may hold to be our truth, there always remains *something else that is not simply untrue for us* but a disquieting possibility with its own original meaning.

And if we say that for us there is an absolute objectiveness whose every disappearance is illuminating; that for us there is an exit from the world that can be taken effectively only within the world; that for us there is danger and the obscurity of beginning and end – if we say all this, there will still be the respective opposites: fixed objectivity; unworldly mysticism; the conclusive way of life in the transcendent framework of an absolute whole that is authoritatively present. These are not nothings. We see them, we make their objective forms our own; and our choice remains in question to the end, though we may believe we have chosen. The *other possibility* will grant no rest to our restlessness. It comes from the fact that we do not obtain definitive possession of the truth that is vital to us; instead, we must struggle for it and transform it in the process of our Existenz. The other, posing as the real truth, would lure me to rest – a temptation which I resist without denying it outright, because I will not close my mind.

NOTE

1. No definable concept – which would presuppose some kind of objective being – can express the being of Existenz. The very word is just one of the German synonyms for 'being.' The philosophical idea began obscurely, as a mere inkling of what Kierkegaard's use of the word has since made historically binding upon us.

2

GABRIEL MARCEL
(1889–1973)

Gabriel Marcel was born in Paris in 1889 and for seventy-five years actively took part in French intellectual life, especially through his work in the theatre. An only child, his mother's death when he was four had a profound effect on his life; for some time he was looked after by his grandmother, his mother's sister and his nurse. His father was a highly cultured person who held several important administrative posts: he was director of the Beaux Arts, adminis-trator in the Bibliotheque Nationale and the Musées Nationaux, and wrote several monographs on French painting. Gabriel's aunt married his father and their joint passion for music and theatre, as well as the bookish, intellectual atmosphere of their home, decisively shaped the principal dimensions of Marcel's character and his artistic ambitions. In 1898, Marcel's father was made ambassador to Sweden; later Marcel recalled with delight the fifteen months they spent in Stockholm and remarked that this was his first taste of an unquenchable hunger for travel and exotic places.

In stark contrast with the excitement of travel his years at the *lycée* were boring, poisonous, annoying and retarded his intellectual development – his own words. The young Marcel's compensations were music lessons, an enthusiasm for the piano, which he shared with his father and aunt, holidays in the mountains and large family gatherings with his many uncles, aunts and cousins. 'Deep down I wanted with all my being to be part of an abundant, substantial family community.' After Marcel's marriage, he said that 'my entry into that family . . . represented an enrichment for me that contributed in a most positive way to enhancing my thought' (1969, p. 13). These three activities, and later his abiding love for his wife, are the sources for the many pathways that became crucial to Marcel's Existentialist philosophy: artistic creativity, the personal journey of philosophy, the root sense of communal being and faithful commitment to the loved one. He later commented on his experience of these multifaceted delights in contrast with the mind-numbing boredom of school-work that 'it was in that obscure and ill-defined region that were born not only my dramatic writings, but also my philosophical thinking, at least from the moment it became existential, that is to say, liberated from what had all in all been high-level training' (1969, p. 14).

But everything changed for the better, he later recalled, when he enrolled in a philosophy course. His first teacher was 'an infirm, deformed dwarf' whose lectures were admittedly uninspiring but whose encouragement stimulated the young boy to devote himself fully to a subject matter in which Marcel, to his surprise, discovered he could excel. 'I felt as if a vise were opening, as if for the first time I were called upon to think for myself, to be myself …' Having earned his degree he enrolled at the Sorbonne where he attended lectures by André Lalande, Victor Delbos and Henri Bergson, at that time one of the most famous philosophers in France. Bergson's teaching *did* inspire Marcel; he was

> the only one whose thought and words took a sure and lasting hold on me … I can testify that by a driving light he cut through the gray and indistinct background of notions that were being inculcated at the Sorbonne by academicians whose knowledge and goodwill were beyond question, but who lacked the spark, the genius. (1969, p. 17)

He gained his *licence* in October 1907 and devoted the next two happy years to his diploma thesis on Coleridge and Schelling; he was admitted to the *agrégation* in philosophy in 1910, along with his good friend Jean Wahl, who would later become one of the first popular exponents of Existentialism. The next year Marcel gained a teaching post at the Lycée de Vendôme but he had only three 'impermeable' students and left shortly after to take up another teaching post in Switzerland. As it turned out, he never made teaching philosophy (at least in the classroom) into his profession, but by the summer of 1914 cataclysmic events were to direct his attention elsewhere.

In Marcel's earliest work, the *Philosophical Fragments* from 1909–14, he argued against the German idealists who made the subject into an object; his struggle was to find 'that living subjectivity which for the Danish thinker [Kierkegaard] was like a fountain of youth, the fruits of which, however, were not to be fully experienced until our own time' (1965, p. 24). He also thought through the issue of suicide which he considered the inevitable consequence of radical despair, but Marcel did not accept death as a finality, rather as the end of one stage of human being. At this time Marcel also wrote about the metaphysics of the American philosopher Josiah Royce whose treatise on loyalty influenced Marcel's ethical vision. According to Royce, loyalty is 'the will to manifest as far as possible the Eternal, that is, the conscious and superhuman unity of life, in the form of the acts of an individual self'; this core concept shows up in Marcel's later work as 'creative fidelity'.

After the outbreak of hostilities in the First World War, one of Marcel's colleagues, the Editor of the prestigious *Revue de métaphysique et morale*, suggested that Marcel go to work for the French Red Cross. For the next four years Marcel worked tirelessly for the bureau which dealt with the families of those missing in action. Without doubt, he later said, these sad, desperate encounters with bereaved and distraught families contributed to 'a boundless compassion for the distress to which each day testified anew'. In addition, his work gave him the opportunity to reflect on the very process of asking questions and the nature of the responses which a concerned inquiry solicits. 'More profoundly, it led me to consider the limits within which any inquiry at all is possible. This in turn led me to reflect on what could lie beyond the question-naire and investigation and on communication involving no such mediation, such as telepathy' (1969, pp. 20–1). During the winter of 1916–17, Marcel took part in some seances with a medium which culminated in some sort of break-through where he felt that he had made contact with 'the other side'. Although he did not pursue this path of unmediated inquiry, he later declared that this experience was an important aspect of his thought and studies – but we cannot pursue this here.

In November 1918, he became engaged to and soon married Jacqueline Boegner, daughter of an influential Protestant minister who had died in 1912. The deep and abiding love between them was a potent shaping factor in Marcel's Existentialist philosophy (somewhat in the same fashion as Jaspers' devotion to his wife Gertrud), but he delicately avoids discussing any intimate details. 'It is enough to say that to the end she was my absolute companion with whom I shared everything' (1969, p. 23). The next year he took up another post as teacher of philosophy in a *lycée* on the outskirts of Paris where, during three contented years, he wrote several of his most important plays. Scholars of Marcel's work (such as Denis Moran and Elizabeth Hanley) emphasise that Marcel considered his dramas and theatre work to be as important, or even more important, than his essays and short treatises in philosophy. Although this topic cannot be pursued here, it is eminently clear that many of his key Existentialist themes are 'bodied forth' or brought to life in the settings and dialogue of plays such as *Un Homme de Dieu, La Soif, Le Fanal* and others. Marcel's plays were not designed as popular forums for the presentation of worked out ideas, as Sam Keen has pointed out; instead they present complex situations in which persons find themselves trapped, challenged and confused, and thus indirectly they explore the soul's exile as it becomes alienated from itself, from those it loves and from God.

When he and his wife became convinced that they could not have their own children, they adopted a little boy, Jean-Marie, who would later become a prominent photographer and documentary film-maker. His commitment to his wife reflects Marcel's firm belief that in heeding the call of a loved one a person partakes of a transcendent domain, and his positive, nourishing sense of fatherhood reflects his belief that a person can embody Christ's incarnation as the son of God. These two dimensions, in conjunction with his affirmation of artistic creativity, define or at least circumscribe the landmarks in Marcel's path through life. His work now took him away from teaching and into publishing; he became the drama critic and editor for Editions Plon and Editions Grasset. Under their auspices, for the next forty years and more, Marcel introduced a number of important French and foreign playwrights to the literary public. From 1927 to 1960, with Charles Du Bos, he edited Editions Plon's series of foreign authors under the series title Feux croisés.

In 1927, Gallimard published Marcel's *Metaphysical Journal*, a collection of short essays, diary entries and sketches written between 1914 and 1923, with an essay-appendix 'Existence and Objectivity' from 1925. Many of the central Existentialist themes later explored by Marcel, Jaspers, Sartre and others are prefigured in this collection: his phenomenological analysis of being and having, the individual's participation in transcendence, the infinite within the finite through Christ's incarnation, human being and being-in-the-world, and the priority of human action in a concrete situation over theoretical abstraction. Like his great Existentialist forebears, Kierkegaard and Nietzsche, Marcel's philosophical writings are non-systematic, fragmentary and aphoristic; the charm and conviction of his conclusions are inseparable from his itinerant, tentative and exploratory philosophical method, in Sam Keen's words.

Perhaps the most important and well-known crossroads in Marcel's life occurred in 1929. François Mauriac, a celebrated writer whose novels reflected a strong Catholic sentiment, read Marcel's review of his own book, *Souffrance du chrétien*, and wrote to Marcel to persuade him to convert to the Catholic Church. 'Is it even honest', Mauriac queried, 'to continue to think and to speak like someone who believes in the faith of others, and who is convinced that this faith is everything but illusion, but who nevertheless does not resolve to take it unto himself? ... Is it not like a leap before which you must decide?' (1969, p. 29). The call for a leap of faith was a summons which a thinker like Marcel, with a deep admiration for Kierkegaard's notion of a demand to move beyond the ethical into a personal faith, was unable to resist. After his conversion to Roman Catholicism he took lessons in the philosophy of St Thomas Aquinas from an abbot but found the lessons disappointing; instead he and his friend Du Bos went to weekly tutorials with the great Catholic theologian-philosopher Jacques Maritain. During the three ominous years before the war broke out, Marcel travelled several times with his wife and old friend Jean Wahl to Eastern Europe; his experiences in Hungary, Bosnia and Dalmatia made a lasting impression on his political sentiments. During the war he and Jacqueline, and later his son Jean-Marie, lived in relative safety and isolation in the Corréze region where they had purchased an old house. After the war, he began to travel again, first to the International Congress of Philosophy in Rome, where he learned that he was considered to be the pre-eminent Christian Existentialist, a label which he was very reluctant to accept. Later he went to visit Heidegger in Freiburg, where, Marcel reported, the German philosopher told him that he (Heidegger) did not wish to be represented as an atheist; they met again in 1955 on Heidegger's first visit to France.

Shortly before the war's end, his wife had learned that she had only a few years to live – a terminal illness carried her away in November 1947. But under her careful musical tutelage, she and Marcel spent many months setting poems to music. In his 'Autobiography', twenty years later, Marcel clearly indicates the importance he attached to making music as a form of creative activity. After his wife's death, he said that his life became 'somewhat becalmed', although he did travel even more extensively than before on many lecture tours to Morocco, Lebanon, Japan, South America and the United States, where among others he met Hubert Dreyfus, today one of the foremost expositors of Continental Philosophy in America. A serious automobile accident in Corréze in August 1953 ended Marcel's lifelong passion for hill walking and mountain climbing; he later said that most of his best thinking was done while rambling. But the accident didn't stop him thinking and writing; he organised the production of many of his plays throughout the 1950s and 1960s. In September 1964, he was awarded the Peace Prize at the Frankfurt International Book Fair, the same award which Jaspers had received in 1958. In his 'Autobiography' written for Open Court in 1969, four years before his death, Marcel closed his memoirs with the ringing statement that:

> Never since the [First World War] have I ceased to feel, I can say in my flesh, the unutterable ordeal that our moral condition imposes on those who love ... My thought has a been a committed thinking – not for the benefit of any party or ideology, but *for my fellow beings*. (1969, p. 64)

In his 1930 essay 'The Ontological Mystery' several important Marcelian themes are introduced. Here he says that many common events in a person's life are *problems*, that is obstacles and hindrances which must be sorted out, reconnected in a more advantageous manner and so forth. The thinking that is involved in such problem-solving Marcel calls primary reflection; it does not involve the unique individual but only thinking as a thinking being, and the information needed is accessible to any thinking person. But some special events, such as birth, marriage and death, and some special issues or concerns, such as God, freedom, love and death, are not problems to be solved, but *mysteries* that demand a response from the individual in his uniqueness. Personal mysteries, in Marcel's view, centre around the unique self and the presence of others and not around a subject confronted with objects. The thinking engaged in dealing with a mystery Marcel calls secondary reflection; it is a thinking which begins not with doubt and curiosity, but with wonder and astonishment; it is concrete, practical and open, that is open to its solution as a lover is open to the beloved.

Openness is the principal dimension in Marcel's Existentialist ethics. In contrast with Sartre's emphasis on commitment as the free, self-conscious, clear-headed dedication to a great project, Marcel proposes *disponsibilité*, usually translated as 'availableness', but perhaps better rendered as 'disponsibility' along the lines of 'responsibility'. Marcel argues that an engaged moral agent, having eschewed a detached, theoretical stance, should also be on guard against imposing his or her own great project on others, becoming deaf and blind to others' needs. Unavailability, on the other hand, is a crispation or sclerosis, 'a hardening of the categories in accordance with which we conceive and evaluate the world'. The unavailable person draws concentric circles around himself, allowing only those experiences that fall within the closest zones to influence his concepts and values. Those that fall further out are ignored or filtered through in order to confirm a previous conviction. In *Being and Having*, Marcel says that there should be nothing 'about which we can be certain that its spell could hold out against the attack of a fearless critical reflection' (1965 [1923–53], p. 119). Such reflection is demanded when one is caught up in the ontological mystery, so in this context the mystery is an address or summons to the exigency of being. Being can be affirmed only when or if a person discovers within a concrete experience some presence that testifies to Being. Marcel says that there are two sources of such testimony: the impulse within every human to transcend the given situation, to achieve a level of experience saturated with meaning and value, and the origin or author of the summons to transcendence.

The ultimate presence that testifies to the possibility of such human transcendence can never be some thing which one *has* or holds, but rather it is some thing *created* anew each time the person enters into a loving relation with the other. David Cooper argues that in the final analysis Sartrean commitment and Marcelian availability are compatible:

> The remedy for such unavailability is commitment: for it is only through this that others have come to 'have a hold' on me. And it is through this hold and the reciprocal one which I have on them, that our lives interpenetrate and we become truly 'present' to one another. But what are the constituents of this reciprocal commitment? In particular, the mutual exercise of the Christian virtues of faith, hope and charity ... Availability then is a reciprocal relation through which each party is committed not only to treating the other as a free person, but to enabling and collaborating with his freedom. (Cooper, 1999, p. 176)

In Marcel's most mature Existentialist vision, the concrete approaches to Being are the same as the approaches to other persons, as Sam Keen says. To enter into a loving relation with another requires that a person exorcise the egocentric spirit and make a vow of creative fidelity. Through an intimate, deeply personal attitude toward God, fidelity becomes faith and *disponsibilité* becomes hope. Through the rapport established by love, hope and faith the human being approaches the mystery of being and becomes filled with the assurance that one's life is lived in the company of an eternal presence.

PRINCIPAL WORKS

(1909–14) *Philosophical Fragments*. Notre Dame, IN: University of Notre Dame Press, 1965.
(1914–23) *Metaphysical Journal*, trans. Bernard Wall. Chicago: Regnery, 1952.
(1923–53) *Being and Having*, trans. Katherine Farrer. Boston: Beacon Press, 1965.
(1933) *The Philosophy of Existence*, trans. Manya Harari. New York: Citadel Press, 1949/61.
(1940) *Creative Fidelity*, trans. Robert Rosthal. New York: Crossroad Press, 1964.
(1944) *Homo Viator*, trans. Emma Crauford. Chicago: Regnery, 1952.
(1950) *The Mystery of Being*, 2 vols, trans. G. S. Fraser and René Hauge. Chicago: Regnery, 1950.
(1951) *Presence and Immortality*. Pittsburg: Duquesne University Press, 1967.
(1955) *Problematic Man*. New York: Herder & Herder, 1967.
(1969) *Tragic Wisdom and Beyond*. Evanston, IL: Northwestern University Press, 1973.
(1969) 'Autobiography', in Paul Schilpp (ed.), *The Philosophy of Gabriel Marcel*. Chicago: Open Court, 1969.

RECOMMENDED READING

Cooney, William (ed.) (1989) *Contributions of Gabriel Marcel to Philosophy*. Lewiston, ME: Edwin Mellon.
Cooper, David E. (1999) *Existentialism: A Reconstruction*, 2nd edn. Oxford and New York: Blackwell.
Gallagher, Kenneth (1962) *The Philosophy of Gabriel Marcel*. New York: Fordham University Press.
Gillman, Neil (1986) *Gabriel Marcel on Religious Knowledge*. Lanham, MA: University Presses of America.
Godfrey, Joseph (1987) *A Philosophy of Human Hope*. Dordrecht: Martinus Nijhoff.
Hanley, Katherine (1987) *Dramatic Approaches to Creative Fidelity*. Lanham, MA: University Presses of America.
Keen, Sam (1967) *Gabriel Marcel*. Richmond, VA: John Knox Press.
Keen, Sam (1967) 'Gabriel Marcel', in Paul Edwards (ed.), *Encyclopedia of Philosophy*. New York: Macmillan, vol. 5, pp. 153–5.
Moran, Denis (1992) *Gabriel Marcel*. Lanham, MA: University Presses of America.
O'Malley, John (1966) *The Fellowship of Being*. The Hague: Martinus Nijhoff.
Ricoeur, Paul (1947) *Gabriel Marcel et Karl Jaspers*. Paris: Temps Present.
Troisfontaines, Roger (1968) *De l'existence à l'être*, 2 vols. Louvain: Nauwelaerts.
Zaner, Richard (1964) *The Problem of Embodiment*. The Hague: Martinus Nijhoff, Part Two.

'ON THE ONTOLOGICAL MYSTERY' (1933)[*]

Gabriel Marcel

The title of this essay is likely to annoy the philosopher as much as to startle the layman, since philosophers are inclined to leave mystery either to the theologians or else to the vulgarizers, whether of mysticism or of occultism, such as Maeterlinck. Moreover, the term *ontological*, which has only the vaguest meaning for the layman, has become discredited in the eyes of idealist philosophers; while the term *mystery* is reserved by those thinkers who are imbued with the ideas of scholasticism for the revealed mysteries of religion.

Thus my terminology is clearly open to criticism from all sides. But I can find no other which is adequate to the body of ideas which I intend to put forward and on which my whole outlook is based. Readers of my *Journal Métaphysique* will see that they represent the term of the whole spiritual and philosophical evolution which I have described in that book.

Rather than to begin with abstract definitions and dialectical arguments, which may be discouraging at the outset, I should like to start with a sort of global and intuitive characterization of the man in whom the sense of the ontological – the sense of being – is lacking, or to speak more correctly, of the man who has lost the awareness of this sense. Generally speaking, modern man is in this condition; if ontological demands worry him at all, it is only dully, as an obscure impulse. Indeed, I wonder if a psychoanalytical method deeper and more discerning than any that has been evolved until now would not reveal the morbid effects of the repression of this sense and of the ignoring of this need.

The characteristic feature of our age seems to me to be what might be called the misplacement of the idea of function, taking function in its current sense, which includes both the vital and the social functions.

The individual tends to appear both to himself and to others as an agglomeration of functions. As a result of deep historical causes, which can as yet be understood only in part, he has been led to see himself more and more as a mere assemblage of functions, the hierarchical interrelation of which seems to him questionable, or at least, subject to conflicting interpretations.

To take the vital functions first. It is hardly necessary to point out the role which historical materialism on the one hand, and Freudian doctrines on the other, have played in restricting the concept of man.

---

[*] From *The Philosophy of Existence*, trans. Manya Harari. New York: Citadel Press, 1949/61.

Then there are the social functions – those of the consumer, the producer, the citizen, etc.

Between these two there is, in theory, room for the psychological functions as well; but it is easy to see how these will tend to be interpreted in relation either to the social or the vital functions, so that their independence will be threatened and their specific character put in doubt. In this sense, Comte, served by his total incomprehension of psychical reality, displayed an almost prophetic instinct when he excluded psychology from his classification of sciences.

So far we are still dealing only with abstractions, but nothing is easier than to find concrete illustrations in this field.

Traveling on the underground, I often wonder with a kind of dread what can be the inward reality of the life of this or that man employed on the railway – the man who opens the doors, for instance, or the one who punches the tickets. Surely everything both within him and outside him conspires to identify this man with his functions – meaning not only with his functions as worker, as trade-union member, or as voter, but with his vital functions as well. The rather horrible expression 'time table' perfectly describes his life. So many hours for each function. Sleep, too, is a function which must be discharged, so that the other functions may be exercised in their turn. The same with pleasure, with relaxation; it is logical that the weekly allowance of recreation should be determined by an expert on hygiene; recreation is a psycho-organic function which must not be neglected any more than, for instance, the function of sex. We need go no further; this sketch is sufficient to suggest the emergence of a kind of vital schedule; the details will vary with the country, the climate, the profession, etc., but what matters is that there is a schedule.

It is true that certain disorderly elements – sickness, accidents of every sort – will break in on the smooth working of the system. It is therefore natural that the individual should be overhauled at regular intervals, like a watch (this is often done in America). The hospital plays the part of the inspection bench or the repair shop. And it is from this same standpoint of function that such essential problems as birth control will be examined.

As for death, it becomes, objectively and functionally, the scrapping of what has ceased to be of use and must be written off as total loss.

I need hardly insist on the stifling impression of sadness produced by this functionalized world. It is sufficient to recall the dreary image of the retired official, or those urban Sundays when the passers-by look like people who have retired from life. In such, a world, there is something mocking and sinister even in the tolerance awarded to the man who has retired from his work.

But besides the sadness felt by the onlooker, there is the dull, intolerable unease of the actor himself, who is reduced to living as though he were in fact submerged by his functions. This uneasiness is enough to show that there is in all this some appalling mistake, some ghastly misinterpretation, implanted in defenseless minds by an increasingly inhuman social order and an equally inhuman philosophy (for if the philosophy has prepared the way for the order, the order has also shaped the philosophy).

I have written on another occasion that, provided it is taken in its metaphysical and not its physical sense, the distinction between the *full* and the *empty* seems to me more fundamental than that between the *one* and the *many*. This is particularly applicable to the case in point. Life in a world centered on function is liable to despair because in reality this world is *empty*, it rings hollow; and if it resists this temptation, it is only to the extent that there come into play from within it, and in its favor, certain hidden forces which are beyond its power to conceive or to recognize.

It should be noted that this world is, on the one hand, riddled with problems, and on the other, determined to allow no room for mystery. I shall come back to this distinction between problem and mystery, which I believe to be fundamental. For the moment I shall only point out that to eliminate or to try to eliminate mystery is (in this functionalist world) to bring into play in the face of events which break in on the course of existence – such as birth, love, and death – that psychological and pseudoscientific category of the 'purely natural,' which deserves a study to itself. In reality, this is nothing more than the remains of a degraded rationalism from whose standpoint cause explains effect and accounts for it exhaustively. There exist in such a world, nevertheless, an infinity of problems, since the causes are not known to us in detail and thus leave room for unlimited research. And in addition to these theoretical puzzles, there are innumerable technical problems, bound up with the difficulty of knowing how the various functions, once they have been inventoried and labeled, can be made to work together without doing one another harm. These theoretical and technical questions are interdependent, for the theoretical problems arise out of the different techniques while the technical problems cannot be solved without a measure of pre-established theoretical knowledge.

In such a world the ontological need, the need of being, is exhausted in exact proportion to the breaking up of personality on the one hand, and on the other, to the triumph of the category of the 'purely natural' and the consequent atrophy of the faculty of *wonder*.

But to come at last to the ontological need itself; can we not approach it directly and attempt to define it? In reality this can only be done to a limited extent. For reasons which I shall develop later, I suspect that the characteristic of this need is that it can never be wholly clear to itself.

To try to describe it without distorting it we shall have to say something like this:

Being is – or should be – necessary. It is impossible that everything should be reduced to a play of successive appearances which are inconsistent with each other ('inconsistent' is essential), or in the words of Shakespeare, to 'a tale told by an idiot.' I aspire to participate in this being, in this reality – and perhaps this aspiration is already a degree of participation, however rudimentary.

Such a need, it may be noted, is to be found at the heart of the most inveterate pessimism. Pessimism has no meaning unless it signifies: it would surely be well if there were being, but there is no being, and I, who observe this fact, am therefore nothing.

As for defining the word 'being,' let us admit that is extremely difficult. I would merely suggest this method of approach: being is what withstands – or what would withstand – an exhaustive analysis bearing on the data of experience and aiming to reduce them step by step to elements increasingly devoid of intrinsic or significant value. (An analysis of this kind is attempted in the theoretical works of Freud.)

When the pessimist Besme says in *La Ville* that *nothing is*, he means precisely this, that there is no experience that withstands this analytical test. And it is always toward death regarded as the manifestation, the proof, of this ultimate nothingness that the kind of inverted apologetic which arises out of absolute pessimism will inevitably gravitate.

A philosophy which refuses to endorse the ontological need is, nevertheless, possible; indeed, generally speaking, contemporary thought tends toward this abstention. But at this point a distinction must be made between two different attitudes which are sometimes confused: one which consists in a systematic reserve (it is that of agnosticism in all its forms), and the other, bolder and more coherent, which regards the ontological need as the expression of an outworn body of dogma liquidated once and for all by the idealist critique.

The former appears to me to be purely negative: it is merely the expression of an intellectual policy of 'not raising the question.'

The latter, on the contrary, claims to be based on a positive theory of thought. This is not the place for a detailed critical study of this philosophy. I shall only note that it seems to me to tend toward an unconscious relativism, or else toward a monism which ignores the personal in all its forms, ignores the tragic and denies the transcendent, seeking to reduce it to its caricatural expressions, which distort its essential character. I shall also point out that, just because this philosophy continually stresses the activity of verification, it ends by ignoring *presence* – that inward realization of presence through love which infinitely transcends all possible verification because it exists in an immediacy beyond all conceivable mediation. This will be clearer to some extent from what follows.

Thus I believe for my part that the ontological need cannot be silenced by an arbitrary dictatorial act which mutilates the life of the spirit at its roots. It remains true, nevertheless, that such an act is possible, and the conditions of our life are such that we can well believe that we are carrying it out; this must never be forgotten.

These preliminary reflections on the ontological need are sufficient to bring out its indeterminate character and to reveal a fundamental paradox. To formulate this need is to raise a host of questions: Is there such a thing as being? What is it? etc. Yet immediately an abyss opens under my feet: I who ask these questions about being, how can I be sure that I exist?

Yet surely I, who formulate this problem, should be able to remain *outside* it – *before* or *beyond* it? Clearly this is not so. The more I consider it the more I find that this problem tends inevitably to invade the proscenium from which it is excluded in theory: it is only by means of a fiction that idealism in its traditional form seeks to maintain on the margin of being the consciousness which asserts it or denies it.

So I am inevitably forced to ask: Who am I – I who question being? How am I qualified to begin this investigation? If I do not exist, how can I succeed in it? And if I do exist, how can I be sure of this fact?

Contrary to the opinion which suggests itself at this point, I believe that on this plane the *cogito* cannot help us at all. Whatever Descartes may have thought of it himself, the only certainty with which it provides us concerns only the epistemological subject as organ of objective cognition. As I have written elsewhere, the *cogito* merely guards the threshold of objective validity, and that is strictly all; this is proved by the indeterminate character of the *I*. The *I am* is, to my mind, a global statement which it is impossible to break down into its component parts.

There remains a possible objection; it might be said: Either the being designated in the question 'What am I?' concerns the subject of cognition, and in this case we are on the plane of the *cogito*; or else that which you call the ontological need is merely the extreme point (or perhaps only the fallacious transposition) of a need which is, in reality, vital, and with which the metaphysician is not concerned.

But is it not a mistake arbitrarily to divide the question 'Who am I?' from the ontological 'problem' taken as a whole? The truth is that neither of the two can be dealt with separately, but that when they are taken together, they cancel one another out as *problems*.

It should be added that the Cartesian position is inseparable from a form of dualism which I, for my part, would unhesitatingly reject. To raise the ontological problem is to raise the question of being as a whole and of oneself seen as a totality.

But should we not ask ourselves if we must not reject this disassociation between the intellectual and the vital, with its resultant over- or underestimation of the one or the other? Doubtless it is legitimate to establish certain distinctions within the unity of the being who thinks and who endeavors to *think himself*; but it is only beyond such distinctions that the ontological problem can arise, and it must relate to that being seen in his all-comprehensive unity.

To sum up our reflections at this point, we find that we are dealing with an urge toward an affirmation – yet an affirmation which it seems impossible to make, since it is not until it has been made that I can regard myself as qualified to make it.

It should be noted that this difficulty never arises at a time when I am actually faced with a problem to be solved. In such a case I work on the data, but everything leads me to believe that I need not take into account the *I* who is at work – it is a factor which is presupposed, and nothing more.

Here, on the contrary, what I would call the ontological status of the investigator assumes a decisive importance. Yet so long as I am concerned with thought itself, I seem to follow an endless regression. But by the very fact of recognizing it as endless, I transcend it in a certain way: I see that process takes place within an affirmation of being – an affirmation which I *am* rather than an affirmation which I *utter:* by uttering it I break it, I divide it, I am on the point of betraying it.

It might be said, by way of an approximation, that my inquiry into being presupposes an affirmation in regard to which I am, in a sense, passive, *and of which I am the stage rather than the subject.* But this is only at the extreme limit of thought, a limit which I cannot reach without falling into contradiction. I am therefore led to assume or to recognize a form of participation which has the reality of a subject; this participation cannot be, by definition, an *object* of thought; it cannot serve as a solution – it appears beyond the realm of problems: it is metaproblematical.

Conversely, it will be seen that if the metaproblematical can be asserted at all, it must be conceived as transcending the opposition between the subject who asserts the existence of being, on the one hand, and being *as asserted by that subject*, on the other, and as underlying it in a given sense. To postulate the metaproblematical is to postulate the primacy of being over knowledge (not of being as *asserted*, but of being as *asserting itself*); it is to recognize that knowledge is, as it were, environed by being, that it is interior to it in a certain sense – a sense perhaps analogous to that which Paul Claudel tried to define in his *Art Poétique*. From this standpoint, contrary to what epistemology seeks vainly to establish, there exists well and truly a mystery of cognition; knowledge is contingent on a participation in being for which no epistemology can account because it continually presupposes it.

At this point we can begin to define the distinction between mystery and problem. A mystery is a problem which encroaches upon its own data, invading them, as it were, and thereby transcending itself as a simple problem. A set of examples will help us to grasp the content of this definition.

It is evident that there exists a mystery of the union of the body and the soul. The indivisible unity always inadequately expressed by such phrases as *I have a body, I make use of my body, I feel my body*, etc., can be neither analyzed nor reconstituted out of precedent elements. It is not only data, I would say that it is the basis of data, in the sense of being my own presence to myself, a presence of which the act of self-consciousness is, in the last analysis, only an inadequate symbol.

It will be seen at once that there is no hope of establishing an exact frontier between problem and mystery. For in reflecting on a mystery we tend inevitably to degrade it to the level of a problem. This is particularly clear in the case of the problem of evil.

In reflecting upon evil, I tend, almost inevitably, to regard it as a disorder which I view from outside and of which I seek to discover the causes or the secret aims. Why is it that the 'mechanism' functions so defectively? Or is the defect merely apparent and due to a real defect of my vision? In this case the defect is in myself, yet it remains objective in relation to my thought, which discovers it and observes it. But evil which is only stated or observed is no longer evil which is suffered: in fact, it ceases to be evil. In reality, I can only grasp it as evil in the measure in which it *touches* me – that is to say, in the measure in which I am *involved*, as one is involved in a lawsuit. Being 'involved' is the fundamental fact; I cannot leave it out of account except by an unjustifiable fiction, for in doing so, I proceed as though I were God, and a God who is an onlooker at that.

This brings out how the distinction between what is *in me* and what is only *before me* can break down. This distinction falls under the blow of a certain kind of thought: thought at one remove.

But it is, of course, in love that the obliteration of this frontier can best be seen. It might perhaps even be shown that the domain of the metaproblematical coincides with that of love, and that love is the only starting point for the understanding of such mysteries as that of body and soul, which, in some manner, is its expression.

Actually, it is inevitable that, in being brought to bear on love, thought which had not thought itself – unreflected reflection – should tend to dissolve its metaproblematical character and interpret it in terms of abstract concepts such as the will to live, the will to power, the libido, etc. On the other hand, since the domain of the problematical is that of the objectively valid, it will be extremely difficult – if not impossible – to refute these interpretations without changing to a new ground: a ground on which, to tell the truth, they lose their meaning. Yet I have the assurance, the certainty – and it envelops me like a protective cloak – that for as much as I really love I must not be concerned with these attempts at devaluation.

It will be asked: What is the criterion of true love? It must be answered that there is no criteriology except in the order of the objective and the problematical; but we can already see at a distance the eminent ontological value to be assigned to fidelity.

Let us take another illustration, more immediate and more particular, which may shed some light on the distinction between problem and mystery.

Say that I have made an encounter which has left a deep and lasting trace on all my life. It may happen to anyone to experience the deep spiritual significance of such a meeting – yet this is something which philosophers have commonly ignored or disdained, doubtless because it affects only the particular person as person – it cannot be universalized, it does not concern the rational being in general.

It is clear that such a meeting raises, if you will, a problem; but it is equally clear that the solution of this problem will always fall short of the only question that matters. Suppose that I am told, for instance: 'The reason you have met this person in this place is that you both like the same kind of scenery,' or, 'that you both need the same kind of treatment for your health' – the explanation means nothing. Crowds of people who apparently share my tastes were in the Engadine or in Florence at the time I was there; and there are always numbers of patients suffering from the same disease as myself at the health resort I frequent. But neither this supposed identity of tastes nor this common affliction has brought us together in any real sense; it has nothing to do with that intimate and unique affinity with which we are dealing. At the same time, it would be transgression of this valid reasoning to treat this affinity as if it were in itself the cause, and to say: It is precisely this which has determined our meeting.

Hence I am in the presence of a mystery. That is to say, of a reality rooted in what is beyond the domain of the problematical properly so called. Shall we avoid the difficulty by saying that it was after all nothing but a coincidence, a lucky chance? But the whole of me immediately protests against this empty formula, this vain negation of what I apprehend with the deepest of my being. Once again we are brought back to our first definition of a mystery as a problem which encroaches upon its own data: I who inquire into the meaning and the possibility of this meeting, I cannot place myself outside it or before it; I am engaged in this encounter, I depend upon it, I am inside it in a certain sense, it envelops me and it comprehends me – even if it is not comprehended by me. Thus it is only by a kind of betrayal or denial that I can say: After all, it might not have happened, I would still have been what I was, and what I am today. Nor must it be said: I have been changed by it as by an outward cause. No, it has developed in me from within, it has acted in me as an inward principle.

But this is very difficult to grasp without distortion. I shall be inevitably tempted to react against this sense of the inwardness of the encounter, tempted by my probity itself, by what from a certain standpoint I must judge to be the best – or at least, the safest – of myself.

There is a danger that these explanations may strengthen in the minds of my readers a preliminary objection, which must be stated at once.

It will be said: The metaproblematical of which you speak is after all a content of thought; how then should we not ask ourselves what is its mode of existence? What assures us of its existence at all? Is it not itself problematical in the highest degree?

My answer is categorical: To think, or rather, to assert, the metaproblematical is to assert it as indubitably real, as a thing of which I cannot doubt without falling into contradiction. We are in a sphere where it is no longer possible to dissociate the idea itself from the certainty or the degree of certainty which pertains to it. Because this idea *is* certainty, it *is* the assurance of itself; it is, in this sense, something other and something more than an idea. As for the term *content of thought*, which figured in the objection, it is deceptive in the highest degree. For content is, when all is said and done, derived from experience; whereas it is only by a way of liberation and detachment from experience that we can possibly rise to the level of the metaproblematical and of mystery. This liberation must be *real*; this detachment must be *real*; they must not be an abstraction, that is to say, a fiction recognized as such.

And this at last brings us to recollection, for it is in recollection and in this alone that this detachment is accomplished. I am convinced, for my part, that no ontology – that is to say, no apprehension of ontological mystery in whatever degree – is possible except to a being who is capable of recollecting himself, and of thus proving that he is not a living creature pure and simple, a creature, that is to say, which is at the mercy of its life and without a hold upon it.

It should be noted that recollection, which has received little enough attention from pure philosophers, is very difficult to define – if only because it transcends the dualism of being and action, or more correctly, because it reconciles in itself these two aspects of the antinomy. The word means what it says – the act where I recollect myself as a unity – but this hold, this grasp upon myself, is also relaxation and abandon. *Abandon to, ... relaxation in the presence of ...* – yet there is no noun for these propositions to govern. The way stops at the threshold.

Here, as in every other sphere, problems will be raised, and it is the psychologist who will raise them. All that must be noted is that the psychologist is no more in a position to shed light on the metaphysical bearing of recollection than on the poetic value of knowledge.

It is within recollection that I take up my position – or rather, I become capable of taking up my position – in regard to my life; I withdraw from it in a certain way, but not as the pure subject of cognition; *in this withdrawal I carry with me that which I am and which perhaps my life is not*. This brings out the gap between my being and my life. I am not my life; and if I can judge my life – a fact I cannot deny without falling into a radical skepticism which is nothing other than despair – it is only on condition that I encounter myself within recollection beyond all possible judgment, and, I would add, beyond all representation. Recollection is doubtless what is least spectacular in the soul; it does not consist in looking at something, it is an inward hold, an inward reflection, and it might be asked in passing whether it should not be seen as the ontological basis of memory – that principle of effective and nonrepresentational unity on which the possibility of remembrance rests. The double meaning of 'recollection' in English is revealing.

It may be asked: Is not recollection identical with that dialectical moment of the turning to oneself (*retour sur soi*) or else with the *für sich sein* which is the central theme of German idealism?

I do not think so. To withdraw into oneself is not to be for oneself nor to mirror oneself in the intelligible unity of subject and object. On the contrary. I would say that here we come up against the paradox of that actual mystery whereby the I into which I withdraw ceases, for as much, to belong to itself. 'You are not your own' – this great saying of St Paul assumes in this connection its full concrete and ontological significance; it is the nearest approach to the reality for which we are groping. It will be asked: Is not this reality an object of intuition? Is not that which you term 'recollection' the same as what others have termed 'intuition'?

But this again seems to me to call for the utmost prudence. If intuition can be mentioned in this context at all, it is not an intuition which is, or can be, given as such.

The more an intuition is central and basic in the being whom it illuminates, the less it is capable of turning back and apprehending itself.

Moreover, if we reflect on what an intuitive knowledge of being could possibly be, we see that it could never figure in a collection, a procession of simple experiences or *Erlebnisse*, which all have this characteristic that they can be at times absorbed and at others isolated, and as it were, uncovered. Hence, any effort to remember such an intuition, to represent it to oneself, is inevitably fruitless. From this point of view, to be told of an intuitive knowledge of being is like being invited to play on a soundless piano. Such an intuition cannot be brought out into the light of day, for the simple reason that we do not possess it.

We are here at the most difficult point of our whole discussion. Rather than to speak of intuition in this context, we should say that we are dealing with an assurance which underlies the entire development of thought, even of discursive thought; it can therefore be approached only by a second reflection – a reflection whereby I ask myself how and from what starting point I was able to proceed in my initial reflection, which itself postulated the ontological, but without knowing it. This second reflection is recollection in the measure in which recollection can be self-conscious.

It is indeed annoying to have to use such abstract language in a matter which is not one of dialectics *ad usum philosophorum*, but of what is the most vital and, I would add, the most dramatic moment in the rhythm of consciousness seeking to be conscious of itself.

It is this dramatic aspect which must now be brought out.

Let us recall what we said earlier: that the ontological need, the need of being, can deny itself. In a different context we said that being and life do not coincide; my life, and by reflection all life, may appear to me as forever inadequate to something which I carry within me, which in a sense, I am, but which reality rejects and excludes. Despair is possible in any form, at any moment, and to any degree, and this betrayal may seem to be counseled, if not forced upon us, by the very structure of the world we live in. The deathly aspect of this world may, from a given standpoint, be regarded as a ceaseless incitement to denial and to suicide. It could even be said in this sense that the fact that suicide is always possible is the essential starting point of any genuine metaphysical thought.

It may be surprising to find in the course of this calm and abstract reasoning such verbal star turns – words so emotionally charged – as 'suicide' and 'betrayal.' They are not a concession to sensationalism. I am convinced that it is in drama and through drama that metaphysical thought grasps and defines itself *in concreto*. Two years ago, in a lecture on the 'Problem of Christian Philosophy' which he delivered at Louvain, M. Jacques Maritain said: 'There is nothing easier for a philosophy than to become tragic, it has only to let itself go to its human weight.' The allusion was doubtless to the speculation of a Heidegger. I believe, on the contrary, that the natural trend of philosophy leads it into a sphere where it seems that tragedy has simply vanished – evaporated at the touch of abstract thought. This is borne out by the work of many contemporary idealists. Because they ignore the person, offering it up to I know not what ideal truth, to what principle of pure inwardness, they are unable to grasp those tragic factors of human existence to which I have alluded above; they banish them, together with illness and everything akin to it, to I know not what disreputable suburb of thought outside the ken of any philosopher worthy of the name. But, as I have stressed earlier, this attitude is intimately bound up with the rejection of the ontological need; indeed, it is the same thing.

If I have stressed despair, betrayal, and suicide, it is because these are the most manifest expressions of the will to negation as applied to being.

Let us take despair, I have in mind the act by which one despairs of reality as a whole, as one might despair of a person. This appears to be the result, or the immediate translation into other terms, of a kind of balance sheet. Inasmuch as I am able to evaluate the world of reality (and, when all is said and done, what I am unable to evaluate is for me as if it were not), I can find nothing in it that withstands that process of dissolution at the heart of things which I have discovered and traced. I believe that at the root of despair there is always this affirmation: There is nothing in the realm of reality to which I can give credit – no security, no guarantee. It is a statement of complete insolvency.

As against this, hope is what implies credit. Contrary to what was thought by Spinoza, who seems to me to have confused two quite distinct notions, fear is correlated to desire and not to hope, whereas what is negatively correlated to hope is the act which consists in putting things at their worst – an act which is strikingly illustrated by what is known as defeatism, and which is ever in danger of being degraded into the desire of the worst. Hope consists in asserting that there is at the heart of being, beyond all data, beyond all inventories and all calculations, a mysterious principle which is in connivance with me, which cannot but will that which I will, if what I will deserves to be willed and is, in fact, willed by the whole of my being.

We have now come to the center of what I have called the ontological mystery, and the simplest illustrations will be the best. To hope against all hope that a person whom I love will recover from a disease which is said to be incurable is to say: It is impossible that I should be alone in willing this cure; it is impossible that reality in its inward depth should be hostile or so much as indifferent to what I assert is in itself a good. It is quite useless to tell me of discouraging *cases* or *examples*: beyond all experience, all probability, all statistics, I assert that a given order shall be re-established, that reality *is* on my side in willing it to be so. I do not wish: I assert; such is the prophetic tone of true hope.

No doubt I shall be told: In the immense majority of cases this is an illusion. But it is of the essence of hope to exclude the consideration of cases; moreover, it can be shown that there exists an ascending dialectic of hope, whereby hope rises to a plane which transcends the level of all possible empirical disproof – the plane of salvation as opposed to that of success in whatever form.

It remains true, nevertheless, that the correlation of hope and despair subsists until the end; they seem to me inseparable. I mean that while the structure of the world we live in permits – and may even seem to counsel – absolute despair, yet it is only such a world that can give rise to an unconquerable hope. If only for this reason, we cannot be sufficiently thankful to the great pessimists in the history of thought; they have carried through an inward experience which needed to be made, of which the radical possibility no apologetics should disguise; they have prepared our minds to understand that despair can be what it was for Nietzsche (though on an infraontological level and in a domain fraught with mortal dangers), the springboard to the loftiest affirmation.

At the same time, it remains certain that, forasmuch as hope is a mystery, its mystery can be ignored or converted into a problem. Hope is then regarded as a desire which wraps itself up in illusory judgments to distort an objective reality which it is interested in disguising from itself. What happens in this case is what we have already observed in connection with encounter and with love; it is because mystery can – and, in a sense, logically must – be degraded into a problem, that an interpretation such as that of Spinoza, with all the confusion it implies, had to be put forward sooner or later. It is important and must be stressed that this attitude has nothing against it so long as our standpoint is on the hitherside of the realm of the ontological. Just as long as my attitude toward reality is that of someone who is not involved in it, but who judges it his duty to draw up its minutes as exactly as possible (and this is by definition the attitude of the scientist), I am justified in maintaining in regard to it a sort of principle of mistrust, which in theory is unlimited in its application; such is the legitimate standpoint of the workman in the laboratory, who must in no way prejudge the result of his analysis, and who can all the better envisage *the worst*, because at this level the very notion of worst is empty of meaning. But an investigation of this sort, which is just like that of an accountant going through the books, takes place on the hitherside of the order of mystery, an order in which the problem encroaches upon its own data.

It would indeed be a profound illusion to believe that I can still maintain this same attitude when I undertake an inquiry, say, into the value of life; it would be a paralogism to suppose that I can pursue such an inquiry as though my own life were not at issue.

Hence, between hope – the reality of hope in the heart of the one whom it inhabits – and the judgment brought to bear upon it by a mind chained to objectivity there exists the same barrier as that which separates a pure mystery from a pure problem.

This brings us to a nodal point of our subject, where certain intimate connections can be traced.

The world of the problematical is the world of fear and desire, which are inseparable; at the same time, it is that world of the functional – or of what can be functionalized – which was defined at the beginning of this essay; finally, it is the kingdom of technics of whatever sort. Every technique serves, or can be made to serve, some desire or some fear; conversely, every desire, as every fear, tends to invent its appropriate technique. From this standpoint, despair consists in the recognition of the ultimate inefficacy of all technics, joined to the inability or the refusal to change over to a new ground – a ground where all technics are seen to be incompatible with the fundamental nature of being, which itself escapes our grasp (insofar as our grasp is limited to the world of objects and to this alone). It is for this reason that we seem nowadays to have entered upon the very era of despair; we have not ceased to believe in technics, that is to envisage reality as a complex of problems; yet at the same time the failure of technics *as a whole* is as discernible to us as its *partial* triumphs. To the question 'What can man achieve?' we continue to reply: he can achieve as much as his technics – yet we are obliged to admit that these technics are unable *to save man himself*, and even that they are apt to conclude the most sinister alliance with the enemy he bears within him.

I have said that man is *at the mercy of his technics*. This must be understood to mean that he is increasingly incapable of controlling his technics, or rather, of *controlling his own control*. This control of his own control, which is nothing else than the expression on the plane of active life of what I have called thought at one remove, cannot find its center or its support anywhere except in recollection.

It will be objected that even those whose faith in technics is strongest are bound to admit that there exist enormous realms which are outside man's control. But what matters is the spirit in which this admission is made. We have to recognize that we have no control over meteorological conditions, but the question is: Do we consider it desirable and just that we should have such control? The more the sense of the ontological tends to disappear, the more unlimited become the claims of the mind which has lost it to a kind of cosmic governance, because it is less and less capable of examining its own credentials to the exercise of such dominion.

It must be added that the more the disproportion grows between the claims of the technical intelligence on the one hand, and the persisting fragility and precariousness of what remains its material substratum on the other, the more acute becomes the constant danger of despair which threatens this intelligence. From this standpoint there is truly an intimate dialectical correlation between the optimism of technical progress and the philosophy of despair which seems inevitably to emerge from it – it is needless to insist on the examples offered by the world of today.

It will perhaps be said: This optimism of technical progress is animated by great hope. How is hope in this sense to be reconciled with the ontological interpretation of hope?

I believe it must be answered that, *speaking metaphysically, the only genuine hope is hope in what does not depend on ourselves,* hope springing from humility, and not from pride. This brings us to the consideration of another aspect of the mystery – a mystery which, in the last analysis, is one and unique – on which I am endeavoring to throw some light.

The metaphysical problem of pride – *hubris* – which was perceived by the Greeks and which has been one of the essential themes of Christian theology, seems to me to have been almost completely ignored by modern philosophers other than theologians. It has become a domain reserved for the morality. Yet from my own standpoint it is an essential – if not the vital – question. It is sufficient to recall Spinoza's definition of *superbia*, in his *Ethics* (III, def. 28), to see how far he was from grasping the problem: 'Pride is an exaggeratedly good opinion of ourselves which arises from self-love.' In reality, this is a definition of vanity. As for pride, it consists in drawing one's strength solely from oneself. The proud man is cut off from a certain form of communion with his fellow men, which pride, acting as a principle of destruction, tends to break down. Indeed, this destructiveness can be equally well directed against the self; pride is in no way incompatible with self-hate; this is what Spinoza does not seem to have perceived.

An important objection may be raised at the point we have now reached.

It will perhaps be said: Is not that which you are justifying ontologically, in reality a kind of moral quietism which is satisfied by passive acceptance, resignation, and inert hope? But what, then, becomes of man as man, as active being? Are we to condemn action itself inasmuch as it implies a self-confidence which is akin to pride? Can it be that action itself is a kind of degradation?

This objection implies a series of misunderstandings.

To begin with, the idea of inert hope seems to me a contradiction in terms. Hope is not a kind of listless waiting; it underpins action or it runs before it, but it becomes degraded and lost once the action is spent. Hope seems to me, as it were, the prolongation into the unknown of an activity which is central – that is to say, rooted in beings. Hence it has affinities, not with desire, but with the will. The will implies the same refusal to calculate possibilities, or at any rate, it suspends this calculation. Could not hope therefore be defined as the will when it is made to bear on what does not depend on itself?

The experimental proof of this connection is that it is the most active saints who carry hope to its highest degree; this would be inconceivable if hope were simply an inactive state of the soul. The mistake so often made here comes from a stoical representation of the will as a stiffening of the soul, whereas it is, on the contrary, relaxation and creation.

The term 'creation,' which occurs here for the first time, is, nevertheless, decisive. Where there is creation there can be no degradation, and to the extent that technics are creative, or imply creativity, they are not degrading in any way. Degradation begins at the point where creativeness falls into self-imitation and self-hypnotism, stiffening and falling back on itself. This may, indeed, bring out the origin of the confusion which I denounced in the context of recollection.

Great is the temptation to confuse two distinct movements of the soul, whose opposition is blurred by the use of spatial metaphors. The stiffening, the contraction, the falling back on the self, which are inseparable from pride, and which are indeed its symbol, must not be confused with the humble withdrawal which befits recollection and whereby I renew my contact with the ontological basis of my being.

There is every reason to think that such withdrawal in recollection is a presupposition of aesthetic creativity itself. Artistic creation, like scientific research, excludes the act of self-centering and self-hypnotism which is, onto-logically speaking, pure negation.

It may perhaps seem that my thesis comes so near to that of Bergson as to coincide with it, but I do not think that this is the case. The terms almost invariably used by Bergson suggest that for him the essential character of creativity lay in its inventiveness, in its spontaneous innovation. But I wonder if by limiting our attention to this aspect of creation, we do not lose sight of its ultimate significance, which is its deep-rootedness in being. It is at this point that I would bring in the notion of *creative fidelity*; it is a notion which is the more difficult to grasp, and above all, to define conceptually, because of its underlying and unfathomable paradox, and because it is at the very center of the realm of the metaproblematical.

It is important to note that the idea of fidelity seems difficult to maintain in the context of Bergsonian metaphysics, because it will tend to be interpreted as a routine, as an observance in the pejorative sense of the word, as an arbitrary safeguard *against* the power of renewal which is the spirit itself.

I am inclined to think that there is something in this neglect of the values of fidelity which deeply vitiates the notion of static religion as it is put forward in *Les Deux Sources de la Morale et de la Religion*. It may perhaps be useful to devote some thought to creative fidelity in order to elucidate this point.

Faithfulness is, in reality, the exact opposite of inert conformism. It is the active recognition of something permanent, not formally, after the manner of a law, but ontologically; in this sense, it refers invariably to a presence, or to something which can be maintained within us and before us as a presence, but which, *ipso facto*, can be just as well ignored, forgotten, and obliterated; and this reminds us of that menace of betrayal which, to my mind, overshadows our whole world.

It may perhaps be objected that we commonly speak of fidelity to a principle. But it remains to be seen if this is not an arbitrary transposition of the notion of fidelity. A principle, insofar as it is a mere abstract affirmation, can make no demands upon me because it owes the whole of its reality to the act whereby I sanction it or proclaim it. Fidelity to a principle as a principle is idolatry in the etymological sense of the word; it might be a sacred duty for me to deny a principle from which life has withdrawn and which I know that I no longer accept, for by continuing to conform my actions to it, it is myself – myself as presence – that I betray.

So little is fidelity akin to the inertia of conformism that it implies an active and continuous struggle against the forces of interior dissipation, as also against the sclerosis of habit. I may be told: This is nevertheless no more than a sort of active conservation which is the opposite of creation. We must, I think, go much further into the nature of fidelity and of presence before we can reply to this point.

If presence were merely an *idea* in us whose characteristic was that it was nothing more than itself, then indeed the most we could hope would be to maintain this idea in us or before us, as one keeps a photograph on a mantel-piece or in a cupboard. But it is of the nature of presence as presence to be uncircumscribed; and this takes us once again beyond the frontier of the problematical. Presence is mystery in the exact measure in which it is presence. Now fidelity is the active perpetuation of presence, the renewal of its benefits – of its virtue, which consists in a mysterious incitement to create. Here again we may be helped by the consideration of aesthetic creativeness; for if artistic creation is conceivable, it can only be on condition that the world is present to the artist in a certain way – present to his heart and to his mind, present to his very being.

Thus if creative fidelity is conceivable, it is because fidelity is conceivable, it is because fidelity is ontological in its principle, because it prolongs presence, which itself corresponds to a certain kind of hold which being has upon us; because it multiplies and deepens the effect of this presence almost unfathomably in our lives. This seems to me to have almost inexhaustible consequences, if only for the relationships between the living and the dead.

I must insist once again: A presence to which we are faithful is not at all the same thing as the carefully preserved effigy of an object which has vanished; an effigy is, when all is said and done, nothing but a likeness; metaphysically it is *less* than the object, it is a diminution of the object. Whereas presence, on the contrary, is *more* than the object, it exceeds the object on every side. We are here at the opening of a vista at whose term death will appear as the *test of presence*. This is an essential point and we must consider it carefully.

It will no doubt be said: What a strange way of defining death! Death *is* a phenomenon definable in biological terms; it *is not* a test.

It must be answered: It is what it signifies, and moreover, what it signifies to a being who rises to the highest spiritual level to which it is possible for us to attain. It is evident that if I read in the newspaper of the death of Mr So-and-so, who is for me nothing but a name, this event *is* for me nothing more than the subject of an announcement. But it is quite another thing in the case of a being who has been granted to me as a presence. In this case, everything depends on me, on my inward attitude of maintaining this presence which could be debased into an effigy.

It will be objected: This is nothing more than a description in recondite and unnecessarily metaphysical terms of a common psychological fact. It is evident that it depends upon us in a certain measure to enable the dead to survive in our memory, but this existence is no more than subjective.

I believe that the truth is altogether different and infinitely more mysterious. In saying 'It depends upon us that the dead should live on in our memory,' we are still thinking of the idea in terms of a diminution or an effigy. We admit that the object has disappeared, but that there remains a likeness which it is in our power to keep, as a woman daily 'keeps' a flat or a set of furniture. It is all too evident that this manner of keeping can have no ontological value whatsoever. But it is altogether different in the case where fidelity is creative in the sense which I have tried to define. A presence is a reality; it is a kind of influx: it depends upon us to be permeable to this influx, but not, to tell the truth, to call it forth. Creative fidelity consists in maintaining ourselves actively in a permeable state; and there is a mysterious interchange between this free act and the gift granted in response to it.

An objection which is the converse of the preceding one may be expected at this point. I will be told: All right. You have now ceased to decorate a psychological platitude with metaphysical ornaments, but only to make a gratuitous assertion which is unproved and which is beyond all possible experimental proof; this was inevitable as soon as you replaced the ambiguous and neutral term 'presence' by the much more compromising term 'influx.'

To reply to this objection, we must refer again to what I have already said of mystery and of recollection. Indeed, it is only on the metaproblematical level that the notion of influx can possibly be accepted. If it were taken in its objective sense, as an accretion of strength, we would indeed be faced with a thesis, not of metaphysics, but of physics, which would be open to every possible objection. When I say that a being is granted to me as a presence or as a being (it comes to the same, for he is not a being for me unless he is a presence), this means that I am unable to treat him as if he were merely placed in front of me; between him and me there arises a relationship which, in a sense, surpasses my awareness of him; he is not only before me, he is also within me – or rather, these categories are transcended, they have no longer any meaning. The word 'influx' conveys, though in a manner which is far too physical and spatial, the kind of interior accretion, of accretion from within, which comes into being as soon as presence is effective. Great and almost invincible is the temptation to think that such effective presence can be only that of an object; but if we believed this, we would fall back to the level of the problematical and remain on the hitherside of mystery; and against this belief fidelity raises up its voice: 'Even if I cannot see you, if I cannot touch you, I feel that you are with me; it would be a denial of you not to be assured of this.' *With* me: note the metaphysical value of this word, so rarely recognized by philosophers, which corresponds neither to a relationship of inherence or immanence nor to a relationship of exteriority. It is of the essence of genuine *coesse* – I must use the Latin word – that is to say, of genuine intimacy, to lend itself to the decomposition to which it is subjected by critical thought; but we already know that there exists another kind of thought, a thought which bears upon that thought itself, and is related to a bottled-up yet efficacious underlying intuition, of which it suffers the attraction.

It must be added (and this brings us to the verge of another sphere) that the value of such intimacy, particularly in regard to the relation between the living and the dead, will be the higher and the more assured the more this intimacy is grounded in the realm of total spiritual availability – that is to say, of pure charity; and I shall note in passing that an ascending dialectic of creative fidelity corresponds to the dialectic of hope to which I have already referred.

The notion of availability is no less important for our subject than that of presence, with which it is bound up.

It is an undeniable fact, though it is hard to describe in intelligible terms, that there are some people who reveal themselves as 'present' – that is to say, at our disposal – when we are in pain or need to confide in someone, while there are other people who do not give us this feeling, however great is their good will. It should be noted at once that the distinction between presence and absence is not at all the same as that between attention and distraction. The most attentive and the most conscientious listener may give me the impression of not being present; he gives me nothing, he cannot make room for me in himself, whatever the material favors which he is prepared to grant me. The truth is that there is a way of listening which is a way of giving, and another way of listening which is a way of refusing, of refusing *oneself*; the material gift, the visible action, do not necessarily witness to presence. We must not speak of proof in this connection; the word would be out of place. Presence is something which reveals itself immediately and unmistakably in a look, a smile, an intonation, or a handshake.

It will perhaps make it clearer if I say that the person who is at my disposal is the one who is capable of being with me with the whole of himself when I am in need; while the one who is not at my disposal seems merely to offer me a temporary loan raised on his resources. For the one, I am a presence; for the other, I am an object. Presence involves a reciprocity which is excluded from any relation of subject to object or of subject to subject-object. A concrete analysis of unavailability is no less necessary for our purpose than that of betrayal, denial, or despair.

Unavailability is invariably rooted in some measure of alienation. Say, for instance, that I am told of some misfortune with which I am asked to sympathize: I understand what I am told; I admit in theory that the sufferers deserve my sympathy; I see that it is a case where it would be logical and just for me to respond with sympathy; I even offer my sympathy, but only with my mind;

because, when all is said and done, I am obliged to admit that I feel absolutely nothing. Indeed, I am sorry that this should be so; the contradiction between the indifference which I feel in fact and the sympathy which I know I ought to feel is humiliating and annoying; it diminishes me in my own eyes. But it is no use; what remains in me is the rather embarrassing awareness that, after all, these are people I do not know – if one had to be touched by every human misfortune, life would not be possible; it would indeed be too short. The moment I think: After all, this is only a case, No. 75,627 – it is no good, I can feel nothing.

But the characteristic of the soul which is present and at the disposal of others is that it cannot think in terms of *cases*; in its eyes there are *no cases at all*.

And yet it is clear that the normal development of a human being implies an increasingly precise, and as it were, automatic, division between what concerns him and what does not, between things for which he is responsible and those for which he is not. Each one of us becomes the center of a sort of mental space arranged in concentric zones of decreasing interest and participation. It is as though each one of us secreted a kind of shell which gradually hardened and imprisoned him; and this sclerosis is bound up with the hardening of the categories in accordance with which we conceive and evaluate the world.

Fortunately, it can happen to anyone to make an encounter which breaks down the framework of this egocentric topography; I know by my own experience how, from a stranger met by chance, there may come an irresistible appeal which overturns the habitual perspectives, just as a gust of wind might tumble down the panels of a stage set – what had seemed near becomes infinitely remote, and what had seemed distant seems to be close. Such cracks are repaired almost at once. But it is an experience which leaves us with a bitter taste, an impression of sadness and almost of anguish; yet I think it is beneficial, for it shows us as in a flash all that is contingent and – yes – artificial in the crystallized pattern of our personal system.

But it is, above all, the sanctity realized in certain beings which reveals to us that what we call the normal order is, from a higher point of view, from the standpoint of a soul rooted in ontological mystery, merely the subversion of an order which is its opposite. In this connection, the study of sanctity with all its concrete attributes seems to me to offer an immense speculative value; indeed, I am not far from saying that it is the true introduction to ontology.

Once again a comparison with the soul which is not at the disposal of others will throw light on our subject.

To be incapable of presence is to be in some manner not only occupied but encumbered with one's own self. I have said 'in some manner'; the immediate object of the preoccupation may be one of any number; I may be preoccupied with my health, my fortune, or even with *my inward perfection*. This shows that to be occupied with oneself is not so much to be occupied with a *particular object* as to be occupied in a *particular manner*. It must be noted that the contrary of this state is not a state of emptiness or indifference. The real contrast is rather between the being who is opaque and the being who is transparent. But this inward opacity remains to be analyzed. I believe that it consists in a kind of obduracy or fixation; and I wonder if, by generalizing and adapting certain psychoanalytical data, we would not find that it is the fixation in a given zone or in a given key of a certain disquiet which, in itself, is something quite different. But what is remarkable is that the disquiet persists within this fixation and gives it that character of constriction which I mentioned in connection with the degradation of the will. There is every reason to believe that this indefinite disquiet should be identified with the anguish of temporality and with that aspiration of man, not toward, but *by*, death, which is at the heart of pessimism.

Pessimism is rooted in the same soil as the inability to be at the disposal of others. If the latter grows in us as we grow old, it is only too often because, as we draw near to what we regard as the term of our life, anxiety grows in us almost to the point of choking us; to protect itself, it sets up an increasingly heavy, exacting, and I would add, vulnerable mechanism of self-defense. The capacity to hope diminishes in proportion as the soul becomes increasingly chained to its experience and to the categories which arise from it, and as it is given over more completely and more desperately to the world of the problematical.

Here at last can be brought together the various motifs and thematic elements which I have had to bring out one by one. In contrast to the captive soul we have described, the soul which is at the disposal of others is consecrated and inwardly dedicated; it is protected against suicide and despair, which are interrelated and alike, because it knows that it is not its own, and that the most legitimate use it can make of its freedom is precisely to recognize that it does not belong to itself; this recognition is the starting point of its activity and creativeness.

The difficulties of a philosophy of this sort must not be disguised. It is inevitably faced by a disquietening alternative: Either it will try to solve these difficulties – to give all the answers; in that case it will fall into the excesses of a dogmatism which ignores its vital principles and, I would add, into those of a sacrilegious theodicy; or else it will allow these difficulties to subsist, labeling them as mysteries.

Between these two I believe that there exists a middle way – a narrow, difficult, and dangerous path which I have tried to discover. But, like Karl Jaspers in his *Philosophy of Existence*, I can only proceed in this kind of country by calling out to other travelers. If, as it occasionally happened, certain minds respond – not the generality, but this being and that other – then there is a way. But, as I believe Plato perceived with incomparable clarity, it is a way which is undiscoverable except through love, to which alone it is visible, and this brings us to what is perhaps the deepest characteristic of that realm of the metaproblematical of which I have tried to explore certain regions.

A serious objection remains to be mentioned. It will perhaps be said: All that you have said implies an unformulated reference to the data of Christianity and can only be understood in the light of these data. Thus we understand what you mean by presence if we think of the Eucharist and what you mean by creative fidelity if we think of the Church. But what can be the value of such a philosophy for those who are anti-Christian – for those who ignore Christianity or who do not accept it? I would answer: It is quite possible that the existence of the fundamental Christian data may be necessary *in fact* to enable the mind to conceive some of the notions which I have attempted to analyze; but these notions cannot be said to depend on the data of Christianity, and *they do not presuppose it*. On the other hand, should I be told that the intellect must leave out of account anything which is not a universal datum of thinking as such, I would say that this claim is exaggerated, and in the last analysis, illusory. Now, as at any other time, the philosopher is placed in a given historical situation from which he is most unlikely to abstract himself completely; he would deceive himself if he thought that he could create a complete void both within and around himself. Now this historical situation implies as one of its essential data the existence of the Christian fact – quite independently of whether the Christian religion is accepted and its fundamental assertions are regarded as true or false. What appears to me evident is that we cannot reason today as though there were not behind us centuries of Christianity, just as, in the domain of the theory of knowledge, we cannot pretend that there have not been centuries of positive science. But neither the existence of Christianity nor that of positive science plays in this connection more than the role of a fertilizing principle. It favors the development of certain ideas which we might not have conceived without it. This development may take place in what I would call para-Christian zones; for myself, I have experienced it more than twenty years before I had the remotest thought of becoming a Catholic.

Speaking more particularly to Catholics, I should like to note that from my own standpoint the distinction between the natural and the supernatural must be rigorously maintained. It will perhaps be objected that there is a danger that the word 'mystery' might confuse this very issue.

I would reply that there is no question of confusing those mysteries which are enveloped in human experience as such with those mysteries which are revealed, such as the Incarnation or redemption, and to which no effort of thought bearing on experience can enable us to attain.

It will be asked: Why, then, do you use the same word for two such distinct notions? But I would point out that no revelation is, after all, conceivable unless it is addressed to a being who is *involved – committed* – in the sense which I have tried to define – that is to say, to a being who participates in a reality which is nonproblematical and which provides him with his foundation as subject. Supernatural life *must*, when all is said and done, find a hold in the natural – which is not to say that it is the flowering of the natural. On the contrary, it seems to me that any study of the notion of created nature, which is fundamental for the Christian, leads to the conclusion that there is in the depth of nature, as of reason, which is governed by it, a fundamental principle of inadequacy to itself which is, as it were, a restless anticipation of a different order.

To sum up my position on this difficult and important point, I would say that the recognition of the ontological mystery, in which I perceive as it were the central redoubt of metaphysics, is, no doubt, only possible through a sort of radiation which proceeds from revelation itself and which is perfectly well able to affect souls who are strangers to all positive religion of whatever kind; that this recognition, which takes place through certain higher modes of human experience, in no way involves the adherence to any given religion; but it enables those who have attained to it to perceive the possibility of a revelation in a way which is not open to those who have never ventured beyond the frontiers of the realm of the problematical and who have therefore never reached the point from which the mystery of being can be seen and recognized. Thus, a philosophy of this sort is carried by an irresistible movement toward the light which it perceives from afar and of which it suffers the secret attraction.

3

JOSÉ ORTEGA Y GASSET
(1883–1955)

'Man is not a thing, but a drama,' Ortega said in 1935. 'His life [is] a pure and universal happening which happens to each one of us and in which each one in his turn is nothing but happening.' Ortega's own life was certainly dramatic and he was never content to be a mere spectator, but instead chose to be an actor on a global stage of events. 'Life is a task,' he went on to say in the same context. 'Life, in fact, sets us plenty of tasks ... Life's mode of being is formally a being difficult, a being which consists in problematic toil.' In these words he may have been referring in an exemplary fashion to the many dangers and obstacles that beset his own path through life. Ortega's personal heritage itself attested to a deep-seated commitment to be a witness to historical reason, one of his key concepts. He was the son of José Ortega Munilla and grandson of Eduardo Gasset, both important and highly regarded Spanish journalists. He studied at the Jesuit College in Miraflores near Malaga, then for another year at Deusto, before switching to the University of Madrid, where he was awarded his doctorate in 1904 for his thesis on *The Terrors of the Year 1000: Critique of a Legend*. In 1905 he began his postdoctoral studies at various German universities, first at Berlin, then at Leipzig and finally at Marburg, where he became a research student under the neo-Kantian Hermann Cohen. He also attended lectures by Ernst Cassirer, Georg Simmel and Paul Natorp, from whom he learned about Husserl's teaching in phenomenology. Husserl's *Logical Investigations* (published in 1900) had little impact at his own University of Göttingen; his initial influence began to make itself felt among a group of students of Theodor Lipps, then at the University of Munich. One gifted young researcher, Johannes Daubert, organised these dissident students and persuaded them to adopt Husserl's work as their future programme. But only after members of this group, especially Adolf Reinach, had moved to Göttingen to join with Husserl in an effective 'movement', did his teaching begin to spread through other German universities, including the otherwise fairly provincial Marburg University.

Due to his achievements at these renowned German universities, Ortega was appointed to the Chair of Metaphysics at the University of Madrid in 1910. In that year he published an article, 'Adam and Paradise', which sets out some of his principal themes for the first time. In talking about Adam, Ortega stresses the importance of the human environment, everything that surrounds the individual, not only directly but also remotely, not only in the physical dimension, but also in the historical and spiritual dimension. Human being, he says here, is the problem of life, and the concept of life that he employs is something that is concrete, incomparable and unique. Moreover, in terms of humans' social being, 'life is an exchange of substances; therefore, [it is] a living together, a coexisting.' The image of Adam in Paradise signifies oneself in the world, but a world that is not a collection of things, rather a stage setting since human life is a drama, a series of events that humans perform. Ortega began to write a regular column for the Madrid newspapers in which he kept his literate readers up to date with wide-ranging reports about philosophy, the fine arts, theatre and fiction outside Spain. His first major book was *Meditations on Don Quixote* (1914) in which he set out to go beyond the opposition between idealism and realism, an attempt to find a third way that also characterised Husserl's work after 1913, and much later the work of Sartre, Jaspers and Merleau-Ponty. Ortega claimed that idealism asserts the ontological priority of the self, while realism asserts the ontological priority of the things the self comes to know about. Striking off on his own, Ortega argued that self and things were constitutive of each other, that each pole required the other pole in order to exist. The true reality could be termed self-with-things, or in his words, 'the ego and its circumstances'. The things which literally 'stand-around' oneself are 'the other half of my personality', but not in the form of static coexistence, rather through ongoing activity, in which the self acts on things and realises itself through these actions. This special form of self-willed activity is the dynamic interplay (*quehacer*) of self and circum-stances, in relations of mutual depen-dence in the course of which the self carries out a mission of self-fulfilment. 'The fundamental reality is our life. And life is made up of what we do and what happens to us. To live is to deal with the world, to direct oneself toward it, to act in it, to concern oneself with it.'

Ortega's lifelong emphasis on the concept of human *life*, of living, not being, reflects the influence of several important elements in his background. He was in regular correspondence with the great elder Spanish philosopher Miguel de Unamuno (1864–1936), whose book *The Tragic Sense of Life* (1912) had a profound impact on the intellectual milieu of pre-Republican Spain. On the opening page Unamuno demands the reader's attention in considering an entirely new subject of philosophical discourse, 'the man of flesh and bone; the man who is born, suffers, and dies – above all, who dies; the man who eats and drinks and plays and sleeps and thinks and wills; the man who is seen and heard; the brother, the real brother.' This incarnate being is the subject of all Ortega's books, and the very notion of *incarnation*, Merleau-Ponty later argued, is the core of the Existential overthrow of traditional metaphysics. As well as Unamuno, Ortega also felt the powerful force of his former teacher Georg Simmel who argued that authentic culture as the product of human social being was the best synthesis of the opposed values of life as process and life as cultural principle. Ortega was also committed to wedding the phenomenological approach with some elements from vitalist philosophy, especially through the works of Henri Bergson, Wilhelm Dilthey and Nietzsche. This attempt at a synthesis of phenomenology and lifeforce philosophy becomes most apparent in his next important work, *The Theme of Our Time* (1923). Here Ortega elevates life above thought and proposes one of his most famous catchwords, 'vital reason'; this concept is designed to replace the pure reason of traditional metaphysics, as transmitted to him through his neo-Kantian education. Vital reason comprises thought and emotion and volition; it must be subordinated to human life and requires truth in thought, beauty and affect, as well as generosity in the will to action.

In this context he brings into play Nietzsche's doctrine that reality is comprised of multiple perspectives, that each person has an irreducible point of view which presents his or her own truth. 'Perspective is one of the components of reality. Far from being a deformation of reality, it is its organization. A reality that would always turn out to be the same no matter what point it was viewed from is an absurd concept.' And further, 'every life is a viewpoint on the universe'; in this formula Ortega seems to be moving away from the Husserlian claim that every human being experiences the *one* world, the earth as horizon of space and time, even though such experiences have an egocentric point of view. But Ortega's response to this focuses on the immediate, concrete character of an individual's lived experience, as opposed to his or her 'objective' experience. 'The reduction or conversion of the world into a horizon does not in the least rob it of reality; it merely relates it to the living subject, whose world it is, and endows it with a vital dimension.' It seems clear that in order to make this point cohere with his perspectival thesis Ortega needs to rely on Husserl's distinction between *lived*-experience (*Erlebnis*) and 'object'-experience (*Erfahrung*). An individual life is an irreducible event or happening that amounts to a person's ongoing struggle with his or her circumstances. If one wants to consider this happening in terms of 'lived'-experiences, then this concept has to be stripped of its idealist overtones; what underscores this concept is that some things befall an individual in an absolute sense. This befalling, or happening to one, demands that the individual *make sense* of these events, in order to be able to go on living. As Suzanne Cunningham puts it, the meaning of Descartes' *cogito ergo sum* has to be reversed:

I do not exist because I think, but the other way round: *cogito quia vivo*. I think because I experience my being, without meditation or choice, as my struggle to exist in the world. In fact, I am a being who is condemned to translate this necessity into freedom. Freedom is born in and conditioned by such an encounter. I am thus a *dramatic thing*, the drama enacted by myself in the world with things of the world.

Ortega carried forward his journalist legacy as early as 1914 when he founded the magazine *España*, and in 1917 he was instrumental in founding the Madrid daily newspaper *El Sol*. When *España* ceased publication in 1923, he inaugurated one of the greatest Spanish journals *Revista de Occidente*, comparable in its scope and influence to the famous British review *Encounter*. Although the *Revista* was shut down in 1936 under Franco, at the same time that Ortega left Spain, it was revived for its second period after the war. An eight-volume edition of his collected journalism from 1916 to 1928, including reviews, editorials and columns, is available as *El espectador: colección de ensayos filosoficos y literarios*. While at the University of Madrid, Ortega always maintained a strong commitment to bring philosophy into the public arena, and to resist the temptation to keep its privileged, elitist niche among the intellectuals.

In 1929, intervention in university affairs by the dictator Primo de Rivera provoked Ortega into resigning his chair, but he didn't give up addressing his public, and instead rented theatres to deliver his lectures. Ortega's popular, direct voice comes across very clearly in the printed texts of these lectures, *What is Philosophy?*, where he organises some of his early reflections under four main principles: first, that my life is the 'radical reality', the framework in which all other realities, including that of pure reason, have their place; second, that my life is a self-conscious problem that demands personal realisation; third, that my problem amounts to deciding among specific possibilities in order to achieve an authentic being for myself; and fourth, that the plurality of these possibilities defines my freedom in this life. Under Ortega's guidance several works on phenomenology appeared before the war: José Gaos, *La critica del psicologismo en Husserl* (1933); Xavier Zubiri, *Ensayo de una idea fenomenologica del juicio* (1927), and the Spanish translation of Theodor Celms, *El idealismo fenomenologico de Husserl* (1928). José Gaos was professor at the Universities of Zaragoza and Madrid until 1939, and then professor at the University of Mexico, where he was responsible for the Spanish translation of Heidegger's *Being and Time* in 1951, more than ten years before it appeared in English. If Ortega never really managed to complete a systematic treatise in Existential Phenomenology, one of his students and younger colleagues, Xavier Zubiri, did. Zubiri studied with Heidegger at Freiburg from 1929 to 1931, was professor at Madrid from 1926 to 1936 and at Barcelona from 1940 to 1942 (though he did not return to teaching after the war), and in 1962 published his great work *On Essence* which shows the decisive influence of Ortega's philosophical vocabulary and phenomenological orientation.

In his 1930 book, *The Revolt of the Masses*, Ortega launched an attack on the current type of herd or crowd culture, reminiscent of Nietzsche's savage denunciations of herd mentality. Here Ortega offered diagnoses of the cultural malaise of the 1930s: large-scale aggression in public affairs, opposition to liberalism, ignorance of European history, excessive reliance on the central state and demoralized conformism. Ortega himself never shied away from political engagement; he was one of the leaders of the intellectual opposition to the dictator, ousted in 1930, and played some part in the overthrow of King Alfonso XIII in 1931. He was elected deputy for the Leon province in the assembly of the Second Spanish Republic, became the leader of an opposition group in parliament called *La Agrupación al servicio de la república*, and was named civil governor of Madrid. But these political commitments compelled him to leave Spain in 1936 at the outbreak of the Civil War and he spent the next twelve years in exile. He moved from house to house in France, Holland, Argentina, Portugal and Germany before returning to live in Spain in 1945. In Germany in 1936, during Heidegger's itinerant lecture tours, Hans-Georg Gadamer recalls that on one occasion, Ortega followed Heidegger to the Kurhaus Buhlerhohe, 'drawn in by this seeker after the gold of speech and thought.' Much of the research and lecture material for his great systematic work *The Idea of Principle in Leibniz and the Evolution of Deductive Theory* was carried out in Buenos Aires, where in fact it was first published in 1958. In 1948, in collaboration with his protégé Julian Marias, Ortega founded the Institute for Humanities in Madrid, in which he continued to lecture until his death in 1955.

> By the time of his death, Ortega was the acknowledged head of the most productive school of thinkers Spain had known for three centuries, and he had placed philosophy in Spain beyond the reach, not of opposition and criticism, but of the centuries-old reproach that it was un-Spanish or antinational and therefore either a foreign affectation or a subversive danger. (McInnes, 1967)

Ortega was a superb literary stylist who managed to blend vivid, concrete details into philosophical arguments whose framework he had imported and transformed from the German original. His penchant for pithy epigrams and slogan-like pronouncements, no doubt inspired by his years working to tight deadlines and short word-counts in newspaper columns, tends to sometimes occlude his efforts to carry through a complex train of thought. Many of his topically driven essays repeat, in slightly different forms, statements that he made in previous essays. But in his one comprehensive historical work, *The Idea of Principle*, Ortega set out to trace in meticulous detail, from Aristotle through the Scholastics to the present, the tension and polarity between counterposed tendencies in philosophical reflection. He wanted to reverse the direction of Husserl's phenomenological reduction by showing that consciousness itself cannot be suspended or revoked, since it is not contemplation, but human being situated in the world, that comprises our first reality. Modern philosophy since Descartes has given the realm of thought priority over the realm of being, but the being that we know is not the theoretical conclusion of an abstract argument, rather it is the primary datum that all experience begins with. 'The activity of knowing used to seem to consist in an effort to reflect, mirror, or copy in our mind the world of real things, but it turns out to be just the opposite, namely, the invention, construction, or fabrication of an unreal world.'

Julian Marias, one of Ortega's early postgraduate students and junior colleagues, became one of the most significant Spanish philosophers of the next generation. In his excellent *History of Philosophy* (1967), Marias summarises Ortega's distinctive contribution to twentieth-century ethical debate in words that are particularly appropriate to our exposition of Existentialist thought:

> Since I have to decide what I am going to do at every moment, I need to *justify myself to myself* for doing one thing and not another; life is responsibility; in its ultimate substance, it is *moral*. Like all human reality life admits of *degrees of being* . . . Since the being of life is not already and immediately given, it can be realized *fully* or *insufficiently*, it can be *falsified*. When one's life is made from one's own standpoint, when a man is true to the voice which calls him to be a determined thing, and which is therefore known as his *vocation*, his life is *authentic*; when man abandons himself to what is trite and handed down, when he is unfaithful to his intimate and original vocation, he falsifies his life and changes it into *inauthentic* life. Morality consists in authenticity, in bringing life to its maximum reality, to live is *to live more*. Morality consists in each man's realizing his own unique and unsubstitutable destiny. (Marias, 1967, p. 458)

PRINCIPAL WORKS

(1914) *Meditations on Quixote*, trans. E. Rugg and D. Marin. New York: W. W. Norton, 1961.

(1915) *Psychological Investigations*, trans. Jorge Garcia-Gomez. New York: W. W. Norton, 1987.

(1923) *The Theme of Our Time*, trans. James Cleugh. New York: Harper & Row, 1961.

(1929) *What is Philosophy?*, trans. by M. Adams. New York: W. W. Norton, 1960.

(1930) *The Revolt of the Masses*, trans. A. Kerrigan. Notre Dame, IN: University of Notre Dame Press, 1986.

(1932) *Some Lessons in Metaphysics*, trans. M. Adams. New York: W. W. Norton, 1969.

(1935) *History as a System*, trans. W. C. Atkinson. In *Philosophy and History*. Oxford: Oxford University Press, 1941; and in *History as a System and Other Essays*. New York: W. W. Norton, 1941.

(1940–4) *Historical Reason*, trans. Philip Silver. New York: W. W. Norton, 1984.

(1947–50) *The Idea of Principle in Leibniz and the Evolution of Deductive Theory*, trans. M. Adams. New York: W. W. Norton, 1971.

RECOMMENDED READING

Note: There is no entry, not even a single reference, to Ortega or Unamuno in *A Companion to Continental Philosophy*, eds Simon Critchley and William Schroeder (Oxford: Blackwell, 1998), nor in *Twentieth-Century Continental Philosophy*, ed. Richard Kearney (London and New York: Routledge, 1994).

Ferrater Mora, José (1957) *Ortega y Gasset: An Outline of His Philosophy*. New Haven, CT: Yale University Press.

McInnes, Neil (1967) 'José Ortega y Gasset', in Paul Edwards (ed.), *Encyclopedia of Philosophy*. New York: Macmillan, vol. 6, pp. 2–5.

Marias, Julian (1967) *History of Philosophy*, trans. Stanley Appelbaum and Clarence Strowbridge. New York: Dover, pp. 442–68.

Marias, Julian (1970) *José Ortega y Gasset: Circumstance and Vocation*, trans. Frances Lopez-Morillas. Norman: University of Oklahoma Press.

Orringer, N. (1984) 'Ortega y Gasset's Critique of Method', in *Comparative Criticism*, vol. 6, pp. 135–54.

Ouimette, V. (1982) *José Ortega y Gasset*. Boston: Twayne Publishers.

Rodriguez Huéscar, Antonio (1994) *José Ortega y Gasset's Metaphysical Innovation*, trans. Jorge Garcia-Gomez. Albany: State University of New York Press.

Silver, Philip W. (1978) *Ortega as Phenomenologist*. New York: Columbia University Press.

Zubiri, Xavier (1980) *On Essence*, trans. A. R. Caponigri. Washington, DC: Catholic University of America Press.

'HISTORY AS A SYSTEM' (1935)[*]

José Ortega y Gasset

I

Human life is a strange reality concerning which the first thing to be said is that it is the basic reality, in the sense that to it we must refer all others, since all others, effective or presumptive, must in one way or another appear within it.

The most trivial and at the same time the most important note in human life is that man has no choice but to be always doing something to keep himself in existence. Life is given to us; we do not give it to ourselves, rather we find ourselves in it, suddenly and without knowing how. But the life which is given us is not given us ready-made; we must make it for ourselves, each one his own. Life is a task. And the weightiest aspect of these tasks in which life consists is not the necessity of performing them but, in a sense, the opposite: I mean, that we find ourselves always under compulsion to do something but never, strictly speaking, under compulsion to do something in particular, that

---

[*] Trans. William C. Atkinson, from *Philosophy and History*, eds R. Klibansky and H. J. Paton. Oxford: Clarendon Press, 1936.

there is not imposed on us this or that task as there is imposed on the star its course or on the stone its gravitation. Each individual before doing anything must decide for himself and at his own risk what he is going to do. But this decision is impossible unless one possesses certain convictions concerning the nature of things around one, the nature of other men, of oneself. Only in the light of such convictions can one prefer one act to another, can one, in short, live.

It follows that man must ever be grounded on some belief, and that the structure of his life will depend primordially on the beliefs on which he is grounded; and further that the most decisive changes in humanity are changes of belief, the intensifying or weakening of beliefs. The diagnosis of any human existence, whether of an individual, a people or an age, must begin by establishing the repertory of its convictions. For always in living one sets out from certain convictions. They are the ground beneath our feet, and it is for this reason we say that man is grounded on them. It is man's beliefs that truly constitute his state. I have spoken of them as a repertory to indicate that the plurality of beliefs on which an individual, a people or an age is grounded never possesses a completely logical articulation, that is to say, does not form a system of ideas such as, for example, a philosophy constitutes or aims at constituting. The beliefs that coexist in any human life, sustaining, impelling, and directing it, are on occasion incongruous, contradictory, at the least confused. Be it noted that all these qualifications attach to beliefs in so far as they partake of ideas. But it is erroneous to define belief as an idea. Once an idea has been thought it has exhausted its role and its consistency. The individual, moreover, may think whatever the whim suggests to him, and even many things against his whim. Thoughts arise in the mind spontaneously, without will or deliberation on our part and without producing any effect whatever on our behaviour. A belief is not merely an idea that is thought, it is an idea in which one also believes. And believing is not an operation of the intellectual mechanism, but a function of the living being as such, the function of guiding his conduct, his performance of his task.

This observation once made, I can now withdraw my previous expression and say that beliefs, a mere incoherent repertory in so far as they are merely ideas, always constitute a system in so far as they are effective beliefs; in other words, that while lacking articulation from the logical or strictly intellectual point of view, they do none the less possess a vital articulation, they *function* as beliefs resting one on another, combining with one another to form a whole: in short, that they always present themselves as members of an organism, of a structure. This causes them among other things always to possess their own architecture and to function as a hierarchy. In every human life there are beliefs that are basic, fundamental, radical, and there are others derived from these, upheld by them and secondary to them. If this observation is supremely trivial, the fault is not mine that with all its triviality it remains of the greatest importance. For should the beliefs by which one lives lack structure, since their number in each individual life is legion there must result a mere pullulation hostile to all idea of order and incomprehensible in consequence.

The fact that we should see them, on the contrary, as endowed with a structure and a hierarchy allows us to penetrate their hidden order and consequently to understand our own life and the life of others, that of to-day and that of other days.

Thus we may now say that the diagnosing of any human existence, whether of an individual, a people, or an age, must begin by an ordered inventory of its system of convictions, and to this end it must establish before all else which belief is fundamental, decisive, sustaining and breathing life into all the others.

Now in order to determine the state of one's beliefs at a given moment the only method we possess is that of comparing this moment with one or more other moments. The more numerous the terms of comparison the more exact will be the result – another banal observation whose far-reaching consequences will emerge suddenly at the end of this meditation.

II

A comparison of the state of beliefs in which the European finds himself to-day with that obtaining a mere thirty years ago makes it clear that this has changed profoundly, because the fundamental conviction has changed.

The generation that flourished about the year 1900 was the last of a very long cycle, a cycle which began towards the end of the sixteenth century and was characterized by the fact that men lived on their faith in reason. In what does this faith consist?

If we open the *Discours de la Méthode*, the classical programme of the new age, we find that it culminates in the following sentences:

> 'Those long chains composed of very simple and easy reasonings, which geometers customarily use to arrive at their most difficult demonstrations, had given me occasion to suppose that all the things which can fall under human knowledge are interconnected in the same way. And I thought that, provided we refrain from accepting anything as true which is not, and always keep to the order required for deducing one thing from another, *there can be nothing too remote to be reached in the end or too well hidden to be discovered.*'[1]

These words are the cockcrow of rationalism, the moving reveille that ushers in a whole new age, our so-called modern age, that modern age whose death agony, whose swan-song, as it seems to many, we are to-day witnessing.

There is at least no denying that between the Cartesian attitude of mind and our own no slight difference exists. What joy, what a tone of vigorous challenge to the universe, what an early-morning presumptuousness these magnificent words of Descartes reveal! The reader has observed: apart from the divine mysteries which his courtesy bids him leave on one side, to this man there is no problem that cannot be solved. He assures us that in the universe there are no arcana, no unconquerable secrets before which humanity must halt in defenceless terror. The world that surrounds man all about, existence within which constitutes his life, is to become transparent, even to its farthest recesses, to the human mind. At last man is to know the truth about everything. It suffices that he should not lose heart at the complexity of the problems, and that he should allow no passion to cloud his mind. If with serene self-mastery he uses the apparatus of his intellect, if in particular he uses it in orderly fashion, he will find that his faculty of thought is *ratio*, reason, and that in reason he possesses the almost magic power of reducing everything to clarity, of turning what is most opaque to crystal, penetrating it by analysis until it is become self-evident. According to this the world of reality and the world of thought are each a cosmos corresponding one to the other, each compact and continuous, wherein nothing is abrupt, isolated, or inaccessible, but rather such that from any point in it we may without intermission and without leaping pass to all other points and contemplate the whole. Man with his reason may thus plunge tranquilly into the abysmal depths of the universe, certain of extracting from the remotest problem, from the closest enigma, the essence of its truth, even as the Coromandel diver plunges into the deeps of ocean to reappear straightway bearing between his teeth the pearl of great price.

In the closing years of the sixteenth century and these early years of the seventeenth in which Descartes is meditating western man believes, then, that the world possesses a rational structure, that is to say, that reality possesses an organization coincident with the organization of the human intellect, taking this, of course, in its purest form, that of mathematical reason. Here accordingly is a marvellous key giving man a power over things around him that is theoretically illimitable. Such a discovery was a pretty stroke of fortune. For suppose that Europe had not then come by this belief. In the fifteenth century it had lost its faith in God, in revelation, either because man had completely lost that faith or because it had ceased to be in him a living faith. Theologians make a very shrewd distinction, one capable of throwing light on not a few things of to-day, between a live and a sluggish faith. Generalizing this, I should formulate it thus: we believe in something with a live faith when that belief is sufficient for us to live by, and we believe in something with a dead, a sluggish faith when, without having abandoned it, being still grounded on it, it no longer acts efficaciously on our lives. It is become a drag, a dead-weight; still part of us, yet useless as lumber in the attic of the soul. We no longer rest our existence on that something believed in; the stimuli, the pointers we live by no longer spring spontaneously from that faith. The proof is that we are constantly forgetting we still believe in it, whereas a living faith is the constant and most active presence of the entity we believe in. (Hence the perfectly natural phenomenon that the mystic calls 'the presence of God'. For a living love is likewise distinguished from a lifeless, dragging love in this, that the object loved is present to us without need of trance or fear of eclipse. We do not need to go in search of it with our attention, on the contrary we have difficulty in removing it from before our inner eye. And this is not to say that we are always nor even frequently *thinking* about it, but simply that we constantly 'count on it'.) An illustration of this difference in the present situation of the European I shall shortly adduce.[2]

Throughout the Middle Ages the European had lived on revelation. Lacking it, limited to his own naked strength, he would have felt incapable of dealing with the mysterious surroundings that made up his world, with the misfortunes and trials of existence. But he believed with a living faith that an all-powerful, all-knowing being would unfold to him gratuitously all that was essential to his life. We may follow the vicissitudes of this faith and witness, almost generation by generation, its progressive decay. It is a melancholy story. Gradually the living faith ceases to take nutriment, loses its colour, becomes paralysed, until, from whatever motives – these lie outside my present inquiry – towards the middle of the fifteenth century that living faith is clearly seen to have changed to a tired, ineffective faith, if indeed the individual soul has not uprooted it entirely. The man of that age begins to perceive that revelation does not suffice to illumine his relations to the world; once more he is conscious of being lost in the trackless forest of the universe, face to face with which he lacks alike a guide and a mediator. The fifteenth and the sixteenth centuries are, therefore, two centuries of tremendous restlessness, of fierce disquiet, two centuries, as we should say to-day, of crisis. From this crisis western man is saved by a new faith, a new belief: faith in reason, in the *nuove scienze* [new science]. Man, having again fallen, is born again. The Renaissance is the parturient disquiet of a new confidence based on physico-mathematical science, the new mediator between man and the world.

III

Beliefs constitute the basic stratum, that which lies deepest, in the architecture of our life. By them we live, and by the same token we rarely think of them. Whatever is still to us more or less in debate, that we think of. Hence we say that we *hold* such and such ideas, whereas rather than holding our beliefs we are them.

One may symbolize the individual life as a bank of issue. The bank lives on the credit of a gold reserve which is rarely seen, which lies at the bottom of metal coffers hidden in the vaults of the building. The most elementary caution will suggest that from time to time the effective condition of these guarantees – of these *credences*, one might say, that are the basis of *credit* – be passed in review.

To-day it is become urgent that we should do the same with the faith in reason by which the European, obedient to tradition – a tradition of close on three centuries – has been living. It may be said that until twenty years ago the state of this belief had not suffered modification in its general outline, but that in the last few years it has changed most profoundly. So much is demonstrated by innumerable facts, facts that are only too well known and that it would be depressing to enunciate once more.

It will be superfluous to point out that in speaking of the traditional faith in reason and of its present-day modification I am not referring to what happens in this or that individual as such. Apart from what individuals as individuals, that is to say, each for himself and on his own account, may believe, there exists always a collective state of belief. This social faith may or may not coincide with that felt by such and such an individual. The decisive factor in the matter is that whatever may be the private belief of each one of us we are confronted with a state of faith collectively constituted and established, a faith, in short, that is socially operative.

The faith in science to which I refer was not merely and firstly an individual opinion. It was on the contrary a collective opinion, and when something is a collective or social opinion it is a reality independent of individuals, outside them as stones are outside the landscape, a reality with which individuals must reckon willy-nilly. Our personal opinion may run counter to social opinion, but this will not invalidate one iota the reality of the latter. What constitutes and gives a specific character to collective opinion is the fact that its existence does not depend on its acceptance or rejection by any given individual. From the view-point of each individual life public belief has, as it were, the appearance of a physical object. The tangible reality, so to speak, of collective belief does not consist in its acceptance by you or by me; instead it is it which, whether we acquiesce or not, imposes on us its reality and forces us to reckon with it. To this characteristic of social faith I apply the term 'operative'. A law is said to be operative when, far from its effectiveness hingeing on my recognition of it, it acts and functions independently of my adhesion. And in like manner collective belief has no need of my belief in it as a particular individual in order to exist and weigh upon me and even, perchance, crush me. If now it be agreed, for our better understanding, to apply the term 'social dogma' to the content of a collective belief, we are in a position to continue our meditation.

When, equipped with these instrumental concepts, we compare the situation in which the European found himself about the year 1910 with that of to-day, the perception of the change, the mutation, that has occurred ought to cause in us a salutary terror. A mere twenty years, that is to say only a portion of a man's life, in itself so short, have sufficed to invert the order of things to the point that, whereas then one might in any part of Europe have invoked faith in science and the rights of science as the maximum human value, and this urge functioned automatically, the social body accepting in all docility its imperative and reacting thereto with efficacy, energy, and promptitude, to-day there are already nations where such an invocation would provoke only smiles – nations that some years ago were considered precisely as being in the van of science – and I do not believe there is any, at the time of writing, in which it would call forth even a throb from the social body.

IV

Science is in danger. In saying this I do not think I exaggerate. For this is not to say that Europe collectively has made a radical end of its belief in science, but only that its faith, once living, is in our day become sluggish. This is sufficient to cause science to be in danger and to make it impossible for the scientist to go on living as he has lived till now, sleep-walking at his work, believing that the society around him still supports, sustains, and venerates him. What has happened to bring about such a situation? Science to-day knows with incredible precision much of what is happening on remote stars and galaxies. Science is rightly proud of the fact, and because of it, although with less right, it spreads its peacock feathers at academic gatherings. But meanwhile it has come about that this same science, once a living social faith, is now almost looked down upon by society in general. And although this has not happened on Sirius but only on our own planet, it is not, I conceive, bereft of importance. Science cannot be merely science about Sirius; it claims also to be science about man. What then has science, reason, got to say to-day, with reasonable precision, concerning this so urgent fact that so intimately concerns it? Just nothing. Science has no clear knowledge on the matter. One perceives the enormity of the position, the shame of it. The upshot is that, where great human changes are concerned, science, strictly so called, has got nothing exact to say. The thing is so enormous that it straightway reveals to us the reason. For it causes us to note that the science, the reason, in which modern man placed his social faith is, speaking strictly, merely physico-mathematical science together with biological science, the latter based directly on the former and benefiting, in its weakness, from the other's prestige – in short, summing both up together, what is called natural science or reason.

The present position of physical science or reason is in consequence somewhat paradoxical. If there is anything in the repertory of human activities and pursuits that has not proved a failure, it is precisely this science, when one considers it circumscribed within its genuine territory, nature. Within this order and ambit, far from having failed, it has transcended all our hopes. For the first time in history the powers of realization, of achievement, have outstripped those of mere fantasy. Science has achieved things that irresponsible imaginings had never so much as dreamed of. This is so unquestionable that one has difficulty in understanding straightway why man is not to-day on his knees before science as before some magic power. The fact remains that he is not on his knees; on the contrary he is beginning to turn his back. He does not deny, he is not unaware of, its marvellous power, its triumph over nature, but he realizes at the same time that nature is only one dimension of human life and that a resounding success with regard to nature does not preclude failure with regard to the totality of our existence. Life at any instant is an inexorable balance, in which 'physical reason' (*la razón física*) for all its partial splendour does not rule out the possibility of a heavy deficit. Even more, the lack of equilibrium between the perfection of its partial efficiency and its failure from the comprehensive point of view, which is final, is such in my opinion that it has contributed to the aggravation of our universal disquiet.

Man thus finds himself, when confronted with physical reason, in a state of mind comparable to that of Cristina of Sweden, as described by Leibniz, when, after her abdication, she caused a coin to be struck bearing the effigy of a crown and had these words inscribed in the exergue: *Non mi bisogna e non mi basta.*[3]

In the upshot the paradox resolves itself into a supremely simple observation. What has not collapsed in physics is physics. What has collapsed in it is the rhetoric, the trimmings of childish presumption, of irrational and arbitrary additions it gave rise to, what, many years ago, I styled 'the terrorism of the laboratory'. This is why ever since I began to write I have combated what I called scientific *Utopianism*. Open, for example, *El tema de nuestro tiempo* [*The Theme of Our Time*] at the chapter entitled 'The historic sense of Einstein's theory', written about 1921. There the following passage will be found:

> 'It is incomprehensible that science, whose only pleasure lies in attaining to a true image of things, should nourish itself on illusions. I recall a detail whose influence on my thought was decisive. Many years ago I was reading a lecture of the physiologist Loeb on tropism. The tropism is a concept which has been invoked to describe and throw light on the law governing the elemental movements of the Infusoria. The concept serves, indifferently well and with corrections and additions, to help us understand some of these phenomena. But at the close of this lecture Loeb adds: "The day will come when what we now call moral acts in man will be explained simply as tropisms." Such temerity perturbed me exceedingly, for it opened my eyes to many other judgements of modern science that are guilty, if less ostentatiously, of the same error. So then, I thought, a concept like the tropism, which is scarce capable of plumbing the secret of phenomena so simple as the antics of the Infusoria, may at some vague future date suffice to explain phenomena as mysterious and complex as man's ethical acts! What sense is there here? Science has to solve its problems in the present, not transport us to the Greek kalends. If its present methods are insufficient to master now the enigmas of the universe, discretion would suggest that they be replaced by other and more effective ones. But the science *à la mode* is full of problems which are left intact because they are incompatible with its methods. As if it was the former that were under obligation to subordinate themselves to the latter, and not the other way round! Science is full of anachronisms, of Greek kalends.
>
> When we emerge from a science so devoutly simple, bowing in idolatrous worship before pre-established methods, and approach the thought of Einstein there comes upon us as it were a fresh morning breeze. Einstein's attitude is radically different from that of tradition. With the dash of a young athlete we see him make straight for his problems and

take them by the horns, using the method that lies nearest to his hand. Out of the apparent defects and limitations of science he draws virtue and tactical efficiency.'

From this idea of the Greek kalends[4] all my philosophic thought has emanated. There in germ is my whole conception of life as the basic reality and of knowledge as an internal – and not an independent or Utopian – function of life. Just as Einstein was then telling us that in physics it is necessary to elaborate concepts such as will make perpetual motion impossible (perpetual motion is immeasurable and before what cannot be measured physics is impotent), I considered it essential to elaborate a philosophy that should take its point of departure, its formal principle, from the exclusion of the Greek kalends. Because life is the opposite of these kalends. Life is haste and has urgent need to know what it is up against, and it is out of this urgency that truth must derive its method. The idea of progress, placing truth in a vague to-morrow, has proved a dulling opiate to humanity. Truth is what is true now and not what remains to be discovered in an undetermined future. Herr Loeb – and his whole generation is with him – gives up his claim to a present truth of morality on the strength of the future attaining to a physics of morality: a curious way of existing at the expense of posterity while leaving one's own life shorn of foundations, of roots, of any profound implications in the scheme of things. The viciousness of this attitude is so radical that it appears already in the 'provisional morality' of Descartes.[5] And so it happens that the first blow directed against the superficial framework of our civilization, our economics, our morals, our politics, finds man possessed of no truths of his own, of no clear, firm position on anything of importance.

The only thing he believed in was physical science, and when this received the urgent call to propound its truth on the most human problems, it did not know what to say. And suddenly western man has received the impression of losing his footing, of finding himself without support, and has known a panic terror and believed himself to be sinking, making shipwreck in the void.

And yet, a measure of serenity is all that is needed for our feet once more to experience the delicious sensation of touching hard, solid mother earth, an element capable of sustaining man. As always, it is essential – and sufficient – instead of giving way to panic and losing one's head, to convert into a source of support the very factor that had engendered the impression of an abyss. Physical science can throw no clear light on the human element. Very well. This means simply that we must shake ourselves free, radically free, from the physical, the natural, approach to the human element. Let us instead accept this in all its spontaneity, just as we see it and come upon it. In other words, the collapse of physical reason leaves the way clear for vital, historical reason.[6]

V

Nature is a thing, a great thing, that is composed of many lesser things. Now, whatever be the differences between things, they all have one basic feature in common, which consists simply in the fact that things *are*, they have their being. And this signifies not only that they exist, that there they are, in front of us, but also that they possess a given, fixed structure or consistency. Given a stone, there exists forthwith, for all to see, what a stone is. Its every change and mutation, world without end, will be in specific combinations of its fundamental consistency. The stone can never be something new and different. This consistency, given and fixed once and for all, is what we customarily understand when we speak of the being of a thing. An alternative expression is the word 'nature'. And the task of natural science is to penetrate beneath changing appearances to that permanent nature or texture.

When naturalist reason studies man it seeks, in consistence with itself, to reveal his nature. It observes that man has a body, which is a thing, and hastens to submit it to physics; and since this body is also an organism, it hands it over to biology. It observes further that in man as in animals there functions a certain mechanism incorporeally, confusedly attached to the body, the psychic mechanism, which is also a thing, and entrusts its study to psychology, a natural science. But the fact is that this has been going on for three hundred years and that all the naturalist studies on man's body and soul put together have not been of the slightest use in throwing light on any of our most strictly human feelings, on what each individual calls his own life, that life which, intermingling with others, forms societies, that in their turn, persisting, make up human destiny. The prodigious achievement of natural science in the direction of the knowledge of things contrasts brutally with the collapse of this same natural science when faced with the strictly human element. The human element escapes physico-mathematical reason as water runs from a sieve.

And here we have the explanation why our faith in reason has entered upon a phase of lamentable decadence. Man cannot wait any longer. He demands that science illumine for him the problems of humanity. At bottom he is somewhat tired by now of stars and nervous reactions and atoms. The earliest generations of rationalists believed that with their physical science they could throw light on human destiny. Descartes himself wrote a treatise *De homine*.[7] To-day we know that all the marvels of the natural sciences, inexhaustible though they be in principle, must always come to a full stop before the strange reality of human life. Why? If all things have given up a large part of their secret to physical science, why does this alone hold out so stoutly? The explanation must go deep, down to the roots. Perchance it is no less than this: that man is not a thing, that it is false to talk of human nature, that man has no nature. I conceive that a physicist, on hearing this, may well feel his hair stand on end, since it signifies, in other words, an assertion that physics is radically incompetent to speak of man. But it is useless to shelter behind illusions: whether our consciousness of this be clear or not so clear, whether we suspect or not the existence of another mode of knowledge, another reason capable of speaking of man, the conviction of this incompetence is to-day a fact of the first magnitude on the European horizon. Physicists in the presence of it may feel irritated or pained – although both attitudes may here seem somewhat puerile – but this conviction is the historical precipitate of three centuries of failure.

Human life, it would appear then, is not a thing, has not a nature, and in consequence we must make up our minds to think of it in terms of categories and concepts that will be *radically* different from such as shed light on the phenomena of matter. The enterprise is no easy one, since for the last three centuries 'physicism' has accustomed us to leaving behind us, as an entity having neither importance nor reality, precisely this strange reality of human life. And so, while the naturalists devoted themselves with pious absorption to their professional tasks, the whim has taken this strange reality to veer to another point of the compass, and on enthusiasm for science there have followed lukewarmness and aversion. To-morrow, who knows, it may be frank hostility.

VI

It will be said that the more patent became the resistance of the human phenomenon to physical science, the more prominent became another form of science opposed to this: against the natural sciences, in effect, there arose and developed the so-called sciences of the spirit, the moral or cultural sciences. To this I reply, to begin with, that these sciences of the spirit, *Geisteswissenschaften*, have not so far been successful in moving the European to belief in the way that the natural sciences were.

And this is easily understood. The representatives of the spiritual sciences were combating the avowed intent of the others to investigate the human element by means of naturalistic ideas; but it happens that the spiritual sciences have in fact represented so far no more than a disguised attempt to do the same. Let me explain.

Geist? Wer ist der Bursche?[8] asked Schopenhauer, with an ill-humoured insolence that was not lacking in common sense. This great Utopian concept of the spirit sought to oppose itself to nature. One felt intuitively that nature was not the only reality, and above all, that it was not the primary or fundamental one. The more one got to grips with it, the more it appeared to depend on the human element. German idealism, like the positivism of Comte, signifies the attempt to place man before nature. It was the former that gave man, in so far as he is not nature, the name *Geist*, spirit.

But it happened that in the effort to comprehend the human element as a spiritual reality things did not go any better: human phenomena showed the same resistance, the same stubborn reluctance to let themselves be hemmed in by concepts. Further, it was a privilege reserved to the thought of that age to indulge in the most scandalous and irresponsible Utopias. One readily appreciates Schopenhauer's ill-humour and insolence. Hegel's *Philosophy of History* and Comte's 'law of the three estates' are, beyond a doubt, two works of genius. In affixing to them this qualification of genius, however, all we are clearly doing is to applaud a man's magnificent dexterity as such, to applaud him for his agility, for what he has of the juggler or the athlete. If we study these works, chiefly Hegel's, from the decisive point of view, that of intellectual responsibility, and consider them as symptomatic of a moral climate, we soon perceive that they would have been impossible, *ceteris paribus*, in any normal epoch of thought, in any age of restraint, proportion, and sensitive respect for the function of the intellect.

I am bold to say this solely as an extrinsic indication of the fact that the interpretation of man as a spiritual reality could not but be violent, arbitrary, and a failure. Because in this context it is not permissible to continue using the word 'spirit' vaguely; it must needs be referred to the cycle of exact meanings it has borne in the philosophy of the past two centuries.

If now we ask why the concept of spirit has shown itself insufficient to explain the human element we are led to the following fundamental consideration.

When the knights-errant of the spirit sallied forth to wage war on naturalism, determined to give a scrupulous representation of human phenomena in their genuine essence and putting far from them the concepts and categories that nature imposes on our thinking, they did not take heed that, as they set out, they had already left the enemy behind. In nature they saw only certain peculiar attributes, spatiality, force, their sensorial manifestation, and the like, and they believed it sufficient to replace these by other antagonistic attributes, *cogitatio*, consciousness, apperception, and the like, in order to place themselves outside nature. In short, they were guilty of the same mistake Descartes made when he held it enough, in order to define the self, to oppose it as a *res cogitans* to the *res extensa*. But can the fundamental difference between that strange reality, man, the *ego*, and that other reality, things, consist in the fact that the *ego* thinks while things have extent? What difficulty would there be in the *res* that thinks having extent and the *res* that has extent thinking? Descartes is wont to add, astutely, that the *res* that thinks has no extent and the *res* that has extent does not think. But this denial, coming as an afterthought, is wholly arbitrary, and Spinoza, who was not easily imposed upon, calmly draws the inference that one and the same *res – Natura sive Deus* – thinks and has extent. To compose the issue it would be necessary to do what Descartes did not do, to wit, to ask oneself what is this *res* business, what is its structure, before proceeding to classify it as thinking or as having extent. For if the attributes of *cogitatio* and *extensio* are in such wise antagonistic that they cannot coexist in the same *res*, the suspicion arises that each of them must react on the very structure of the *res* as *res*. Or, which comes to the same thing, that the term *res* is equivocal in both expressions.

Now, the concept *res* had already been established by traditional ontology. The error made by Descartes and by the knights-errant of the spirit lay in not carrying down to bedrock their reform of philosophy, in applying unthinkingly to the new reality they aspired to establish – *pensée, Geist* – the old doctrine of being. Can an entity that consists in thinking have *being* in the same sense as one that consists in having extent has *being*? Apart from the difference implied in the fact that one thinks while the other has extent, are they not differentiated also in their very being, as entities *sensu stricto*?

In traditional ontology the term *res* is always linked with the term *natura*, whether as a synonym or in the sense that *natura* is the real *res*, the beginning of *res*. The concept of nature we know to be of pure Greek descent: it is first stabilized in Aristotle, then, modified by the Stoics, it comes into the Renaissance, and through that mighty portal inundates the modern age. In Robert Boyle it finds the expression that still holds: '*natura* is the rule or system of rules according to which phenomena behave – in short, their law.'[9]

To go back over the history of the concept of nature is not possible here, and any summary of it must be futile. For the sake of brevity I shall content myself with a single allusion: is it not surprising that the term 'nature' should have come, with unbroken continuity, from meaning what it meant to Aristotle to mean the law of phenomena? Is not the distance between the two meanings enormous? That distance, be it noted, implies nothing less than the whole change in our way of thinking of the universe from ancient to modern man. What then, down this long evolution, has remained constant in the concept of nature?

There are few themes in which one may see so clearly as here the extent to which European man is heir to the Greek. Inheritance, however, is not only treasure; it is, at the same time, a charge and a bond. Concealed in the concept of nature we have received the bonds that make us the slaves of Hellenic destiny.

Greek thought is formulated in Parmenides. Parmenides represents beyond question the pure essence of Hellenism, for it is a fact that Eleaticism has always held sway in Hellenic minds. What was not Eleaticism, simple or compound, was merely opposition. This Greek destiny continues to weigh on us, and in spite of some notable rebellions we are still prisoners within the magic circle described by Eleatic ontology.[10]

Ever since Parmenides, the orthodox thinker in search of an object's being holds that he is searching for a fixed, static consistency,[11] hence something that the entity *already* is, which already composes or constitutes it. The prototype of this mode of being, possessed of the characteristics of fixity, stability, and actuality (a being *already* what it is), was the being of mathematical concepts and objects, an invariable being, a being-always-the-same. Since observation showed that the things in the world around were changeable, were 'movement', he begins by denying their reality. Aristotle, more prudent, renounces such absolutism and adopts a solution of the *juste milieu*. In the changeable object he seeks that which in the midst of change does not vary, that which in its movement remains motionless. This accordingly is what he called the 'nature' of things, that which in the real object *appears* to shrink from having a being similar to the being of mathematical concepts and objects. The *phusis* was the invariable principle of variations. In this way it became possible to retain the fundamental Eleatism of being and yet to conceive as realities those objects which in the eyes of absolute Eleaticism lacked authentic reality, *ousia*. The idea of time, interposing itself between the invariable *ousia* and the diverse states of the object served as bridge between the latent unity of being and its apparent multiplicity. The *res* was thus conceived of as something possessing at heart – in its *arché* – the same ontological condition as the concept and the triangle: identity, radical invariability, stability – the profound tranquillity that the term *being* signified to the Greek.[12]

The process that causes the *natura* of Aristotelianism to evolve into Boyle's stable rule or law of unstable phenomena, far from being a degeneration, is a purification of the original concept and as it were a sincere confession of it. Thus in Comte and Stuart Mill everything hangs as from a nail on 'the invariability of the laws of nature'. The nature of positivism is already pure and declared 'invariability', a being fixed, static ... Eleatic.[13]

Now, in laying down as a condition of reality, before admitting it as such, that it should consist in an element of identity, Parmenides and the orthodox Greeks in general revealed their colossal arbitrariness. Into the origin of what I call sublime 'arbitrariness' I do not propose here to inquire, although the theme is one of infinite attractiveness. The word is an express concept, and the concept is a reality that is peculiar among realities in consisting of identity, one might say in being made of identity. When we speak of reality – *onto-logy* – we are under obligation to be faithful at once to the conditions of the reality of which we are thinking and to the conditions of the thought with which we 'manipulate' the reality.

One can readily understand that philosophy, in its first phase, should have lacked the agility necessary to distinguish, in thinking of reality, between that element in the resulting thought that belonged to the intellect and that which belonged properly to the object. Until Kant, strictly speaking, no one had even begun to see clearly that thought is not a copy and mirror of reality but a transitive operation performed on it, a surgical intervention. Hence philosophy since Kant has embarked on what Plato would call its *deuteros plous* its second voyage, its second apprenticeship. This rests on the observation that if there be possible a knowledge of authentic reality, *auto to on* [being itself] (and only philosophic knowledge claims to be such), it must consist in a duplicate thinking, a going and coming – that is to say, in a thinking that, having once thought something concerning reality, turns back on the thought and strips it of what is mere intellectual form, leaving only the intuition of reality in all its nakedness. This is fearsome, and paradoxical, but there is no other way out. In the formidable crusade for the liberation of man that constitutes the mission of the intellect there has come a moment when man needs to deliver himself from his most intimate slavery, to wit, from himself. It follows from this that, precisely because Kant has taught us that thought has its own forms and projects these on to the real, the end of the process initiated by him consists in uprooting from reality all those forms that are at once inevitable and foreign to it, and in learning to think with a mind ever on the alert, in an unceasing *modus ponendo tollens*. In short, we must learn to disintellectualize the real if we are to be faithful to it.

Eleatism was the radical intellectualization of being. It is this that constitutes the magic circle already referred to, that we so urgently need to rise above. In naturalism what prevents our conceiving of human phenomena, what veils them to our minds, is not the secondary attributes of things, *res*, but the very idea of *res* founded on identical being and, since identical, fixed, static, predetermined. Wherever this subtle attribute persists, there naturalism, invariable being, is still to be found. Naturalism is, at bottom, intellectualism, i.e. the projection on to the real of the mode of being peculiar to concepts. Let us renounce valiantly, joyously, this convenient presumption that the real is logical and recognize that thought alone is logical.[14] Even the mathematical object presents chasms of illogicality as tremendous as the 'labyrinth of the difficulties of continuity' and all the problems that inspired Brouwer's attempt to overthrow the *principium tertii exclusi*.[15] To-day physics too has sprung a dramatic surprise on us with its states of indeterminateness of the atomic elements.

This article, I need not point out, is not a treatise, quite the contrary; it is a series of theses that are submitted without defence to the meditative fair play of the reader. I believe none the less that some meaning will now attach to my previous enigmatic assertion according to which the concept of spirit is a disguised naturalism and in consequence inoperative when faced with naturalistic conceptions, its presumed enemies.

Spirit, if it is anything in this world, is identity, and hence *res*, a thing – though as subtle and ethereal as you please. Spirit possesses a static consistency: it is already, to begin with, what it is going to be. The revolt of the human element against any conception of it as static was so obvious that soon, with Leibniz, there came the attempt to rise above the static by making spirit consist in dynamic activity.[16] A vain attempt, for that activity, like all activity, is always one and the same, fixed, prescribed, ontologically motionless! Hegel's movement of the spirit is a pure fiction, since it is a movement within the spirit, whose consistency lies in its fixed, static, pre-established truth. Now the entity whose being consists in identical being evidently possesses already, to begin with, all it needs in order to be. For this reason identical being is substantive being, substance, a being that suffices to itself, sufficient being. This is the *thing*. Spirit is no other than a thing. It appears indeed that other things are things in virtue of their materiality, their spatiality, their force. But all this would serve them in no stead if they were not also and previously identical, *that is to say, concepts*. The *proto*-thing, the *Urding*, is the intellect. It identi-fies, thing-ifies – *ver-dinglicht* – all the rest.

The knights-errant of the spirit have no right to the revulsion, that amusing Plotinian revulsion, they feel where nature is concerned. Because the profound error of naturalism is the reverse of what is supposed: it does not consist in our treating ideas as though they were corporeal realities, but on the contrary in our treating realities – corporeal or no – as if they were ideas, concepts, in short, identities.

When Heine, assuredly after reading Hegel, asked his coachman, 'What are ideas?' the answer he got was: 'Ideas? . . . Ideas are the things they put into your head.' But the fact is that we can say, more formally, that things are the ideas that come out of our heads and are taken by us as realities.

The need to rise above, to transcend the idea of nature comes precisely from this, that this idea can have no validity as an authentic reality: it is something relative to the human intellect, which in its turn has no detached, independent reality – herein lies the error of all idealism or 'spiritualism' – but is only real when functioning in a human life, by whose constitutive urgencies it is moved. Nature is a transitory interpretation that man has given to what he finds around him in life. To this then, as to a radical reality, including and preforming all others, we are referred.

Faced with this, what we are indeed now conscious of is a liberation from naturalism, because we have learnt to immunize ourselves from intellectualism and its Greek kalends. Here is the 'fact' previous to all facts, that which holds all others in solution and from which all flow: human life as it is lived by each one of us. *Hic Rhodus, hic salta.* Our need is to think on it with urgency, just as we behold it in all its primary nakedness, by the aid of concepts bent only on describing it and which admit no imperative whatever from traditional ontology.

That undertaking, needless to say, is not one that can be pursued within the bounds of the present article. My purpose here is limited to the suggestion of so much as is indispensable if my title – 'History as a System' – is to have an exact meaning.

VII

Physico-mathematical reason, whether in its crude form of naturalism or in its beatific form of spiritualism, was in no state to confront human problems. By its very constitution it could do no other than search for man's nature. And, naturally, it did not find it. For man has no nature. Man is not his body which is a thing, nor his soul, psyche, conscience, or spirit which is also a thing. Man is no thing, but a drama – his life a pure and universal happening which happens to each one of us and in which each one in his turn is nothing but happening. All things, be they what they may, are now mere interpretation, which he exercises himself in giving to whatever he comes upon. Things he does not come upon: he poses or supposes them. What he comes upon are pure difficulties and pure facilities for existing. Existence itself is not presented to him ready-made, as it is to the stone; rather, shall we say, looping the loop begun in the opening words of this article, on coming up against the fact of his existence, on existence happening to him, all he comes up against, all that happens to him is the realization that he has no choice but to do something in order not to cease existing. This shows that the mode of being of life, even as simple existing, is not a *being already*, since the only thing that is given us and that *is* when there is human life is the having to make it, each one for himself.[17] Life is a gerundive, not a participle: a *faciendum*, not a *factum*. Life is a task. Life, in fact, sets us plenty of tasks. When the doctor, surprised at Fontenelle's having reached the age of a hundred in full health, asked him what he felt, the centenarian replied: *Rien, rien du tout ... seulement une certain difficulté d'être.*[18] We ought to generalize and say that life always and not only at a hundred, consists in *difficulté d'être*. Its mode of being is formally a being difficult, a being which consists in problematic toil. Compared with the sufficient being of the substance or thing, life is an indigent being, an entity which possesses, properly speaking, only needs, *Bedürfnisse*. The star, on the other hand, continues ever on the line of its orbit, asleep like a child in the cradle.

At every moment of my life there open before me divers possibilities: I can do this or that. If I do this, I shall be A the moment after; if I do that, I shall be B. At the present moment the reader may stop reading me or may go on. And, however slight the importance of this article, according as he does the one or the other the reader will be A or will be B, will have made of himself an A or a B. Man is the entity that makes itself, an entity which traditional ontology only stumbled upon precisely as its course was drawing to a close, and which it in consequence gave up the attempt to understand: the *causa sui*. With this difference, that the *causa sui* had only to 'exert itself' in being the *cause* of itself and not in determining what *self* it was going to cause. It had, to begin with, a *self* previously determined and invariable, consistent, for example, to infinity.

But man must not only make himself: the weightiest thing he has to do is to determine *what* he is going to be. He is *causa sui* to the second power. By a coincidence that is not casual, the doctrine of the living being, when it seeks in tradition for concepts that are still more or less valid, finds only those which the doctrine of the divine being tried to formulate. If the reader has resolved now to go on reading into the next moment, it will be, in the last instance, because doing this is what is most in accordance with the general programme he has mapped out for his life, and hence with the man of determination he has resolved to be. This vital programme is the *ego* of each individual, his choice out of divers possibilities of being which at every instant open before him.[19]

Concerning these possibilities of being the following remarks fall to be made:

1. That they likewise are not presented to me. I must find them for myself, either on my own or through the medium of those of my fellows with whom my life brings me in contact. I invent projects of being and of doing in the light of circumstance. This alone I come upon, this alone is given me: circumstance.[20] It is too often forgotten that man is impossible without imagination, without the capacity to invent for himself a conception of life, to 'ideate' the character he is going to be. Whether he be original or a plagiarist, man is the novelist of himself.[21]

2. That among these possibilities I must choose. Hence, I am free. But, be it well understood, I am free *by compulsion*, whether I wish to be or not. Freedom is not an activity pursued by an entity that, apart from and previous to such pursuit, is already possessed of a fixed being. To be free means to be lacking in constitutive identity, not to have subscribed to a determined being, to be able to be other than what one was, to be unable to instal oneself once and for all in any given being. The only attribute of the fixed, stable being in the free being is this constitutive instability.

In order to speak, then, of man's being we must first elaborate a non-Eleatic concept of being, as others have elaborated a non-Euclidean geometry. The time has come for the seed sown by Heraclitus to bring forth its mighty harvest.

Man is an infinitely plastic entity of which one may make what one will, precisely because of itself it is nothing save only the mere potentiality to be 'as you like'. Let the reader pass in review for a moment all the things that man has been – that is to say, that he has made of himself – and has then ceased to be – that is to say, has cast off from himself – from the palaeolithic 'savage' to the young *surréaliste* of Paris. I do not say that at any moment he may make of himself anything whatever. At each moment there open before him limited possibilities – what these limits are we shall see straightway. But if instead of one moment we take all moments, it is impossible to see what frontiers can be set to human plasticity. From the palaeolithic female there have issued Madame Pompadour and Lucile de Chateaubriand, from the indigene of Brazil, unable to count above five, have come Newton and Henri Poincaré. Lessening the distance in time, be it remembered that in 1873 the liberal Stuart Mill, in 1903 the most liberal Herbert Spencer, were still alive, and that already in 1921 Stalin and Mussolini are in power.

Meanwhile man's body and psyche, his *nature*, have experienced no change of importance to which these effective mutations may be clearly ascribed. What has taken place, on the contrary, is the 'substantial' change in the reality 'human life' implied by man's passing from the belief that he must exist in a world composed only of arbitrary wills to the belief that he must exist in a world where there are 'nature', invariable consistencies, identity, &c. Human life is thus not an entity that changes accidentally, rather the reverse: in it the 'substance' is precisely change, which means that it cannot be thought of Eleatically as substance. Life being a 'drama' that happens, and the 'subject' to whom it happens being, not a thing apart from and previous to his drama, but a function of it, it follows that the 'substance' of the drama would be its argument. And if this varies, it means that the variation is 'substantial'.

Since the being of whatever is alive is a being always distinct from itself – in the terms of the schools, a being that is metaphysically and not only physically mobile – it must be thought of in concepts that annul their own inevitable identity. This is not so terrifying as it may appear at first sight, though it is a question that I cannot even touch the fringe of here. I would only recall to the reader, that I may not leave his mind adrift on an uncharted sea, that thought has a much greater capacity for avoiding itself than is commonly supposed. Thought is constitutively generous, it is the great altruist. It is capable of thinking what lies at the opposite extreme to thought. One example will suffice. There are concepts called by some 'occasional'; e.g. the concept 'here', the concept 'I', the concept 'this'. Such concepts or significations have a formal identity that serves precisely to guarantee the constitutive non-identity of the matter signified or thought of through them. All concepts that seek to think of the authentic reality, life, must be 'occasional' in this sense. There is nothing strange in this, since life is pure occasion. It is for this reason Cardinal Nicholas of Cusa calls man a *Deus occasionatus*, for, according to him, man once he is free is a creator like God inasmuch as he is a being creating its own entity. Unlike God, however, his creation is not absolute but is limited by the occasion. Whence, literally, what I am bold to affirm: that man makes himself in the light of circumstance, that he is a God as occasion offers, a 'second-hand God' (*un Dios de ocasión*).

Every concept, in Husserl's phrase, is a universal meaning (*allgemeine Bedeutung*). But whereas in other concepts the universality consists in the fact that when applying them to one singular case we must always think the *same* as when applying them to another singular case, in the occasional concept it functions precisely by inviting us never to think the *same* when we apply it. The supreme example is this very concept 'life' in the sense of human life. Its signification *qua* signification is, of course, identical, but what it signifies is something not merely singular, but unique. Life is the life of each one of us.

And here, for the sake of brevity, I may be allowed to interrupt these considerations and to refrain from dealing with the most obvious difficulties they give rise to.[22]

VIII

Yesterday I made the acquaintance of Hermione. She is a fascinating woman. Towards me she was deferential, insinuating. I think of making love to her, and of attempting to win her love in return. But can my authentic being, what I call *I*, consist in 'being Hermione's lover'? Scarcely have I conjured up my love for Hermione in the mind's eye with a measure of precision when I emphatically turn down such a project of being. Why? I can find no objection to raise against Hermione, only the fact is ... that I am fifty, and at fifty, although the body may have retained all the elasticity of thirty and the psychic impulses have lost none of their vigour, I cannot now 'be Hermione's lover'. But why? The point is this, that being a man of years I have already had time to be the lover of Cidalisa and the lover of Arsinoe and the lover of Glykeia, and I know now what 'being a lover' is. I know its excellences, I know also its limitations. In short, I have experienced to the full that form of life that is called 'loving a woman', and, frankly, I have had enough. And so it happens that the 'cause' of my not being a lover to-morrow is precisely the fact that I have been one. If I had not been a lover, if I had not already experienced love to the full, I should be Hermione's lover.

Here, then, is a new dimension in this strange reality of life. Before us lie the diverse possibilities of being, but behind us lies what we have been. And what we have been acts negatively on what we can be. When I was a child I was a Christian; now I am one no longer. Does this mean, strictly speaking, that I do not go on being a Christian? The Christian I was, is he dead, annihilated? Of course not; of course I am still a Christian, but in the form of having been a Christian. Had I not known the experience of being a Christian, did I not have it behind me and go on being a Christian in this form of having been one, it is possible that, faced with the difficulties of life to-day, I might now resolve to be a Christian. And what has happened to me in this matter is happening to many Europeans, who *were* Christians either on their own account or vicariously, from the recollection of their forefathers. Who knows, if one got to the bottom of things, whether it might not be said that it is happening to everybody, including those who believe in all good faith that they still are Christians? That it is possible to be a Christian to-day, just like that, in the fullness of the term and without reservations, is not so very certain. And the same might be said about being 'a democrat', being 'a liberal', being *ancien régime*, being 'feudal'.

If I do not make love to Hermione, if I do not turn Christian, accordingly, if the reality of my life at the moment is what it is, what it is going to be depends on what is commonly called 'experience of life'. This is a knowledge of what we have been that memory has preserved for us and that lies always to hand, accumulated in our to-day, in our actuality or reality. And it happens that this knowledge determines my life negatively in its 'real' aspect, in its being. And from this it follows that constitutively my life is experience of life. My fifty years signify an absolute reality, not because the body may be growing weak or the psyche losing its grip, things that do not always happen, but because at that age one has accumulated a longer living past, one has been more things and one 'has more experience'. The conclusion to be drawn from which is that man's being is irreversible, he is compelled ontologically always to advance on himself, and this not because a given instant of time cannot recur: on the contrary, time does not recur because man cannot go back to being what he has been.

But experience of life is not made up solely of my past, of the experiences that I personally have had. It is built up also of the past of my forbears, handed down to me by the society I live in. Society consists primarily in a repertory of usages, intellectual, moral, political, technical, of play and pleasure. Now, in order that a form of life – an opinion, a line of conduct – may become a usage, a thing of social validity, it is necessary, first, that time should elapse, and second, that the form in question should cease to be a spontaneous form of personal life. Usage is tardy in taking shape. Every usage is old. Expressed differently, society is, primarily, the past and, relatively to man, tardigrade. For the rest, the establishing of a new usage – a new 'public opinion' or 'collective belief', a new morality, a new form of government, – the determination of *what* at each moment society *is going to be*, depends on what it has been, just as in the individual life. Western societies are finding in the present political crisis that they cannot, without more ado, be 'liberal', 'democratic', 'monarchical', 'feudal' or … 'Pharaonic', precisely because they have already been these things, either in themselves or from experience of how others have been them. In the 'political public opinion' of to-day, in the usage at present in force, an enormous amount of the past continues active; that opinion, that usage, is accordingly this past in the form of having been it.[23]

Let the reader simply take note of what happens to him when, faced with the great political problems of the day, he desires to take up an attitude. First there arises in his mind a certain form of government, let us say, authoritarianism. In it he sees, rightly, a means of surmounting some of the difficulties of the public situation. But if this solution is the first or one of the first to occur to him it is not by chance. It thrusts itself upon him precisely because it already lay there to his hand, because he did not need to invent it for himself. And it lay to his hand not merely as a project but as an experiment already made. The reader knows, from personal experience or from reference, that there have been absolute monarchies, Caesarisms, unipersonal or collective dictatorships. And he knows further that all these forms of authoritarianism, if they solve some difficulties, leave others unsolved and in fact bring new ones of their own. The reader is thus led to reject this solution and to essay another in his mind which will avoid the drawbacks of authoritarianism. But here the same thing happens over again, and so it goes on until he has exhausted all the obvious forms of government, those that lay already to his hand, those he knew about because they had already been tried. At the end of this intellectual journey through forms of government he finds that, if he is to be sincere and act with full conviction, there is only one he could accept: to wit, a new one, one different from any that has been before, one invented by himself. He must either invent a new being of the State himself – even though it be only a *new* authoritarianism or a *new* liberalism – or search around for some one who has invented such or who is capable of inventing it. Here, then, may be seen how in our present political attitude, in our political being, there persists all the past of mankind that is known to us. That past is past not because it happened to others but because it forms part of our present, of what we are in the form of having been, because, in short, it is *our* past. Life as a reality is absolute presence: we cannot say that *there is* anything unless it be present, of this moment. If, then, *there is* a past, it must be as something present, something active in us *now*. And, in effect, if we analyse what we are now, if we take the consistency of our present and hold it up against the light in order to reduce it to its component elements as the chemist or the physicist may an object, we find to our surprise that this life of ours that is always this, the life of this present, actual moment, is *composed* of what, personally or collectively, we have been. And if we speak of *being* in the traditional sense as a *being already* what one is, as a fixed, static, invariable and given being, we shall have to say that the only element of being, of 'nature', in man is what he has been. The past is man's moment of identity, his only element of the thing: nothing besides is inexorable and fatal. But, for the same reason, if man's only Eleatic being is what he has been, this means that his authentic being, what in effect he is – and not merely 'has been' – is distinct from the past, and consists precisely and formally in 'being what one has not been', in non-Eleatic being. And since we cannot hope ever to rid the term 'being' of its traditional static signification, we should be well advised to dispense with it. Man *is* not, he 'goes on being' this and that. The concept 'to go on being' is, however, absurd: under promise of something logical it turns out in the end to be completely irrational. The term we can apply, without absurdity, to 'going on being' is 'living'. Let us say, then, not that man *is*, but that he *lives*.

On the other hand, it is advisable to take due note of the strange mode of knowledge, of comprehension, represented by this analysis of what, concretely, our life, that of the present, is. In order to understand my conduct with regard to Hermione and to Christianity, or the reader's with regard to public problems, in order to discover the reason of our being or, what comes to the same thing, *why* we are as we are, what have we done? What was it that made us understand, *conceive*, our being? Simply the telling, the narrating that *formerly* I was the lover of this and that woman, that *formerly* I was a Christian, that the reader in himself or through others he has heard of was an absolutist, a Caesarist, a democrat, &c. In short, the reasoning, the *reason*, that throws light here consists in a narration. Alongside pure physico-mathematical reason there is, then, a narrative reason. To comprehend anything human, be it personal or collective, one must tell its history. This man, this nation does such a thing and is in such a manner, *because* formerly he or it did that other thing and was in such another manner. Life only takes on a measure of transparency in the light of *historical reason*.

The most disparate forms of being *happen* to man. To the despair of the intellectualist, *being* is in man mere *happening, happening to him*: it 'happens to him to be' a Stoic, a Christian, a rationalist, a vitalist. It happens to him to be the palaeolithic female and the Marquise de Pompadour, Jenghiz Khan and Stefan George, Pericles and Charles Chaplin. Man does not actively subscribe to any of these forms: he passes through them – he lives them – like Zeno's arrow, moving, in spite of Zeno, during the whole of its flight.

Man invents for himself a programme of life, a static form of being, that gives a satisfactory answer to the difficulties posed for him by circumstance. He essays this form of life, attempts to realize this imaginary character he has resolved to be. He embarks on the essay full of illusions and prosecutes the experiment with thoroughness. This means that he comes to *believe* deeply that this character is his real being. But meanwhile the experience has made apparent the shortcomings and limitations of the said programme of life. It does not solve all the difficulties, and it creates new ones of its own. When first seen it was full face, with the light shining upon it: hence the illusions, the enthusiasm, the delights believed in store. With the back view its inadequacy is straightway revealed. Man thinks out another programme of life. But this second programme is drawn up in the light, not only of circumstance, but also of the first. One aims at avoiding in the new project the drawbacks of the old. In the second, therefore, the first is still active; it is preserved in order to be avoided. Inexorably man shrinks from being what he was. On the second project of being, the second thorough experiment, there follows a third, forged in the light of the second and the first, and so on. Man 'goes on being' and 'unbeing' – living. He goes on accumulating being – the past; he goes on making for himself a being through his dialectical series of experiments. This is a dialectic not of logical but precisely of historical reason – the *Realdialektik* dreamt of somewhere in his papers by Dilthey,[24] the writer to whom we owe more than to any one else concerning the idea of life, and who is, to my mind, the most important thinker of the second half of the nineteenth century.

In what does this dialectic that will not tolerate the facile anticipations of logical dialectic consist? This is what we have to find out on the basis of facts. We must know what is this series, what are its stages, and of what nature is the link between one and the next. Such a discovery is what would be called history were history to make this its objective, were it, that is to say, to convert itself into historical reason.

Here, then, awaiting our study, lies man's authentic 'being' – stretching the whole length of his past. Man is what has happened to him, what he has done. Other things might have happened to him or have been done by him, but what did in fact happen to him and was done by him, this constitutes a relentless trajectory of experiences that he carries on his back as the vagabond his bundle of all he possesses. Man is a substantial emigrant on a pilgrimage of being, and it is accordingly meaningless to set limits to what he is capable of being. In this initial illimitableness of possibilities that characterizes one who has no nature there stands out only one fixed, pre-established, and given line by which he may chart his course, only one limit: the past. The experiments already made with life narrow man's future. If we do not know what he is going to be, we know what he is not going to be. Man lives in view of the past.

Man, in a word, has no nature; what he has is ... history. Expressed differently: what nature is to things, history, *res gestae*, is to man. Once again we become aware of the possible application of theological concepts to human reality. *Deus, cui hoc est natura quod fecerit ...* , says St Augustine.[25] Man, likewise, finds that he has no nature other than what he has himself done.

It is comic in the extreme that 'historicism' should be condemned because it produces or corroborates in us the consciousness that the human factor is changeable in its every direction, that in it there is nothing concrete that is stable. As if the stable being – the stone, for instance – were preferable to the unstable! 'Substantial' mutation is the condition on which an entity as such can be progressive, the condition on which its being may consist in progress. Now concerning man it must be said, not only that his being is variable, but also that his being grows and, in this sense, that it progresses. The error of the old doctrine of progress lay in affirming *a priori* that man progresses towards the better. That is something that can only be determined *a posteriori* by concrete historical reason: it is precisely the great discovery we await from this, since to it we look for the clarifying of human reality and, along with this, for light on the nature of the good, the bad, the better and the worse. But that our life does possess a simply progressive character, this we can affirm *a priori* with full evidence and with a surety very different from that which has led to the supposition of the improgressivity of nature, that is to say, the 'invariability of its laws'. The same knowledge that discovers to us man's variation makes patent his progressive consistency. The European of to-day is not only different from what he was fifty years ago, his being now includes that of fifty years ago. The European of to day finds himself without a living faith in science precisely *because* fifty years ago he did believe wholeheartedly in it. That faith that held sway half a century ago may now be defined with reasonable precision; were this done it would be seen that it was such *because* about 1800 the same faith in science wore a different profile, and so successively until we come to the year 1700 or thereabouts, at which date faith in reason is constituted as a 'collective belief', as something socially operative. (Earlier than 1700 faith in reason is an individual belief or the belief of particular small groups that live submerged in societies where faith in God, if already more or less inert, yet continues operative.) In our present 'crisis', in our present doubt concerning reason, we find then included the whole of that earlier life. We are, that is to say, all those forms of faith in reason, and we are in addition the doubt engendered by that faith. We are other than the man of 1700, and we are more.

There is no cause, therefore, for weeping overmuch concerning the mutability of everything human. This is precisely our ontological privilege. Progress is only possible to one who is not linked to-day to what he was yesterday, who is not caught for ever in that being which is already, but can migrate from it into another. But this is not enough: it is not sufficient that man should be able to free himself from what he is already and take on a new form, as the serpent sloughs its skin and is left with another. Progress demands that this new form should rise above the old and to this end should preserve it and turn it to account, that it should take off from the old, climbing on its shoulders as a high temperature mounts on lower ones. To progress is to accumulate being, to store up reality. This increase of being, it is true, when referred only to the individual, might be interpreted naturalistically as the mere development or *enodatio* of an initial disposition. With the evolutionary thesis still unproved, whatever its probability, it can be said that the tiger of to-day is neither more nor less a tiger than was that of a thousand years ago: it is being a tiger for the first time, it is always a first tiger. But the human individual is not putting on humanity for the first time. To begin with, he finds around him, in his 'circumstance', other men and the society they give rise to. Hence his humanity, that which begins to develop in him, takes its point of departure from another, already developed, that has reached its culmination: in short, to his humanity he adds other humanities. He finds at birth a form of humanity, a mode of being a man, already forged, that he need not invent but may simply take over and set out from for his individual development. This does not begin for him – as for the tiger, which must always start again – at zero but at a positive quantity to which he adds his own growth. Man is not a first man, an eternal Adam: he is formally a second man, a third man, &c.

Mutable condition has thus its ontological virtue and grace, and invites one to recall Galileo's words: *I detrattori della corruttibilità meriterebber d'esser cangiati in statue.*[26]

Let the reader reflect closely on his life, studying it against the light as one looks at a glass of water to study its Infusoria. If he asks himself why his life is thus and not otherwise, it will appear to him that not a few details had their origin in inscrutable chance. But he will find the broad lines of its reality perfectly comprehensible once he sees that he is thus because, in the last resort, the society – 'collective man' – in which he lives is thus. And in its turn the mode of being of society will stand revealed, once there is discovered within it what that society was – what it believed, felt, preferred – at an earlier stage. That is to say that in his individual and fleeting to-day man will see, foreshortened, the whole of man's past still active and alive. For we can only throw light on yesterday by invoking the day before yesterday; and so with all yesterdays. History is a system, the system of human experiences linked in a single, inexorable chain. Hence nothing can be truly clear in history until everything is clear. We cannot properly understand what this 'rationalist' European is unless we know exactly what it was to be a Christian, nor what it was to be a Christian unless we know what it was to be a Stoic: and so the process goes on. And this systematism of *res gestae* becomes re-operative and potent in history as *cognitio rerum gestarum*. Every historic term whatsoever, to have exactness, must be determined as a function of all history, neither more nor less than each concept in Hegel's *Logic* has value only in respect of the niche left for it by the others.

History is the systematic science of that radical reality, my life. It is therefore a science of the present in the most rigorous and actual sense of the word. Were it not a science of the present, where should we find that past that is commonly assigned to it as theme? The opposite – and customary – interpretation is equivalent to making of the past an abstract, unreal something lying lifeless just where it happened in time, whereas the past is in truth the live, active force that sustains our to-day. There is no *actio in distans*. The past is not yonder, at the date when it happened, but here, in me. The past is I – by which I mean, my life.

IX

Man stands in need of a new revelation. And whenever man feels himself in contact with a reality distinct from himself, there is always revelation. It does not matter what the reality be, provided it appear to us absolute reality and not a mere idea, presumption, or imagination of our own concerning a reality.

Physical reason was, in its day, a revelation. Astronomy previous to Kepler and Galileo was a mere play of ideas, and when one *believed* in any of the various systems then current or in such and such a modification of those systems, it was always a pseudo- belief that was at issue. One believed in this theory or in that as a theory. Its content was not reality but simply a 'saving of appearances'. Now the adhesion that a certain reasoning or combination of ideas commands in us does not go beyond these. Called forth by ideas as such, with them it ends. One believes that *within the sphere and play of ideas* these ideas are those best worked out, the strongest, the most subtle, but one does not on that account experience the devastating impression that in these ideas reality itself is breaking through, hence that they are not merely 'ideas' but pores opening in us through which there penetrates into our consciousness something ultramental, something transcendent throbbing fearfully directly beneath our touch.

Ideas represent, then, two very distinct roles in human life. At times they are *mere ideas*. Man is aware that, in spite of the subtlety and even the exactitude and logical rigour of his thoughts, these are no more than inventions of his own, in the last instance an intrahuman, subjective, and non-transcendent activity. The idea in this case is the opposition of a revelation – it is an invention. But at other times the idea *qua* idea disappears, converted into a pure mode of sensitive presence elected by an absolute reality. The idea now appears to us neither as an idea nor as our own. The transcendent reveals itself to us on its own account, invades and inundates us – and this is the revelation.[27]

For over a century now we have been using the word 'reason', giving to it a meaning that has become more and more degraded until to-day it signifies in effect the mere play of ideas. That is why faith appears as opposed to reason. We forget that at its birth in Greece, as at its rebirth in the sixteenth century, reason was not the play of ideas but a radical and tremendous conviction that in astronomic thought man was in indubitable contact with an absolute order of the cosmos, that through the medium of physical reason cosmic nature loosed within man its formidable and transcendent secret. Reason was, therefore, a faith. On this account, and on this account only – not in virtue of its other peculiar attributes and graces – it was able to wage war with the religious faith that till then had held the field. Vice versa, it has not been realized that religious faith is also reason, because of the narrow and fortuitous conception one held of reason. It was claimed that reason did not pass beyond what took place in laboratories or the cabalism of the mathematicians. The claim as we see it to-day is ridiculous enough – one form, it might be called, out of a thousand intellectual provincialisms. The truth is that the specific characteristic of religious faith rests on a structure every bit as conceptual as dialectics or physics. It is a matter of profound surprise to me that there should not yet exist – that I am aware of – any exposition of Christianity as a pure system of ideas, expounded as one may expound Platonism, Kantianism, or positivism. Did such exist – and it would not be a difficult task – its relationship to all other theories as such would become evident, and religion would no longer seem so abruptly separated from ideology.

All the definitions of reason that made its essence consist in certain particular modes of setting the intellect in operation have not only been narrow, they have sterilized reason by amputating or devitalizing its decisive dimension. To me reason, in the true and rigorous sense of the word, is every such act of the intellect as brings us into contact with reality, every act by means of which we come upon the transcendent. The rest is nothing but . . . intellect, a mere homely exercise leading nowhere, that first amuses, then depraves, and finally causes man to despair and to despise himself.

Hence the necessity in the present state of humanity to leave behind, as archaic fauna, the so-called 'intellectuals' and to set our course anew towards the man of reason, of revelation.

Man has need of a new revelation. He loses himself in the infinite arbitrariness of his inner cabalism when he cannot assay this and discipline it in the impact with something that smacks of authentic, relentless reality. Reality is man's only true pedagogue and ruler. Without its inexorable and sensitive presence culture, seriously speaking, does not exist, the State does not exist, even – and this is the most terrible of all – reality in his own personal life does not exist. When man is left, or believes himself left, alone with no reality other than his ideas to impose its stern limits on him, he loses the sensation of his own reality, he becomes to himself an imaginary, spectral, phantasmagoric entity. It is only under the formidable pressure of something transcendent that our person becomes compact and solid and we are enabled to discriminate between what, in effect, we are and what we merely imagine ourselves to be.

Now, physical reason by its very evolution, by its changes and vicissitudes, is come to a point where it recognizes itself as being mere intellect, if indeed as the highest form of this. To-day we are beginning to see that physics is a mental combination and nothing more. Physicists themselves have discovered the merely symbolic, that is to say, domestic, immanent, intrahuman, character of their knowledge. In natural science these or those mutations may come about, Einstein's physics may give way to another, the quantum theory be followed by other theories, the electron conception of the structure of matter by other conceptions: no one looks for these modifications and advances ever to leap beyond their symbolic horizon. Physics brings us into contact with no transcendence. So-called nature, at least what the physicist examines under this name, turns out to be an apparatus of his own manufacture that he interposes between authentic reality and himself. And, correlatively, the physical world appears not as a reality but as a great machine ready to man's hand for him to manage and exploit. The faith that still attaches to physics to-day comes down to faith in the uses to which it can be put. What is real in it – and not mere idea – is only its utility.[28] That is why we have lost our fear of physics, and with fear our respect, and with respect our enthusiasm.

But whence, then, can there come to us this new revelation that man stands in need of?

Every disillusionment consequent on depriving man of faith in some reality on which he had set store brings into the foreground and permits the discovery of the reality of what remains to him, a reality that had previously escaped his attention. So the loss of faith in God leaves man alone with his nature, with what he has. Of this nature the intellect forms a part, and man, obliged to have recourse to it, forges for himself his faith in physico-mathematical reason. Now, having lost his faith – in the manner here described – in that reason also, man finds himself compelled to take his stand on the only thing still left to him, his disillusioned life. And here we see the reason why in our day we are beginning to discover the great reality of life as such, in which the intellect is no more than a simple function, and which possesses in consequence a more radical character of reality than all the worlds constructed by the intellect. We find ourselves, then, in a disposition that might be styled 'Cartesianism of life' and not of *cogitatio*.

Man asks himself, What is this solitary thing that remains to me – my life, my disillusioned life? How has it come to being nothing but this? And the answer is the discovery of man's trajectory, of the dialectical series of his experiences, which, I repeat, though it might have been different, has been what it has been, and which must be known because it is ... *the* transcendent reality. Man set outside himself is brought up against himself as reality, as history. And, for the first time, he sees himself forced to a concern with his past, not from curiosity nor in the search for examples which may serve as norms, but because it is all he *has*. Things are never done seriously until the lack of them has been seriously felt. For this reason the present hour is the appointed time for history to re-establish itself as historical reason.

Until now history has been the contrary of reason. In Greece the two terms reason and history were opposed. And it is in fact the case that scarcely any one up till now has set himself to seek in history for its rational substance. At most, attempts have been made to impose on it a reason not its own, as when Hegel injected into history the formalism of his logic or Buckle his physiological and physical reason. My purpose is the exact reverse: to discover in history itself its original, autochthonous reason. Hence the expression 'historical reason' must be understood in all the rigour of the term: not an extra-historical reason which appears to be fulfilled in history but, literally, *a substantive reason constituted by what has happened to man*, the revelation of a reality transcending man's theories and which is himself, the self underlying his theories.

Until now what we have had of reason has not been historical and what we have had of history has not been rational.

Historical reason is, then, *ratio*, *logos*, a rigorous concept. It is desirable that there should not arise the slightest doubt about this. In opposing it to physico-mathematical reason there is no question of granting a licence to irrationalism. On the contrary, historical reason is still more rational than physical reason, more rigorous, more exigent. Physical reason does not claim to understand what it is that it is talking about. It goes farther, and makes of this ascetic renunciation its formal method, the result being that the term 'understanding' takes on a paradoxical sense against which Socrates already protested in the *Phaedo* when describing to us his intellectual education. The protest has been repeated by every subsequent philosopher down to the establishment of empirical rationalism at the end of the seventeenth century. We can understand in physics the analytical operation it performs in reducing complex facts to a repertory of simpler facts. But these elemental, basic facts of physics are unintelligible. Impact conveys exactly nothing to intellection. And this is inevitable since it is a fact. Historical reason, on the contrary, accepts nothing as a mere fact: it makes every fact fluid in the *fieri* whence it comes, it *sees* how the fact takes place. It does not believe it is throwing light on human phenomena by reducing them to a repertory of instincts and 'faculties' which would, in effect, be crude facts comparable to impact and attraction. Instead it shows what man does with these instincts and faculties and even expounds to us how these facts – the instincts and faculties – have come about: they are, of course, nothing more than ideas – interpretations – that man has manufactured at a given juncture of his life.

NOTES

1. *Oeuvres*, ed. Adam et Tannery, vi, p. 19; Descartes, *The Philosophical Writings*, trans. by Cottingham, Stoothoff and Murdoch, Cambridge University Press, 1985, vol. I, p. 120.
2. In his book *On Liberty*, chap. ii (London, 1859), Stuart Mill makes very opportune use of this same distinction, expressed in the same terms of 'living faith' and 'dead, inert faith'.
3. 'I do not need it and it is not enough.' Queen Christina (1626–89), Descartes' one-time patroness, abdicated the Swedish crown in June 1654, after which she converted to Catholicism and moved to Rome, where she hoped to have a wider sphere for her ambitions than the mere sovereign of a small northern state. – Ed.
4. In the Greek and Roman calendar, the kalends is the first day of each month, when interest on debts was due and worship of the God (e.g. Janus, Mars or Juno) was observed. – Ed.
5. *Discourse on the Method*, Part Three, in *The Philosophical Writings*, vol. I, pp. 122–5. – Ed.
6. The form I first gave to this thought, in my youth, may be found in *El tema de nuestro tiempo*, 1923 (English translation by James Cleugh, 1932).
7. *Treatise on Man*, incomplete, composed in 1630–33, in *The Philosophical Writings*, vol. I, pp. 99–108. – Ed.
8. 'Spirit? Who is the boy?' *Bursche* also means 'student' or 'lad', as in 'he's a real lad.'
9. Cassirer, *Das Erkenntnisproblem in der Philosophie und Wissenschaft der neueren Zeit* (Berlin, 1907) ii, 433.
10. Parmenides of Elea (*c*. 515 – *c*. 450 bce), claimed that there is no real change or motion in the cosmos, that perception of change and motion is illusory. – Ed.
11. Alongside the term *existence* I use that of *consistency*. The entity that exists has a consistency, that is to say, it *consists of* something or other.
12. These are key terms from Aristotle's Metaphysics: *phusis* is 'the indwelling character', usually translated as 'nature'; *ousia* is 'essence', whose paradigmatic case is 'substance'; and *arché* means both 'beginning' in the temporal sense and 'original principle'. – Ed.
13. I do not enter here into the question whether this is compatible with the relativism of Comte. This is a theme which I hope to develop in a forthcoming study on *The Unknown Comte*.
14. See '"La Filosofia de la Historia" de Hegel y la historiologia', *Revista de Occidente*, February, 1928.
15. Early in his remarkable career, the Dutch mathematician Luitzen Brouwer (1881–1966) developed a three-valued logic to avoid the constraints of the 'principle of the excluded third term' or 'excluded middle'. – Ed.
16. Only Fichte constitutes a case apart. One is aware that he touches the true being of life, but his intellectualism does not allow him to see what it is he is touching, and he is compelled forcibly to think Eleatically. Whence the pathetic resemblance to a blind traveller we see in Fichte as he journeys across the mountain ranges of metaphysics.

17. Bergson, the least Eleatic of thinkers. Whom we must allow to-day to have been right on so many points, constantly uses the expression *l'être en se faisant*. But a comparison of his sense with that which I here give to the same words shows a radical difference. In Bergson the term *se faisant* is merely a synonym for *devenir*. In my text *making oneself* is not merely *becoming* but in addition the way in which human reality *becomes*, which is the effective and literal *making oneself*, a *fabricating oneself*, we might say.

18. 'Nothing, nothing at all ... only a certain difficulty of being.' Bernard de Fontenelle (1657–1757), forerunner of the French Enlightenment, author of *Dialogues of the Dead* (1683), *Conversations on the Plurality of Worlds* (1686) and *The Origin of Fables* (1680) among other works, was sceptical about human credulity and superstition, especially in religious beliefs. – Ed.

19. See my *Goethe desde dentro*, 1932; 'In Search of Goethe from within', trans. by William R. Trask, in *Dehumanization of Art and Other Writings*, New York: Doubleday, 1956. – Ed.

20. See my *Meditaciones del Quijote*, 1914. In this early book of mine it is already suggested that *I am* no more than one ingredient in that radical reality 'my life', whose other ingredient is circumstance.

21. Let it be recalled that the Stoics spoke of an 'imagining of oneself', *phantasia heautou*.

22. For example, whether two lives whose attributes were the same and, in consequence, indistinguishable, would not be the *same* life. The idea of life obliges us, in fact, to invert the Leibnizian principle and to speak of 'the discernibility of identities'. Or again, how, if life is unique, it is at the same time multiple, since we can speak of the lives of others, &c., &c. All these difficulties are engendered in the old intellectualist habits. The most interesting and fruitful of them consists in asking how it is that we 'define' life by means of general characteristics, saying that in all its possible cases it is this and this and this.

23. I have already shown excessive temerity, and incurred excessive risk, in thus attacking at the gallop, like the Median warriors of old, the most fearsome themes of general ontology. Now that I have come to the point where, if I were to be moderately clear, it would be necessary to establish carefully the difference between so-called 'collective or social life' and personal life, I would ask permission to renounce emphatically any intention of doing so. Should the reader be moved to curiosity concerning my ideas on the matter or, in general, concerning the development of all that has preceded, he will find both set forth, as adequately as may be, in two books shortly to be published. In the first, under the title *El hombre y la gente*, I have tried faithfully to expound a sociology which does not, as in the past, avoid the truly basic problems. The second, *Sobre la razón viviente*, is an attempt at a *prima philosophia*.

24. Wilhelm Dilthey (1833–1911) was one of the founders of modern hermeneutics, the investigation of the philosophical basis of human understanding; his principal work, in several volumes, is *Introduction to the Human Sciences* (1883) and he discusses 'real-dialectic' through the Hegelian concept of 'objective spirit' in the *Formation of the Historical World* (1910). – Ed.

25. 'God, whose nature is what he has made', St Augustine, *De Genesi ad Litteram* (*On the Literal Meanings in Genesis*), Book vi, 13. 24.

26. 'Taking away (or deduction) from corruptibility has the merit to have accomplished change in condition', i.e. of the thing's properties. – Ed.

27. See the series of articles, 'Ideas y creencias', published in *La Nación*, Buenos Aires, for October and November, 1935.

28. It is not extravagant to see a resemblance between what physics means to man to-day and what 'divinatio artificiosa' that Posidonius speaks of (see Cicero, *De divinatione*, Book I) meant to the ancients.

4

ALBERT CAMUS
(1913–1960)

I call the accident that killed Camus shameful, because it revealed the absurdity of our most profound demands within the midst of the human world. Camus, at the age of twenty, suddenly struck down by a disease which upset his life, discovered the absurd, the idiotic negation of man. He made himself by it, he *thought* his insufferable condition, he got over it ... The absurd would be this question which no one will any longer ask him, which he will no longer ask anyone, this silence which isn't even silence, which is absolutely *nothing* anymore. (Sartre, 1965, p. 111)

So wrote his old friend, rival and associate Jean-Paul Sartre in his obituary for Camus after Camus' death at the age of forty-seven. The absurd was inscribed in his premature violent death, in the tuberculosis he contracted as a young man and which made living or dying a real issue for him, but perhaps the absurd was also inscribed in his birth. His father Lucien was an employee of the Ricôme wine company in Algeria; in November 1910, Lucien Camus had married Hélène Sintès, three years his elder, and three months later their first son, also called Lucien, was born. The poor, small family lived on an estate at the vineyard, where in November 1913 their second son Albert was born. Following the German declaration of war in August 1914, Albert's father Lucien was called up for service. Sent to the front in the uniform of the First Zouave Regiment, a dark fez, wide red pants and a blue vest, the Algerian soldiers were an easy target for the German machine-gunners. Lucien was seriously wounded at the Battle of the Marne and two months later died in hospital in France. Albert's father left in their Algerian home some military documents, sepia photos, a war medal that arrived after his death and some shrapnel from the shell that killed him. Albert was an orphan in infancy, just as his father himself had been, and the search for the lost father plays an important role in some of his stories, especially his final incomplete novel, *The First Man*.

Albert's mother's family had come from Minorca; she was partly deaf, unable to read and probably backward. After her husband's death, she moved with her two sons to her parents' house in the mixed-race, working-class Algiers suburb of Belcourt. Albert's grandmother tyrannised the household and reduced Hélène to the status of an indentured servant in her own home, and laid down severe moral guidelines for Albert and his brother. His Uncle Etienne was an ugly, rough and moody man, who worked long hours as a barrel-maker, but he treated Albert with affection, teaching the young boy adult card-games, the delights of café life and how to hunt small animals in the hills; the narrator of *The First Man* recalls his uncle with respect and fondness. Albert grew up on the streets of this noisy, overcrowded quarter of Algiers; his everyday contact with the lower-class French, Arabs, Jews, Italians, Spanish and Corsicans infused in him an abiding tolerance for other cultures and sympathy with the down-trodden and oppressed. He did well at the primary school and received a bursary to study at the local *lycée*, where, as well as his schoolwork, he excelled at sports, especially soccer, which was to remain one of his lifelong passions. One of his *lycée* teachers, Louis Germain, left an indelible mark on young Albert, the privative exemplar of an overly strict teacher who inculcated severe standards of French grammar and syntax.

In December 1930 Camus came down with a high fever, coughing fits and spitting blood; in his diary, Camus blamed his poor health on too much sports and sunbathing. But the doctors diagnosed tuberculosis, which in the poor unsanitary conditions of Belcourt and other nearby areas was little less than a death sentence. Camus eventually returned to school where his new teacher Jean Grenier introduced him to philosophical subjects; Grenier was more than a talented teacher, he took a personal interest in the well-being of his students, Camus included. Years later, when he thought that Albert was best suited to further education in the university, Grenier personally intervened with Camus' grandmother to overcome her opposition to such 'unworldly' and 'impractical' studies. The eighteen-year-old Camus admired Grenier immensely and avidly read his teacher's book. In his diaries, Camus recorded his reaction to Grenier's teaching:

> Of him it can be said that he assumes the greatest possible humanity precisely by trying to keep his distance from it. The unity of his book is the constant presence of death. This makes it clear why the very sight of Grenier, though not changing anything about the way I am, makes me graver, more deeply concerned about the gravity of life ... Grenier: 'Independence can be nothing else than the free choice of a dependence.' Variant [on this]: 'Freedom from slavery is given in order to be free.' (Camus, 1976 [1932–5], p. 178)

In these very early comments one can clearly detect the glimmers of one of his later great themes: an individual overcomes the absurd through his freedom to commit himself to a great project.

With Grenier's advice and encouragement Camus published in June 1932 his first short pieces in the local Algerian magazine *Sud*: an article on Bergson's *Two Sources of Morality and Religion*, an overly ambitious article on Nietzsche's and Schopenhauer's musical aesthetics and other topical reviews. In his working notes, under the heading 'Intuitions', Camus also played with another Nietzschean motif – a series of brief dialogues between the young thinker and a madman who espouses some sort of 'going-over', like Nietzsche's Zarathustra. As someone who hoped to become a writer one day he was most impressed with the works of André Gide and André Malraux, the latter an important French novelist who vigorously expressed the belief that intellectuals should have an active engagement with social and political affairs. On the strength of his teachers' recommendations, Camus was awarded a scholarship to study philosophy at the University of Algiers, where he attended lectures by Jean Grenier, René Poirier (on science) and Jacques Heurgon (on classics). It was Heurgon who introduced Camus to the Roman emperors, especially Caligula, whom Camus would make into the centrepiece of his first play. Camus' course through his university years was rather patchy, due in part to his recurrent bouts of TB, but also due to the stormy and troubled state of his marriage. In June 1934 he married Simone Hié, the daughter of an upper middle-class medical doctor. Simone was an uninhibited and sensuous woman, who captured the attention of all the young men, but there was a downside to her beauty – she was a morphine addict. In this alliance, Simone gambled that Albert's strong-willed character would help her overcome her addiction, and Albert gambled that marriage to Simone would help him out of his lower-class status – neither gamble paid off.

Simone went into a medical clinic for treatment and Camus began to drift; already he felt thwarted, as though real life was elsewhere. He wanted to study philosophy in Paris, where reputations were made, but his poor health and lack of money made that seem impossible. However, under these very difficult circumstances, he did manage to finish his graduate thesis in May 1936 and was awarded his degree the same month. His thesis was 'Christian Metaphysics and Neoplatonism' (see McBride, 1992, pp. 93–165), an important document in Camus' philosophical development, and one that is usually overlooked in accounts of his early existentialist thought. This text cannot be fairly relegated to the status of juvenilia; it shows a great deal of hard work on a hard subject, but more than that it shows real confidence in its treatment of issues that will later become central to his more famous works, especially the presence of evil, the absurdity of one's being alive, and the power of human beings to transcend their limits. In an effort to keep their marriage alive and healthy, Camus and Simone, in the company of one of their close friends, took an extended vacation in Central Europe, walking and canoeing through some of the great cities he had until then only read about. They spent several miserable weeks in August 1936 in Czechoslovakia, 'deadly days filled with anxiety' in Prague, as he noted in a letter, 'an immense city ... where I feel completely out of my depth. Since yesterday I haven't been able to shake a stupid depression which prevents me from enjoying what is admirable here'. It's sad to think that, if he had looked harder he might have found an immense amount of philosophical activity in this magical city at the crossroads of Central Europe. But the eerie atmosphere and architecture of Prague made an impression on his imaginative landscape, since his first novel (abandoned and published only after his death) A Happy Death and his play Le Malentendu (translated into English as 'Cross Purpose') have important scenes set in Prague.

One source of his 'deadly anxiety' and feeling of unrelieved dread came from his growing suspicion that Simone was still addicted to morphine, a suspicion confirmed within the next few months when he learned that she was exchanging sexual favours for her favourite drug. Back in Algiers, his marriage over, Camus threw himself into work in his first real job, at the newspaper Alger-Republicain, the forum for the Popular Front. At one time or another he did every job that needed doing: general dogsbody, deputy editor, chief reporter, special correspondent, book reviewer and fund-raiser. Olivier Todd claims that Camus published over 150 articles in the newspaper: about crime, senatorial elections, the city budget, welfare aid to North African emigrants in France and the desperate poverty of the Arabs in Kabyllia, among others (Todd, 1997, p. 78). The paper's owner had hired Pascal Pia to be the editor-in-chief, and Pia would remain Camus' oldest and most trusted friend, helping him out on many occasions. In addition to the little time left for his own writing he also became more and more involved in many aspects of stage production at the Théâtre de l'Equipe. At about this time, he fell in love with Francine Faure, a middle-class girl from the Algerian city of Oran; they crossed the northern desert to visit each other whenever they could, but Camus knew that it was time for him to move on. The only place he thought would give him a chance to become a real writer, and not just an odd-job journalist, was Paris.

In March 1940, Camus arrived in Paris, with contact names for newspaper work and cheap hotels supplied by Pascal Pia. At first he didn't like Paris. He missed the sea most of all, and missed Francine enough to suggest that she come to France so that they could get married. When the paper he worked for, Paris-Soir, moved to Clermont-Ferrand after the Nazi occupation, and then moved on again to Lyons, Francine joined him there and they were married in December 1940. He shared some of his thoughts on the current situation with his wife:

> I don't think I'm the only person to find all this absurd. On the contrary, I think that it's a useful view for us all ... People say 'that's absurd', but then they pay their taxes and put their daughter into a religious school, because they think that there's nothing else to do, after one has said that things are absurd, whereas in reality, that's only the beginning. I can't

explain in a few words what would take a whole book to say ... Philosophical thought only begins when we challenge the logic of clichés with rigor and honesty. (Todd, 1997, p. 92)

Camus had a whole book to say this in – in fact, two books: the connected essays in *The Myth of Sisyphus* and his novel *The Stranger*, both of which were published in 1942 by Gallimard. He had hoped that his play *Caligula* would be released at the same time, but, as it turned out, it wasn't staged until September 1945. *The Stranger* made an immediate impact on the literary public, although some critics didn't know quite what to make of it. The story unfolds from the narrator's point of view; Meursault's voice is neutral and distant, even when he describes the events that change his life forever. Without colour or tone he recounts various trivial details in his daily life; in the same matter-of-fact style he tells the reader that he attended his mother's funeral, discusses with his girlfriend whether they love each other enough to get married, and mentions almost in passing that he shot and killed an Arab on the beach. The second part tells about Meursault's arrest and trial, his lack of interest in whether or not the jurors think him guilty, and his apparent indifference to his sentence of execution – the 'stranger' is an alien in his own skin. André Malraux, whose opinion Camus valued highly, wrote to him via Pascal Pia: 'The power and simplicity of the means which finally force the reader to accept his character's point of view are all the more remarkable in that the book's destiny depends on whether this character is convincing or not.' Camus was concerned that readers would understand that *The Stranger* and *The Myth of Sisyphus* made a joint statement, that they approached the same issues from different perspectives and reinforced their separate conclusions. Malraux understood this straightaway: 'The essay gives the other book its full meaning and, above all, changes what in the novel first seemed monotonous and impoverished into a positive austerity, with primitive force' (Todd, 1997, pp. 131, 133).

The startling lesson that Camus' unheroic character conveys is that human existence lacks any ground, there is no reason why *this* individual should exist, rather than not exist. Human life lacks any meaning; it is absurd because human beings have a desire for understanding and the limitations of their reason do not allow for the satisfaction of that desire. The world in itself is simply unintelligible and humans attempt in vain to discover a meaning that is never there to begin with. For Camus, death is the principal source of this absurdity, since death is the annihilation of a creature that was made for God, but there is *no* God, and hence no life beyond this life. Sartre wrote in his explication of Camus' novel that the absurd is

> nothing less than man's relation to the world. Primary absurdity manifests the cleavage between man's aspirations to unity and the insurmountable dualism of mind and nature, between man's drive toward the eternal and the finite character of his existence, between the 'concern' which constitutes his very essence and the vanity of his efforts. (Brée, 1962, p. 109)

Jacques Maritain referred to Camus as 'an absolute, positive atheist', that is, that Camus' purpose was not merely to reject religious belief and the Christian meaning bestowed on human life, but to replace these values with a philosophical perspective that would give humans a secular meaning, locating their destiny within this world and not another world beyond, making them, at the moral level, masters in their own house (McBride, 1992, p. 8).

Becoming masters in their own house was what the French were most concerned with after the liberation from Nazi occupation. During the war years Camus had continued his journalist work, but now in a more dangerous environment, as editor-in-chief of the Resistance newspaper *Combat*. Although his frail health prevented him from taking part in one of the 'active units', his own life was often 'on the line'; his whole-hearted commitment to the cause of revolt against the hated 'master race' *left him no choice*, as he would have said. Camus was not afraid to die, but perhaps he felt this sense of one's own mortality more than others did; in 1943 he said:

> From now on the feeling of death is familiar to me, although it is no longer accompanied by pain. Pain makes us hang on to the present, and requires a struggle that keeps one busy. But death, foretold by the mere sight of a blood-covered handkerchief, without any other symptom, means being plunged back into time in a vertiginous way, which is the fear of becoming something else. (Todd, 1997, p. 162)

After the liberation Camus became seriously ill again and he and his wife moved back to Algiers where they rented an apartment from the writer André Gide. For several years Camus had been working on another novel, *The Plague*, which finally appeared in 1947 and was an instant success. Unlike his earlier works. *The Plague* sold very well, earning the author enough money to buy his own house and pay off some of his debts.

> By the 'plague', I want to express the suffocation which all have suffered and the atmosphere of danger and exile which we have all lived in. At the same time, I want to extend this interpretation to the notion of life in general. *The Plague* will show people who have taken the part of reflection, silence and moral suffering during the war. (Todd, 1997, p. 158)

Camus and Sartre had been great friends during the occupation and the years of jubilation and optimism after liberation, but soon their paths began to diverge, leading to one of the most acrimonious intellectual disputes of the 1950s. Camus had joined the Communist party in 1935 and, though he had officially withdrawn as a member within two years, he still maintained an interest in the one movement which he and many of his friends thought offered the best hope for amelioration of suffering and poverty in oppressive societies. But in the course of events in the late 1940s, especially the public release of information about the Soviet 'show-trials' and their forced labour camps, Camus' political sentiments began to change. His criticisms of the missed opportunities and loss of intelligent leaders in the Marxist-Socialist revolution are one of the sharpest features of his next book *L'Homme révolté (The Rebel)* which appeared in 1951 to much critical acclaim and angry counter-attacks. His arguments in this text are grouped under five headings: man in revolt, metaphysical revolt, historical revolt, artistic revolt and 'Southern thought', by which he meant the Mediterranean spirit of 'good measure', in contrast with the North European spirit of domination. Camus attacked the symbolist poets, the surrealists, Louis Aragon, André Breton, even his old friend André Malraux, and many other notable (and powerful) French artists and writers, but especially those who still clung to Marxist-Socialism in the form of Stalin's new regime, in which he said 'absurdity outdid itself'. One of the editors of *Les Temps Modernes* launched the first counter-attack, but this was followed by an even more vitriolic denunciation from Sartre himself. The French literate public, always sensitive to nuances of political debate, was divided between support for Camus and for his enemies.

Although he had fallen out with some of his friends, Camus was a revered figure in France and other European countries whose democracy had been restored. Camus was seen as one of the principal exponents of political self-determination, an intellectual who had actively taken part in the Resistance and whose own life testified to his firm belief in the dignity and sovereignty of the individual. In recognition of these and other achievements he was awarded the Nobel Prize for Literature in 1957; when he was informed his first reaction was one of disbelief and 'suffocation'. In order to escape the public spotlight and find the solitude he needed to work, he bought a large house in Provence where he moved with his wife and twin children in 1958. His publisher Michel Gallimard was one of the Camus couple's closest friends, and it was on one of Gallimard's visits, when they were returning by car to Paris, that Camus was killed in a road accident. In the wrecked car rescuers found a nearly complete manuscript of Camus' final novel, *The First Man*; his widow had strong reservations about its being made public and it wasn't until twelve years after her death in 1979 that their son and daughter decided to release it for publication. Sartre concluded his obituary for Camus with these words:

> For all those who loved him, there was an unbearable absurdity in this death. But we shall have to learn to see this mutilated life-work as a whole life-work … We shall recognize in this work and in the life which is inseparable from it, the pure and victorious endeavor of a man to recover each instant of his existence from his future death. (Sartre, 1965, p. 112)

PRINCIPAL WORKS

(1932–5) *Youthful Writings*, trans. Ellen Kennedy, intro. Paul Viallaneix. New York: Alfred Knopf, 1976.
(1935–42) *Notebooks 1935–42*, trans. Philip Thody. London: Hamish Hamilton, 1963.
(1936) 'Christian Metaphysics and Neoplatonism', in Joseph McBride, *Albert Camus: Philosopher and Litterateur*. New York: St. Martin's Press, 1992.

(1942) *The Stranger*, trans. Justin O'Brien; also as *The Outsider*, trans. Stuart Gilbert Penguin Books, 1961.

(1942) *The Myth of Sisyphus*, trans. Justin O'Brien. Penguin Books, 1975.

(1942–51) *Notebooks 1942–1951*, trans. Philip Thody. London: Hamish Hamilton, 1966.

(1947) *The Plague*, trans. Stuart Gilbert. Penguin Books, 1960.

(1951) *The Rebel*, trans. Anthony Bower. Penguin Books, 1971.

(1954) *The Fall*, trans. Justin O'Brien. Penguin Books, 1957.

(1957) *Exile and the Kingdom*, trans. Justin O'Brien. Penguin Books, 1962.

(1960) *The First Man*, trans. David Hapgood. Penguin Books, 1995.

RECOMMENDED READING

Barnes, Hazel (1961) *The Literature of Possibility*. London: Tavistock Press.

Brée, Germaine (ed.) (1962) *A Collection of Critical Essays*. Eaglewood Cliffs, NJ: Prentice-Hall.

Bronner, Stephen (1999) *Camus: Portrait of a Moralist*. Minneapolis: University of Minnesota Press.

Cruickshank, John (1959) *Albert Camus and the Literature of Revolt*. Oxford: Oxford University Press.

Isaac, Jeffrey (1992) *Arendt, Camus and Modern Rebellion*. New Haven CT: Yale University Press.

Lazere, Donald (1973) *The Unique Creation of Albert Camus*. New Haven CT: Yale University Press.

Lottman, Herbert (1979) *Albert Camus: A Biography*. London: Weidenfeld & Nicolson.

McBride, Joseph (1992) *Albert Camus: Philosopher and Litterateur*. New York: St. Martin's Press.

McCarthy, Patrick (1982) *Camus: A Critical Analysis of His Life and Work*. London: Hamish Hamilton.

O'Brien, Conor Cruise (1970) *Camus*, Modern Masters Series. London: Fontana.

Sprintzen, David (1988) *Camus: A Critical Examination*. Philadelphia: Temple University Press.

Todd, Olivier (1997) *Albert Camus: A Life*, trans. Benjamin Ivry. New York: Alfred Knopf.

'AN ABSURD REASONING' (1942)[*]

Albert Camus

The pages that follow deal with an absurd sensitivity that can be found widespread in the age and not with an absurd philosophy which our time, properly speaking, has not known. It is therefore simply fair to point out, at the outset, what these pages owe to certain contemporary thinkers. It is so far from my intention to hide this that they will be found cited and commented upon throughout this work.

---

[*] From *The Myth of Sisyphus*, trans. Justin O'Brien. New York: Penguin Books, 1975.

But it is useful to note at the same time that the absurd, hitherto taken as a conclusion, is considered in this essay as a starting point. In this sense it may be said that there is something provisional in my commentary: one cannot pre-judge the position it entails. There will be found here merely the description, in the pure state, of an intellectual malady. No metaphysic, no belief is involved in it for a moment. These are the limits and the only bias of this book. Certain personal experiences urge me to make this clear.

ABSURDITY AND SUICIDE

There is but one truly serious philosophical problem and that is suicide. Judging whether life is or is not worth living amounts to answering the fundamental question of philosophy. All the rest – whether or not the world has three dimensions, whether the mind has nine or twelve categories – comes afterwards. These are games; one must first answer. And if it is true, as Nietzsche claims, that a philosopher, to deserve our respect, must preach by example, you can appreciate the importance of that reply, for it will precede the definitive act. These are facts the heart can feel; yet they call for careful study before they become clear to the intellect.

If I ask myself how to judge that this question is more urgent than that, I reply that one judges by the actions it entails. I have never seen anyone die for the ontological argument. Galileo who held a scientific truth of great importance abjured it with the greatest ease as soon as it endangered his life. In a certain sense, he did right.[1] That truth was not worth the stake. Whether the earth or the sun revolves around the other is a matter of profound indifference. To tell the truth, it is a futile question. On the other hand, I see many people die because they judge that life is not worth living. I see others paradoxically getting killed for the ideas or illusions that give them a reason for living (what is called a reason for living is also an excellent reason for dying). I therefore conclude that the meaning of life is the most urgent of questions. How to answer it? On all essential problems (I mean thereby those that run the risk of leading to death or those that intensify the passion of living) there are probably but two methods of thought: the method of La Palisse and the method of Don Quixote. Solely the balance between evidence and lyricism can allow us to achieve simultaneously emotion and lucidity. In a subject at once so humble and so heavy with emotion, the learned and classical dialectic must yield, one can see, to a more modest attitude of mind deriving at one and the same time from common sense and understanding.

Suicide has never been dealt with except as a social phenomenon. On the contrary, we are concerned here, at the outset, with the relationship between individual thought and suicide. An act like this is prepared within the silence of the heart, as is a great work of art. The man himself is ignorant of it. One evening he pulls the trigger or jumps. Of an apartment-building manager who had killed himself I was told that he had lost his daughter five years before, that he had changed greatly since and that that experience had 'undermined' him. A more exact word cannot be imagined. Beginning to think is beginning to be undermined. Society has but little connection with such beginnings. The worm is in man's heart. That is where it must be sought. One must follow and understand this fatal game that leads from lucidity in the face of experience to flight from light.

There are many causes for a suicide and generally the most obvious ones were not the most powerful. Rarely is suicide committed (yet the hypothesis is not excluded) through reflection. What sets off the crisis is almost always unverifiable. Newspapers often speak of 'personal sorrows' or of 'incurable illness'. These explanations are plausible. But one would have to know whether a friend of the desperate man had not that very day addressed him indifferently. He is the guilty one. For that is enough to precipitate all the rancours and all the boredom still in suspension.[2]

But if it is hard to fix the precise instant, the subtle step when the mind opted for death, it is easier to deduce from the act itself the consequences it implies. In a sense, and as in melodrama, killing yourself amounts to confessing. It is confessing that life is too much for you or that you do not understand it. Let's not go too far in such analogies, however, but rather return to everyday words. It is merely confessing that that 'is not worth the trouble'. Living, naturally, is never easy. You continue making the gestures commanded by existence for many reasons, the first of which is habit. Dying voluntarily implies that you have recognized, even instinctively, the ridiculous character of that habit, the absence of any profound reason for living, the insane character of that daily agitation and the uselessness of suffering.

What then is that incalculable feeling that deprives the mind of the sleep necessary to life? A world that can be explained even with bad reasons is a familiar world. But, on the other hand, in a universe suddenly divested of illusions and lights, man feels an alien, a stranger. His exile is without remedy since he is deprived of the memory of a lost home or the hope of a promised land. This divorce between man and his life, the actor and his setting, is properly the feeling of absurdity. All healthy men having thought of their own suicide, it can be seen, without further explanation, that there is a direct connection between this feeling and the longing for death.

The subject of this essay is precisely this relationship between the absurd and suicide, the exact degree to which suicide is a solution to the absurd. The principle can be established that for a man who does not cheat what he believes to be true must determine his action. Belief in the absurdity of existence must then dictate his conduct. It is legitimate to wonder, clearly and without false pathos, whether a conclusion of this importance requires forsaking as rapidly as possible an incomprehensible condition. I am speaking, of course, of men inclined to be in harmony with themselves.

Stated clearly, this problem may seem both simple and insoluble. But it is wrongly assumed that simple questions involve answers that are no less simple and that evidence implies evidence. A priori and reversing the terms of the problem, just as one does or does not kill oneself, it seems that there are but two philosophical solutions, either yes or no. This would be too easy. But allowance must be made for those who, without concluding, continue questioning. Here I am only slightly indulging in irony: this is the majority. I notice also that those who answer 'no' act as if they thought 'yes'. As a matter of fact, if I accept the Nietzschean criterion, they think yes in one way or another. On the other hand, it often happens that those who commit suicide were assured of the meaning of life. These contradictions are constant. It may even be said that they have never been so keen as on this point where, on the contrary, logic seems so desirable. It is a commonplace to compare philosophical theories and the behaviour of those who profess them. But it must be said that of the thinkers who refused a meaning to life none except Kirilov who belongs to literature, Peregrinos who is born of legend,[3] and Jules Lequier who belongs to hypothesis, admitted his logic to the point of refusing that life. Schopenhauer is often cited, as a fit subject for laughter, because he praised suicide while seated at a well-set table. This is no subject for joking. That way of not taking the tragic seriously is not so grievous, but it helps to judge a man.

In the face of such contradictions and obscurities must we conclude that there is no relationship between the opinion one has about life and the act one commits to leave it? Let us not exaggerate in this direction. In a man's attachment to life there is something stronger than all the ills in the world. The body's judgement is as good as the mind's and the body shrinks from annihilation. We get into the habit of living before acquiring the habit of thinking. In that race which daily hastens us towards death, the body maintains its irreparable lead. In short, the essence of that contradiction lies in what I shall call the act of eluding because it is both less and more than diversion in the Pascalian sense. Eluding is the invariable game. The typical act of eluding, the fatal evasion that constitutes the third theme of this essay, is hope. Hope of another life one must 'deserve' or trickery of those who live, not for life itself, but for some great idea that will transcend it, refine it, give it a meaning, and betray it.

Thus everything contributes to spreading confusion. Hitherto, and it has not been wasted effort, people have played on words and pretended to believe that refusing to grant a meaning to life necessarily leads to declaring that it is not worth living. In truth, there is no necessary common measure between these two judgements. One merely has to refuse to be misled by the confusions, divorces, and inconsistencies previously pointed out. One must brush everything aside and go straight to the real problem. One kills oneself because life is not worth living, that is certainly a truth – yet an unfruitful one because it is a truism. But does that insult to existence, that flat denial in which it is plunged come from the fact that it has no meaning? Does its absurdity require one to escape it through hope or suicide – this is what must be clarified, hunted down and elucidated while brushing aside all the rest. Does the Absurd dictate death? This problem must be given priority over others, outside all methods of thought and all exercises of the disinterested mind. Shades of meaning, contradictions, the psychology that an 'objective' mind can always introduce into all problems have no place in this pursuit and this passion. It calls simply for an unjust, in other words logical, thought. That is not easy. It is always easy to be logical. It is almost impossible to be logical to the bitter end. Men who die by their own hand consequently follow to its conclusion their emotional inclination. Reflection on suicide gives me an opportunity to raise the only problem to interest me: is there a logic to the point of death? I cannot know unless I pursue, without reckless passion, in the sole light of evidence, the reasoning of which I am here suggesting the source. This is what I call an absurd reasoning. Many have begun it. I do not yet know whether or not they kept to it.

When Karl Jaspers, revealing the impossibility of constituting the world as a unity, exclaims: 'This limitation leads me to myself, where I can no longer withdraw behind an objective point of view that I am merely representing, where neither I myself nor the existence of others can any longer become an object for me,' he is evoking after many others those waterless deserts where thought reaches its confines. After many others, yes indeed, but how eager they were to get out of them! At that last crossroad where thought hesitates, many men have arrived and even some of the humblest. They then abdicated what was most precious to them, their life. Others, princes of the mind, abdicated likewise, but they initiated the suicide of their thought in its purest revolt. The real effort is to stay there, rather, in so far as that is possible, and to examine closely the odd vegetation of those distant regions. Tenacity and acumen are privileged spectators of this inhuman show in which absurdity, hope and death carry on their dialogue. The mind can then analyse the figures of that elementary yet subtle dance before illustrating them and reliving them itself.

ABSURD WALLS

Like great works, deep feelings always mean more than they are conscious of saying. The regularity of an impulse or a repulsion in a soul is encountered again in habits of doing or thinking, is reproduced in consequences of which the soul itself knows nothing. Great feelings take with them their own universe, splendid or abject. They light up with their passion an exclusive world in which they recognize their climate. There is a universe of jealousy, of ambition, of selfishness or of generosity. A universe – in other words a metaphysic and an attitude of mind. What is true of already specialized feelings will be even more so of emotions basically as indeterminate, simultaneously as vague and as 'definite', as remote and as 'present' as those furnished us by beauty or aroused by absurdity.

At any street corner the feeling of absurdity can strike any man in the face. As it is, in its distressing nudity, in its light without effulgence, it is elusive. But that very difficulty deserves reflection. It is probably true that a man remains for ever unknown to us and that there is in him something irreducible that escapes us.

But *practically* I know men and recognize them by their behaviour, by the totality of their deeds, by the consequences caused in life by their presence. Likewise, all those irrational feelings which offer no purchase to analysis. I can define them *practically*, appreciate them *practically*, by gathering together the sum of their consequences in the domain of the intelligence, by seizing and noting all their aspects, by outlining their universe. It is certain that apparently, though I have seen the same actor a hundred times, I shall not for that reason know him any better personally. Yet if I add up the heroes he has personified and if I say that I know him a little better at the hundredth character counted off, this will be felt to contain an element of truth. For this apparent paradox is also an apologue. There is a moral to it. It teaches that a man defines himself by his make-believe as well as by his sincere impulses. There is thus a lower key of feelings, inaccessible in the heart but partially disclosed by the acts they imply and the attitudes of mind they assume. It is clear that in this way I am defining a method. But it is also evident that that method is one of analysis and not of knowledge. For methods imply metaphysics; unconsciously they disclose conclusions that they often claim not to know yet. Similarly the last pages of a book are already contained in the first pages. Such a link is inevitable. The method defined here acknowledges the feeling that all true knowledge is impossible. Solely appearances can be enumerated and the climate make itself felt.

Perhaps we shall be able to overtake that elusive feeling of absurdity in the different but closely related worlds of intelligence, of the art of living, or of art itself. The climate of absurdity is in the beginning. The end is the absurd universe and that attitude of mind which lights the world with its true colours to bring out the privileged and implacable visage which that attitude has discerned in it.

All great deeds and all great thoughts have a ridiculous beginning. Great works are often born on a street-corner or in a restaurant's revolving door. So it is with absurdity. The absurd world more than others derives its nobility from that abject birth. In certain situations, replying 'nothing' when asked what one is thinking about may be pretence in a man. Those who are loved are well aware of this. But if that reply is sincere, if it symbolizes that odd state of soul in which the void becomes eloquent, in which the chain of daily gestures is broken, in which the heart vainly seeks the link that will connect it again, then it is as it were the first sign of absurdity.

It happens that the stage-sets collapse. Rising, tram, four hours in the office or factory, meal, tram, four hours of work, meal, sleep and Monday, Tuesday, Wednesday, Thursday, Friday and Saturday, according to the same rhythm – this path is easily followed most of the time. But one day the 'why' arises and everything begins in that weariness tinged with amazement. 'Begins' – this is important. Weariness comes at the end of the acts of a mechanical life, but at the same time it inaugurates the impulse of consciousness. It awakens consciousness and provokes what follows. What follows is the gradual return into the chain or it is the definitive awakening. At the end of the awakening comes, in time, the consequence: suicide or recovery. In itself weariness has something sickening about it. Here. I must conclude that it is good. For everything begins with consciousness and nothing is worth anything except through it. There is nothing original about these remarks. But they are obvious; that is enough for a while, during a sketchy reconnaissance in the origins of the absurd. Mere 'anxiety', as Heidegger says, is at the source of everything.

Likewise and during every day of an unillustrious life, time carries us. But a moment always comes when we have to carry it. We live on the future: 'tomorrow', 'later on', 'when you have made your way', 'you will understand when you are old enough'. Such irrelevancies are wonderful, for, after all, it's a matter of dying. Yet a time comes when a man notices or says that he is thirty. Thus he asserts his youth. But simultaneously he situates himself in relation to time. He takes his place in it. He admits that he stands at a certain point on a curve that he acknowledges having to travel to its end. He belongs to time and, by the horror that seizes him, he recognizes his worst enemy. Tomorrow, he was longing for tomorrow, whereas everything in him ought to reject it. The revolt of the flesh is the absurd.[4]

A step lower and strangeness creeps in: perceiving that the world is 'dense', sensing to what degree a stone is foreign and irreducible to us, with what intensity nature or a landscape can negate us. At the heart of all beauty lies something inhuman, and these hills, the softness of the sky, the outline of these trees at this very minute lose the illusory meaning with which we had clothed them, henceforth more remote than a lost paradise. The primitive hostility of the world rises up to face us across millennia. For a second we cease to understand it because for centuries we have understood in it solely the images and designs that we had attributed to it beforehand, because henceforth we lack the power to make use of that artifice. The world evades us because it becomes itself again. That stage-scenery masked by habit becomes again what it is. It withdraws at a distance from us. Just as there are days when, under the familiar face of a woman, we see as a stranger her we had loved months or years ago, perhaps we shall come even to desire what suddenly leaves us so alone. But the time has not yet come. Just one thing: that denseness and that strangeness of the world is the absurd.

Men, too, secrete the inhuman. At certain moments of lucidity, the mechanical aspect of their gestures, their meaningless pantomime make silly everything that surrounds them. A man is talking on the telephone behind a glass partition; you cannot hear him but you see his incomprehensible dumb-show: you wonder why he is alive. The discomfort in the face of man's own inhumanity, this incalculable tumble before the image of what we are, this 'nausea', as a writer of today calls it, is also the absurd. Likewise the stranger who at certain seconds comes to meet us in a mirror, the familiar and yet alarming brother we encounter in our own photographs is also the absurd.

I come at last to death and to the attitude we have towards it. On this point everything has been said and it is only proper to avoid pathos. Yet one will never be sufficiently surprised that everyone lives as if no one 'knew'. This is because in reality there is no experience of death. Properly speaking, nothing has been experienced but what has been lived and made conscious. Here, it is barely possible to speak of the experience of others' deaths. It is a substitute, an illusion, and it never quite convinces us. That melancholy convention cannot be persuasive. The horror comes in reality from the mathematical aspect of the event. If time frightens us, this is because it works out the problem and the solution comes afterwards. All the pretty speeches about the soul will have their contrary convincingly proved, at least for a time. From this inert body on which a slap makes no mark the soul has disappeared. This elementary and definitive aspect of the adventure constitutes the absurd feeling. Under the fatal lighting of that destiny, its uselessness becomes evident. No code of ethics and no effort are justifiable *a priori* in the face of the cruel mathematics that command our condition.

Let me repeat: all this has been said over and over. I am limiting myself here to making a rapid classification and to pointing out these obvious themes. They run through all literatures and all philosophies. Everyday conversation feeds on them. There is no question of re-inventing them. But it is essential to be sure of these facts in order to be able to question oneself subsequently on the primordial question. I am interested – let me repeat again – not so much in absurd discoveries as in their consequences. If one is assured of these facts, what is one to conclude, how far is one to go to elude nothing? Is one to die voluntarily or to hope in spite of everything? Beforehand, it is necessary to take the same rapid inventory on the plane of the intelligence.

The mind's first step is to distinguish what is true from what is false. However, as soon as thought reflects itself, what it first discovers is a contradiction. Useless to strive to be convincing in this case. Over the centuries no one has furnished a clearer and more elegant demonstration of the business than Aristotle: 'The often ridiculed consequence of these opinions is that they destroy themselves. For by asserting that all is true we assert the truth of the contrary assertion and consequently the falsity of our own thesis (for the contrary assertion does not admit that it can be true). And if one says that all is false, that assertion is itself false. If we declare that solely the assertion opposed to ours is false or else that solely ours is not false, we are nevertheless forced to admit an infinite number of true or false judgements. For the one who expresses a true assertion proclaims simultaneously that it is true, and so on *ad infinitum*.'

This vicious circle is but the first of a series in which the mind that studies itself gets lost in a giddy whirling. The very simplicity of these paradoxes makes them irreducible. Whatever may be the plays on words and the acrobatics of logic, to understand is above all to unify. The mind's deepest desire, even in its most elaborate operations, parallels man's unconscious feelings in the face of his universe: it is an insistence upon familiarity, an appetite for clarity. Understanding the world for a man is reducing it to the human, stamping it with his seal. The cat's universe is not the universe of the ant-hill. The truism 'All thought is anthropomorphic' has no other meaning. Likewise the mind that aims to understand reality can consider itself satisfied only by reducing it to terms of thought. If man realized that the universe like him can love and suffer, he would be reconciled. If thought discovered in the shimmering mirrors of phenomena eternal relations capable of summing them up and summing themselves up in a single principle, then would be seen an intellectual joy of which the myth of the blessed would be but a ridiculous imitation. That nostalgia for unity, that appetite for the absolute illustrates the essential impulse for the human drama. But the fact of that nostalgia's existence does not imply that it is to be immediately satisfied. For if, bridging the gulf that separates desire from conquest, we assert with Parmenides the reality of the One (whatever it may be) we fall into the ridiculous contradiction of a mind that asserts total unity and proves by its very assertion its own difference and the diversity it claimed to resolve. This other vicious circle is enough to stifle our hopes.

These are again truisms. I shall again repeat that they are not interesting in themselves but in the consequences that can be deduced from them. I know another truism: it tells me that man is mortal. One can nevertheless count the minds that have deduced the extreme conclusions from it. It is essential to consider as a constant point of reference in this essay the regular hiatus between what we fancy we know and what we really know, practical assent and simulated ignorance which allows us to live with ideas which, if we truly put them to the test, ought to upset our whole life. Faced with this inextricable contradiction of the mind, we shall fully grasp the divorce separating us from our own creations. So long as the mind keeps silent in the motionless world of its hopes, everything is reflected and arranged in the unity of its nostalgia. But with its first move this world cracks and tumbles: an infinite number of shimmering fragments is offered to the understanding. We must despair of ever reconstructing the familiar, calm surface which would give us peace of heart. After so many centuries of inquiries, so many abdications among thinkers, we are well aware that this is true for all our knowledge. With the exception of professional rationalists, today people despair of true knowledge. If the only significant history of human thought were to be written, it would have to be the history of its successive regrets and its impotences.

Of whom and of what indeed can I say: 'I know that!' This heart within me I can feel, and I judge that it exists. This world I can touch, and I likewise judge that it exists. There ends all my knowledge, and the rest is construction. For if I try to seize this self of which I feel sure, if I try to define and to summarize it, it is nothing but water slipping through my fingers. I can sketch one by one all the aspects it is able to assume, all those likewise that have been attributed to it, this upbringing, this origin, this ardour or these silences, this nobility or this vileness. But aspects cannot be added up. This very heart which is mine will for ever remain indefinable to me. Between the certainty I have of my existence and the content I try to give to that assurance, the gap will never be filled. For ever I shall be a stranger to myself. In psychology as in logic, there are truths but no truth. Socrates' 'Know thyself' has as much value as the 'be virtuous' of our confessionals. They reveal a nostalgia at the same time as an ignorance. They are sterile exercises on great subjects. They are legitimate only precisely in so far as they are approximate.

And here are trees and I know their gnarled surface, water and I feel its taste. These scents of grass and stars at night, certain evenings when the heart relaxes – how shall I negate this world whose power and strength I feel? Yet all the knowledge on earth will give me nothing to assure me that this world is mine. You describe it to me and you teach me to classify it. You enumerate its laws and in my thirst for knowledge I admit that they are true. You take apart its mechanism and my hope increases. At the final stage you teach me that this wondrous and multi-coloured universe can be reduced to the atom and that the atom itself can be reduced to the electron. All this is good and I wait for you to continue. But you tell me of an invisible planetary system in which electrons gravitate around a nucleus. You explain this world to me with an image. I realize then that you have been reduced to poetry: I shall never know. Have I the time to become indignant? You have already changed theories. So that science that was to teach me everything ends up in a hypothesis, that lucidity founders in metaphor, that uncertainty is resolved in a work of art. What need had I of so many efforts? The soft lines of these hills and the hand of evening on this troubled heart teach me much more. I have returned to my beginning. I realize that if through science I can seize phenomena and enumerate them. I cannot for all that apprehend the world. Were I to trace its entire relief with my finger, I should not know any more. And you give me the choice between a description that is sure but that teaches me nothing and hypotheses that claim to teach me but that are not sure. A stranger to myself and to the world, armed solely with a thought that negates itself as soon as it asserts, what is this condition in which I can have peace only by refusing to know and to live, in which the appetite for conquest bumps into walls that defy its assaults? To will is to stir up paradoxes. Everything is ordered in such a way as to bring into being that poisoned peace produced by thoughtlessness, lack of heart or fatal renunciations.

Hence the intelligence, too, tells me in its way that this world is absurd. Its contrary, blind reason, may well claim that all is clear. I was waiting for proof and longing for it to be right. But, despite so many pretentious centuries and over the heads of so many eloquent and persuasive men, I know that is false. On this plane, at least, there is no happiness if I cannot know. That universal reason, practical or ethical, that determinism, those categories that explain everything are enough to make a decent man laugh. They have nothing to do with the mind. They negate its profound truth which is to be enchained. In this unintelligible and limited universe, man's fate henceforth assumes its meaning. A horde of irrationals has sprung up and surrounds him until his ultimate end. In his recovered and now studied lucidity, the feeling of the absurd becomes clear and definite. I said that the world is absurd but I was too hasty. This world in itself is not reasonable, that is all that can be said. But what is absurd is the confrontation of the irrational and the wild longing for clarity whose call echoes in the human heart. The absurd depends as much on man as on the world. For the moment it is all that links them together. It binds them one to the other as only hatred can weld two creatures together. This is all I can discern clearly in this measureless universe where my adventure takes place. Let us pause here. If I hold to be true that absurdity that determines my relationship with life, if I become thoroughly imbued with that sentiment that seizes me in face of the world's scenes, with that lucidity imposed on me by the pursuit of a science, I must sacrifice everything to these certainties and I must see them squarely to be able to maintain them. Above all, I must adapt my behaviour to them and pursue them in all their consequences. I am speaking here of decency. But I want to know beforehand if thought can live in those deserts.

I already know that thought has at least entered those deserts. There it found its bread. There it realized that it had previously been feeding on phantoms. It justified some of the most urgent themes of human reflection.

From the moment absurdity is recognized, it becomes a passion, the most harrowing of all. But whether or not one can live with one's passions, whether or not one can accept their law, which is to burn the heart they simultaneously exalt, that is the whole question. It is not, however, the one we shall ask just yet. It stands at the centre of this experience. There will be time to come back to it. Let us recognize rather those themes and those impulses born of the desert. It will suffice to enumerate them. They, too, are known to all today. There have always been men to defend the rights of the irrational. The tradition of what may be called humiliated thought has never ceased to exist. The criticism of rationalism has been made so often that it seems unnecessary to begin again. Yet our epoch is marked by the rebirth of those paradoxical systems that strive to trip up the reason as if truly it has always forged ahead. But that is not so much a proof of the efficacy of the reason as of the intensity of its hopes. On the plane of history, such a constancy of two attitudes illustrates the essential passion of man torn between his urge towards unity and the clear vision he may have of the walls enclosing him.

But never, perhaps, at any time has the attack on reason been more violent than in ours. Since Zarathustra's great outburst: 'By chance it is the oldest nobility in the world. I conferred it upon all things when I proclaimed that above them no eternal will was exercised'; since Kierkegaard's fatal illness, 'that malady that leads to death with nothing else following it', the significant and tormenting themes of absurd thought have followed one another. Or, at least, and this proviso is of capital importance, the themes of irrational and religious thought. From Jaspers to Heidegger, from Kierkegaard to Chestov, from the phenomenologists to Scheler, on the logical plane and on the moral plane, a whole family of minds related by their nostalgia but opposed by their methods or their aims, have persisted in blocking the royal road of reason and in recovering the direct paths of truth. Here I assume these thoughts to be known and lived. Whatever may be or have been their ambitions, all started out from that indescribable universe where contradiction, antinomy, anguish or impotence reigns. And what they have in common is precisely the themes so far disclosed. For them, too, it must be said that what matters above all is the conclusions they have managed to draw from those discoveries. That matters so much that they must be examined separately. But for the moment we are concerned solely with their discoveries and their initial experiments. We are concerned solely with noting their agreement. If it would be presumptuous to try to deal with their philosophies, it is possible and sufficient in any case to bring out the climate that is common to them.

Heidegger considers the human condition coldly and announces that that existence is humiliated. The only reality is 'anxiety' in the whole chain of beings. To the man lost in the world and its diversions this anxiety is a brief, fleeting fear. But if that fear becomes conscious of itself, it becomes anguish, the perpetual climate of the lucid man 'in whom existence is concentrated'. This professor of philosophy writes without trembling and in the most abstract language in the world that 'the finite and limited character of human existence is more primordial than man himself.' His interest in Kant extends only to recognizing the restricted character of his 'pure Reason'. This is to conclude at the end of his analyses that 'the world can no longer offer anything to the man filled with anguish'. This anxiety seems to him so much more important than all the categories in the world that he thinks and talks only of it. He enumerates its aspects: boredom when the ordinary man strives to quash it in him and benumb it; terror when the mind contemplates death. He, too, does not separate consciousness from the absurd. The consciousness of death is the call of anxiety and 'existence then delivers itself its own summons through the intermediary of consciousness'. It is the very voice of anguish and it adjures existence 'to return from its loss in the anonymous They'. For him, too, one must not sleep but must keep alert until the consummation. He stands in this absurd world and points out its ephemeral character. He seeks his way amidst these ruins.

Jaspers despairs of any ontology because he claims that we have lost 'naïveté'. He knows that we can achieve nothing that will transcend the fatal game of appearances. He knows that the end of the mind is failure. He tarries over the spiritual adventures revealed by history and pitilessly discloses the flaw in each system, the illusion that saved everything, the preaching that hid nothing. In this ravaged world in which the impossibility of knowledge is established, in which everlasting nothingness seems the only reality and irremediable despair seems the only attitude, he tries to discover the 'Ariadne's thread' that leads to divine secrets.

Chestov, for his part, throughout a wonderfully monotonous work, constantly straining towards the same truths, tirelessly demonstrates that the tightest system, the most universal rationalism always stumbles eventually on the irrational of human thought. None of the ironic facts or ridiculous contradictions that depreciate the reason escapes him. One thing only interests him and that is the exception, whether in the domain of the heart or of the mind. Through the Dostoyevskian experiences of the condemned man, the exacerbated adventures of the Nietzschean mind, Hamlet's imprecations, or the bitter aristocracy of an Ibsen, he tracks down, illuminates and magnifies the human revolt against the irremediable. He refuses the reason its seasons and begins to advance with some decision only in the middle of that colourless desert where all certainties have become stones.

Of all, perhaps the most engaging, Kierkegaard, for a part of his existence at least, does more than discover the absurd, he lives it. The man who writes: 'The surest of stubborn silences is not to hold one's tongue but to talk' makes sure in the beginning that no truth is absolute or can render satisfactory an existence that is impossible in itself. Don Juan of the understanding, he multiplies pseudonyms and contradictions, writes his *Discourses of Edification* at the same time as that manual of cynical spiritualism, *The Diary of the Seducer*. He refuses consolations, ethics, reliable principles. As for that thorn he feels in his heart, he is careful not to quiet its pain. On the contrary, he awakens it and, in the desperate joy of a man crucified and happy to be so, he builds up piece by piece – lucidity, refusal, make-believe – a category of the man possessed. That face both tender and sneering, those pirouettes followed by a cry from the heart are the absurd spirit itself grappling with a reality beyond its comprehension. And the spiritual adventure that leads Kierkegaard to his beloved scandals begins likewise in the chaos of an experience divested of its setting and relegated to its original incoherence.

On quite a different plane, that of method, Husserl and the phenomenologists, by their very extravagances, reinstate the world in its diversity and deny the transcendent power of the reason. The spiritual universe becomes incalculably enriched through them. The rose petal, the milestone, or the human hand are as important as love, desire, or the laws of gravity. Thinking ceases to be unifying or making a semblance familiar in the guise of a major principle. Thinking is learning all over again to see, to be attentive, to focus consciousness; it is turning every idea and every image, in the manner of Proust, into a privileged moment. What justifies thought is its extreme consciousness. Though more positive than Kierkegaard's or Chestov's, Husserl's manner of proceeding, in the beginning, nevertheless negates the classic method of reason, disappoints hope, opens to intuition and to the heart a whole proliferation of phenomena, the wealth of which has about it something inhuman. These paths lead to all sciences or to none. This amounts to saying that in this case the means are more important than the end. All that is involved is 'an attitude for understanding' and not a consolation. Let me repeat: in the beginning, at very least.

How can one fail to feel the basic relationship of these minds! How can one fail to see that they take their stand around a privileged and bitter moment in which hope has no further place? I want everything to be explained to me or nothing. And the reason is impotent when it hears this cry from the heart. The mind aroused by this insistence seeks and finds nothing but contradictions and nonsense. What I fail to understand is nonsense. The world is peopled with such irrationals. The world itself, whose single meaning I do not understand, is but a vast irrational. If one could only say just once: 'this is clear', all would be saved. But these men vie with one another in proclaiming that nothing is clear, all is chaos, that all man has is his lucidity and his definite knowledge of the walls surrounding him.

All these experiences agree and confirm one another. The mind, when it reaches its limits, must make a judgement and choose its conclusions. This is where suicide and the reply stand. But I wish to reverse the order of the inquiry and start out from the intelligent adventure and come back to daily acts. The experiences called to mind here were born in the desert that we must not leave behind. At least it is essential to know how far they went. At this point of his effort man stands face to face with the irrational. He feels within him his longing for happiness and for reason. The absurd is born of this confrontation between the human need and the unreasonable silence of the world. This must not be forgotten. This must be clung to because the whole consequence of a life can depend on it. The irrational, the human nostalgia, and the absurd that is born of their encounter – these are the three characters in the drama that must necessarily end with all the logic of which an existence is capable.

PHILOSOPHICAL SUICIDE

The feeling of the absurd is not, for all that, the notion of the absurd. It lays the foundations for it, and that is all. It is not limited to that notion, except in the brief moment when it passes judgement on the universe. Subsequently it has a chance of going further. It is alive; in other words, it must die or else reverberate. So it is with the themes we have gathered together. But there again what interests me is not words or minds, criticism of which would call for another form and another place, but the discovery of what their conclusions have in common. Never, perhaps, have minds been so different. And yet we recognize as identical the spiritual landscapes in which they get under way. Likewise, despite such dissimilar zones of knowledge, the cry that terminates their itinerary rings out in the same way. It is evident that the thinkers we have just recalled have a common climate. To say that that climate is deadly scarcely amounts to playing on words. Living under that stifling sky forces one to get away or to stay. The important thing is to find out how people get away in the first case and why people stay in the second case. This is how I define the problem of suicide and the possible interest in the conclusions of existential philosophy.

But first I want to detour from the direct path. Up to now we have managed to circumscribe the absurd from the outside. One can, however, wonder how much is clear in that notion and by direct analysis try to discover its meaning on the one hand and, on the other, the consequences it involves.

If I accuse an innocent man of a monstrous crime, if I tell a virtuous man that he has coveted his own sister, he will reply that this is absurd. His indignation has its comical aspect. But it also has its fundamental reason. The virtuous man illustrates by that reply the definitive antinomy existing between the deed I am attributing to him and his lifelong principles. 'It's absurd' means 'It's impossible' but also: 'It's contradictory'. If I see a man armed only with a sword attack a group of machine-guns, I shall consider his act to be absurd. But it is so solely by virtue of the disproportion between his intention and the reality he will encounter, of the contradiction I notice between his true strength and the aim he has in view. Likewise we shall deem a verdict absurd when we contrast it with the verdict the facts apparently dictated. And similarly a demonstration by the absurd is achieved by comparing the consequences of such a reasoning with the logical reality one wants to set up. In all these cases, from the simplest to the most complex, the magnitude of the absurdity will be in direct ratio to the distance between the two terms of my comparison. There are absurd marriages, challenges, rancours, silences, wars and even peace-treaties. For each of them the absurdity springs from a comparison. I am thus justified in saying that the feeling of absurdity does not spring from the mere scrutiny of a fact or an impression but that it bursts from the comparison between a bare fact and a certain reality, between an action and the world that transcends it. The absurd is essentially a divorce. It lies in neither of the elements compared; it is born of their confrontation.

In this particular case and on the plane of intelligence, I can therefore say that the Absurd is not in man (if such a metaphor could have a meaning) nor in the world, but in their presence together. For the moment it is the only bond uniting them. If I wish to limit myself to facts, I know what man wants, I know what the world offers him, and now I can say that I also know what links them. I have no need to dig deeper. A single certainty is enough for the seeker. He simply has to derive all the consequences from it.

The immediate consequence is also a rule of method. The odd trinity brought to light in this way is certainly not a startling discovery. But it resembles the data of experience in that it is both infinitely simple and infinitely complicated. Its first distinguishing feature in this regard is that it cannot be divided. To destroy one of its terms is to destroy the whole. There can be no absurd outside the human mind. Thus, like everything else, the absurd ends with death. But there can be no absurd outside this world either. And it is by this elementary criterion that I judge the notion of the absurd to be essential and consider that it can stand as the first of my truths. The rule of method alluded to above appears here. If I judge that a thing is true, I must preserve it. If I attempt to solve a problem, at least I must not by that very solution conjure away one of the terms of the problem. For me the sole datum is the absurd. The first and, after all, the only condition of my inquiry is to preserve the very thing that crushes me, consequently to respect what I consider essential in it. I have just defined it as a confrontation and an unceasing struggle.

And carrying this absurd logic to its conclusion, I must admit that that struggle implies a total absence of hope (which has nothing to do with despair), a continual rejection (which must not be confused with renunciation), and a conscious dissatisfaction (which must not be compared to immature unrest). Everything that destroys, conjures away, or exercises these requirements (and, to begin with, consent which overthrows divorce) ruins the absurd and devaluates the attitude that may then be proposed. The absurd has meaning only in so far as it is not agreed to.

There exists an obvious fact that seems utterly moral: namely, that a man is always a prey to his truths. Once he has admitted them, he cannot free himself from them. One has to pay something. A man who has become conscious of the absurd is for ever bound to it. A man devoid of hope and conscious of being so has ceased to belong to the future. That is natural. But it is just as natural that he should strive to escape the universe of which he is the creator. All the foregoing has significance only on account of this paradox. Certain men, starting from a critique of rationalism, had admitted the absurd climate. Nothing is more instructive in this regard than to scrutinize the way in which they have elaborated their consequences.

Now, to limit myself to existential philosophies, I see that all of them without exception suggest escape. Through an odd reasoning, starting out from the absurd over the ruins of reason, in a closed universe limited to the human, they deify what crushes them and find reason to hope in what impoverishes them. That forced hope is religious in all of them. It deserves attention.

I shall merely analyse here as examples a few themes dear to Chestov and Kierkegaard. But Jaspers will provide us, in caricatural form, a typical example of this attitude. As a result the rest will be clearer. He is left powerless to realize the transcendent, incapable of plumbing the depth of experience and conscious of that universe upset by failure. Will he advance or at least draw the con-clusions from that failure? He contributes nothing new. He has found nothing in experience but the confession of his own impotence and no occasion to infer any satisfactory principle. Yet without justification, as he says to himself, he suddenly asserts all at once the transcendent, the essence of experience and the super-human significance of life when he writes: 'Does not the failure reveal, beyond any possible explanation and interpretation, not the absence but the existence of transcendence?' That existence which, suddenly and through a blind act of human confidence, explains everything, he defines as 'the unthinkable unity of the general and the particular'. Thus the absurd becomes god (in the broadest meaning of this word) and that inability to understand becomes the existence that illuminates everything. Nothing logically prepares this reasoning. I can call it a leap. And paradoxically can be understood Jaspers' insistence, his infinite patience devoted to making the experience of the transcendent impossible to realize. For the more fleeting that approximation is, the more empty that definition proves to be, the more real that transcendent is to him; for the passion he devotes to asserting it is in direct proportion to the gap between his powers of explanation and the irrationality of the world and of experience. It thus appears that the more bitterly Jaspers destroys the reason's preconceptions the more radically he will explain the world. That apostle of humiliated thought will find at the very end of humiliation the means of regenerating being to its very depth.

Mystical thought has familiarized us with such devices. They are just as legitimate as any attitude of mind. But for the moment I am acting as if I took a certain problem seriously. Without judging beforehand the general value of this attitude or its educative power, I mean simply to consider whether it answers the conditions I set myself, whether it is worthy of the conflict that concerns me. Thus I return to Chestov. A commentator relates a remark of his that deserves interest: 'The only true solution,' he said, 'is precisely where human judgement sees no solution. Otherwise, what need would we have of God? We turn towards God only to obtain the impossible. As for the possible, men suffice.' If there is a Chestovian philosophy, I can say that it is altogether summed up in this way. For when, at the conclusion of his passionate analyses, Chestov discovers the fundamental absurdity of all existence, he does not say: 'This is absurd', but rather 'This is God: we must rely on him even if he does not correspond to any of our rational categories'. So that confusion may not be possible, the Russian philosopher even hints that this God is, perhaps, full of hatred and hateful, incomprehensible and contradictory; but the more hideous is his face the more he asserts his power. His greatness is his incoherence. His proof is his inhumanity. One must spring into him and by this leap free oneself from rational illusions. Thus, for Chestov, acceptance of the absurd is contemporaneous with the absurd itself. Being aware of it amounts to accepting it, and the whole logical effort of his thought is to bring it out so that at the same time the tremendous hope it involves may burst forth. Let me repeat that this attitude is legitimate. But I am persisting here in considering a single problem and all its consequences. I do not have to examine the emotion of a thought or of an act of faith. I have a whole lifetime to do that. I know that the rationalist finds Chestov's attitude annoying. But I also feel that Chestov is right rather than the rationalist and I merely want to know if he remains faithful to the commandments of the absurd.

Now, if it is admitted that the absurd is the contrary of hope, it is seen that existential thought for Chestov presupposes the absurd but proves it only to dispel it. Such subtlety of thought is a conjuror's emotional trick. When Chestov elsewhere sets his absurd in opposition to current morality and reason, he calls it truth and redemption. Hence there is basically in that definition of the absurd an approbation that Chestov grants it. If it is admitted that all the power of that notion lies in the way it runs counter to our elementary hopes, if it is felt that to remain, the absurd requires not to be consented to, then it can be clearly seen that it has lost its true aspect, its human and relative character in order to enter an eternity that is both incomprehensible and satisfying. If there is an absurd, it is in man's universe. The moment the notion transforms itself into eternity's springboard, it ceases to be linked to human lucidity. The absurd is no longer that evidence that man ascertains without consenting to it. The struggle is eluded. Man integrates the absurd and in that condition causes to disappear its essential character which is opposition, laceration and divorce. This leap is an escape. Chestov, who is fond of quoting Hamlet's remark, 'The time is out of joint', writes it down with a sort of savage hope that seems to belong to him in particular. For it is not in this sense that Hamlet says it or Shakespeare writes it. The intoxication of the irrational and the vocation of rapture turn a lucid mind away from the absurd. To Chestov reason is useless but there is something beyond reason. To an absurd mind reason is useless and there is nothing beyond reason.

This leap can at least enlighten us a little more as to the true nature of the absurd. We know that it is worthless except in an equilibrium, that it is above all in the comparison and not in the terms of that comparison. But it so happens that Chestov puts all the emphasis on one of the terms and destroys the equilibrium. Our appetite for understanding, our nostalgia for the absolute are explicable only in so far, precisely, as we can understand and explain many things. It is useless to negate the reason absolutely. It has its order in which it is efficacious. It is properly that of human experience. Whence we wanted to make everything clear. If we cannot do so, if the absurd is born on that occasion, it is born precisely at the very meeting-point of that efficacious but limited reason with the ever-resurgent irrational. Now, when Chestov rises up against a Hegelian proposition such as 'the motion of the solar system takes place in conformity with immutable laws and those laws are its reason', when he devotes all his passion to upsetting Spinoza's rationalism, he concludes, in effect, in favour of the vanity of all reason. Whence, by a natural and illegitimate reversal, to the pre-eminence of the irrational.[5] But the transition is not evident. For here may intervene the notion of limit and the notion of level. The laws of nature may be operative up to a certain limit, beyond which they turn against themselves to give birth to the absurd. Or else, they may justify themselves on the level of description without for that reason being true on the level of explanation. Everything is sacrificed here to the irrational, and, the demand for clarity being conjured away, the absurd disappears with one of the terms of its comparison. The absurd man on the other hand does not undertake such a levelling process. He recognizes the struggle, does not absolutely scorn reason and admits the irrational. Thus he again embraces in a single glance all the data of experience and he is little inclined to leap before knowing. He knows simply that in that alert awareness there is no further place for hope.

What is perceptible in Leo Chestov will be perhaps even more so in Kierkegaard. To be sure, it is hard to outline clear propositions in so elusive a writer. But, despite apparently opposed writings, beyond the pseudonyms, the tricks and the smiles, can be felt throughout that work as it were the presentiment (at the same time as the apprehension) of a truth which eventually bursts forth in the last works: Kierkegaard likewise takes the leap. His childhood having been so frightened by Christianity, he ultimately returns to its harshest aspect. For him, too, antinomy and paradox become criteria of the religious. Thus the very thing that led to despair of the meaning and depth of this life now gives it its truth and its clarity. Christianity is the scandal, and what Kierkegaard calls for quite plainly is the third sacrifice required by Ignatius Loyola, the one in which God most rejoices: 'The sacrifice of the intellect.'[6] This effect of the 'leap' is odd but must not surprise us any longer. He makes of the absurd the criterion of the other world, whereas it is simply a residue of the experience of this world. 'In his failure,' says Kierkegaard, 'the believer finds his triumph.'

It is not for me to wonder to what stirring preaching this attitude is linked. I merely have to wonder if the spectacle of the absurd and its own character justifies it. On this point, I know that it is not so. Upon considering again the content of the absurd, one understands better the method that inspired Kierkegaard. Between the irrational of the world and the insurgent nostalgia of the absurd, he does not maintain the equilibrium. He does not respect the relationship that constitutes properly speaking the feeling of absurdity. Sure of being unable to escape the irrational, he wants at least to save himself from that desperate nostalgia that seems to him sterile and devoid of implication. But if he may be right on this point in his judgement, he could not be in his negation. If he substitutes for his cry of revolt a frantic adherence, at once he is led to blind himself to the absurd which hitherto enlightened him and to deify the only certainty he henceforth possesses, the irrational. The important thing, as Abbé Galiani said to Mme d'Epinay, is not to be cured, but to live with one's ailments. Kierkegaard wants to be cured. To be cured is his frenzied wish and it runs throughout his whole journal. The entire effort of his intelligence is to escape the antinomy of the human condition. An all the more desperate effort since he intermittently perceives its vanity when he speaks of himself, as if neither fear of God nor piety were capable of bringing him to peace. Thus it is that, through a strained subterfuge, he gives the irrational the appearance and God the attributes of the absurd: unjust, incoherent and incomprehensible. Intelligence alone in him strives to stifle the underlying demands of the human heart. Since nothing is proved, everything can be proved.

Indeed, Kierkegaard himself shows us the path taken. I do not want to suggest anything here, but how can one fail to read in his works the signs of an almost intentional mutilation of the soul to balance the mutilation accepted in regard to the absurd? It is the leitmotiv of the *Journal*. 'What I lacked was the animal which *also* belongs to human destiny . . . But give me a body then.' And further on: 'Oh! especially in my early youth what should I not have given to be a man, even for six months . . . what I lack, basically, is a body and the physical conditions of existence.' Elsewhere, the same man nevertheless adopts the great cry of hope that has come down through so many centuries and quickened so many hearts, except that of the absurd man. 'But for the Christian death is certainly not the end of everything and it implies infinitely more hope than life implies for us, even when that life is overflowing with health and vigour.' Reconciliation through scandal is still reconciliation. It allows one, perhaps, as can be seen, to derive hope of its contrary which is death. But even if fellow-feeling inclines one towards that attitude, still it must be said that excess justifies nothing. That transcends, as the saying goes, the human scale; therefore it must be superhuman. But this 'therefore' is superfluous. There is no logical certainty here. There is no experimental probability either. All I can say is that, in fact, that transcends my scale. If I do not draw a negation from it, at least I do not want to found anything on the incomprehensible. I want to know whether I can live with what I know and with that alone. I am told again that here the intelligence must sacrifice its pride and the reason bow down. But if I recognize the limits of the reason. I do not therefore negate it, recognizing its relative powers. I merely want to remain in this middle path where the intelligence can remain clear. If that is its pride, I see no sufficient reason for giving it up. Nothing more profound, for example, than Kierkegaard's view according to which despair is not a fact but a state: the very state of sin. For sin is what alienates from God. The absurd, which is the metaphysical state of the conscious man, does not lead to God.[7] Perhaps this notion will become clearer if I risk this shocking statement: the absurd is sin without God.

It is a matter of living in that state of the absurd. I know on what it is founded, this mind and this world straining against each other without being able to embrace each other. I ask for the rule of life of that state and what I am offered neglects its basis, negates one of the terms of the painful opposition, demands of me a resignation. I ask what is involved in the condition I recognize as mine; I know it implies obscurity and ignorance; and I am assured that this ignorance explains everything and that this darkness is my light. But there is no reply here to my intent and this stirring lyricism cannot hide the paradox from me. One must therefore turn away. Kierkegaard may shout in warning: 'If man had no eternal consciousness, if, at the bottom of everything, there were merely a wild, seething force producing everything, both large and trifling, in the storm of dark passions, if the bottomless void that nothing can fill underlay all things, what would life be but despair?' This cry is not likely to stop the absurd man. Seeking what is true is not seeking what is desirable. If in order to elude the anxious question: 'What would life be?' one must, like the donkey, feed on the roses of illusion, then the absurd mind, rather than resigning itself to falsehood, prefers to adopt fearlessly Kierkegaard's reply: 'despair'. Everything considered, a determined soul will always manage.

I am taking the liberty at this point of calling the existential attitude philosophical suicide. But this does not imply a judgement. It is a convenient way of indicating the movement by which a thought negates itself and tends to transcend itself in its very negation. For the existentials negation is their

God. To be precise, that god is maintained only through the negation of human reason.[8] But like suicides, gods change with men. There are many ways of leaping, the essential being to leap. Those redeeming negations, those ultimate contradictions which negate the obstacle that has not yet been leapt over, may spring just as well (this is the paradox at which this reasoning aims) from a certain religious inspiration as from rational order. They always lay claim to the eternal and it is solely in this that they take the leap.

It must be repeated that the reasoning developed in this essay leaves out altogether the most widespread spiritual attitude of our enlightened age: the one, based on the principle that all is reason, which aims to explain the world. It is natural to give a clear view of the world after accepting the idea that it must be clear. That is even legitimate but does not concern the reasoning we are following out here. In fact, our aim is to shed light upon the step taken by the mind when, starting from a philosophy of the world's lack of meaning, it ends up by finding a meaning and depth in it. The most touching of those steps is religious in essence; it becomes obvious in the theme of the irrational. But the most paradoxical and most significant is certainly the one that attributes rational reasons to a world it originally imagined as devoid of any guiding principle. It is impossible in any case to reach the consequences that concern us without having given an idea of this new attainment of the spirit of nostalgia.

I shall examine merely the theme of 'the Intention' made fashionable by Husserl and the phenomenologists. I have already alluded to it. Originally Husserl's method negates the classic procedure of the reason. Let me repeat. Thinking is not unifying or making the appearance familiar under the guise of a great principle. Thinking is learning all over again how to see, directing one's consciousness, making of every image a privileged place. In other words, phenomenology declines to explain the world, it wants to be merely a description of actual experience. It confirms absurd thought in its initial assertion that there is no truth, but merely truths. From the evening breeze to this hand on my shoulder, everything has its truth. Consciousness illuminates it by paying attention to it. Consciousness does not form the object of its understanding, it merely focuses, it is the act of attention and, to borrow a Bergsonian image, it resembles the projector that suddenly focuses on an image. The difference is that there is no scenario but a successive and incoherent illustration. In that magic lantern all the pictures are privileged. Consciousness suspends in experience the objects of its attention. Through its miracle it isolates them. Henceforth they are beyond all judgements. This is the 'intention' that characterizes consciousness. But the word does not imply any idea of finality; it is taken in its sense of 'direction': its only face value is topographical.

At first sight, it certainly seems that in this way nothing contradicts the absurd spirit. That apparent modesty of thought that limits itself to describing what it declines to explain, that intentional discipline whence results paradoxically a profound enrichment of experience and the rebirth of the world in its prolixity are absurd procedures. At least at first sight. For methods of thought, in this case as elsewhere, always assume two aspects, one psychological and the other metaphysical.[9] Thereby they harbour two truths. If the theme of the intentional claims to illustrate merely a psychological attitude, by which reality is drained instead of being explained, nothing in fact separates it from the absurd spirit. It aims to enumerate what it cannot transcend. It affirms solely that without any unifying principle thought can still take delight in describing and understanding every aspect of experience. The truth involved then for each of those aspects is psychological in nature. It simply testifies to the 'interest' that reality can offer. It is a way of awaking a sleeping world and of making it vivid to the mind. But if one attempts to extend and give a rational basis to that notion of truth, if one claims to discover in this way the 'essence' of each object of knowledge, one restores its depth to experience. For an absurd mind that is incomprehensible. Now it is this wavering between modesty and assurance that is noticeable in the intentional attitude and this shimmering of phenomenological thought will illustrate the absurd reasoning better than anything else.

For Husserl speaks likewise of 'extra-temporal essences' brought to light by the intention, and he sounds like Plato. All things are not explained by one thing but by all things. I see no difference. To be sure those ideas or those essences that consciousness 'effectuates' at the end of every description are not yet to be considered perfect models. But it is asserted that they are directly present in each datum of perception. There is no longer a single idea explaining everything but an infinite number of essences giving a meaning to an infinite number of objects. The world comes to a stop, but also lights up. Platonic realism becomes intuitive but it is still realism. Kierkegaard was swallowed up in his God; Parmenides plunged thought into the One. But here thought hurls itself into an abstract polytheism. But this is not all: hallucinations and fictions likewise belong to 'extra-temporal essences'. In the new world of ideas, the species of centaur collaborates with the more modest species of metropolitan man.

For the absurd man, there was a truth as well as a bitterness in that purely psychological opinion that all aspects of the world are privileged. To say that everything is privileged is tantamount to saying that everything is equivalent. But the metaphysical aspect of that truth is so far-reaching, that through an elementary reaction, he feels closer perhaps to Plato. He is taught, in fact, that every image presupposes an equally privileged essence. In this ideal world without hierarchy, the formal army is composed solely of generals. To be sure, transcendency had been eliminated. But a sudden shift in thought brings back into the world a sort of fragmentary immanence which restores to the universe its depth.

Am I to fear having carried too far a theme handled with greater circumspection by its creators? I read merely these assertions of Husserl, apparently paradoxical yet rigorously logical if what precedes is accepted: 'That which is true is true absolutely, in itself; truth is one, identical to itself, however different the creatures who perceive it, men, monsters, angels or gods.' Reason triumphs and trumpets forth with that voice, I cannot deny. What can its assertions mean in the absurd world? The perception of an angel or a god has no meaning for me. That geometrical spot where divine reason ratifies mine will always be incomprehensible to me. There, too, I discern a leap and, though performed in the abstract, it nonetheless means for me forgetting just what I do not want to forget. When further on Husserl exclaims: 'If all masses subject to attraction were to disappear, the law of attraction would not be destroyed but would simply remain without any possible application', I know that I am faced with a metaphysic of consolation. And if I want to discover the point where thought leaves the path of evidence, I have only to reread the parallel reasoning that Husserl voices regarding the mind: 'If we could contemplate clearly the exact laws of psychic processes, they would be seen to be likewise eternal and invariable, like the basic laws of theoretical natural science. Hence they would be valid even if there were no psychic process.' Even if the mind were not, its laws would be! I see then that of a psychological truth Husserl aims to make a rational rule: after having denied the integrating power of human reason, he leaps by this expedient to eternal Reason.

Husserl's theme of the 'concrete universe' cannot then surprise me. If I am told that all essences are not formal, but that some are material, that the first are the object of logic and the second of science, this is merely a question of definition. The abstract, I am told, indicates but a part, without consistency in itself, of a concrete universal. But the wavering already noted allows me to throw light on the confusion of these terms. For that may mean that the concrete object of my attention, this sky, the reflection of that water on this coat alone preserve the prestige of the real that my interest isolates in the world. And I shall not deny it. But that may mean also that this coat itself is universal, has its particular and sufficient essence, belongs to the world of forms. I then realize that merely the order of the procession has been changed. This world has ceased to have its reflection in a higher universe, but the heaven of forms is figured in the host of images of this earth. This changes nothing for me. Rather than encountering here a taste for the concrete, the meaning of the human condition, I find an intellectualism sufficiently unbridled to generalize the concrete itself.

It is futile to be amazed by the apparent paradox that leads thought to its own negation by the opposite paths of humiliated reason and triumphal reason. From the abstract god of Husserl to the dazzling god of Kierkegaard the distance is not so great. Reason and the irrational lead to the same preaching. In truth the way matters but little; the will to arrive suffices. The abstract philosopher and the religious philosopher start out from the same disorder and support each other in the same anxiety. But the essential is to explain. Nostalgia is stronger here than knowledge. It is significant that the thought of the epoch is at once one of the most deeply imbued with a philosophy of the non-significance of the world and one of the most divided in its conclusions. It is constantly oscillating between extreme rationalization of reality which tends to break up that thought into standard reasons and its extreme irrationalization which tends to deify it. But this divorce is only apparent. It is a matter of reconciliation, and, in both cases, the leap suffices. It is always wrongly thought that the notion of reason is a one-way notion. To tell the truth, however rigorous it may be in its ambition, this concept is nonetheless just as unstable as others. Reason bears a quite human aspect, but it also is able to turn towards the divine. Since Plotinus, who was the first to reconcile it with the eternal climate, it has learned to turn away from the most cherished of its principles, which is contradiction, in order to integrate into it the strangest, the quite magic one of participation.[10] It is an instrument of thought and not thought itself. Above all, a man's thought is his nostalgia.

Just as reason was able to soothe the melancholy of Plotinus, it provides modern anguish the means of calming itself in the familiar setting of the eternal. The absurd mind has less luck. For it the world is neither so rational nor so irrational. It is unreasonable and only that. With Husserl the reason eventually has no limits at all. The absurd on the contrary establishes its limits since it is powerless to calm its anguish. Kierkegaard independently asserts that a single limit is enough to negate that anguish. But the absurd does not go so far. For it that limit is directed solely at the reason's ambitions. The theme of the irrational, as it is conceived by the existentialists, is reason becoming confused and escaping by negating itself. The absurd is lucid reason noting its limits.

Only at the end of this difficult path does the absurd man recognize his true motives. Upon comparing his inner exigence and what is then offered him, he suddenly feels he is going to turn away. In the universe of Husserl the world becomes clear and that longing for familiarity that man's heart harbours becomes useless. In Kierkegaard's apocalypse that desire for clarity must be given up if it wants to be satisfied. Sin is not so much knowing (if it were, everybody would be innocent) as wanting to know. Indeed, it is the only sin of which the absurd man can feel that it constitutes both his guilt and his innocence. He is offered a solution in which all the past contradictions have become merely polemical games. But this is not the way he experienced them. Their truth must be preserved, which consists in not being satisfied. He does not want preaching.

My reasoning wants to be faithful to the evidence that aroused it. That evidence is the absurd. It is that divorce between the mind that desires and the world that disappoints, my nostalgia for unity, this fragmented universe and the contradiction that binds them together. Kierkegaard suppresses my nostalgia and Husserl gathers together that universe. That is not what I was expecting. It was a matter of living and thinking with those dislocations, of knowing whether one had to accept or refuse. There can be no question of masking the evidence, of suppressing the absurd by denying one of the terms of its equation. It is essential to know whether one can live with it or whether, on the other hand, logic commands one to die of it. I am not interested in philosophical suicide but rather in plain suicide. I merely wish to purge it of its emotional content and know its logic and its integrity. Any other position implies for the absurd mind deceit and the mind's retreat before what the mind itself has brought to light. Husserl claims to obey the desire to escape 'the inveterate habit of living and thinking in certain well-known and convenient conditions of existence', but the final leap restores in him the eternal and its comfort. The leap does not represent an extreme danger as Kierkegaard would like it to do. The danger, on the contrary, lies in the subtle instant that precedes the leap. Being able to remain on that dizzying crest – that is integrity and the rest is subterfuge. I know also that never has helplessness inspired such striking harmonies as those of Kierkegaard. But if helplessness has its place in the in different landscapes of history, it has none in a reasoning whose exigence is now known.

ABSURD FREEDOM

Now the main thing is done, I hold certain facts from which I cannot separate. What I know, what is certain, what I cannot deny, what I cannot reject – this is what counts. I can negate everything of that part of me that lives on vague nostalgias, except this desire for unity, this longing to solve, this need for clarity and cohesion. I can refute everything in this world surrounding me that offends or enraptures me, except this chaos, this sovereign chance and this divine equivalence which springs from anarchy. I don't know whether this world has a meaning that transcends it. But I know that I do not know that meaning and that it is impossible for me just now to know it. What can a meaning outside my condition mean to me? I can understand only in human terms. What I touch, what resists me – that is what I understand. And these two certainties – my appetite for the absolute and for unity and the impossibility of reducing this world to a rational and reasonable principle – I also know that I cannot reconcile them. What other truth can I admit without lying, without bringing in a hope I lack, which means nothing within the limits of my condition?

If I were a tree among trees, a cat among animals, this life would have a meaning or rather this problem would not arise, for I should belong to this world. I should *be* this world to which I am now opposed by my whole consciousness and my whole insistence upon familiarity. This ridiculous reason is what sets me in opposition to all creation. I cannot cross it out with a stroke of the pen. What I believe to be true I must therefore preserve. What seems to me so obvious, even against me, I must support. And what constitutes the basis of that conflict, of that break between the world and my mind, but the awareness of it? If, therefore, I want to preserve it, I can, through a constant awareness, ever revived, ever alert. This is what, for the moment, I must remember. At this moment the absurd, so obvious and yet so hard to win, returns to a man's life and finds its home there. At this moment, too, the mind can leave the arid, dried-up path of lucid effort. That path now emerges in daily life. It encounters the world of the anonymous impersonal pronoun 'one', but henceforth man enters in with his revolt and his lucidity. He has forgotten how to cope. This hell of the present is his Kingdom at last. All problems recover their sharp edge. Abstract evidence retreats before the poetry of forms and colours. Spiritual conflicts become embodied and return to the abject and magnificent shelter of man's heart. None of them is settled. But all are transfigured. Is one going to die, escape by the leap, rebuild a mansion of ideas and forms to one's own scale? Is one on the contrary going to take up the heartrending and marvellous wager of the absurd? Let's make a final effort in this regard and draw all our conclusions. The body, affection, creation, action, human nobility will then resume their places in this mad world. At last man will again find there the wine of the absurd and the bread of indifference on which he feeds his greatness.

Let us insist again on the method: it is a matter of persisting. At a certain point on his path the absurd man is tempted. History is not lacking in either religions or prophets, even without gods. He is asked to leap. All he can reply is that he doesn't fully understand, that it is not obvious. Indeed, he does not want to do anything but what he fully understands. He is assured that this is the sin of pride, but he does not understand the notion of sin; that perhaps hell is in store, but he has not enough imagination to visualize that strange future; that he is losing immortal life, but that seems to him an idle consideration. An attempt is made to get him to admit his guilt. He feels innocent. To tell the truth, that is all he feels – his irreparable innocence. This is what allows him everything. Hence what he demands of himself is to live *solely* with what he knows, to accommodate himself to what is and to bring in nothing that is not certain. He is told that nothing is. But this at least is a certainty. And it is with this that he is concerned: he wants to find out if it is possible to live *without appeal*.

Now I can broach the notion of suicide. It has already been felt what solution might be given. At this point the problem is reversed. It was previously a question of finding out whether or not life had to have a meaning to be lived. It now becomes clear on the contrary that it will be lived all the better if it has no meaning. Living an experience, a particular fate, is accepting it fully. Now, no one will live this fate, knowing it to be absurd, unless he does everything to keep before him that absurd brought to light by consciousness. Negating one of the terms of the opposition on which he lives amounts to escaping it. To abolish conscious revolt is to elude the problem. The theme of permanent revolution is thus carried into individual experience. Living is keeping the absurd alive. Keeping it alive is above all contemplating it. Unlike Eurydice, the absurd dies only when we turn away from it. One of the only coherent philosophical positions is thus revolt. It is a constant confrontation between man and his own obscurity. It is an insistence upon an impossible transparency. It challenges the world anew every second. Just as danger provided man with the unique opportunity of seizing awareness, so metaphysical revolt extends awareness to the whole of experience. It is that constant presence of man in his own eyes. It is not aspiration, for it is devoid of hope. That revolt is the certainty of a crushing fate, without the resignation that ought to accompany it.

This is where it is seen to what a degree absurd experience is remote from suicide. It may be thought that suicide follows revolt – but wrongly. For it does not represent the logical outcome of revolt. It is just the contrary by the consent it presupposes. Suicide, like the leap, is acceptance at its extreme. Everything is over and man returns to his essential history. His future, his unique and dreadful future – he sees and rushes towards it. In its way, suicide settles the absurd. It engulfs the absurd in the same death. But I know that in order to keep alive, the absurd cannot be settled. It escapes suicide to the extent that it is simultaneously awareness and rejection of death. It is, at the extreme limit of the condemned man's last thought, that shoelace that despite everything he sees a few yards away, on the very brink of his dizzying fall. The contrary of suicide, in fact, is the man condemned to death.

That revolt gives life its value. Spread out over the whole length of a life, it restores its majesty to that life. To a man devoid of blinkers, there is no finer sight than that of the intelligence at grips with a reality that transcends it. The sight of human pride is unequalled. No disparagement is of any use. That discipline that the mind imposes on itself, that will conjured up out of nothing, that face-to-face struggle have something exceptional about them. To impoverish that reality whose inhumanity constitutes man's majesty is tantamount to impoverishing him himself. I understand then why the doctrines that explain everything to me also debilitate me at the same time. They relieve me of the weight of my own life and yet I must carry it alone. At this juncture, I cannot conceive that a sceptical metaphysics can be joined to an ethics of renunciation.

Consciousness and revolt, these rejections are the contrary of renunciation. Everything that is indomitable and passionate in a human heart quickens them, on the contrary, with its own life. It is essential to die unreconciled and not of one's own free will. Suicide is a repudiation. The absurd man can only drain everything to the bitter end, and deplete himself. The absurd is his extreme tension which he maintains constantly by solitary effort, for he knows that in that consciousness and in that day-to-day revolt he gives proof of his only truth which is defiance. This is a first consequence.

If I remain in that prearranged position which consists in drawing all the conclusions (and nothing else) involved in a newly discovered notion, I am faced with a second paradox. In order to remain faithful to that method, I have nothing to do with the problem of metaphysical liberty. Knowing whether or not man is free doesn't interest me. I can experience only my own freedom. As to it, I can have no general notions, but merely a few clear insights. The problem of 'freedom as such' has no meaning. For it is linked in quite a different way with the problem of God. Knowing whether or not man is free involves knowing whether he can have a master. The absurdity peculiar to this problem comes from the fact that the very notion that makes the problem of freedom possible also takes away all its meaning. For in the presence of God there is less a problem of freedom than a problem of evil. You know the alternative: either we are not free and God the all-powerful is responsible for evil. Or we are free and responsible but God is not all-powerful. All the scholastic subtleties have neither added anything to nor subtracted anything from the acuteness of this paradox.

This is why I cannot get lost in the glorification or the mere definition of a notion which eludes me and loses its meaning as soon as it goes beyond the frame of reference of my individual experience. I cannot understand what kind of freedom would be given me by a higher being. I have lost the sense of hierarchy. The only conception of freedom I can have is that of the prisoner or the individual in the midst of the State. The only one I know is freedom of thought and action. Now if the absurd cancels all my chances of eternal freedom, it restores and magnifies on the other hand my freedom of action. That privation of hope and future means an increase in man's availability.

Before encountering the absurd, the everyday man lives with aims, a concern for the future or for justification (with regard to whom or what is not the question). He weighs his chances, he counts on 'someday', his retirement or the labour of his sons. He still thinks that something in his life can be directed. In truth, he acts as if he were free, even if all the facts make a point of contradicting that liberty. But after the absurd, everything is upset. That idea that 'I am', my way of acting as if everything has a meaning (even if, on occasion, I said that nothing has) – all that is given the lie in vertiginous fashion by the absurdity of a possible death. Thinking of the future, establishing aims for oneself, having preferences – all this presupposes a belief in freedom, even if one occasionally ascertains that one doesn't feel it. But at that moment I am well aware that that higher liberty, that freedom *to be*, which alone can serve as basis for a truth, does not exist. Death is there as the only reality. After death the chips are down. I am not even free either to perpetuate myself, but a slave, and above all a slave without hope of an eternal revolution, without recourse to contempt. And who without revolution and without contempt can remain a slave? What freedom can exist in the fullest sense without assurance of eternity?

But at the same time the absurd man realizes that hitherto he was bound to that postulate of freedom on the illusion of which he was living. In a certain sense, that hampered him. To the extent to which he imagined a purpose to his life, he adapted himself to the demands of a purpose to be achieved and became the slave of his liberty. Thus I could not act otherwise than as the father (or the engineer or the leader of a nation, or the post-office sub-clerk) that I am preparing to be. I think I can choose to be that rather than something else. I think so unconsciously, to be sure. But at the same time, I strengthen my postulate with the beliefs of those around me, with the presumptions of my human environment (others are so sure of being free and that cheerful mood is so contagious!). However far one may remain from any presumption, moral or social, one is partly influenced by them and even, for the best among them (there are good and bad presumptions), one adapts one's life to them. Thus the absurd man *realizes* that he *was* not really free. To speak clearly, to the extent to which

I hope, to which I worry about a truth that might be individual to me, about a way of being or creating, to the extent to which I arrange my life and prove thereby that I accept its having a meaning, I create for myself barriers between which I confine my life. I do as do so many bureaucrats of the mind and heart who only fill me with disgust and whose only vice, I now see clearly, is to take man's freedom seriously.

The absurd enlightens me on this point: there is no future. Henceforth this is the reason for my inner freedom. I shall use two comparisons here. Mystics, to begin with, find freedom in giving themselves. By losing themselves in their god, by accepting his rules, they become secretly free. In spontaneously accepted slavery they recover a deeper independence. But what does that freedom mean? It may be said above all that they *feel* free with regard to themselves and not so much free as liberated. Likewise, completely turned towards death (taken here as the most obvious absurdity), the absurd man feels released from everything outside that passionate attention crystallizing in him. He enjoys a freedom with regard to common rules. It can be seen at this point that the initial themes of existential philosophy keep their entire value. The return to consciousness, the escape from everyday sleep represent the first steps of absurd freedom. But it is existential *preaching* that is alluded to and with it that spiritual leap which basically escapes consciousness. In the same way (this is my second comparison) the slaves of antiquity did not belong to themselves. But they knew that freedom which consists in not feeling responsible.[11] Death, too, has patrician hands which, while crushing, also liberate.

Losing oneself in that bottomless certainty, feeling henceforth sufficiently remote from one's own life to increase it and take a broad view of it – this involves the principle of a liberation. Such new independence has a definite time-limit, like any freedom of action. It does not write a cheque on eternity. But it takes the place of the illusions of *freedom*, which all stopped with death. The divine availability of the condemned man before whom the prison doors open in a certain early dawn, that unbelievable disinterestedness with regard to everything except for the pure flame of life – it is clear that death and the absurd are here the principles of the only reasonable freedom: that which a human heart can experience and live. This is a second consequence. The absurd man thus catches sight of a burning and frigid, transparent and limited universe in which nothing is possible but everything is given, and beyond which all is collapse and nothingness. He can then decide to accept such a universe and draw from it his strength, his refusal to hope, and the unyielding evidence of a life without consolation.

But what does life mean in such a universe? Nothing else for the moment but indifference to the future and a desire to use up everything that is given. Belief in the meaning of life always implies a scale of values, a choice, our preferences. Belief in the absurd, according to our definitions, teaches the contrary. But this is worth examining.

Knowing whether or not one can live *without appeal* is all that interests me. I do not want to get out of my depth. This aspect of life being given me, can I adapt myself to it? Now, faced with this particular concern, belief in the absurd is tantamount to substituting the quantity of experiences for the quality. If I convince myself that this life has no other aspect than that of the absurd, if I feel that its whole equilibrium depends on that perpetual opposition between my conscious revolt and the darkness in which it struggles, if I admit that my freedom has no meaning except in relation to its limited fate, then I must say that what counts is not the best living but the most living. It is not up to me to wonder if this is vulgar or revolting, elegant or deplorable. Once and for all, value judgements are discarded here in favour of factual judgements. I have merely to draw the conclusions from what I can see and to risk nothing that is hypothetical. Supposing that living in this way were not honourable, then true propriety would command me to be dishonourable.

The most living; in the broadest sense, that rule means nothing. It calls for definition. It seems to begin with the fact that the notion of quantity has not been sufficiently explored. For it can account for a large share of human experience. A man's rule of conduct and his scale of values have no meaning except through the quantity and variety of experiences he has been in a position to accumulate. Now the conditions of modern life impose on the majority of men the same quantity of experiences and consequently the same profound experience. To be sure, there must also be taken into consideration the individual's spontaneous contribution, the 'given' element in him. But I cannot judge of that, and let me repeat that my rule here is to get along with the immediate evidence. I see then that the individual character of a common code of ethics lies not so much in the ideal importance of its basic principles as in the norm of an experience that it is possible to measure. To stretch a point somewhat, the Greeks had the code of their leisure just as we have the code of our eight-hour day. But already many men among the most tragic cause us to foresee that a longer experience changes this table of values. They make us imagine that adventurer of the everyday who through mere quantity of experiences would break all records (I am purposely using this sports expression) and would thus win his own code of ethics.[12] Yet let us avoid romanticism and just ask ourselves just what such an attitude may mean to a man with his mind made up to take up his bet and to observe strictly what he takes to be the rules of the game.

Breaking all the records is first and foremost being faced with the world as often as possible. How can that be done without contradictions and without playing on words? For on the one hand the absurd teaches that all experiences are unimportant and, on the other, it urges towards the greatest quantity of experiences. How then can one fail to do as did so many of those men I was speaking of earlier – choose the form of life that brings us the most possible of that human matter, thereby introducing a scale of values that on the other hand one claims to reject?

But again it is the absurd and its contradictory life that teaches us. For the mistake is thinking that that quantity of experiences depends on the circumstances of our life when it depends solely on us. Here we have to be over simple. To two men living the same number of years, the world always provides the same sum of experiences. It is up to us to be conscious of them. Being aware of one's life, one's revolt, one's freedom, and to the maximum, is living, and to the maximum. Where lucidity dominates, the scale of values becomes useless. Let's be even more simple. Let us say that the sole obstacle, the sole deficiency to be made good, is constituted by premature death. Thus it is that no depth, no emotion, no passion and no sacrifice could render equal in the eyes of the absurd man (even if he wished it so) a conscious life of forty years and a lucidity spread over sixty years.[13]? Madness and death are his irreparables. Man does not choose. The absurd and the extra life it involves *therefore do not depend on man's will* but on its contrary which is death[14]. Weighing words carefully, it is altogether a question of luck. One just has to be able to consent to this. There will never be any substitute for twenty years of life and experience.

But with an inconsistency odd in such an alert race, the Greeks claimed that those who died young were beloved of the gods. And that is true only if you are willing to believe that entering the ridiculous world of the gods is for ever losing the purest of joys which is feeling, and feeling on this earth. The present and the succession of presents before a constantly conscious soul is the ideal of the absurd man. But the word ideal rings false in this connection. It is not even his vocation but merely the third consequence of his reasoning. Having started from an anguished awareness of the inhuman, the meditation on the absurd returns at the end of its itinerary to the very heart of the passionate flames of human revolt.[15]

Thus I draw from the absurd three consequences which are my revolt, my freedom and my passion. By the mere activity of consciousness I transform into a rule of life what was an invitation to death – and I refuse suicide. I know, to be sure, the dull resonance that vibrates throughout these days. Yet I have but a word to say: that it is necessary. When Nietzsche writes: 'It clearly seems that the chief thing in heaven and on earth is to *obey* at length and in a single direction: in the long run there results something for which it is worth the trouble of living on this earth as, for example, virtue, art, music, the dance, reason, the mind – something that transfigures, something delicate, mad, or divine,' he elucidates the rule of a really distinguished code of ethics. But he also points the way of the absurd man. Obeying the flame is both the easiest and the hardest thing to do. However, it is good for man to judge himself occasionally. He is alone in being able to do so.

'Prayer,' says Alain, 'is when night descends over thought.' 'But the mind must meet the night,' reply the mystics and the existentials. Yes indeed, but not that night that is born under closed eyelids and through the mere will of man – dark, impenetrable night that the mind calls up in order to plunge into it. If it must encounter a night, let it be rather that of despair which remains lucid – polar night, vigil of the mind – whence will arise perhaps that white and virginal brightness which outlines every object in the light of the intelligence. At that degree, equivalence encounters passionate understanding. Then it is no longer even a question of judging the existential leap. It resumes its place amidst the age-old fresco of human attitudes. For the spectator, if he is conscious, that leap is still absurd. In so far as it thinks it solves the paradox, it reinstates it intact. On this score, it is stirring. On this score, everything resumes its place and the absurd world is reborn in all its splendour and diversity.

But it is bad to stop, hard to be satisfied with a single way of seeing, to go without contradiction, perhaps the most subtle of all spiritual forces. The preceding merely defines a way of thinking. But the point is to live.

NOTES

1. From the point of view of the relative value of truth. On the other hand, from the point of view of virile behaviour, this scholar's fragility may well make us smile.
2. Let us not miss this opportunity to point out the relative character of this essay. Suicide may, indeed, be related to much more honourable considerations – for example, the political suicides of protest, as they were called, during the Chinese revolution.
3. I have heard of an emulator of Peregrinos, a post-war writer who, after having finished his first book, committed suicide to attract attention to his work. Attention was in fact attracted, but the book was judged no good.
4. But not in the proper sense. This is not a definition, but rather an *enumeration* of the feelings that may admit of the absurd. Still, the enumeration finished, the absurd has nevertheless not been exhausted.
5. Apropos of the notion of exception particularly and against Aristotle.
6. It may be thought that I am neglecting here the essential problem, that of faith. But I am not examining the philosophy of Kierkegaard, or of Chestov, or, later on, of Husserl (this would call for a different place and a different attitude of mind); I am simply borrowing a theme from them and examining whether its consequences can fit the already established rules. It is merely a matter of persistence.
7. I did not say 'excludes God', which would still amount to asserting.
8. Let me assert again: it is not the affirmation of God that is questioned here, but rather the logic leading to the affirmation.
9. Even the most rigorous epistemologies imply metaphysics. And to such a degree that the metaphysic of many contemporary thinkers consists in having nothing but an epistemology.
10. A. – At that time reason had to adapt itself or die. It adapts itself. With Plotinus, after being logical it becomes aesthetic. Metaphor takes the place of the syllogism.
    B. – Moreover, this is not Plotinus' only contribution to phenomenology. This whole attitude is already contained in the concept so dear to the Alexandrian thinker that there is not only an idea of man but also an idea of Socrates.
11. I am concerned here with a factual comparison, not with an apology of humility. The absurd man is the contrary of the reconciled man.
12. Quantity sometimes constitutes quality. If I can believe the latest restatements of scientific theory, all matter is constituted by centres of energy. Their greater or lesser quantity makes its specificity more or less remarkable. A billion ions and one ion differ not only in quantity but also in quality. It is easy to find an analogy in human experience.

13. Same reflection on a notion as different as the idea of eternal nothingness. It neither adds anything to nor subtracts anything from reality. In psychological experience of nothingness, it is by the consideration of what will happen in 2,000 years that our own nothingness truly takes on meaning. In one of its aspects, eternal nothingness is made up precisely of the sum of lives to come which will not be ours.

14. The will is only the agent here: it tends to maintain consciousness. It provides a discipline of life and that is appreciable.

15. What matters is coherence. We start out here from acceptance of the world. But Oriental thought teaches that one can indulge in the same effort of logic by choosing *against* the world. That is just as legitimate and gives this essay its perspectives and its limits. But when the negation of the world is pursued just as rigorously one often achieves (in certain Vedantic schools) similar results regarding, for instance, the indifference of works. In a book of great importance, *Le Choix*, Jean Grenier establishes in this way a veritable 'philosophy of indifference'.

5

MAURICE MERLEAU-PONTY
(1908–1961)

To be someone, is something which happens and unhappens, but not without first tracing the ribs of a future, always new and always begun anew. What was he, if not this paradise lost, a wild and undeserved piece of luck, a gratuitous gift transformed, after the fall, into adversity, depopulating the world and disenchanting him in advance? This story is both extraordinary and commonplace.

So Sartre said in his obituary to his long-time friend, adversary and collaborator (Sartre, 1965, p. 228). Merleau-Ponty's extraordinary and commonplace life began in March 1908 in Rochefort-sur-Mer on the west coast of France, where he was born into a bourgeois Catholic family. Both the bourgeois and the Catholic dimensions of his background would become serious issues later in his life, for he would reject them both, but without adopting the opposite extreme; even in these matters he would attempt to find a middle way. After his father, an artillery officer, died in 1913, he went to live in Paris with his mother, brother and sister. He later told Sartre that he had never recovered from an incomparably happy childhood; 'he had known that private world of happiness from which only age drives us'. Having achieved excellent results in his school examinations, he entered the prestigious École Normale Supérieure in 1926, which he attended for the next four years, gaining second place in the *aggréga-tion* in philosophy in 1930. His fellow students during those years, and his five years of independent research, included Jean-Paul Sartre, Simone de Beauvoir, Daniel Lagache, Raymond Aron, Claude Lévi-Strauss, Immanuel Levinas and many other exceptional writers, artists and political activists.

In the first volume of her autobiography, *Memoirs of a Dutiful Daughter*, de Beauvoir paints a vivid picture of the youthful Maurice, under the pseudonym of Jean Pradelle:

> He was a little younger than me, and he had already spent a year in the Normale as a day-student. He too looked as if he came from a good family, though he wasn't at all stuck up. He had a limpid, rather beautiful face, with thick dark lashes, and the gay frank laugh of a schoolboy ... At the École Normale, he was classed among the *tolas* [slang for 'priest']. He disapproved of his fellow students' coarse manners, their indecent songs, rude jokes, brutality, debauchery, and cynical dissipations ... What I thought was most important was that he too was anxiously seeking for the truth: he believed that one day it would be revealed to him through the medium of philosophy.

De Beauvoir summed up her picture of Maurice with the words, 'uncomplicated, unmysterious, a well-behaved scholar' (de Beauvoir, 1963, pp. 245–7). Uncomplex, even simple, in his feelings for other persons, 'Pradelle' was a serious, highly focused scholar who never took part in the outrageous escapades and elaborate hoaxes carried out by Sartre, de Beauvoir, Herbaud and their other notorious cronies. But he was clear-minded in his loyalty to those he considered his friends, as they were to him; when the young Sartre got him into trouble on one occasion, Merleau-Ponty later recalled the incident.

> The École Normale unleashed its fury against one of my schoolmates [Sartre] and myself for having hissed at the traditional songs, too vulgar to suit us. He slipped between us and our persecutors and contrived a way for us to get out of a heroic and ridiculous situation without concessions or damages.

From 1926 to 1930, Merleau-Ponty's main teacher was Professor Leon Brunschvicg who transmitted to his students a profound understanding of the history of philosophical positions, filtered through Kant's critical perspective. Twenty-five years later, Merleau-Ponty recalled that, in addition to Husserl's phenomenology and Bergson's vitalist doctrines, Brunschvicg's Kantian idealism was one of the most potent influences in French philosophy in the 1930s.

> He was, among us students, absolutely and justly famous, perhaps not so much because of the philosophy he advocated and taught us, but because of his quite extraordinary personal qualities ... He was a man of the first order, not so much because of the conclusions of his doctrines, but because of his personal experience and talent, which were considerable.

The context in which Merleau-Ponty extolled his first great philosophy teacher was one where he sought to succinctly capture the principal motifs that shaped his thinking in an Existentialist direction, and his former teacher played a role there also.

There is a quality of thought in which we all participate, and philosophy
begins and ends by returning to this unique principle of all thought. The
entire history of philosophy, which Brunschvicg pursued, was the coming
to consciousness of this spirituality. According to him, philosophies were
worthwhile to the extent that they succeeded in being conscious projects,
and he judged them according to this canon, this rule. (1996, pp. 130)

In the academic year 1928–9, he prepared a thesis on Plotinus, under the
supervision of Emile Bréhier, one of the foremost French historians of ancient
Greek thought. Between 1928 and 1930, he attended a series of lectures at the
Sorbonne by Georges Gurvitch on current German philosophy, especially the
writings and lectures of Husserl, Heidegger and Max Scheler. In February 1929,
along with hundreds of other French intellectuals, everyone who was *anyone* (as
they say), he sat in the audience to listen to a series of lectures by the master
himself, Edmund Husserl. These lectures were edited and translated into French
by Immanuel Levinas under the title *Cartesian Meditations* in 1931 and were to
have a decisive influence on Merleau-Ponty's thinking for the rest of his far too
short life. After gaining his degree, he served one year's compulsory military
service and then taught philosophy in the *lycées* in Beauvais and Chartres.
During this time he taught himself German and read everything he could by the
relatively new German writers who were carrying forward Husserl's project, as
well as major works in Gestalt psychology by Koffka, Kohler, Gelb and
Goldstein. His first published articles were sympathetic critical reviews of the
French translation of Max Scheler's treatise on *Ressentiment* (1935), Gabriel
Marcel's *Etre et Avoir* (1936) and Sartre's first short work, *The Imagination*
(1936) (all three reprinted in 1996). An important document from this period is
his two-part proposal on 'The Nature of Perception' (1933), in which he clearly
outlines a large-scale study that would incorporate recent research in neurol-
ogy, physiology and pathology into a phenomenological investigation into
perception and embodied behaviour (also reprinted in 1996, pp. 74–84). In
1935, he was appointed as a lowly tutor at the École Normale, where he
remained until the military call for conscription in the autumn of 1939.

One crucial episode from his university years is not recorded in the standard
biographical entries about his education and philosophical apprenticeship. It
may help the reader to reach a more mature and fulsome understanding of
Merleau-Ponty's references to affective comportment in the world and the
personal commitment someone in good faith has towards those he or she cares
most about. This story only becomes apparent through a close reading of de
Beauvoir's intermittent record of her close rapport with 'Jean Pradelle' and her
close friend and confidante Zaza Mabille. De Beauvoir depicts herself as a
young woman who rebels against her own bourgeois background, who through
her studies at university, her close companionship with outrageous and exciting
friends, seeks to find her true self, one that she will create for herself alone. Her
lovely, vivacious friend Zaza feels duty bound to please her mother, constrained

by her own bourgeois values to accept only what her family accepts. But she falls in love with Pradelle, and against his own single-minded ambition to excel in philosophy and carry out grand scholarly plans, he too falls in love with Zaza. After numerous hesitant encounters, long promisory letters and attempts to circumvent both Pradelle's and Zaza's mothers' disapproval, Zaza feels that she is about to lose the love of her life, the person who means more to her than the world. De Beauvoir helps to persuade Pradelle to be more resolute, to seize the chance for happiness, and he proposes to Zaza; they become engaged and set a wedding for the near future. Zaza's frail health takes a dramatic downturn, she contracts a raging fever and dies within a week of falling ill, only a few weeks before she and Pradelle are due to marry. The closing pages of *Memoirs of a Dutiful Daughter* are incredibly sad, and in the final line de Beauvoir says, 'we had fought together against the revolting fate that had lain ahead of us, and for a long time I believed that I had paid for my own freedom with her death' (1963, p. 360). One can only wonder at the profound effect that this abrupt end to his (and her) hope for 'a haven or mercy and love' may have had upon the young Merleau-Ponty, but perhaps Sartre had these events in mind when he wrote these moving words in his obituary for his close friend.

> Misunderstandings, estrangements, separations due to mutual wrongs, his private life had already taught him that our acts become inscribed into our little world otherwise than we might have wished, and that they make us other than we were, by giving us, after the fact, intentions which we didn't have, but which we shall have from now on. (Sartre, 1965, pp. 235–6)

The intention he did have at the time was to bring to completion the studies he had first proposed several years earlier; his minor doctoral thesis, *La Structure du comportement* was completed in 1938, though not published in book form until 1942. The use of the word 'comportement' (the normal French word for 'behaviour') in the title is itself significant; 'comportement' resonates with the same connotations as the later Husserl's and Heidegger's concept of corporeal intentionality, the manner in which human being actively engages in the everyday world. Thus Merleau-Ponty's employment of Gestalt theory, abnormal psychology and ethnological studies of 'primitive' mentality showed him that there was a primordial dimension of human being below the level of conscious awareness, a dimension that was genetically and ontologically prior to reflection, judgement formation and explicit calculation. In early 1939, Merleau-Ponty read with avid interest a special issue of the *Revue internationale de philosophie* devoted to Husserl (who had died in April 1938); it contained an essay-synopsis by Husserl's junior colleague, Eugen Fink, of some of Husserl's unpublished works. Just before the outbreak of hostilities, in April 1939, Merleau-Ponty was the very first visitor to the newly established Husserl Archives in Louvain, Belgium, where Husserl's manuscripts had been transported for safekeeping (see 1996, Appendix by H. L. van Breda). In 'a near rhapsody of excitement', he read the complete texts of the master's

Crisis of European Sciences, the Second and Third Books of the *Ideas*, and other texts on intersubjectivity and inner time consciousness. During the Nazi occupation of France he continued to work ever harder at bringing together the many strands of his radical vision of a middle way, one that would not fall foul of the dead ends and 'logical ghosts' of either empiricism or intellectualism. Husserl's manuscripts on the lifeworld, more than any other, played a decisive role in the completion of this project, the monumental and path-breaking *The Phenomenology of Perception* (1945), one of the few landmark works in Existential Phenomenology (see Cullen, 1994, pp. 105–8).

Merleau-Ponty states his picture of a newly founded phenomenology of the lifeworld in the Preface, one of the best (and briefest) precis of the general orientation of phenomenology. It is oriented around

> a philosophy which puts essences back into existence, and does not expect to arrive at an understanding of man and the world from any starting point other than that of their 'facticity' … It is also a philosophy for which the world is always 'already there' before reflection begins – as an unalienable presence; and all its efforts are concentrated upon re-achieving a direct and primitive contact with the world, and endowing that contact with a philosophical status. (1962 [1945], p. vii)

In this brief preamble, we can only hint at some of the central themes in this long and complex work. The third dimension, intermediate between outward observable behaviour and inward mental episodes, takes form in the basic concepts of shape and structure; these are neither things nor ideas, but rather ways of organising reality itself, matched by a correlative self-organisation by the human being. Perception is primary because it is both exemplary and basic: it is exemplary since the openness and indeterminacy of perception are found throughout conscious and sensuous manifestations; and it is basic since it makes an original contact with reality at the level of the lifeworld and forms the background against which all actions and operations are seen.

> As corporeal beings, humans are engaged in a constant *dialogue with the world*, beginning with the communication of the senses, where the sentient and that which is sensed get in contact, even before a subject confronts an object. The dialogue with things is finally intensified in the *dialogue with others*. The anonymity of the body represents itself as 'inter-corporality' (*intercorporéité*), in relation to an 'interworld' (*intermonde*) in which our experiences are interwoven with those of others, our own expressions with those of others, even before the self confronts the other as a strange subject. (Waldenfels, 1998, pp. 283–4)

After the war Merleau-Ponty was appointed lecturer in philosophy at the University of Lyons, where he was made professor in 1948. He combined his teaching duties with the sometimes onerous tasks of jointly editing the left-wing journal *Les Temps modernes*, which he had helped to found, along with Sartre,

Jean Paulhan, Raymond Aron and Albert Ollivier. (On this period, see Sartre, 1965, pp. 248–54.) Merleau-Ponty wrote many of the editorials and book reviews without signing his name (something that really annoyed Sartre), and several feature-length articles, which he did sign. Many of these important pieces were gathered together and published in his collection *Humanism and Terror* (1947), with other articles in the collection *Sense and Non-Sense* (1948). The latter title recalls his comment 'we cannot say that *everything has a sense* or that *everything is non-sense*, but simply, *there is sense.*' He eventually broke away from Sartre over an irresolvable conflict in their respective interpretations of the Soviet institution of Marxist-Socialist principles, and resigned as co-editor of the journal. From 1949 to 1952, he held the chair in Child Psychology and Pedagogy at the Sorbonne, and in 1952, at the early age of forty-four, he was appointed to the most prestigious philosophy post in France, the chair of philosophy at the Collège de France, where he continued to teach until his premature death in May 1961.

In Merleau-Ponty's mature work he came to the conclusion that language, especially in the dialogic interchange between speakers, was of paramount importance in understanding the manner in which humans can make appear that which is hidden; from the realm of the unsaid, speech manifests more than is contained in the mere meaning of the words used. Merleau-Ponty was perhaps the first philosopher to bring structural linguistics, from the work of de Saussure and Roman Jakobson, into the arena of philosophical discussion about language. In his final work *The Visible and the Invisible* (incomplete at his death) the many strands of his previous excavations in the ontology of the lifeworld come together and are made into something new and startling. His earlier espousal of the phenomenology of perception and one's own body becomes an ontology of seeing (*vision*) and flesh (*chair*); seeing is no longer the conscious act of a subject, but an event that occurs between the seer, the visible and the co-seer, all enveloped in a sphere of visibility that he calls the 'flesh'. Here he offers a truly radical innovation on traditional ontological schemas by asserting that there is one dimension (or level of being) that undercuts both subject and object, mind and world, self and other – the flesh of the world. He thought of this flesh as a field of force; in every thing and person it appears *as* some thing and some person; everything is presented *under an aspect* due to this envelope. On other occasions he likens the flesh to an element, in the same (or analogical) fashion as the Greek elements of earth, air, water and fire. Through the elemental constitution of the world, an intertwining (*entrelacs*) forms among things, persons and myself; our conscious being is situated at an intersection between our own being and all other beings. He calls this intertwining the *chiasm*, a term that plays on the Greek letter *chi* (X), an emblem that emphasises the inextricable interlocking of the various aspects of Being. For the Catholic-born Merleau-Ponty, the *chiasm* may also recall the Greek symbols for Christ; *chi rho* (XP), god made flesh, the being who incarnated the finite and the infinite, the visible and the invisible, the kingdoms of earth and heaven.

It is impossible to exaggerate just how ambitious Merleau-Ponty's mature project really is. He proposed to go beyond ... the traditional philosophical categories of realism and idealism, subject and object, consciousness and world, in-itself and for-itself, being and nothingness, the knower and the known, and discover in that scarcely penetrable region what he called 'the flesh of the world', the primordial stuff in which we all inhere and which is the ultimate ground of all human experience. (Cullen, 1994, p. 119)

PRINCIPAL WORKS

(1933–60) *Texts and Dialogues*, eds Hugh Silverman and James Barry, Jr, 2nd edn. Atlantic Highlands, NJ: Humanities Press, 1996.

(1942) *The Structure of Behavior*, trans. Alden L. Fischer. Boston: Beacon Press, 1963.

(1945) *The Phenomenology of Perception*, trans. Colin Smith. London: Routledge, 1962.

(1947) *Humanism and Terror*, trans. John O'Neill. Boston: Beacon Press, 1969.

(1947) *The Primacy of Perception and Other Essays*, ed. James Edie. Evanston, IL: Northwestern University Press, 1964.

(1948) *Sense and Non-Sense*, eds and trans. Hubert and Patricia Dreyfus. Evanston, IL: Northwestern University Press, 1964.

(1950–2) *The Prose of the World*, trans. John O'Neill. Evanston, IL: Northwestern University Press, 1973.

(1955) *Adventures of the Dialectic*, trans. Joseph Bien. Evanston, IL: Northwestern University Press, 1973.

(1960) *Signs*, trans. Richard McCleary. Evanston, IL: Northwestern University Press, 1964.

(1964) *The Visible and the Invisible*, trans. Alphonso Lingis. Evanston, IL: Northwestern University Press, 1968.

RECOMMENDED READING

de Beauvoir, Simone (1963) *Memoirs of a Dutiful Daughter*, trans. James Kirkup. Harmondsworth: Penguin Books.

Busch, Thomas and Gallagher, Shaun (eds) (1992) *Merleau-Ponty: Hermeneutics and Postmodernism*. Albany: State University of New York Press.

Cullen, Bernard (1994) 'Philosophy of Existence 3: Merleau-Ponty', in Richard Kearney Ed (ed.), *Twentieth-Century Continental Philosophy*. London and New York: Routledge.

Dillon, Martin (1988) *Merleau-Ponty's Ontology*. Bloomington: Indiana University Press.

Dillon, Martin (1991) *Merleau-Ponty Vivant*. Albany: State University of New York Press.

Johnson, Galen and Smith, Michael (eds) (1990) *Ontology and Alterity in Merleau-Ponty*. Evanston, IL: Northwestern University Press.

Kwant, Remy (1963) *The Phenomenological Philosophy of Merleau-Ponty*. Pittsburg, PA: Duquesne University Press.

Kwant, Remy (1966) *From Phenomenology to Metaphysics*. Pittsburg: Duquesne University Press.

Langer, Monika (1989) *Merleau-Ponty's Phenomenology of Perception: A Guide and Commentary*. Miami: Florida State University Press.

Macann, Christopher (1993) 'Merleau-Ponty', in *Four Phenomenological Philosophers*. London and New York: Routledge.

Madison, Gary Brent (1973) *The Phenomenology of Merleau-Ponty*. Athens: Ohio University Press.

Pietersma, Henry (ed.) (1989) *Merleau-Ponty: Critical Essays*. Lanham, MA: University Presses of America.

Sallis, John (1981) *Merleau-Ponty: Perception, Structure, Language*. Atlantic Highlands, NJ: Humanities Press.

Sartre, Jean-Paul (1965) 'Merleau-Ponty', in *Situations*, trans. Benita Eisler. New York: Braziller.

Schmidt, James (1985) *Merleau-Ponty: Between Phenomenology and Structuralism*. New York: St Martin's Press.

Silverman, Hugh (1997) *Inscriptions: After Phenomenology and Structuralism*. Evanston, IL: Northwestern University Press.

Waldenfels, Bernhard (1998) 'Merleau-Ponty', in *A Companion to Continental Philosophy*, eds Simon Critchley and William Schroeder. Oxford: Blackwell.

'REFLECTIONS ON THE CARTESIAN COGITO' (1945)[*]

Maurice Merleau-Ponty

I am thinking of the Cartesian *cogito*, wanting to finish this work, feeling the coolness of the paper under my hand, and perceiving the trees of the boulevard through the window. My life is constantly thrown headlong into transcendent things, and passes wholly outside me. The *cogito* is either this thought which took shape three centuries ago in the mind of Descartes, or the meaning of the books he has left for us, or else an eternal truth which emerges from them, but in any case is a cultural being of which it is true to say that my thought strains towards it rather than that it embraces it, as my body, in a familiar surrounding, finds its orientation and makes its way among objects without my needing to have them expressly in mind. This book, once begun, is not a certain set of ideas; it constitutes for me an open situation, for which I could not possibly provide any complex formula, and in which I struggle blindly on until, miraculously, thoughts and words become organized by themselves. *A fortiori* the sensible forms of being which lie around me, the paper under my hand, the trees before my eyes, do not yield their secret to me, rather is it that my consciousness takes flight from itself and, in them, is unaware of itself. Such is the initial situation that realism tries to account for by asserting an actual transcendence and the existence in itself of the world and ideas.

---

[*] From *The Phenomenology of Perception*, trans. Colin Smith. London: Routledge & Kegan Paul, 1962.

There is, however, no question of justifying realism, and there is an element of final truth in the Cartesian return of things or ideas to the self. The very experience of transcendent things is possible only provided that their project is borne, and discovered, within myself. When I say that things are transcendent, this means that I do not possess them, that I do not circumambulate them; they are transcendent to the extent that I am ignorant of what they are, and blindly assert their bare existence. Now what meaning can there be in asserting the existence of one knows not what? If there can be any truth at all in this assertion, it is in so far as I catch a glimpse of the nature or essence to which it refers, in so far, for instance, as my vision of the tree as a mute *ek-stase* into an individual thing already envelops a certain thought about seeing and a certain thought about the tree. It is, in short, in so far as I do not merely encounter the tree, am not simply confronted with it, but discover in this existent before me a certain nature, the notion of which I actively evolve. In so far as I find things round about me, this cannot be because they are actually there, for, *ex hypothesi*, I can know nothing of this factual existence. The fact that I am capable of recognizing it is attributable to my actual contact with the thing, which awakens within me a primordial knowledge of all things, and to my finite and determinate perceptions' being partial manifestations of a power of knowing which is co-extensive with the world and unfolds it in its full extent and depth. If we imagine a space in itself with which the perceiving subject contrives to coincide, for example, if I imagine that my hand perceives the distance between two points as it spans it, how could the angle formed by my fingers, and indicative of that distance, come to be judged, unless it were so to speak measured out by the inner operation of some power residing in neither object, a power which, *ipso facto*, becomes able to know, or rather effect, the relation existing between them? If it be insisted that the 'sensation in my thumb' and that in my first finger are at any rate 'signs' of the distance, how could these sensations come to have in themselves any means of signifying the relationship between points in space, unless they were already situated on a path running from one to the other, and unless this path in its turn were not only traversed by my fingers as they open, but also 'aimed at' by my thought pursuing its intelligible purpose? 'How could the mind know the significance of a sign which it has not itself constituted as a sign?'[1] For the picture of knowledge at which we arrived in describing the subject situated in his world, we must, it seems, substitute a second, according to which it constructs or constitutes this world itself, and this one is more authentic than the first, since the transactions between the subject and the things round about it are possible only provided that the subject first of all causes them to exist for itself, actually arranges them round about itself, and extracts them from its own core. The same applies with greater force in acts of spontaneous thought. The Cartesian *cogito*, which is the theme of my reflection, is always beyond what I bring to mind at the moment. It has a horizon of significance made up of a great number of thoughts which occurred to me as I was reading Descartes and which are not now present, along with others which I feel stirring within me, which I might have, but never have developed. But the fact that it is enough to utter these three syllables in my presence for me to be immediately directed towards a certain set of ideas, shows that in some way all possible developments and clarifications are at once present to me. 'Whoever tries to limit the spiritual light to what is at present before the mind always runs up against the Socratic problem. "How will you set about looking for that thing, the nature of which is totally unknown to you? Which, among the things you do not know, is the one which you propose to look for? And if by chance you should stumble upon it, how will you know that it is indeed that thing, since you are in ignorance of it?" (*Meno*, 80D.)[2] A thought really transcended by its objects would find them proliferating in its path without ever being able to grasp their relationships to each other, or finding its way through to their truth. It is I who reconstitute the historical *cogito*, I who read Descartes' text, I who recognize in it an undying truth, so that finally the Cartesian *cogito* acquires its significance only through my own *cogito*, and I should have no thought of it, had I not within myself all that is needed to invent it. It is I who assign to my thought the objective of resuming the action of the *cogito*, and I who constantly verify my thought's orientation towards this objective, therefore my thought must forestall itself in the pursuit of this aim, and must already have found what it seeks, otherwise it would not seek it. We must define thought in terms of that strange power which it possesses of being ahead of itself, of launching itself and being at home everywhere, in a word, in terms of its autonomy. Unless thought itself had put into things what it subsequently finds in them, it would have no hold upon things, would not think of them, and would be an 'illusion of thought'.[3] A sensible perception or a piece of reasoning cannot be facts which come about in me and of which I take note. When I consider them after the event, they are dispersed and distributed each to its due place. But all this is merely what is left in the wake of reasoning and perception which, seen contemporaneously, must necessarily, on pain of ceasing to hang together, take in simultaneously everything necessary to their realization, and consequently be present to themselves with no intervening distance, in one indivisible intention. All thought of something is at the same time self-consciousness, failing which it could have no object. At the root of all our experiences and all our reflections, we find, then, a being which immediately recognizes itself, because it is its knowledge both of itself and of all things, and which knows its own existence, not by observation and as a given fact, nor by inference from any idea of itself, but through direct contact with that existence. Self-consciousness is the very being of mind in action. The act whereby I am conscious of something must itself be apprehended at the very moment at which it is carried out, otherwise it would collapse. Therefore it is inconceivable that it should be triggered off or brought about by anything whatsoever; it must be *causa sui*.[4] To revert with Descartes from things to thought about things is to take one of two courses: it is either to reduce experience to a collection of psychological events, of which the *I* is merely the overall name or the hypothetical cause, in which case it is not clear how my existence is more certain than that of any thing, since it is no longer immediate, save at a fleeting instant; or else it is to recognize as anterior to events a field and a system of thoughts which is subject neither to time nor to any other limitation, a mode of existence owing nothing to the event and which is existence as consciousness, a spiritual act which grasps at a distance and compresses into itself everything at which it aims, an 'I think' which is, by itself and without any adjunct, an 'I am'.[5] 'The Cartesian doctrine of the *cogito* was therefore bound to lead logically to the assertion of the timelessness of mind, and to the acceptance of a consciousness of the eternal: *experimur nos aeternos esse*.'[6] Accordingly eternity, understood as the power to embrace and anticipate temporal developments in a single intention, becomes the very definition of subjectivity.[7]

Before questioning this interpretation of the *cogito* in terms of eternity, let us carefully observe what follows from it, as this will show the need of some rectification. If the *cogito* reveals to me a new mode of existence owing nothing to time, and if I discover myself as the universal constituent of all being accessible to me, and as a transcendental field with no hidden corners and no outside, it is not enough to say that my mind, 'when it is a question of the form of all the objects of sense ... is the God of Spinoza',[8] for the distinction between form and matter can no longer be given any ultimate value, therefore it is not clear how the mind, reflecting on itself, could in the last analysis find any meaning in the notion of receptivity, or think of itself in any valid way as undergoing modification: for if it is the mind itself which thinks of itself as affected, it does *not* think of itself thus, since it affirms its activity afresh simultaneously with appearing to restrict it: in so far, on the other hand, as it is the mind which places itself in the world, it is *not* there, and the self-positing is an illusion. It must then be said, with no qualification, that my mind is God. How can M. Lachièze-Rey, for example, have avoided this consequence? 'If, having suspended thinking, I resume it again, I return to life, I reconstitute, in its indivisibility, and by putting myself back at the source whence it flows, the movement which I carry on ... Thus, whenever he thinks, the subject makes himself his point of support, and takes his place, beyond and behind his various representations, in that unity which, being the principle of all recognition, is not there to be recognized, and he becomes once more the absolute because that is what he eternally is.'[9] But how could there be several absolutes? How in the first place could I ever recognize other (my)selves? If the sole experience of the subject is the one which I gain by coinciding with it, if the mind, by definition, eludes 'the outside spectator' and can be recognized only from within, my *cogito* is necessarily unique, and cannot be 'shared in' by another. Perhaps we can say that it is 'transferable' to others.[10] But then how could such a transfer ever be brought about? What spectacle can ever validly induce me to posit outside myself that mode of existence the whole significance of which demands that it be grasped from within? Unless I learn within myself to recognize the junction of the *for itself* and the *in itself*, none of those mechanisms called other bodies will ever be able to come to life; unless I have an exterior others have no interior. The plurality of consciousness is impossible if I have an absolute consciousness of myself. Behind the absolute of my thought, it is even impossible to conjecture a divine absolute. If it is perfect, the contact of my thought with itself seals me within myself, and prevents me from ever feeling that anything eludes my grasp; there is no opening, no 'aspiration'[11] towards an Other for this self of mine, which constructs the totality of being and its own presence in the world, which is defined in terms of 'self-possession',[12] and which never finds anything outside itself but what it has put there. This hermetically sealed self is no longer a finite self. 'There is ...' a consciousness of the universe only through the previous consciousness of organization in the active sense of the word, and consequently, in the last analysis, only through an inner communion with the very working of godhead.'[13] It is ultimately with God that the *cogito* brings me into coincidence. While the intelligible and identifiable structure of my experience, when recognized by me in the *cogito*, draws me out of the event and establishes me in eternity, it frees me simultaneously from all limiting attributes and, in fact, from that fundamental event which is my private existence. Hence the same reasoning which necessarily leads from the event to the act, from thoughts to the *I*, equally necessarily leads from the multiplicity of *I*'s to one sole constituting consciousness, and prevents me from entertaining any vain hope of salvaging the finiteness of the subject by defining it as a 'monad'.[14] The constituting consciousness is necessarily unique and universal. If we try to maintain that what it constitutes in each one of us is merely a microcosm, if we keep, for the *cogito*, the meaning of 'existential experience',[15] and if it reveals to me, not the absolute transparency of thought wholly in possession of itself, but the blind act by which I take up my destiny as a thinking nature and follow it out, then we are introducing another philosophy, which does not take us *out of* time. What is brought home to us here is the need to find a middle course between eternity and the atomistic time of empiricism, in order to resume the interpretation of the *cogito* and of time. We have seen once and for all that our relations with things cannot be eternal ones, nor our consciousness of ourself the mere recording of psychic events. We perceive a world only provided that, before being facts of which we take cognizance, that world and that perception are thoughts of our own. What remains to be understood precisely is the way the world comes to belong to the subject and the subject to himself, which is that *cogitatio* which makes experience possible; our hold on things and on our 'states of consciousness'. We shall see that this does not leave the event and time out of account, but that it is indeed the fundamental mode of the event and *Geschichte*, from which objective and impersonal events are derived forms, and finally that any recourse we have to eternity is necessitated solely by an objective conception of time.

There can therefore be no doubt at all that I think. I am not sure that there is over there an ash-tray or a pipe, but I am sure that I think I see an ash-tray or a pipe. Now is it in fact as easy as is generally thought to dissociate these two assertions and hold, independently of any judgement concerning the thing seen, the evident certainty of my 'thought about seeing'? On the contrary, it is impossible. Perception is precisely that kind of act in which there can be not question of setting the act itself apart from the end to which it is directed. Perception and the perceived necessarily have the same existential modality, since perception is inseparable from the consciousness which it has, or rather is, of reaching the thing itself. Any contention that the perception is indubitable, whereas the thing perceived is not, must be ruled out. If I see an ash-tray, *in the full sense of the word see*, there must be an ash-tray there, and I cannot forego this assertion. To see is to see something. To see red, is to see red actively in existence. Vision can be reduced to the mere presumption of seeing only if it is represented as the contemplation of a shifting and anchorless *quale*. But if, as we have shown above, the very quality itself, in its specific texture, is the suggestion of a certain way of existing put to us, and responded to by us, in so far as we have sensory fields; and if the perception of a colour, endowed with a definite structure (in the way of superficial colour or area of colour), at a place or distance away either definite or vague, presupposes our opening on to a reality or a world, how can we possibly dissociate the certainty of our perceptual existence from that of its external counterpart? It is of the essence of my vision to refer not only to an alleged visible entity, but also to a being actually seen. Similarly, if I feel doubts about the presence of the thing, this doubt attaches to vision itself, and if there is no red or blue there, I say that I have not *really seen* these colours, and concede that at no time has there been created that parity between my visual intentions and the visible which constitutes the genuine act of seeing. We are therefore faced with a choice: either I enjoy no certainty with regard to things themselves, in which case neither can I be certain about my own perception, taken as a mere thought, since, taken even in this way, it involves the assertion of a thing. Or else I grasp my thought with certainty, which involves the simultaneous assumption of the existence towards which it is projected. When Descartes tells us that the existence of visible things is doubtful, but that our vision, when considered as a mere thought of seeing is not in doubt, he takes up an untenable position. For thought about seeing can have two meanings. It can in the first place be understood in the restricted sense of alleged vision, or 'the impression of seeing', in which case it offers only the certainty of a possibility or a probability, and the 'thought of seeing' implies that we have had, in certain cases, the experience of genuine or actual vision to which the idea of seeing bears a resemblance and in which the certainty of the thing was, on those occasions, involved. The certainty of a possibility is no more than the possibility of a certainty, the thought of seeing is no more than seeing mentally, and we could not have any such thought unless we had on other occasions really seen. Now we may understand 'thought about seeing' as the consciousness we have of our constituting power. Whatever be the case with our empirical perceptions, which may be true or false, these perceptions are possible only if they are inhabited by a mind able to recognize, identify and sustain before us their intentional object. But if this constituting power is not a myth, if perception is really the mere extension of an inner dynamic power with which I can coincide, my certainty concerning the transcendental premises of the world must extend to the world itself, and, my vision being in its entirety thought about seeing, then the thing seen is in itself what I think about it, so that transcendental idealism becomes absolute realism. It would be contradictory to assert[16] both that the world is constituted by me and that, out of this constitutive operation, I can grasp no more than the outline and the essential structures; I must see the existing world appear at the end of the constituting process, and not only the world as an idea, otherwise I shall have no more than an abstract construction, and not a concrete consciousness, of the world. Thus, in whatever sense we take 'thought about seeing', it is certain only so long as actual sight is equally so. When Descartes tells us that sensation reduced to itself is always true, and that error creeps in through the transcendent interpretation of it that judgement provides, he makes an unreal distinction: it is no less difficult for me to know whether or not I have felt something than it is to know whether there is really something there, for the victim of hysteria feels yet does not know what it is that he feels, as he perceives external objects without being aware of that perception. When, on the other hand, I am sure of having felt, the certainty of some external thing is involved in the very way in which the sensation is articulated and unfolded before me: it is a pain *in the leg*, or it is *red*, and this may be an opaque red on one plane, or a reddish three-dimensional atmosphere. The 'interpretation' of my sensations which I give must necessarily be motivated, and be so only in terms of the structure of those sensations, so that it can be said with equal validity either that there is no transcendent interpretation and no judgement which does not spring from the very configuration of the phenomena – or that there is no sphere of immanence, no realm in which my consciousness is fully at home and secure against all risk of error. The acts of the *I* are of such a nature that they outstrip themselves leaving no interiority of consciousness. Consciousness is transcendence through and through, not transcendence undergone – we have already said that such a transcendence would bring consciousness to a stop – but active transcendence. The consciousness I have of seeing or feeling is no passive noting of some psychic event hermetically sealed upon itself, an event leaving me in doubt about the reality of the thing seen or felt. Nor is it the activation of some constituting power superlatively and eternally inclusive of every possible sight or sensation, and linking up with the object without ever having to be drawn away from itself. It is the actual effecting of vision. I reassure myself that I see by seeing this or that, or at least by bringing to life around me a visual surrounding, a visible world which is ultimately vouched for only by the sight of a particular thing. Vision is an action, not, that is, an eternal operation (which is a contradiction in terms) but an operation which fulfils more than it promises, which constantly outruns its premises and is inwardly prepared only by my primordial opening upon a field of transcendence, that is, once again, by an *ek-stase*. Sight is achieved and fulfils itself in the thing seen. It is of its essence to take a hold upon itself, and indeed if it did not do so it would not be the sight of anything, but it is none the less of its essence to take a hold upon itself in a kind of ambiguous and obscure way, since it is not in possession of itself and indeed escapes from itself into the thing seen. What I discover and recognize through the *cogito* is not psychological immanence, the inherence of all phenomena in 'private states of consciousness', the blind contact of sensation with itself. It is not even transcendental immanence, the belonging of all phenomena to a constituting consciousness, the possession of clear thought by itself. It is the deep-seated momentum of transcendence which is my very being, the simultaneous contact with my own being and with the world's being.

And yet is not the case of perception a special one? It throws me open to a world, but can do so only by outrunning both me and itself. Thus the perceptual 'synthesis' has to be incomplete; it cannot present me with a 'reality' otherwise than by running the risk of error. It is absolutely necessarily the case that the thing, if it is to be a thing, should have sides of itself hidden from me, which is why the distinction between appearance and reality straightway has its place in the perceptual 'synthesis'. It would seem, on the other hand, that consciousness comes back into its rights and into full possession of itself, if I consider my awareness of 'psychic facts'. For example, love and will are inner operations; they forge their own objects, and it is clear that in doing so they may be sidetracked from reality and, in that sense, mislead us; but it seems impossible that they should mislead us about themselves. From the moment I feel love, joy or sadness, it is the case that I love, that I am joyful or sad, even when the object does not in fact (that is, for others or for myself at other times) have the value that I now attribute to it. Appearance is, within me, reality, and the being of consciousness consists in appearing to itself. What is willing, if it is not being conscious of an object as valid (or as valid precisely in so far as it is invalid, in the case of perverse will), and what is loving other than being conscious of an object as lovable? And since the consciousness of an object necessarily involves a knowledge of itself, without which it would escape from itself and fail even to grasp its object, to will and to know that one wills, to love and know one loves are one and the same act; love is consciousness of loving, will is consciousness of willing. A love or a will unaware of itself would be an unloving love, or an unwilling will, as an unconscious thought would be an unthinking one. Will or love would seem to be the same whether their object be artificial or real and, considered independently of the object to which they actually refer, they would appear to constitute a sphere of absolute certainty in which truth cannot elude us. Everything is, then, truth within consciousness. There can never be illusion other than with regard to the external object. A feeling, considered in itself, is always true once it is felt. Let us, however, look at the matter more closely.

It is, in the first place, quite clear that we are able to discriminate, within ourselves, between 'true' and 'false' feelings, that everything felt by us as within ourselves is not *ipso facto* placed on a single footing of existence, or true in the same way, and that there are degrees of reality within us as there are, outside of us, 'reflections', 'phantoms' and 'things'. Besides true love, there is false or illusory love. This last case must be distinguished from misinterpretations, and those errors in which I have deceitfully given the name of love to emotions unworthy of it. For in such cases there was never even a semblance of love, and never for a moment did I believe that my life was committed to that feeling. I conspired with myself to avoid asking the question in order to avoid receiving the reply which was already known to me; my 'love'-making was an attempt to do what was expected of me, or merely deception. In mistaken or illusory love, on the other hand, I was willingly united to the loved one, she was for a time truly the vehicle of my relationships with the world. When I told her that I loved her, I was not 'interpreting', for my life was in truth committed to a form which, like a melody, demanded to be carried on. It is true that, following upon disillusionment (the revelation of my illusion *about myself*), and when I try to understand what has happened to me, I shall find beneath this supposed love *something other* than love: the likeness of the 'loved' woman to another, or boredom, or force of habit, or a community of interests or of convictions, and it is just this which will justify me in talking about illusion. I loved only *qualities* (that smile that is so like another smile, that beauty which asserts itself like a fact, that youthfulness of gesture and behaviour) and not the individual manner of being which is that person herself. And, correspondingly, I was not myself wholly in thrall, for areas of my past and future life escaped the invasion, and I maintained within me corners set aside for other things. In that case, it will be objected, I was either unaware of this, in which case it is not a question of illusory love, but of a true love which is dying – or else I did know, in which case there was never any love at all, even 'mistaken'. But neither is the case. It cannot be said that this love, while it lasted, was indistinguishable from true love, and that it became 'mistaken love' when I repudiated it. Nor can it be said that a mystical crisis at fifteen is without significance, and that it *becomes*, when independently evaluated in later life, an incident of puberty or the first signs of a religious vocation. Even if I reconstruct my whole life on the basis of some incident of puberty, that incident does not lose its contingent character, so that it is my whole life which is 'mistaken'. In the mystical crisis itself as I experienced it, there must be discoverable in it some characteristic which distinguishes vocation from incident: in the first case the mystical attitude insinuates itself into my basic relationship to the world and other people; in the second case, it is within the subject as an impersonal form of behaviour, devoid of inner necessity: 'puberty'. In the same way, true love summons all the subject's resources and concerns him in his entire being, whereas mistaken love touches on only one persona: 'the man of forty' in the case of late love, 'the traveller' in the case of exotic appeal, 'the widower' if the misguided love is sustained by a memory, 'the child' where the mother is recalled. True love ends when I change, or when the object of affection changes; misguided love is revealed as such when I return to my own self. The difference is intrinsic. But as it concerns the place of feeling in my total being-in-the-world, and as mistaken love is bound up with the person I believe I am at the time I feel it, and also as, in order to discern its mistaken nature I require a knowledge of myself which I can gain only through disillusionment, ambiguity remains, which is why illusion is possible.

Let us return to the example of the hysterical subject. It is easy to treat him as a dissembler, but his deception is primarily self-deception, and this instability once more poses the problem we are trying to dispose of: how can the victim of hysteria not feel what he feels, and feel what he does not feel? He does not *feign* pain, sadness or anger, yet his fits of 'pain', 'sadness' or 'rage' are distinguishable from 'real' cases of these afflictions, because he is not wholly given over to them; at his core there is left a zone of tranquillity. Illusory or imaginary feelings are genuinely experienced, but experienced, so to speak, on the outer fringes of ourselves.[17] Children and many grown people are under the sway of 'situational values', which conceal from them their actual feelings – they are pleased because they have been given a present, sad because they are at a funeral, gay or sad according to the countryside around them, and, on the hither side of any such emotions, indifferent and neutral. 'We experience the feeling itself keenly, but inauthentically. It is, as it were, the shadow of an authentic sentiment.' Our natural attitude is not to experience our own feelings or to adhere to our own pleasures, but to live in accordance with the emotional categories of the environment. 'The girl who is loved does not project her emotions like an Isolde or a Juliet, but feels the feelings of these poetic phantoms and infuses them into her own life. It is at a later date, perhaps, that a personal and authentic feeling breaks the web of her sentimental phantasies.'[18] But until this feeling makes its appearance, the girl has no means of discovering the illusory and literary element in her love. It is the truth of her future feelings which is destined to reveal the misguidedness of her present ones, which are genuinely experienced. The girl 'loses her reality'[19] in them as does the actor in the part he plays, so that we are faced, not with representations or ideas which give rise to real emotions, but artificial emotions and imaginary sentiments. Thus we are not perpetually in possession of ourselves in our whole reality, and we are justified in speaking of an inner perception, of an inward sense, an 'analyser' working from us to ourselves which, ceaselessly, goes some, but not all, the way in providing knowledge of our life and our being. What remains on the hither side of inner perception and makes no impression on the inward sense is not an unconscious. 'My life', my 'total being' are not dubious constructs, like the 'deep-seated self' of Bergson, but phenomena which are indubitably revealed to reflection. It is simply a question of what we *are doing*. I make the discovery that I am in love. It may be that none of those facts, which I now recognize as proof of my love, passed unnoticed by me; neither the quickened drive of my present towards my future, nor that emotion which left me speechless, nor my impatience for the arrival of the day we were to meet. Nevertheless I had not seen the thing as a whole, or, if I had, I did not realize that it was a matter of so important a feeling, for I now discover that I can no longer conceive my life without this love. Going back over the preceding days and months, I am made aware that my thoughts and actions were polarized, I pick out the course of a process of organization, a synthesis *in the making*. Yet it is impossible to pretend that I always knew what I now know, and to see as existing, during the months which have elapsed, a self-knowledge which I have only just come by. Quite generally, it is impossible to deny that I have much to learn about myself, as it is to posit ahead of time, in the very heart of me, a knowledge of myself containing in advance all that I am later destined to know of myself, after having read books and had experiences at present unsuspected by me. The idea of a form of consciousness which is transparent to itself, its existence being identifiable with its awareness of existing, is not so very different from the notion of the unconscious: in both cases we have the same retrospective illusion, since there is, introduced into me as an explicit object, everything that I am later to learn concerning myself. The love which worked out its dialectic through me, and of which I have just become aware, was not, from the start, a thing hidden in my unconscious, nor was it an object before my consciousness, but the impulse carrying me towards someone, the transmutation of my thoughts and behaviour – I was not unaware of it since it was I who endured the hours of boredom preceding a meeting, and who felt elation when she approached – it was lived, not known, from start to finish. The lover is not unlike the dreamer. The 'latent content' and the 'sexual significance' of the dream are undoubtedly present to the dreamer since it is he who dreams his dream. But, precisely because sexuality is the general atmosphere of the dream, these elements are not thematized as sexual, for want of any non-sexual background against which they may stand out. When we ask ourselves whether or not the dreamer is conscious of the sexual content of his dream, we are really asking the wrong question. If sexuality, as we have explained above, is indeed one of our ways of entering into a relationship with the world, then whenever our meta-sexual being is overshadowed, as happens in dreams, sexuality is everywhere and nowhere; it is, in the nature of the case, ambiguous and cannot emerge clearly as itself. The fire which figures in the dream is not, for the dreamer, a way of disguising the sexual drive beneath an acceptable symbol, since it is only in the waking state that it appears as a symbol; in the language of dreams, fire is the symbol of the sexual drive because the dreamer, being removed from the physical world and the inflexible context of waking life, uses imagery only in proportion as it has affective value. The sexual significance of the dream is neither unconscious nor 'conscious', because the dream does not 'signify', as does waking life, by relating one order of facts to another, and it is as great a mistake to see sexuality as crystallized in 'unconscious representations' as it is to see lodged in the depths of the dreamer a consciousness which calls it by its true name. Similarly, for the lover whose experience it is, love is nameless; it is not a thing capable of being circumscribed and designated, nor is it the love spoken of in books and newspapers, because it is the way in which he establishes his relations with the world; it is an existential signification. The criminal fails to see his crime, and the traitor his betrayal for what they are, not because they exist deeply embedded within him as unconscious representations or tendencies, but because they are so many relatively closed worlds, so many situations. If we are in a situation, we are surrounded and cannot be transparent to ourselves, so that our contact with ourselves is necessarily achieved only in the sphere of ambiguity.

But have we not overshot our mark? If illusion is possible in consciousness on some occasions, will it not be possible on all occasions? We said that there are imaginary sentiments to which we are committed sufficiently for them to be experienced, but insufficiently for them to be authentic. But are there any absolute commitments? Is it not of the essence of commitment to leave unimpaired the autonomy of the person who commits himself, in the sense that it is never complete, and does it not therefore follow that we have no longer any means of describing certain feelings as authentic? To define the subject in terms of existence, that is to say, in terms of a process in which he transcends himself, is surely by that very act to condemn him to illusion, since he will never be able to *be* anything. Through refraining, in consciousness, from defining reality in terms of appearance, have we not severed the links binding us to ourselves, and reduced consciousness to the status of a mere appearance of some intangible reality? Are we not faced with the dilemma of an absolute consciousness on the one hand and endless doubt on the other? And have we not by our rejection of the first solution, made the *cogito* impossible? This objection brings us to the crucial point. It is true neither that my existence is in full possession of itself, nor that it is entirely estranged from itself, because it is action or doing, and because action is, by definition, the violent transition from what I have to what I aim to have, from what I am to what I intend to be. I can effect the *cogito* and be assured of genuinely willing, loving or believing, provided that in the first place I actually do will, love or believe, and thus fulfil my own existence. If this were not so, an ineradicable doubt would spread over the world, and equally over my own thoughts. I should be for ever wondering whether my 'tastes', 'volitions', 'desires' and 'ventures' were really mine, for they would always seem artificial, unreal and unfulfilled. But then this doubt, not being an actual doubt, could no longer even manage to confer the absolute certainty of doubting.[20] The only way out, and into 'sincerity', is by forestalling such scruples and taking a blind plunge into 'doing'. Hence it is not *because* I think I am that I am certain of my existence; on the contrary the certainty I enjoy concerning my thoughts stems from their genuine existence. My love, hatred and will are not certain as mere thoughts about loving, hating and willing; on the contrary the whole certainty of these thoughts is owed to that of the acts of love, hatred or will of which I am quite sure because I *perform* them. All inner perception is inadequate because I am not an object that can be perceived, because I make my reality and find myself only in the act. 'I doubt': there is no way of silencing all doubt concerning this proposition other than by actually doubting, involving oneself in the experience of doubting, and thus bringing this doubt into existence as the certainty of doubting. To doubt is always to doubt something, even if one 'doubts everything'. I am certain of doubting precisely because I take this or that thing, or even every thing and my own existence too, as doubtful. It is through my relation to 'things' that I know myself; inner perception follows afterwards, and would not be possible had I not already made contact with my doubt in its very object. What has been said of external can equally be said of internal perception: that it involves infinity, that it is a never-ending synthesis which, though always incomplete, is nevertheless self-affirming. If I try to verify my perception of the ash-tray, my task will be endless, for this perception takes for granted more than I can know in an explicit way. Similarly, if I try to verify the reality of my doubt, I shall again be launched into an infinite regress, for I shall need to call into question my thought about doubting, then the thought about that thought, and so on. The certainty derives from the doubt itself as an act, and not from these thoughts, just as the certainty of the thing and of the world precedes any thetic knowledge of their properties. It is indeed true, as has been said, that to know is to know that one knows, not because this second order of knowing guarantees knowledge itself, but the reverse. I cannot reconstruct the thing, and yet there *are* perceived things. In the same way I can never coincide with my life which is for ever fleeing I from itself, in spite of which there *are* inner perceptions. For the same reason I am open to both illusion and truth about myself: that is, there are acts in which I collect myself together in order to surpass I myself. The *cogito* is the recognition of this fundamental fact. In the proposition: 'I think, I am', the two assertions are to be equated with each other, otherwise there would be no *cogito*. Nevertheless we must be clear about the meaning of this equivalence: it is not the 'I am' which is pre-eminently contained in the 'I think,' not my existence which is brought down to the consciousness which I have of it, but conversely the 'I think,' which is re-integrated into the transcending process of the 'I am', and consciousness into existence.

It is true that it seems necessary to concede my absolute coincidence with myself, if not in the case of will and feeling, at least in acts of 'pure thought'. If this were the case, all that we have said would appear to be challenged, so that, far from appearing as a mere manner of existence, thought would truly monopolize us. We must now, therefore, consider the understanding. I think of the triangle, the three-dimensional space to which it is supposed to belong, the extension of one of its sides, and the line that can be drawn through its apex parallel to the opposite side, and I perceive that this line, with the apex, forms three angles the sum of which is equal to the sum of the angles of the triangle, and equal, moreover, to two right angles. I am sure of the result which I regard as proved; which means that my diagrammatic construction is not, as are the strokes arbitrarily added by the child to his drawing, each one of which completely transforms its meaning ('it's a house; no, it's a boat; no it's a man'), a collection of lines fortuitously drawn by my hand. The process from start to finish has a triangle in view. The genesis of the figure is not only a real genesis, but an intelligible one; I make my construction according to rules, and cause *properties* to make their appearance in the figure – properties which are relations belonging to the essence of the triangle. I do not, like the child, reproduce those suggested by the ill-defined figure which is actually there on the paper. I am aware of presenting a proof, because I perceive a necessary link between the collection of data which constitute the hypothesis and the conclusion which I draw from them. It is this necessity which ensures that I shall be able to repeat the operation with an indefinite number of empirical figures, and the necessity itself stems from the fact that at each step in my demonstration, and each time I introduced new relationships, I remained conscious of the triangle as a stable structure conditioned, and left intact, by them. This is why we can say, if we want, that the proof consists in bringing the sum of the angles constructed into two different groupings, and seeing that sum alternately as equal to the sum of the angles of the triangle, and equal to two right angles,[21] but it must be added[22] that here we have not merely two successive configurations, the first of which eliminates the second (as is the case with the child sketching dreamily); the first survives for me while the second is in process of establishing itself, the sum of angles which I equate with two right angles *is* the same as I elsewhere equate with the sum of the angles of the triangle, all of which is possible only provided that I go beyond the order of phenomena or appearances and gain access to that of the *eidos* or of being. Truth would seem to be impossible unless one enjoys an absolute self-possession in active thought, failing which it would be unable to unfold in a set of successive operations, and to produce a permanently valid result.

There would be neither thought nor truth *but for* an act whereby I prevail over the temporal dispersal of the phases of thought, and the mere *de facto* existence of my mental events. The important thing, however, is fully to understand the nature of this act. The necessity of the proof is not an analytic necessity: the construction which enables the conclusion to be reached is not really contained in the essence of the triangle, but merely possible when that essence serves as a starting point. There is no definition of a triangle which includes in advance the properties subsequently to be demonstrated and the intermediate steps leading to that demonstration. Extending one side, drawing through the apex a line parallel to the opposite side, introducing the theorem relating to parallels and their secant, these steps are possible only if I consider the triangle itself as it is drawn on the paper, on the blackboard or in the imagination, with its physiognomy, the concrete arrangement of its lines, in short its *Gestalt*. Is not precisely this the essence or the idea of a triangle? Let us, at the outset, reject any idea of a formal essence of the triangle. Whatever one's opinion of attempts at formalization, it is in any case quite certain that they lay no claim to provide a logic of invention, and that no logical definition of a triangle could equal in fecundity the vision of the figure, or enable us to reach, through a series of formal operations, conclusions not already established by the aid of intuition. This, it will perhaps be objected, touches only on the psychological circumstances of discovery, so that in so far as, after the event, it is possible to establish, between the hypothesis and the conclusion, a link owing nothing to intuition, it is because intuition is not the inevitable mediator of thought and has no place in logic. But the fact that formalization is always retrospective proves that it is never otherwise than apparently complete, and that formal thought feeds on intuitive thought. It reveals those unformulated axioms on which reason is said to rest, and seems to bring to reason a certain added rigour and to uncover the very foundations of our certainty; but in reality the place in which certainty arises and in which a truth makes its appearance is always intuitive thought, even though, or rather *precisely because*, the principles are tacitly assumed there. There would be no experience of truth, and nothing would quench our 'mental volubility' if we thought *vi formae*, and if formal relations were not first presented to us crystallized in some particular thing. We should not even be able to settle on a hypothesis from which to deduce the consequences, if we did not first hold it to be true. A hypothesis is what is presumed to be true, so that hypothetical thinking presupposes some experience of *de facto* truth. The construction relates, then, to the configuration of the triangle, to the way in which it occupies space, to the relations expressed by the words 'on', 'by', 'apex' and 'extend'. Do these relations constitute a kind of material essence of the triangle? If the words 'on', 'through', etc., are to retain any meaning, it is in virtue of my working on a perceptible or imaginary triangle, that is to say, one which is at least potentially situated in my perceptual field, orientated in relation to 'up' and 'down', 'right' and 'left', or again, as we pointed out earlier, implied in my general grip upon the world. The construction makes explicit the possibilities of the triangle, considered not in the light of its definition and as a pure idea, but as a configuration and as the pole towards which my movements are directed. The conclusion follows of necessity from the hypothesis because, in the act of constructing, the geometer has already experienced the possibility of the transition. Let us try to give a better description of this act. We have seen that what occurs is clearly not a purely manual operation, the actual movement of my hand and pen over the paper, for in that case there would be no difference between a construction and any arbitrary set of strokes, and no demonstration would accrue. The construction is a gesture, which means that the actual lines drawn are the outward expression of an intention. But then what is this intention? I 'consider' the triangle, which is for me a set of lines with a certain orientation, and if words such as 'angle' or 'direction' have any meaning for me, it is in so far as I place myself at a point, and from it tend towards another point, in so far as the system of spatial positions provides me with a field of possible movements. Thus do I grasp the concrete essence of the triangle, which is not a collection of objective 'characteristics', but the formula of an attitude, a certain modality of my hold on the world, a structure, in short. When I construct, I commit the first structure to a second one, the 'parallels and secant' structure. How is that possible? It is because my perception of the triangle was not, so to speak, fixed and dead, for the drawing of the triangle on the paper was merely its outer covering; it was traversed by lines of force, and everywhere in it new directions not traced out yet possible came to light. In so far as the triangle was implicated in my hold on the world, it was bursting with indefinite possibilities of which the construction actually drawn was merely one. The construction possesses a demonstrative value because I cause it to emerge from the dynamic formula of the triangle. It expresses my power to make apparent the sensible symbols of a certain hold on things, which is my perception of the triangle's structure. It is an act of the productive imagination and not a return to the eternal idea of the triangle. Just as the localization of objects in space, according to Kant himself, is not merely a mental operation, but one which utilizes the body's motility,[23] movement conferring sensations at the particular point on its trajectory at which those sensations are produced, so the geometer, who, generally speaking, studies the objective laws of location, knows the relationships with which he is concerned only by describing them, at least potentially, with his body. The subject of geometry is a motor subject. This means in the first place that our body is not an object, nor is its movement a mere change of place in objective space, otherwise the problem would be merely shifted, and the movement of one's own body would shed no light on the problem of the location of things, since it would be itself nothing but a thing. There must be, as Kant conceded, a 'motion which generates space'[24] which is our intentional motion, distinct from 'motion in space', which is that of things and of our passive body. But there is more to be said: if motion is productive of space, we must rule out the possibility that the body's motility is a mere 'instrument'[25] for the constituting consciousness. If there is a constituting consciousness, then bodily movement is movement only in so far as that consciousness thinks of it in that light;[26] the constructive power rediscovers in it only what it has put there, and the body is not even an instrument in this respect: it is an object among objects. There is no psychology in a philosophy of constituting consciousness. Or at least there can be nothing valid for such a psychology to say, for it can do nothing but apply the results of analytical reflection to each particular content, while nevertheless distorting them, since it deprives them of their transcendental significance. The body's motion can play a part in the perception of the world only if it is itself an original intentionality, a manner of relating itself to the distinct object of knowledge. The world around us must be, not a system of objects which we synthesize, but a totality of things, open to us, towards which we project ourselves. The 'motion which generates space' does not deploy the trajectory from some metaphysical point with no position in the real world, but from a certain here towards a certain yonder, which are necessarily interchangeable. The project towards motion is an act, which means that it traces out the spatio-temporal distance by actually covering it. The geometer's thought, in so far as it is necessarily sustained by this act, does not, therefore, coincide with itself: it is purely and simply transcendence. In so far as, by adding a construction, I can bring to light the properties of a triangle, and yet find that the figure thus transformed does not cease to be the same figure as I began with, and in so far, moreover, as I am able to effect a synthesis retaining the character of necessity, this is not because my construction is upheld by a concept of the triangle in which all its properties are included, or because, starting from perceptual consciousness, I arrive at the *eidos*: it is because I perform the synthesis of the new property by means of my body, which immediately implants me in space, while its autonomous motion enables me, through a series of definite procedures, to arrive once more at an all-inclusive view of space. Far from its being the case that geometrical thinking transcends perceptual consciousness, it is from the world of perception that I borrow the notion of essence. I believe that the triangle has always had, and always will have, angles the sum of which equals two right angles, as well as all the other less obvious properties which geometry attributes to it, because I have had the experience of a real triangle, and because, as a physical thing, it necessarily *has* within itself everything that it has ever been able, or ever will be able, to display. Unless the perceived thing has for good and ever implanted within us the ideal notion of a being which is what it is, there would be no phenomenon of being, and mathematical thought would appear to us in the light of a creative activity. What I call the essence of the triangle is nothing but this presumption of a completed synthesis, in terms of which we have defined the thing.

Our body, to the extent that it moves itself about, that is, to the extent that it is inseparable from a view of the world and is that view itself brought into existence, is the condition of possibility, not only of the geometrical synthesis, but of all expressive operations and all acquired views which constitute the cultural world. When we say that thought is spontaneous, this does not mean that it coincides with itself; on the contrary it means that it outruns itself, and speech is precisely that act through which it immortalizes itself as truth. It is, indeed, obvious that speech cannot be regarded as a mere clothing for thought, or expression as the translation, into an arbitrary system of symbols, of a meaning already clear to itself. It is said again and again that sounds and phonemes have no meaning in themselves, and that all our consciousness can find in language is what it has put there. But it would follow from this that language can teach us nothing, and that it can at the most arouse in us new combinations of those meanings already possessed by us. But this is just what the experience of language refutes. It is true that communication presupposes a system of correspondences such as the dictionary provides, but it goes beyond these, and what gives its meaning to each word is the sentence. It is because it has been used in various contexts that the word gradually accumulates a significance which it is impossible to establish absolutely. A telling utterance or a good book impose their meaning upon us. Thus they carry it within them in a certain way. As for the speaking subject, he too must be enabled to outrun what he thought before, and to find in his own words more than the thought he was putting into them, otherwise we should not see thought, even solitary thought, seeking expression with such perseverance. Speech is, therefore, that paradoxical operation through which, by using words of a given sense, and already available meanings, we try to follow up an intention which necessarily outstrips, modifies, and itself, in the last analysis, stabilizes the meanings of the words which translate it. Constituted language plays the same limited rôle in the work of expression as do colours in painting. Had we not eyes, or more generally senses, there would be no painting at all for us, yet the picture 'tells' us more than the mere use of our senses can ever do. The picture over and above the sense-data, speech over and above linguistic data must, therefore, in themselves possess a signifying virtue, independently of any meaning that exists for itself, in the mind of the spectator or listener. 'By using words as the painter uses colours and the musician notes, we are trying to constitute, out of a spectacle or an emotion, or even an abstract idea, a kind of equivalent or *specie* soluble in the mind. Here the expression becomes the principal thing. We mould and animate the reader, we cause him to participate in our creative or poetic action, putting into the hidden mouth of his mind the message of a certain object or of a certain feeling.'[27] In the painter or the speaking subject, picture and utterance respectively do not illustrate a ready-made thought, but make that thought their own. This is why we have been led to distinguish between a secondary speech which renders a thought already acquired, and an originating speech which brings it into existence, in the first place for ourselves, and then for others. Now all words which have become mere signs for a univocal thought have been able to do so only because they have first of all functioned as originating words, and we can still remember with what richness they appeared to be endowed, and how they were like a landscape new to us, while we were engaged in 'acquiring' them, and while they still fulfilled the primordial function of expression. Thus self-possession and coincidence with the self do not serve to define thought, which is, on the contrary, an outcome of expression and always an illusion, in so far as the clarity of what is acquired rests upon the fundamentally obscure operation which has enabled us to immortalize within ourselves a moment of fleeting life. We are invited to discern beneath thinking which basks in its acquisitions, and offers merely a brief resting-place in the unending process of expression, another thought which is struggling to establish itself, and succeeds only by bending the resources of constituted language to some fresh usage. This operation must be considered as an ultimate fact, since any explanation of it – whether empiricist, reducing new meanings to given ones; or idealist, positing an absolute knowledge immanent in the most primitive forms of knowledge – would amount to a denial of it. Language outruns us, not merely because the use of speech always presupposes a great number of thoughts which are not present in the mind and which are covered by each word, but also for another reason, and a more profound one: namely, that these thoughts themselves, when present, were not at any time 'pure' thoughts either, for already in them there was a surplus of the signified over the signifying, the same effort of thought already thought to equal thinking thought, the same provisional amalgam of both which gives rise to the whole mystery of expression. That which is called an idea is necessarily linked to an act of expression, and owes to it its appearance of autonomy. It is a cultural object, like the church, the street, the pencil or the Ninth Symphony. It may be said in reply that the church can be burnt down, the street and pencil destroyed, and that, if all the scores of the Ninth Symphony and all musical instruments were reduced to ashes, it would survive only for a few brief years in the memory of those who had heard it, whereas on the other hand the idea of the triangle and its properties are imperishable. In fact, the idea of the triangle with its properties, and of the quadratic equation, have their historical and geographical area, and if the tradition in which they have been handed down to us, and the cultural instruments which bear them on, were to be destroyed, fresh acts of creative expression would be needed to revive them in the world. What is true, however, is that, once they have made their first appearance, subsequent 'appearances', if successful, add nothing and if unsuccessful, subtract nothing, from the quadratic equation, which remains an inexhaustible possession among us. But the same may be said of the Ninth Symphony, which lives on in its intelligible abode, as Proust has said, whether it is played well or badly; or rather which continues its existence in a more occult time than natural time. The time of ideas is not to be confused with that in which books appear and disappear, and musical works are printed or lost: a book which has always been reprinted one day ceases to be read, a musical work of which there were only a few copies extant is suddenly much sought after. The existence of the idea must not be confused with the empirical existence of the means of expression, for ideas endure or fall into oblivion, and the intelligible sky subtly changes colour. We have already drawn a distinction between empirical speech – the word as a phenomenon of sound, the fact that a certain word is uttered at a certain moment by a certain person, which may happen independently of thought – and transcendental or authentic speech, that by which an idea begins to exist. But if there had been no mankind with phonatory or articulatory organs, and a respiratory apparatus – or at least with a body and the ability to move himself – there would have been no speech and no ideas. What remains true is that in speech, to a greater extent than in music or painting, thought seems able to detach itself from its material instruments and acquire an eternal value. There is a sense in which all triangles which will ever exist through the workings of physical causality will always have angles the sum of which equals two right angles, even if a time comes when men have forgotten their geometry, and there is not a single person left who knows any. But in this case it is because speech is applied to nature, whereas music, and painting, like poetry, create their own object, and as soon as they become sufficiently aware of themselves, deliberately confine themselves within the cultural world. Prosaic, and particularly scientific, utterance is a cultural entity which at the same time lays claim to translate a truth relating to nature in itself. Now we know that this is not the case, for modern criticism of the sciences has clearly shown the constructive element in them. 'Real', i.e. perceived, triangles, do not necessarily have, for all eternity, angles the sum of which equals two right angles, if it is true that the space in which we live is no less amenable to non-Euclidean than to Euclidean geometry. Thus there is no fundamental difference between the various modes of expression, and no privileged position can be accorded to any of them on the alleged ground that it expresses a truth in itself. Speech is as dumb as music, music as eloquent as speech. Expression is everywhere creative, and what is expressed is always inseparable from it. There is no analysis capable of making language crystal clear and arraying it before us as if it were an object. The act of speech is clear only for the person who is actually speaking or listening; it becomes obscure as soon as we try to bring explicitly to light those reasons which have led us to understand thus and not otherwise. We can say of it what we have said of perception, and what Pascal says about opinions: in all three cases we have the same miracle of an immediately apprehended clarity, which vanishes as soon as we try to break it down to what we believe to be its component elements. I speak, and I understand myself and am understood quite unambiguously; I take a new grip on my life, and others take a new grip on it too. I may say that 'I have been waiting for a long time', or that someone 'is dead', and I think I know what I am saying. Yet if I question myself on time or the experience of death, which were implied in my words, there is nothing clear in my mind. This is because I have tried to speak about speech, to re-enact the act of expression which gave significance to the words 'dead' and 'time', to extend the brief hold on my experience which they ensure for me. These second or third order acts of expression, like the rest, have indeed in each case their convincing clarity, without, however, ever enabling me to dispel the fundamental obscurity of what is expressed, or to eliminate the distance separating my thought from itself. Must we conclude from this[28] that, born and developed in obscurity, yet capable of clarity, language is nothing but the obverse of an infinite Thought, and the message of that Thought as communicated to us? This would mean losing contact with the analysis which we have just carried out, and reaching a conclusion in conflict with what has been established as we have gone along. Language transcends us and yet we speak. If we are led to conclude from this that there exists a transcendent thought spelt out by our words, we are supposing that an attempt at expression is brought to completion, after saying that it can never be so, and invoking an absolute thought, when we have just shown that any such thought is beyond our conception. Such is the principle of Pascal's apologetics; but the more it is shown that man is without absolute power, the more any assertion of an absolute is made, not probable, but on the contrary suspect. In fact analysis demonstrates, not that there is behind language a transcendent thought, but that language transcends itself in speech, that speech itself *brings about* that concordance between me and myself, and between myself and others, on which an attempt is being made to base that thought. The phenomenon of language, in the double sense of primary fact and remarkable occurrence, is not explained, but eliminated, if we duplicate it with some transcendent thought, since it consists in this: that an act of thought, once expressed, has the power to outlive itself. It is not, as is often held, that the verbal formula serves us as a mnemonic means: merely committed to writing or to memory, it would be useless had we not acquired once and for all the inner power of interpreting it. To give expression is not to substitute, for new thought, a system of stable signs to which unchangeable thoughts are linked, it is to ensure, by the use of words already used, that the new intention carries on the heritage of the past, it is at a stroke to incorporate the past into the present, and weld that present to a future, to open a whole temporal cycle in which the 'acquired' thought will remain present as a dimension, without our needing henceforth to summon it up or reproduce it. What is known as the non-temporal in thought is what, having thus carried forward the past and committed the future, is presumptively of all time and is therefore anything but transcendent in relation to time. The non-temporal is the acquired.

Time itself presents us with the prime model of this permanent acquisition. If time is the dimension in accordance with which events drive each other successively from the scene, it is also that in accordance with which each one of them wins its unchallengeable place. To say that an event *takes place* is to say that it will always be true that it has taken place. Each moment of time, in virtue of its very essence, posits an existence against which the other moments of time are powerless. After the construction is drawn, the geometrical relation is acquired; even if I then forget the details of the proof, the mathematical gesture establishes a tradition. Van Gogh's paintings have their place in me for all time, a step is taken from which I cannot retreat, and, even though I retain no clear recollection of the pictures which I have seen, my whole subsequent aesthetic experience will be that of someone who has become acquainted with the painting of Van Gogh, exactly as a middle class man turned workman always remains, even in his manner of being a workman, a middle-class-man-turned-workman, or as an act confers a certain quality upon us for ever, even though we may afterwards repudiate it and change our beliefs. Existence always carries forward its past, whether it be by accepting or disclaiming it. We are, as Proust declared, perched on a pyramid of past life, and if we do not see this, it is because we are obsessed by objective thought. We believe that our past, for ourselves, is reducible to the express memories which we are able to contemplate. We sever our existence from the past itself, and allow it to pick up only those threads of the past which are present. But how are these threads to be recognized as threads of the past unless we enjoy in some other way a direct opening upon that past? Acquisition must be accepted as an irreducible phenomenon. What we have experienced is, and remains, permanently ours; and in old age a man is still in contact with his youth. Every present as it arises is driven into time like a wedge and stakes its claim to eternity. Eternity is not another order of time, but the atmosphere of time. It is true that a false thought, no less than a true one, possesses this sort of eternity: if I am mistaken at this moment, it is for ever true that I am mistaken. It would seem necessary, therefore, that there should be, in true thought, a different fertility, and that it should remain true not only as a past actually lived through, but also as a perpetual present for ever carried forward in time's succession. This, however, does not secure any essential difference between truths of fact and truths of reason. For there is not one of my actions, not one of even my fallacious thoughts, once it is adhered to, which has not been directed towards a value or a truth, and which, in consequence, does not retain its permanent relevance in the subsequent course of my life, not only as an indelible fact, but also as a necessary stage on the road to the more complete truths or values which I have since recognized. My truths have been built out of these errors, and carry them along in their eternity. Conversely, there is not one truth of reason which does not retain its coefficient of facticity: the alleged transparency of Euclidean geometry is one day revealed as operative for a certain period in the history of the human mind, and signifies simply that, for a time, men were able to take a homogeneous three-dimensional space as the 'ground' of their thoughts, and to assume unquestioningly what generalized science will come to consider as a contingent account of space. Thus every truth of fact is a truth of reason, and *vice versa*. The relation of reason to fact, or eternity to time, like that of reflection to the unreflective, of thought to language or of thought to perception is this two-way relationship that phenomenology has called *Fundierung*: the founding term, or originator – time, the unreflective, the fact, language, perception – is primary in the sense that the originated is presented as a determinate or explicit form of the originator, which prevents the latter from reabsorbing the former, and yet the originator is not primary in the empiricist sense and the originated is not simply derived from it, since it is through the originated that the originator is made manifest. It is for this reason that it is a matter of indifference whether we say that the present foreshadows eternity or that the eternity of truth is merely a sublimation of the present. This ambiguity cannot be resolved, but it can be understood as ultimate, if we recapture the intuition of real time which preserves everything, and which is at the core of both proof and expression. 'Reflection on the creative power of the mind,' says Brunschvicg,[29] 'implies, in every certainty of experience, the feeling that, in any determinate truth that one may have managed to demonstrate, there exists a soul of truth which outruns it and frees itself from it, a soul which can detach itself from the particular expression of that truth in order to adumbrate a deeper and more comprehensive expression, although this drive forward in no way impairs the eternity of the true.' What is this eternally true that no one possesses? What is this thing expressed which lies beyond all expression, and, if we have the right to posit it, why is it our constant concern to arrive at a more precise expression? What is this One round which minds and truths are disposed, as if they tended towards it, while it is maintained at the same time that they tend towards no pre-established term? The idea of a transcendent Being had at least the advantage of not stultifying the actions through which, in an ever difficult process of carrying forward, each consciousness and intersubjectivity themselves forge their own unity. It is true that, if these actions belong to that most intimate part of ourselves accessible to us, the positing of God contributes nothing to the elucidation of our life. We experience, not a genuine eternity and a participation in the One, but concrete acts of taking up and carrying forward by which, through time's accidents, we are linked in relationships with ourselves and others. In short, we experience a *participation in the world*, and 'being-in-truth' is indistinguishable from being in the world.

We are now in a position to make up our minds about the question of evidence, and to describe the experience of truth. There are truths just as there are perceptions: not that we can ever array before ourselves in their entirety the reasons for any assertion – there are merely motives, we have merely a hold on time and not full possession of it – but because it is of the essence of time to take itself up as it leaves itself behind, and to draw itself together into visible things, into firsthand evidence. All consciousness is, in some measure, perceptual consciousness. If it were possible to lay bare and unfold all the presuppositions in what I call my reason or my ideas at each moment, we should always find experiences which have not been made explicit, large-scale contributions from past and present, a whole 'sedimentary history'[30] which is not only relevant to the *genesis* of my thought, but which determines its *significance*. For an absolute evidence, free from any presupposition, to be possible, and for my thought to be able to pierce through to itself, catch itself in action, and arrive at a pure 'assent of the self to the self', it would, to speak the language of the Kantians, have to cease to be an event and become an act through and through: in the language of the Schoolmen, its formal reality would have to be included in its objective reality; in the language of Malebranche, it would have to cease to be 'perception', 'sentiment' or 'contact' with truth, to become pure 'idea' and 'vision' of the truth. It would be necessary, in other words, that instead of being myself, I should become purely and simply one who knows myself, and that the world should have ceased to exist around me in order to become purely and simply an object before me. In relation to what we are by reason of our acquisitions and this pre-existent world, we have a power of placing in abeyance, and that suffices to ensure our freedom from determinism. I may well close my eyes, and stop up my ears, I shall nevertheless not cease to see, if it is only the blackness before my eyes, or to hear, if only silence, and in the same way I can 'bracket' my opinions or the beliefs I have acquired, but, whatever I think or decide, it is always against the background of what I have previously believed or done. *Habemus ideam veram*, we possess a truth, but this experience of truth would be absolute knowledge only if we could thematize every motive, that is, if we ceased to be in a situation. The actual possession of the true idea does not, therefore, entitle us to predicate an intelligible abode of adequate thought and absolute productivity, it establishes merely a 'teleology'[31] of consciousness which, from this first instrument, will forge more perfect ones, and these in turn more perfect ones still, and so on endlessly. 'Only through an eidetic intuition can the essence of eidetic intuition be elucidated,' says Husserl.[32] The intuition of some particular essence necessarily precedes, in our experience, the essence of intuition. The only way to think of thought is in the first place to think of something, and it is therefore essential to that thought not to take itself as an object. To think of thought is to adopt in relation to it an attitude that we have initially learned in relation to 'things'; it is never to eliminate, but merely to push further back the opacity that thought presents to itself. Every halt in the forward movement of consciousness, every focus on the object, every appearance of a 'something' or of an idea presupposes a subject who has suspended self-questioning at least in that particular respect. Which is why, as Descartes maintained, it is true both that certain ideas are presented to me as irresistibly self-evident *de facto*, and that this fact is never valid *de jure*, and that it never does away with the possibility of doubt arising as soon as we are no longer in the presence of the idea. It is no accident that self-evidence itself may be called into question, because *certainty is doubt*, being the carrying forward of a tradition of thought which cannot be condensed into an evident 'truth' without my giving up all attempts to make it explicit. It is for the same reasons that a self-evident truth is irresistible in fact, yet always questionable, which amounts to two ways of saying the same thing: namely, that it is irresistible because I take for granted a certain acquisition of experience, a certain field of thought, and precisely for this reason it appears to me as self-evident for a certain thinking nature, the one which I enjoy and perpetuate, but which remains contingent and given to itself. The consistency of a thing perceived, of a geometrical relationship or of an idea, is arrived at only provided that I give up trying by every means to make it more explicit, and instead allow myself to come to rest in it. Once launched, and committed to a certain set of thoughts, Euclidean space, for example, or the conditions governing the existence of a certain society, I discover evident truths; but these are not unchallengeable, since perhaps this space or this society are not the only ones possible. It is therefore of the essence of certainty to be established only with reservations; there is an *opinion* which is not a provisional form of knowledge destined to give way later to an absolute form, but on the contrary, both the oldest or most rudimentary, and the most conscious or mature form of knowledge – an opinion which is primary in the double sense of 'original' and 'fundamental'. This is what calls up before us *something in general*, to which positing thought – doubt or demonstration – can subsequently relate in affirmation or denial. There is significance, something and not nothing, there is an indefinite train of concordant experiences, to which this ash-tray in its permanence testifies, or the truth which I hit upon yesterday and to which I think I can revert today.

This evidentness of the phenomenon, or again of the 'world', is no less misunderstood when we try to reach being without contact with the phenomenon, that is, when we make being necessary, as when we cut the phenomenon off from being, when we degrade it to the status of mere appearance or possibility. The first conception is Spinoza's. Primary opinion is here subordinated to absolute self-evidence, and the notion, 'there is something' which is an amalgam of being and nothingness, to the notion 'Being exists'. One rejects as meaningless any questioning of being: it is impossible to ask why there is something rather than nothing, and why this world rather than a different one, since the shape of this world and the very existence of a world are merely consequences of necessary being. The second conception reduces self-evidence to appearance: all my truths are after all self-evident only for me, and for a thought fashioned like mine; they are bound up with my psycho-physiological constitution and the existence of this world. Other forms of thought functioning in accordance with other rules, and other possible worlds, can be conceived as having the same claim to reality as this one. And here the question why there is something rather than nothing seems apposite, and why this particular world has come into being, but the reply is necessarily out of our reach, since we are imprisoned in our psycho-physiological make-up, which is a simple fact like the shape of our face or the number of our teeth. This second conception is not so different from the first as it might appear: it implies a tacit reference to an absolute knowledge and an absolute being in relation to which our factual self-evidences, or synthetic truths, are considered inadequate. According to the phenomenological conception, this dogmatism on the one hand and scepticism on the other are both left behind. The laws of our thought and our self-evident truths are certainly facts, but they are not detachable from us, they are implied in any conception that we may form of being and the possible. It is not a question of confining ourselves to phenomena, of imprisoning consciousness in its own states, while retaining the possibility of another being beyond apparent being, nor of treating our thought as one fact among many, but of defining being as that which appears, and consciousness as a universal fact. I think, and this or that thought appears to me as true; I am well aware that it is not unconditionally true, and that the process of making it totally explicit would be an endless task; but the fact remains that at the moment I think, I think something, and that any other truth, in the name of which I might wish to discount this one, must, if it is to be called a truth for me, square with the 'true' thought of which I have experience. If I try to imagine Martians, or angels, or some divine thought outside the realm of my logic, this Martian, angelic or divine thought must figure in my universe without completely disrupting it.[33] My thought, my self-evident truth is not one fact among others, but a value-fact which envelops and conditions every other possible one. There is no other world possible in the sense in which mine is, not because mine is necessary as Spinoza thought, but because any 'other world' that I might try to conceive would set limits to this one, would be found on its boundaries, and would consequently merely fuse with it. Consciousness, if it is not absolute truth or *aletheia*, at least rules out all absolute falsity. Our mistakes, illusions and questions are indeed mistakes, illusions and questions. Error is not consciousness of error; it even excludes such consciousness. Our questions do not always admit of answers, and to say with Marx that man poses for himself only problems that he can solve is to revive a theological optimism and postulate the consummation of the world. Our errors become truths only once they are recognized, and there remains a difference between their revealed and their latent content of truth, between their alleged and their actual significance. The truth is that neither error nor doubt ever cut us off from the truth, because they are surrounded by a world horizon in which the teleology of consciousness summons us to an effort at resolving them. Finally, the contingency of the world must not be understood as a deficiency in being, a break in the stuff of necessary being, a threat to rationality, nor as a problem to be solved as soon as possible by the discovery of some deeper-laid necessity. That is ontic contingency, contingency within the bounds of the world. Ontological contingency, the contingency of the world itself, being radical, is, on the other hand, what forms the basis once and for all of our ideas of truth. The world is that reality of which the necessary and the possible are merely provinces.

To sum up, we are restoring to the *cogito* a temporal thickness. If there is not endless doubt, and if 'I think', it is because I plunge on into provisional thoughts and, by deeds, overcome time's discontinuity. Thus vision is brought to rest in a thing seen which both precedes and outlasts it. Have we got out of our difficulty? We have admitted that the certainty of vision and that of the thing seen are of a piece. Must we conclude from this that, since the thing seen is never absolutely certain, as illusions show, vision also is involved in this uncertainty, or, on the contrary, that, since vision on its own is absolutely certain, so is the thing seen, so that I am never really mistaken? The second solution would amount to reinstating the immanence which we have banished. But if we adopted the first, thought would be cut off from itself, there would no longer be anything but 'facts of consciousness' which might be called internal by nominal definition, but which, for me, would be as opaque as things; there would no longer be either inner experience or consciousness, and the experience of the *cogito* would be once more forgotten. When we describe consciousness as involved through its body in a space, through its language in a history, through its prejudices in a concrete form of thought, it is not a matter of setting it back in a series of objective events, even though they be 'psychic' events, and in the causal system of the world. He who doubts cannot, while doubting, doubt that he doubts. Doubt, even when generalized, is not the abolition of my thought, it is merely a pseudo-nothingness, for I cannot extricate myself from being; my act of doubting itself creates the possibility of certainty and is there for me, it occupies me, I am committed to it, and I cannot pretend to be nothing at the time I execute it. Reflection, which moves all things away to a distance, discovers itself as at least given to itself in the sense that it cannot think of itself as eliminated, or stand apart from itself. But this does not mean that reflection and thought are elementary facts there to be observed as such. As Montaigne clearly saw, one can call into question thought which is loaded with a sediment of history and weighed down with its own being, one can entertain doubts about doubt itself, considered as a definite modality of thought and as consciousness of a doubtful object, but the formula of radical reflection is not: 'I know nothing' – a formula which it is all too easy to catch in flat contradiction with itself – but: 'What do I know?' Descartes was not unmindful of this. He has frequently been credited with having gone beyond sceptical doubt, which is a mere state, and with making doubt into a method, an act, and with having thus provided consciousness with a fixed point and reinstated certainty. But, in fact, Descartes did not suspend doubt in the face of the certainty of doubt itself, as if the act of doubting were sufficient to sweep doubt away by entailing a certainty. He took it further. He does not say: 'I doubt, therefore I am', but 'I think, therefore I am', which means that doubt itself is certain, not as actual doubt, but as pure thought about doubting and, since the same might be said in turn about this thought, the only proposition which is absolutely certain and which halts doubt in its tracks because it is implied by that doubt, is: 'I think,' or again, 'something appears to me'. There is no act, no particular experience which exactly fills my consciousness and imprisons my freedom, 'there is no thought which abolishes the power to think and brings it to a conclusion – no definite position of the bolt that finally closes the lock. No, there is no thought which is a resolution born of its own very development and, as it were, the final chord of this permanent dissonance.'[34] No particular thought reaches through to the core of our thought in general, nor is any thought conceivable without another possible thought as a witness to it. And this is no imperfection from which we may imagine consciousness freed. If there must be consciousness, if something must appear to someone, it is necessary that behind all our particular thoughts there should lie a retreat of not-being, a Self. I must avoid equating myself with a series of 'consciousnesses', for each of these, with its load of sedimentary history and sensible implications, must present itself to a perpetual absentee. Our situation, then, is as follows: in order to know that we think, it is necessary in the first place that we actually should think. Yet this commitment does not dispel all doubts, for my thoughts do not deprive me of my power to question; a word or an idea, considered as events in my history, have meaning for me only if I take up this meaning from within. I know that I think through such and such particular thoughts that I have, and I know that I have these thoughts because I carry them forward, that is, because I know that I think in general. The aim at a transcendent objective and the view of myself aiming at it, the awareness of the connected and of connecting are in a circular relationship. The problem is how I can be the constituting agent of my thought in general, failing which it would not be thought by anybody, would pass unnoticed and would therefore not be thought at all – without ever being that agent of my particular thoughts, since I never see them come into being in the full light of day, but merely know myself through them. The question is how subjectivity can be both dependent yet irremovable.

Let us tackle this by taking language as our example. There is a consciousness of myself which makes use of language and is humming with words. I read, let us say, the *Second Meditation*. It has indeed to do with me, but a me in idea, an idea which is, strictly speaking, neither mine nor, for that matter, Descartes', but that of any reflecting man. By following the meaning of the words and the argument, I reach the conclusion that indeed because I think, I am; but this is merely a verbal *cogito*, for I have grasped my thought and my existence only through the medium of language, and the true formula of this *cogito* should be: 'One thinks, therefore one is.' The wonderful thing about language is that it promotes its own oblivion: my eyes follow the lines on the paper, and from the moment I am caught up in their meaning, I lose sight of them. The paper, the letters on it, my eyes and body are there only as the minimum setting of some invisible operation. Expression fades out before what is expressed, and this is why its mediating rôle may pass unnoticed, and why Descartes nowhere mentions it. Descartes, and *a fortiori* his reader, begin their meditation in what is already a universe of discourse. This certainty which we enjoy of reaching, beyond expression, a truth separable from it and of which expression is merely the garment and contingent manifestation, has been implanted in us precisely by language. It appears as a mere sign only once it has provided itself with a meaning, and the coming to awareness, if it is to be complete, must rediscover the expressive unity in which both signs and meaning appear in the first place. When a child cannot speak, or cannot yet speak the adult's language, the linguistic ritual which unfolds around him has no hold on him, he is near us in the same way as is a spectator with a poor seat at the theatre; he sees clearly enough that we are laughing and gesticulating, he hears the nasal tune being played, but there is nothing at the end of those gestures or behind those words, nothing *happens* for him. Language takes on a meaning for the child when it *establishes a situation* for him. A story is told in a children's book of the disappointment of a small boy who put on his grandmother's spectacles and took up her book in the expectation of being able himself to find in it the stories which she used to tell him. The tale ends with these words: 'Well, what a fraud! Where's the story? I can see nothing but black and white.' For the child the 'story' and the thing expressed are not 'ideas' or 'meanings', nor are speaking or reading 'intellectual operations'. The story is a world which there must be some way of magically calling up by putting on spectacles and leaning over a book. The power possessed by language of bringing the thing expressed into existence, of opening up to thought new ways, new dimensions and new landscapes, is, in the last analysis, as obscure for the adult as for the child. In every successful work, the significance carried into the reader's mind exceeds language and thought as already constituted and is magically thrown into relief during the linguistic incantation, just as the story used to emerge from grandmother's book. In so far as we believe that, through thought, we are in direct communication with a universe of truth in which we are at one with others, in so far as Descartes' text seems merely to arouse in us thoughts already formed, and we seem never to learn anything from outside, and finally in so far as a philosopher, in a meditation purporting to be thoroughgoing, never even mentions language as the condition of the *reading* of the *cogito*, and does not more overtly invite us to pass from the idea to the practice of the *cogito*, it is because we take the process of expression for granted, because it figures among our acquisitions. The *cogito* at which we arrive by reading Descartes (and even the one which Descartes effects in relation to expression and when, looking back on his past life, he fastens it down, objectifies it and 'characterizes' it as indubitable) is, then, a spoken *cogito*, put into words and understood in words, and for this very reason not attaining its objective, since that part of our existence which is engaged in fixing our life in conceptual forms, and thinking of it as indubitable, is escaping focus and thought. Shall we therefore conclude that language envelops us, and that we are led by it, much as the realist believes he is subject to the determinism of the external world, or as the theologian believes he is led on by Providence? This would be to forget half the truth. For after all, words, 'cogito' and 'sum' for example, may well have an empirical and statistical meaning, for it is the case that they are not directed specifically to my own experience, but form the basis of a general and anonymous thought. Nevertheless, I should find them not so much derivative and inauthentic as meaningless, and I should be unable even to read Descartes' book, were I not, before any speech can begin, in contact with my own life and thought, and if the spoken *cogito* did not encounter within me a tacit *cogito*. This silent *cogito* was the one Descartes sought when writing his *Meditations*. He gave life and direction to all those expressive operations which, by definition, always miss their target since, between Descartes' existence and the knowledge of it which he acquires, they interpose the full thickness of cultural acquisitions. And yet Descartes would not even have tried to put these expressive operations into operation had he not in the first place caught a glimpse of his existence. The whole question amounts to gaining a clear understanding of the unspoken *cogito*, to putting into it only what is really there, and not making language into a product of consciousness on the excuse that consciousness is not a product of language.

Neither the word nor the meaning of the word is, in fact *constituted* by consciousness. Let us make this clear. The word is certainly never reducible to one of its embodiments. The word 'sleet', for example, is not the set of characters which I have just written on the paper, nor that other set of signs that I once read in a book for the first time, nor again the sound that runs through the air when I pronounce it. Those are merely reproductions of the word, in which I recognize it but which do not exhaust it. Am I then to say that the word 'sleet' is the unified idea of these manifestations, and that it exists only for my consciousness and through a synthesis of identification? To do so would be to forget what psychology has taught us about language. To speak, as we have seen, is not to call up verbal images and articulate words in accordance with the imagined model. By undertaking a critical examination of the verbal image, and showing that the speaking subject plunges into speech without imagining the words he is about to utter, modern psychology eliminates the word as a representation, or as an object for consciousness, and reveals a motor presence of the word which is not the knowledge of the word. The word 'sleet', when it is known to me, is not an object which I recognize through any identificatory synthesis, but a certain use made of my phonatory equipment, a certain modulation of my body as a being in the world. Its generality is not that of the idea, but that of a behavioural style 'understood' by my body in so far as the latter is a behaviour-producing power, in this case a phoneme-producing one. One day I 'caught on' to the word 'sleet', much as one imitates a gesture, not, that is, by analysing it and performing an articulatory or phonetic action corresponding to each part of the word as heard, but by hearing it as a single modulation of the world of sound, and because this acoustic entity presents itself as 'something to pronounce' in virtue of the all-embracing correspondence existing between my perceptual potentialities and my motor ones, which are elements of my indivisible and open existence. The word has never been inspected, analysed, known and constituted, but caught and taken up by a power of speech and, in the last analysis, by a motor power given to me along with the first experience I have of my body and its perceptual and practical fields. As for the meaning of the word, I learn it as I learn to use a tool, by seeing it used in the context of a certain situation. The word's meaning is not compounded of a certain number of physical characteristics belonging to the object; it is first and foremost the aspect taken on by the object in human experience, for example my wonder in the face of these hard, then friable, then melting pellets falling ready-made from the sky. Here we have a meeting of the human and the non-human and, as it were, a piece of the world's behaviour, a certain version of its style, and the generality of its meaning as well as that of the vocable is not the generality of the concept, but of the world as typical. Thus language presupposes nothing less than a consciousness of language, a silence of consciousness embracing the world of speech in which words first receive a form and meaning. This is why consciousness is never subordinated to any empirical language, why languages can be translated and learned, and finally, why language is not an attribute of external origin, in the sociologist's sense. Behind the spoken *cogito*, the one which is converted into discourse and into essential truth, there lies a tacit *cogito*, myself experienced by myself. But this subjectivity, albeit imperious, has upon itself and upon the world only a precarious hold. It does not constitute the world, it divines the world's presence round about it as a field not provided by itself; nor does it constitute the word, but speaks as we sing when we are happy; nor again the meaning of the word, which instantaneously emerges for it in its dealing with the world and other men living in it, being at the intersection of many lines of behaviour, and being, even once 'acquired', as precise and yet as indefinable as the significance of a gesture. The tacit *cogito*, the presence of oneself to oneself, being no less than existence, is anterior to any philosophy, and knows itself only in those extreme situations in which it is under threat: for example, in the dread of death or of another's gaze upon me. What is believed to be thought about thought, as pure feeling of the self, cannot yet be thought and needs to be revealed. The consciousness which conditions language is merely a comprehensive and inarticulate grasp upon the world, like that of the infant at its first breath, or of the man about to drown and who is impelled towards life, and though it is true that all particular knowledge is founded on this primary view, it is true also that the latter waits to be won back, fixed and made explicit by perceptual exploration and by speech. Silent consciousness grasps itself only as a generalized 'I think' in face of a confused world 'to be thought about'. Any particular seizure, even the recovery of this generalized project by philosophy, demands that the subject bring into action powers which are a closed book to him and, in particular, that he should become a speaking subject. The tacit *cogito* is a *cogito* only when it has found expression for itself.

Such formulations may appear puzzling: if ultimate subjectivity cannot think of itself the moment it exists, how can it ever do so? How can that which does not think take to doing so? And is not subjectivity made to amount to a thing or a force which produces its effects without being capable of knowing it? We do not mean that the primordial *I* completely overlooks itself. If it did, it would indeed be a thing, and nothing could cause it subsequently to become consciousness. We have merely withheld from it objective thought, a positing consciousness of the world and of itself. What do we mean by this? Either these words mean nothing at all, or else they mean that we refrain from assuming an explicit consciousness which duplicates and sustains the confused grasp of primary subjectivity upon itself and upon its world. My vision, for example, is certainly 'thinking that I see', if we mean thereby that it is not simply a bodily function like digestion or respiration, a collection of processes so grouped as to have a significance in a larger system, but that it is itself that system and that significance, that anteriority of the future to the present, of the whole to its parts. There is vision only through anticipation and intention, and since no intention could be a true intention if the object towards which it tends were given to it ready made and with no motivation, it is true that all vision assumes in the last resort, at the core of subjectivity, a total project or a logic of the world which empirical perceptions endow with specific form, but to which they cannot give rise. But vision is not thinking that one sees, if we understand thereby that it itself links up with its object, and that it becomes aware of itself as absolutely transparent, and as the originator of its own presence in the visible world. The essential point is clearly to grasp the project towards the world that we are. What we have said above about the world's being inseparable from our views of the world should here help us to understand subjectivity conceived as inherence in the world. There is no *hylé*, no sensation which is not in communication with other sensations or the sensations of other people, and *for this very reason* there is no *morphe*, no apprehension or apperception, the office of which is to give significance to a matter that has none, and to ensure the *a priori* unity of my experience, and experience shared with others. Suppose that my friend Paul and I are looking at a landscape. What precisely happens? Must it be said that we have both private sensations, that we know things but cannot communicate them to each other – that, as far as pure, lived-through experience goes, we are each incarcerated in our separate perspectives – that the landscape is not numerically the same for both of us and that it is a question only of a specific identity? When I consider my perception itself, before any objectifying reflection, at no moment am I aware of being shut up within my own sensations. My friend Paul and I point out to each other certain details of the landscape; and Paul's finger, which is pointing out the church tower, is not a finger-for-me that I *think of* as orientated towards a church-tower-for-me, it is Paul's finger which itself shows me the tower that Paul sees, just as, conversely, when I make a movement towards some point in the landscape that I can see, I do not imagine that I am producing in Paul, in virtue of some pre-established harmony, inner visions merely analogous to mine: I believe, on the contrary, that my gestures invade Paul's world and guide his gaze. When I think of Paul, I do not think of a flow of private sensations indirectly related to mine through the medium of interposed signs, but of someone who has a living experience of the same world as mine, as well as the same history, and with whom I am in communication through that world and that history. Are we to say, then, that what we are concerned with is an ideal unity, that my world is the same as Paul's, just as the quadratic equation spoken of in Tokyo is the same as the one spoken of in Paris, and that in short the ideal nature of the world guarantees its intersubjective value? But ideal unity is not satisfactory either, for it exists no less between Mount Hymettus seen by the ancient Greeks and the same mountain seen by me. Now it is no use my telling myself, as I contemplate those russet mountain sides, that the Greeks saw them too, for I cannot convince myself that they are the same ones. On the other hand, Paul and I 'together' see this landscape, we are jointly present in it, it is the same for both of us, not only as an intelligible significance, but as a certain accent of the world's style, down to its very thisness. The unity of the world crumbles and falls asunder under the influence of that temporal and spatial distance which the ideal unity traverses while remaining (in theory) unimpaired. It is precisely because the landscape makes its impact upon me and produces feelings in me, because it reaches me in my uniquely individual being, because it is my own view of the landscape, that I enjoy possession of the landscape itself, and the landscape for Paul as well as for me. Both universality and the world lie at the core of individuality and the subject, and this will never be understood as long as the world is made into an ob-ject. It is understood immediately if the world is the *field* of our experience, and if we are nothing but a view of the world, for in that case it is seen that the most intimate vibration of our psycho-physical being already announces the world, the quality being the outline of a thing, and the thing the outline of the world. A world which, as Malebranche puts it, never gets beyond being an 'unfinished work', or which, as Husserl says of the body, is 'never completely constituted', does not require, and even rules out, a constituting subject. There must be, corresponding to this adumbration of being which appears through the concordant aspects of my own experience, or of the experience I share with others – experience which I presume capable of being consummated through indefinite horizons, from the sole fact that my phenomena congeal into a thing, and display, as they occur, a certain consistency of style – there must be, then, corresponding to this open unity of the world, an open and indefinite unity of subjectivity. Like the world's unity, that of the *I* is invoked rather than experienced each time I perform an act of perception, each time I reach a self-evident truth, and the universal *I* is the background against which these effulgent forms stand out: it is through one present thought that I achieve the unity of all my thoughts. What remains, on the hither side of my particular thoughts, to constitute the tacit *cogito* and the original project towards the world, and what, ultimately, am I in so far as I can catch a glimpse of myself independently of any particular act? I am a field, an experience. One day, once and for all, something was set in motion which, even during sleep, can no longer cease to see or not to see, to feel or not to feel, to suffer or be happy, to think or rest from thinking, in a word to 'have it out' with the world. There then arose, not a new set of sensations or states of consciousness, not even a new monad or a new perspective, since I am not tied to any one perspective but can change my point of view, being under compulsion only in that I must always have one, and can have only one at once – let us say, therefore, that there arose a fresh *possibility of situations*. The event of my birth has not passed completely away, it has not fallen into nothingness in the way that an event of the objective world does, for it committed a whole future, not as a cause determines its effect, but as a situation, once created, inevitably leads on to some outcome. There was henceforth a new 'setting', the world received a fresh layer of meaning. In the home into which a child is born, all objects change their significance; they begin to await some as yet indeterminate treatment at his hands; another and different person is there, a new personal history, short or long, has just been initiated, another account has been opened. My first perception, along with the horizons which surrounded it, is an ever-present event, an unforgettable tradition; even as a thinking subject, I still am that first perception, the continuation of that same life inaugurated by it. In one sense, there are no more acts of consciousness or distinct *Erlebnisse* in a life than there are separate things in the world. Just as, as we have seen, when I walk round an object, I am not presented with a succession of perspective views which I subsequently co-ordinate thanks to the idea of one single flat projection, there being merely a certain amount of 'shift' in the thing which, in itself, is journeying through time, so I am not myself a succession of 'psychic' acts, nor for that matter a nuclear *I* who brings them together into a synthetic unity, but one single experience inseparable from itself, one single 'living cohesion',[35] one single temporality which is engaged, from birth, in making itself progressively explicit, and in confirming that cohesion in each successive present. It is this advent or again this event of transcendental kind that the *cogito* reveals. The primary truth is indeed 'I think', but only provided that we understand thereby 'I belong to myself'[36] while belonging to the world. When we try to go deeper into subjectivity, calling all things into question and suspending all our beliefs, the only form in which a glimpse is vouchsafed to us of that non-human ground through which, in the words of Rimbaud, 'we are not of the world', is as the horizon of our particular commitments, and as the potentiality of something in the most general sense, which is the world's phantom. Inside and outside are inseparable. The world is wholly inside and I am wholly outside myself. When I perceive this table, the perception of the top must not overlook that of the legs, otherwise the object would be thrown out of joint. When I hear a melody, each of its moments must be related to its successor, otherwise there would be no melody. Yet the table is there with its external parts, and succession is of the essence of melody. The act which draws together at the same time takes away and holds at a distance, so that I touch myself only by escaping from myself. In one of his celebrated *pensées*, Pascal shows that in one way I understand the world, and in another it understands me. We must add that it is in the same way: I understand the world because there are for me things near and far, foregrounds and horizons, and because in this way it forms a picture and acquires significance before me, and this finally is because I am situated in it and it understands me. We do not say that the *notion* of the world is inseparable from that of the subject, or that the subject *thinks himself* inseparable from the idea of his body and the idea of the world; for, if it were a matter of no more than a conceived relationship, it would *ipso facto* leave the absolute independence of the subject as thinker intact, and the subject would not be in a situation. If the subject *is* in a situation, even if he is no more than a possibility of situations, this is because he forces his ipseity into reality only by actually being a body, and entering the world through that body. In so far as, when I reflect on the essence of subjectivity, I find it bound up with that of the body and that of the world, this is because my existence as subjectivity is merely one with my existence as a body and with the existence of the world, and because the subject that I am, when taken concretely, is inseparable from this body and this world. The ontological world and body which we find at the core of the subject are not the world or body as idea, but on the one hand the world itself contracted into a comprehensive grasp, and on the other the body itself as a knowing-body.

But, it will be asked, if the unity of the world is not based on that of consciousness, and if the world is not the outcome of a constituting effort, how does it come about that appearances accord with each other and group themselves together into things, ideas and truths? And why do our random thoughts, the events of our life and those of collective history, at least at certain times assume common significance and direction, and allow themselves to be subsumed under one idea? Why does my life succeed in drawing itself together in order to project itself in words, intentions and acts? This is the problem of rationality. The reader is aware that, on the whole, classical thought tries to explain the concordances in question in terms of a world in itself, or in terms of an absolute mind. Such explanations borrow all the forces of conviction which they can carry from the phenomenon of rationality, and therefore fail to explain that phenomenon, or ever to achieve greater clarity than it possesses. Absolute Thought is no clearer to me than my own finite mind, since it is through the latter that I conceive the former. We are in the world, which means that things take shape, an immense individual asserts itself, each existence is self-comprehensive and comprehensive of the rest. All that has to be done is to recognize these phenomena which are the ground of all our certainties. The belief in an absolute mind, or in a world in itself detached from us is no more than a rationalization of this primordial faith.

NOTES

1. P. Lachièze-Rey, *Réflexions sur l'activité spirituelle constituante*, Paris: Recherches Philosophiques, 1933, p. 134.
2. P. Lachièze-Rey, *L'Idéalisme kantien*, Paris: Alcan, 1932, pp. 17–18.
3. Ibid., p. 25.
4. Ibid., p. 55.
5. Ibid., p. 184.
6. Ibid., pp. 17–18.
7. P. Lachièze-Rey, *Le Moi, le Monde et Dieu*, Paris: Boivin, 1938, p. 68.
8. Kant, quoted in P. Lachièze-Rey, *L'Idéalisme kantien*, p. 464.
9. P. Lachièze-Rey, *Réflexions*, p. 145.
10. P. Lachièze-Rey, *L'Idéalisme kantien*, p. 477.
11. Ibid., p. 477; P. Lachièze-Rey, *Le Moi, le Monde et Dieu*, p. 83.
12. P. Lachièze-Rey, *L'Idéalisme kantien*, p. 472.
13. P. Lachièze-Rey, *Le Moi, le Monde et Dieu*, p. 33.
14. As does P. Lachièze-Rey, ibid., pp. 69–70.
15. Ibid., p. 72.
16. As Husserl, for example, does when he concedes that any transcendental reduction is at the same time an eidetic one. The necessity of proceeding by essences, and the stubborn opacity of existences, cannot be taken for granted as facts, but contribute to determining the significance of the *cogito* and of ultimate subjectivity. I am not a constituting thought, and my 'I think' is not an 'I am', unless by thought I can equal the world's concrete richness, and re-absorb facticity into it.
17. Max Scheler, *Idole der Selbsterkenntis*, Leipzig: Der Neue Geist, 1919, pp. 63ff.
18. Ibid., pp. 89–95.
19. Jean-Paul Sartre, *L'Imaginaire*, Paris: Gallimard, 1940, p. 243.
20. '... in which case, that too, that cynical distaste at her own persona, was deliberately put on! And that scorn for the distaste which she was busy contriving, was so much play-acting too! And her doubt about her scorn ... it was maddening. Once you started being sincere, was there no end to it?' Simone de Beauvoir, *L'Invitée*, Paris: Gallimard, 1943, p. 232.
21. Max Wertheimer, Über Schlussprozess im produktiven denken', in *Drei Abhandlungen zur Gestalttheorie*, Erlangen, 1925, pp. 164–84.
22. Aron Gurwitsch, 'Quelques aspects et quelques developpements de la psychologie de la forme', in *Journal de Psychologie Normale et Pathologique*, xxxiii, 1936, p. 460.
23. P. Lachièze-Rey, *Utilisation possible du schématisme kantien*, Marseilles, 1938; and *Réflexions*.
24. P. Lachièze-Rey, *Réflexions*, p. 132.
25. P. Lachièze-Rey, *Utilisation possible*, p. 7.
26. 'It must disclose intrinsically the immanence of a spatial trajectory, which alone can enable it to be thought of as motion', ibid., p. 6.
27. Paul Claudel, *Réflexions sur le vers français*, Paris, 1930, pp. 11–12.

28. As does B. Parain, *Recherches sur la nature et les fonctions du langage*, Paris: Gallimard, 1942, chapter XI.
29. L. Brunschvicg, *Les Progrès de la Conscience dans la Philosophie occidentale*, Paris: Alcan, 1927, p. 794.
30. E. Husserl. *Formale und Transzendentale Logik*, in *Jahrbuch für Philosophie*, 10 (1929), p. 221; English trans. by Dorion Cairns, The Hague: Nijhoff, 1969, p. 250.
31. This notion recurs frequently in the later writings of Husserl.
32. E. Husserl. *Formale und Transzendentale Logik*, p. 220; English trans. p. 249.
33. See E. Husserl, *Logische Untersuchungen*, 4th edn, Halle: Niemeyer, 1928, vol. I, p. 117; English trans. by J. N. Findlay, London: Routledge, 1970. What is sometimes termed Husserl's rationalism is in reality the recognition of subjectivity as an inalienable fact, and of the world to which it is directed as *omnitudo realitatis*.
34. Paul Valéry, *Introduction à la méthode de Léonard de Vinci*, in *Nouvelle Revue Français*, 1895.
35. M. Heidegger, *Sein und Zeit*, in *Jahrbuch für Philosophie*, 8 (1927), p. 388; English trans. by John Macquarrie and Edward Robinson, New York: Harper & Row, 1962, p. 425 (H373).
36. Ibid., p. 124–5; English trans., p. 150–2 (H115–17).

6

MARTIN HEIDEGGER
(1889–1976)

One of Heidegger's recent biographers broaches the subject of his birth with the provocative statement that, 'It should not be forgotten that coming into the world is not completed by being born. Several births are necessary during a human life, and it may well be that one never fully arrives in the world. But let us, for the moment, stay with his first birth' (Safranski, 1998, p. 2). He was born in 1889 in the small town of Messkirch, between Lake Constance and the Upper Danube; his father was a master cooper and sexton of the local Catholic church, and his mother's family had been farmers for centuries in a nearby village. His brother Fritz was an eccentric, likeable fellow who lived his whole life in this small district and worked as an official in the local credit bank. He was utterly loyal to his famous philosopher brother and once remarked that Heidegger's thought would only be understood in the future, 'when the Americans have long set up a huge supermarket on the moon.' Young Martin did very well in school and received a grant in 1903 to attend the Catholic seminary in Constance, the Konradihaus. In the autumn of 1906, he transferred to the seminary of St George in Freiburg, where he was expected to continue his theological studies and perhaps enter the Jesuit order. This ambition came to an abrupt end three years later; instead he entered university through the Freiburg Theological Seminary where his principal interest was in the medieval scholastics. Thus, until he completed his studies in 1916, Heidegger was supported in a financial and sometimes a pastoral manner by the Catholic Church. Throughout his life, in his lectures, publications and private letters, he was to maintain an ambivalent and puzzling relation to Mother Church.

In 1907, one of his former teachers had given his pupil Franz Brentano's treatise 'On the Manifold Meaning of Being in Aristotle'. In this dense text Heidegger found 'a strict, icy cold logic', a form of philosophical investigation for strong intellects who do not wish to live by their opinions and emotions alone. Brentano had been the teacher of Edmund Husserl, the founding figure in phenomenology, already at that time an important and well-known professor at Göttingen University. Heidegger read Husserl's *Logical Investigations* (first published in 1900) with great diligence; in fact, he kept the library copy in his room for two years since no one else seemed to want it. Fifty years later he recalled the spell which Husserl's early work exerted on him: 'I remained so fascinated by Husserl's work that I read in it again and again in the years to follow . . . The spell emanating from the work extended to the outer appearance of the sentence structure and the title page' (1972, p. 81).

Under the impact of the successful new empirical psychology in the early and mid 1800s many psychological theorists attempted to extend the natural-scientific method of research and the causal model of lawful explanation into the realm of logic and other normative disciplines. Husserl's thorough and meticulous refutation of the psychologistic derivation of logical laws was the prolegomenon for his radical new approach to consciousness – phenomenological analysis. Phenomenology can be defined as a universal a priori science which is the self-founding First Philosophy (*prima philosophia*), articulated through rigorous and exhaustive descriptive investigations of the phenomena of consciousness, *exactly as and only as* the phenomena are given to consciousness, and where such descriptive analyses are the consequences of a specific methodological procedure, the phenomenological *reduction*. The phenomenological approach had a profound influence on Heidegger's early thinking, though right from the start he rejected Husserl's insistence on a proper theoretical detachment. At this time Heidegger made the decision to leave his theological studies and switched to the science faculty at Freiburg University, although he still had to rely on a private loan from Catholic sources. In the summer of 1913, he received his doctorate with his thesis on 'The Theory of Propositions in Psychologism'.

Although he had hoped to continue his philosophical research on the concept of number (as Husserl had done thirty years earlier), his acceptance of a scholarship stipulated that his work would have to be on a scholastic subject, especially the philosophy of St Thomas Aquinas. For the next three years he endeavoured to fulfil this obligation, an endeavour which resulted in his habilitation thesis (a requirement to teach in a German university) on 'Duns Scotus' Doctrine of Categories and Meaning'. In October 1914, with the German and French armies engaged in battle, Heidegger's heart trouble exempted him from enlistment, though from autumn 1915 until early 1918 he worked part-time for the postal service with the task of censoring letters for sensitive information. But the First World War undoubtedly had an impact on his thinking and career plans. Perhaps he had read Max Scheler's brilliant 1915 essay on 'The Genius of War' in which he might have thought these remarks by Scheler were addressed to a reluctant scholastic philosopher: from this time onward, Scheler said, no one will be content with 'purely formalistic hair-litting', there will be a growing hunger for 'an independent original view of the world' (Safranski, 1998, p. 59). But Heidegger's study of Duns Scotus was far more than a pedantic exposition of the twelfth-century theologian-philosopher. In Duns Scotus, he discovered a medieval precursor to the phenomenological concept of intentionality, something Brentano himself had already carefully pointed out in 1873. In addition, he found in Duns Scotus the notion that human consciousness embraces transcendence in the limit concept of God, and the insight, which was to become central in *Being and Time*, that 'everything that really exists is a "this-here-now".'

In the spring of 1917, Heidegger married Elfride Petri, the daughter of a senior Saxon officer and an economics student. She was an emancipated young woman and an early advocate of women's rights; her strongly held opinions, especially some shocking ones about Jews, were later to be a sticking point with some of Heidegger's colleagues and students. By this time, Heidegger had gained the status of Privatdozent, an unsalaried lecturer, and was working hard to make himself eligible for a better position. In 1916 Husserl had taken up the chair at Freiburg University and Heidegger began to make overtures to gain the elder philosopher's attention. In the winter of 1917–18, Husserl's assistant Edith Stein had given up her thankless task of preparing the endless beginner's manuscripts for publication and Heidegger soon assumed this role. In the next few years his lectures became widely and extravagantly praised by his students, who were astonished that their philosophy teacher could spend weeks evoking in minute detail, for example, the experience of standing at the lectern. He was seen by many as a radical visionary and his ascendancy to a pre-eminent position eclipsed that of Husserl himself. The 'little magician from Messkirch' (Karl Lowith's nickname for his teacher) hypnotised his students with an uncanny mixture of intense scrutiny of the intimate details of everyday life and a cool, elaborate and technical apparatus. One of his students at the time, Hans-Georg Gadamer, later recalled the impact Heidegger's lectures had on him.

> What he provided was the full investment of his energy, and what brilliant energy it was. It was the energy of a revolutionary thinker who himself visibly shrank from the boldness of his increasingly radical questions and who was so filled with the passion of his thinking that he conveyed to his listeners a fascination that was not to be broken ... Who among those who then followed him can forget the breathtaking swirl of questions that he developed in the introductory hours of the semester for the sake of entangling himself in the second or third of these questions and then, in the final hours of the semester, rolling up the deep-dark clouds of sentences from which the lightning flashed to leave us half stunned. (Gadamer, 1985, p. 48)

In those early lectures one can clearly discern elements of what would later become central themes in Heidegger's distinctive Existential interpretation of the phenomenological method.

The 1920s were Heidegger's most productive years; he drove himself very hard, filled with a sense of mission. In 1925, he edited Husserl's lectures from 1907 to 1914 on the *Phenomenology of Inner Time Consciousness*, and read the manuscript of the unpublished Second and Third Books of Husserl's *Ideas* (see 1962 [1927], p. 489, note ii). At the early age of thirty, Heidegger's teaching was definitely making a mark; he had ambitions for the post of ordinary professor but so far had published very little. In order to have a better chance he worked frantically to complete the manuscript of *Being and Time*, which was quickly published in 1927 in a series supervised by Husserl himself. Professor and Frau Husserl held regular evening parties at their home for the privileged colleagues and students who had been taken into the Freiburg philosophical circle; at one of these soirées Heidegger met Karl Jaspers and his wife Gertrud. Heidegger and Jaspers immediately felt a strong rapport, a mutual desire to tread new paths in a forward-looking philosophical enterprise. In one of his early letters to Jaspers, he spoke of 'a rare and original comradeship-in-arms'; he was very favourably impressed with Jaspers' *Philosophy of Worldviews* published in 1919. Jaspers invited him to Heidelberg where the two spent several days in such intense philosophical intimacy that Jaspers proposed founding a journal which the two young beginners would write for. Although no collaborative project would ever emerge from this partnership, their close friendship would continue until the fraught years of 1933–6.

At the same time that he formed a strong bond with Jaspers, he actually put more and more distance between his own thinking and Husserl's phenomenological project. In a private letter Heidegger stated bluntly that 'Husserl has totally gone to pieces ... he vacillates this way and that and utters trivialities such as would reduce one to tears' (Safranski, 1998, p. 128). Husserl was not aware of his young protégé's sarcastic attitude and wrote a glowing testimonial for Heidegger's application for the chair of philosophy at Marburg University. With the support of Paul Natorp, the great Kant scholar and head of the Marburg School of Philosophy, Heidegger was awarded the professorship in June 1923. His five years at Marburg were to be immensely productive and successful, though he seemed to find the town itself unhappy and uninteresting. Years later he was to remark that his time in Marburg was 'the most exciting, the most concentrated and the most eventful' in his life. Perhaps his vivid memory of this excitement and eventfulness was connected with his recently acquired cottage in the Black Forest, where so much of his writing was done in complete solitude and contemplation.

At Marburg Heidegger formed a strong alliance with the theologian Rudolf Bultmann whose *Theology of the New Testament* draws heavily, in some places, on Heidegger's existential analysis of human Dasein, as does Hans

Jonas' *Gnosis and the Spirit of Late Antiquity*. He formed an alliance of another kind with one of his most promising and gifted students, Hannah Arendt. The eighteen-year-old Jewish woman was without doubt, according to her own peers, the most striking, alluring and intelligent of the Marburg students. Heidegger became her private tutor, meeting in secret in her attic room, and then her lover. According to Ettinger, Heidegger loved Arendt as his 'great passion', she was the only woman who understood his philosophy, she was the secret muse behind the composition of *Being and Time*. Even when she had left Marburg, Heidegger repeatedly sought her out; they had to make elaborate arrangements for clandestine rendezvous so that his colleagues and Frau Heidegger wouldn't discover their liaison. Despite the joy and delight that he experienced with Arendt, positive and affirmative states-of-mind (or attunements) are not explored in *Being and Time*; rather the focus there is on anxiety, alienation and distance. When it was published in 1927 only Part One, Division One, 'Preparatory Fundamental Analysis of Dasein', and Division Two, 'Dasein and Temporality', had been completed. At the end of the Introduction, the author lays out the scheme for the entire work: Part One, Division Three, 'Time and Being', and the three divisions of Part Two. The English translators' footnote at this point, as well as brief dictionary-style entries on *Being and Time*, state that these four divisions never appeared, but that is simply inaccurate.

The lectures in the summer semester of 1927, 'Basic Problems of Phenomenology' opens with the explicit statement that they are a new version of Part One, Division Three, 'the explication of time as the transcendental horizon of the question of Being'. Part Two, Division One, 'Kant's Doctrine of Schematism and Time', received book-length treatment in his *Kant and the Problem of Metaphysics* (1929). Part Two, Division Two, 'The Ontological Foundation of Descartes' Cogito', is covered by Chapter Three of *Basic Problems* and preceded by an additional chapter on medieval ontology as an expansion of his projected 'destruction' of western substance-based ontology; he returned to this theme in his 1938 lectures on 'Establishing the Metaphysics of the Modern World Picture'. Part Two, Division Three, 'On Aristotle's Concept of Time' was explored in detail in his lectures on 'Aristotle's Metaphysics' in the summer of 1931.

Heidegger's magisterial 1927 work *Being and Time* is devoted to the question of the meaning of Being, specifically to the kind of being for whom this question has meaning – human being. The unique manner of Being of this being he calls Dasein, 'being-there'. Dasein does not exist like an object just lying around, nor is Dasein merely a subject of conscious awareness, for whom or to whom objects appear. Rather, Heidegger says, Dasein finds itself already out there in the world, not the world as an aggregate of objects and object-relations, but the world as a referential totality of meanings, equipment and possibilities. The difference between Being and beings *makes a difference* for Dasein, and the stages of this difference-making are the moments of the existential analytic.

'The understanding of being is in our background practices; an account of this sense of being is what our investigation is to produce. It must lay out the structure of our access to entities and account for our ability to make sense of making sense' (Dreyfus, 1991, p. 11). Some beings or things Dasein finds already invested with meaning or uses for service, such things as tools, in an exemplary fashion, are available for Dasein as things-to-be-used. Other things are merely lying around, they are occurrent or merely occur to Dasein, though sometimes they too can be turned into tools. Dasein itself cannot be adequately characterised as either available or occurrent, though sometimes indeed humans treat other humans in an object-like manner. Dasein is *in* the world in a special manner also, not as an object is in the world, the way sand is in a bucket, but *in* the world the way one says a person is *in* love.

Moreover, Dasein does not have its essence in advance; rather it is aware of the many possibilities which it can make its own – its being lies ahead of itself, in the future. Dasein's comportment towards things, other humans and its own future reveals a mode of understanding which cannot be reduced to rational insight. The kind of 'sight' required is the seeing which takes place in an open clearing: the clearing reveals that light is not itself an object that can be transparent to reflection; rather light illuminates everything in one's environment. In the way that Dasein is concerned with beings in its environment, is solicitous for other Daseins' concerns and is resolute in its decisions to carry out its own projects, Being-there manifests the temporal structure of care. The fact that Dasein cares for the possibilities which it attempts to actualise and hence for the being it will become means that Dasein is (or can be) aware that death brings about the non-being of the self which it has thrown ahead. This awareness of an always possible severance from the ground of its being is the source of the basic existential attunement or 'mood' of anxiety. Conscience is the call or summons to face squarely the null basis of our being, to recognize our lostness in an everyday, average self and to live instead in an authentic manner the ownness of our own choices. Dasein always already has an attunement though sometimes this 'mood' may have little flavour; in his 1929 lectures, Heidegger develops meticulous analyses of boredom as an emptied 'mood' and in his 1930 'Contributions' he devotes some attention to joy or jubilation.

On the strength of *Being and Time* and the superlative reports on his lectures, in February 1928 Heidegger was appointed professor at Freiburg to succeed his former mentor Husserl. (*Being and Time* in fact had been dedicated to Husserl, but later editions deleted this.) He wrote to Jaspers at that time that 'Freiburg for me will once more be a test of whether anything of philosophy is left there or whether it has all turned into learnedness.' For the next decade his unique version of philosophy held sway in Freiburg and beyond. His lectures reached an apogee in his 1929–30 course 'The Fundamental Concepts of Metaphysics' in which he explored an 'event-thinking', that is bringing about an event in the lecture hall and then opening it up through an existential inquiry. Heidegger 'wants to make his audience plunge into the great emptiness – they are to hear the fundamental roar of existence; he wants to open up the moment when nothing really matters any longer, when no world content offers itself to provide a handhold or something to fill oneself with' (Safranski, p. 192). The moment of the pure lapse of time is revealed in the state of boredom; the person is gripped by the world whole just because he or she is not gripped through interest, but left behind, empty. After meticulous, fine-grained analyses, he returns to this summary question three times, 'Have things ultimately gone so far with us that a profound boredom draws us back and forth like a silent fog in the abysses of Dasein?' (1995 [1929], p. 77).

In the lectures of the early 1930s, Heidegger turned toward the ancient Greek thinkers, those who in his view still grasped an understanding of the primordial meaning of Being before it was covered over by Aristotle and his commentators' taxonomy of categories. This period famously marks the 'turn' or the 'turning' in his thought, about which there has been a great of deal of disagreement. It is simply not feasible here to explore even the main features of Heidegger's later thinking; suffice it to state that he moves away from an investigation of humans' mode of existence toward a thoughtful, thankful and open encounter with Being, primarily through an attempt to construct a hybrid poetic language that reveals, instead of refers to, the manifold dimensions of Being. This supreme effort on his part to evoke Being's presence comes through in many lectures and books, but especially so in a concentrated distillation in his 'secret manuscript', the *Contributions (On Enownment)*.

During this period Heidegger often made reference to an 'advent' or impending event; in March 1933, with Hitler and the Nazi seizure of power, it seems that he thought the event had arrived. He joined the Nazi party, offered his services as 'leader' to the National Socialist Ministry of Education and was made Rector of Freiburg University. Although he resigned a year later, this was not due to any insight into the evil of the Nazi regime; rather Heidegger the administrator felt completely frustrated that the faculty, teachers' union and delegates had failed to bring about the radical, even extreme reforms which he envisaged. (On this controversial topic, see Farias, 1989, Ott, 1993, and Wolin, 1993.) However, the rumour which Hannah Arendt heard and spread, that Heidegger had banned Husserl from entering the library or had carried out an anti-Semitic policy, was not true. Arendt herself had moved to Paris in the autumn of 1933, and in 1941 she fled to the United States, from where after the war she was to be instrumental in getting his work published in English. Until the allied bombing of Freiburg in November 1944, he continued to give lectures and seminars; after retreating to his hometown of Messkirch he held seminars in the Abbey until the town too was bombed.

Following the occupation of Germany in April 1945, Heidegger was brought before the French authorities who were keen to extirpate anyone tainted with Nazi guilt. In desperation, Heidegger wrote to his old friend Jaspers, who with his wife had just moved to Basel after years of fear and hiding. He wanted

Jaspers to give an expert testimony on his good character. Although initially he was quite reluctant, Jaspers eventually wrote a detailed report which concluded that Heidegger's thinking was dangerous and that he should not be allowed to influence young Germans of the postwar generation. As a result of this report Heidegger was deprived of the right to teach, but not his pension or property, though soon after Freiburg granted him emeritus status and in 1952 lifted the ban on teaching.

Meanwhile, Heidegger's thinking had been taken up in France with great enthusiasm. Through the mediation of Jean Beaufret, Heidegger was invited to respond to Sartre's public lecture, 'Existentialism is a Humanism' – his long essay in reply was published in France with the title 'Letter on Humanism'. Having returned to France in 1946, Arendt renewed her contact with Jaspers and informed him of her love affair with Heidegger twenty years earlier, she visited the now disgraced German philosopher for the first time in 1950. In her private diary (or day book), she described Heidegger as a fox who, unable to tell the difference between a trap and a non-trap, built his own burrow out of a trap and thought it was home. Although he no longer had an official university venue, Heidegger continued to lecture on a regular basis for the next thirty years: at the Bremen Club, the Bavarian Academy of Fine Arts and Zollikon, the home of the psychiatrist Medard Boss. In the 1960s, he made three trips to Greece, his spiritual homeland about whose philosophical inspiration he had written so much. In 1966, he was invited to respond to charges of Nazi sympathies by *Der Spiegel* magazine and agreed on the condition that the interview would not be published until after his death (May 1976). Perhaps one can best conclude this synoptic account of an eventful and event-making thinker's life with Arendt's startling words:

> The gale that blows through Heidegger's thinking – like that which still, after thousands of years, blows to us from Plato's work – is not of our century. It comes from the primordial, and what it leaves behind is something perfect which, like everything perfect, falls back into the primordial.

PRINCIPAL WORKS

Heidegger's *Collected Works (Gesamtausgable)* have reached seventy volumes already and are expected to reach one hundred volumes, about forty-five of which have been translated into English; those cited below are highlights.

(1927–64) *Basic Writings*, ed. David Farrell Krell, 2nd edn. New York and San Francisco: Harper & Row, 1993. (The best edited volume of Heidegger's works and an excellent starting point.)
(1927) *Being and Time*, trans. John Macquarrie and Edward Robinson. New York: Harper & Row, 1962. *Being and Time*, trans. Joan Stambaugh. Albany: State University of New York Press, 1996.
(1927) *Basic Problems of Phenomenology*, trans. Alfred Hofstadter. Bloomington: Indiana University Press, 1982.

(1929) *The Essence of Reasons*, trans. Terence Malick. Evanston, IL: Northwestern University Press, 1969.

(1929) *The Fundamental Concepts of Metaphysics*, trans. William McNeill and Nicholas Walker. Bloomington: Indiana University Press, 1995.

(1929) *Kant and the Problem of Metaphysics*, trans. Richard Taft. Bloomington: Indiana University Press, 1996.

(1929) *The Metaphysical Foundations of Logic*, trans. Michael Heim. Bloomington: Indiana University Press, 1984.

(1931) *The Essence of Truth*, trans. T. Sadler. London: Athlone Press, 1998.

(1935) *Introduction to Metaphysics*, trans. G. Fried and R. Polt. New Haven, CT: Yale University Press, 1999.

(1935) *What is a thing?*, trans. W. B. Barton and Vera Deutsch. Chicago: Henry Regnery, 1967.

(1936–46) *Nietzsche*, ed. David Farrell Krell, 4 vols. New York: Harper & Row, 1979–67.

(1938–55) *Question Concerning Technology*, trans. William Lovitt. New York: Harper & Row, 1977.

(1950–9) *Poetry, Language, Thought*, trans. Alfred Hofstadter. New York: Harper & Row, 1971.

(1953–9) *On the Way to Language*, trans. Peter D. Hertz. New York: Harper & Row, 1971.

(1954) *What is Called Thinking?*, trans. F. D. Wieck and J. Glenn Gray. New York: Harper & Row, 1968.

(1972) *On Time and Being*, trans. Joan Stambough. New York: Harper & Row, 1972.

RECOMMENDED READING

Cooper, David E. (1996) *Heidegger*. London: Claridge Press.

Dreyfus, Hubert (1991) *Being-in-the-World: A Commentary on Being and Time*. Cambridge, MA: MIT Press.

Dreyfus, Hubert and Hall, Harrison (eds) (1992) *Heidegger: A Critical Reader*. Oxford: Blackwell.

Farias, Victor (1989) *Heidegger and Nazism*. Philadelphia: Temple University Press.

Gadamer, Hans-Georg (1985) *Philosophical Apprenticeships*. Cambridge, MA: MIT Press.

Gelven, Michael (1989) *A Commentary on Heidegger's Being and Time*, 2nd edn. DeKalb, IL: Northern Illinois University Press.

Guignon, Charles (1983) *Heidegger and the Problem of Knowledge*. Indianapolis: Hackett.

Guignon, Charles (ed.) (1993) *Cambridge Companion to Heidegger*. Cambridge: Cambridge University Press.

Mulhall, Stephen (1996) *Guidebook to Heidegger and Being and Time*. London: Routledge.

Ott, Hugo (1993) *Heidegger: A Political Life* trans. A. Blunden. New York: Basic Books.

Poggeler, Otto (1987) *Martin Heidegger's Path of Thinking*, trans. Daniel Magurshak and Sigmund Barber. Atlantic Highlands, NJ: Humanities Press.

Polt, Richard (1999) *Heidegger: An Introduction*. Ithaca, NY: Cornell University Press.

Richardson, William J. (1974) *Heidegger: Through Phenomenology to Thought*, 3rd edn. The Hague: Martinus Nijhoff. (Still to date the most complete and thorough account of his entire work.)

Safranski, Rudiger (1998) *Heidegger: Between Good and Evil*, trans. Ewald Osers. Cambridge, MA: Harvard University Press. (The most authoritative intellectual and political biography.)

Wolin, Richard (ed.) (1993) *The Heidegger Controversy: A Critical Reader*. Cambridge, MA: MIT Press.

'LETTER ON HUMANISM' (1947)*

Martin Heidegger

EDITOR'S PREFACE

In Brussels during the spring of 1845, not long after his expulsion from Paris, Karl Marx jotted down several notes on the German philosopher Ludwig Feuerbach. The second of these reads: 'The question whether human thought achieves objective truth is not a question of theory but a *practical* question. . . . Dispute over the actuality or non-actuality of any thinking that isolates itself from *praxis* is a purely *scholastic* question.' Ever since that time – especially in France, which Marx exalted as the heart of the Revolution – the relation of philosophy to political practice has been a burning issue. It is not surprising that the impulse for Heidegger's reflections on action, Marxism, existentialism, and humanism in the 'Letter on Humanism' came from a French colleague.

On November 10, 1946, a century after Marx sketched his theses on Feuerbach, Jean Beaufret addressed a number of questions to Heidegger, who responded to Beaufret's letter in December with the following piece. (Actually Heidegger reworked and expanded the letter for publication in 1947.) Both Beaufret's inquiry and Heidegger's response refer to a brief essay by Jean-Paul Sartre, originally a public address, with the title *Existentialism Is a Humanism* (Paris: Nagel, 1946). There Sartre defined existentialism as the conviction 'that existence precedes essence, or . . . that one must take subjectivity as one's point of departure' (p. 17). In Sartre's view no objectively definable 'human nature' underlies man conceived as *existence*: man is nothing more than how he *acts*, what he *does*. This because he has lost all otherworldly underpinnings, has been abandoned to a realm where there are only human beings who have no choice but to make choices. For Sartre man is in the predicament of having to choose and to act without appeal to any concept of human nature that would guarantee the rightness of his choice and the efficacy of his action. 'There is reality only in action,' Sartre insists (p. 55), and existentialism 'defines man by action' (p. 62), which is to say, 'in connection with an *engagement*' (p. 78). Nevertheless, Sartre reaffirms (pp. 64ff.) that man's freedom to act is rooted in subjectivity, which alone grants man his dignity, so that the Cartesian *cogito*

---

* From *Basic Writings*, ed. David Farrell Krell. San Francisco: Harper & Row, 1993.

becomes the only possible *point de départ* for existentialism and the only possible basis for a humanism (p. 93).

Heidegger responds by keeping open the question of action but strongly criticizing the tradition of subjectivity, which celebrates the 'I think' as the font of liberty. Much of the 'Letter' is taken up with renewed insistence that Dasein or existence is and remains beyond the pale of Cartesian subjectivism. Again Heidegger writes *Existenz* as *Ek-sistenz*, in order to stress man's 'standing out' into the 'truth of Being.' Humanism underestimates man's unique position in the clearing of Being (*Lichtung des Seins*), Heidegger argues, conceding that to this extent he rejects the humanistic tradition. For it remains stamped in the mold of metaphysics, engrossed in beings, oblivious to Being.

But any opposition to humanism sounds like a rejection of humanity and of humane values. Heidegger therefore discusses the meaning of 'values' and of the 'nihilism' that ostensibly results when such things are put in question. He finds – as Nietzsche did – that not the denial of such values but their installation in the first place is the source of nihilism. For establishment of values anticipates eventual disestablishment, both actions amounting to a willful self-congratulation of the representing subject.

As Sartre tries to clear a path between the leading competitive 'humanisms,' those of Christianity and Communism, Heidegger attempts to distinguish his understanding of ek-sistence from man as *imago dei* or *homo faber*. He tries to prevent the question of the clearing of Being from collapsing into the available answers of divine or human light. In so doing he comments on basic questions of religion and ethics. He rejects Sartre's 'over-hasty' identification with atheism, not in order to embrace theism but to reflect freely on the nature of the holy and the hale, as of malignancy and the rage of evil. His reflections remain highly relevant at a time when discourses on ethics abound – whether avowedly 'metaphysical' or professedly 'nonmetaphysical,' whether as 'practical reason' or 'applied ethics.'

Returning at the end to the question of action, Heidegger claims that thought of Being occurs prior to the distinction between theory and practice or contemplation and deed. Such thinking seems of the highest importance to Heidegger – yet he warns us not to overestimate it in terms of practical consequences.

Hannah Arendt was fond of calling the 'Letter' Heidegger's *Prachtstück*, his most splendid effort. Yet a number of questions might continue to plague us. Is Heidegger's self-interpretation, his account of the 'turning,' adequate here, even when we note that it is part of an ongoing 'immanent critique' of *Being and Time?* More important, are the motivations of Heidegger's critique of humanism and of the *animal rationale* altogether clear? Why, for instance, insist that there be an 'abyss of essence' separating humanity from animality? Perhaps most disturbing, can Heidegger invoke 'malignancy' and 'the rage of evil' without breaking his silence and offering some kind of reflection on the Extermination? And how can Heidegger's thought help us to think about those evils that continue to be so very much at home in *our* world? However splendid the 'Letter on Humanism,' it should only serve to call *us* to *thinking*.

David Farrell Krell*

LETTER ON HUMANISM[1]

We are still far from pondering the essence of action decisively enough. We view action only as causing an effect. The actuality of the effect is valued according to its utility. But the essence of action is accomplishment. To accomplish means to unfold something into the fullness of its essence, to lead it forth into this fullness – *producere*. Therefore only what already is can really be accomplished. But what 'is' above all is Being. Thinking accomplishes the relation of Being to the essence of man. It does not make or cause the relation. Thinking brings this relation to Being solely as something handed over to it from Being. Such offering consists in the fact that in thinking Being comes to language. Language is the house of Being. In its home man dwells. Those who think and those who create with words are the guardians of this home. Their guardianship accomplishes the manifestation of Being insofar as they bring the manifestation to language and maintain it in language through their speech. Thinking does not become action only because some effect issues from it or because it is applied. Thinking acts insofar as it thinks. Such action is presumably the simplest and at the same time the highest, because it concerns the relation of Being to man. But all working or effecting lies in Being and is directed toward beings. Thinking, in contrast, lets itself be claimed by Being so that it can say the truth of Being. Thinking accomplishes this letting. Thinking is *l'engagement par l'Être pour l'Être* [engagement by Being for Being]. I do not know whether it is linguistically possible to say both of these ('*par*' and '*pour*') at once, in this way: *penser, c'est l'engagement de l'Être* [thinking is the engagement of Being]. Here the possessive form '*de l'* ...' is supposed to express both subjective and objective genitives. In this regard 'subject' and 'object' are inappropriate terms of metaphysics, which very early on in the form of Occidental 'logic' and 'grammar' seized control of the interpretation of language. We today can only begin to descry what is concealed in that occurrence. The liberation of language from grammar into a more original essential framework is reserved for thought and poetic creation. Thinking is not merely *l'engagement dans l'action* for and by beings, in the sense of the actuality of the present situation. Thinking is *l'engagement* by and for the truth of Being. The history of Being is never past but stands ever before; it sustains and defines every *condition et situation humaine*. In order to learn how to experience the aforementioned essence of thinking purely, and that means at the same time to carry it through, we must free ourselves from the technical interpretation of thinking. The beginnings of that interpretation reach back to Plato and Aristotle. They take thinking itself to be a *technē*, a process of reflection in service to doing and making. But here reflection is already seen from the perspective of *praxis* and *poiēsis*. For this reason thinking, when taken for itself, is not 'practical.' The characterization of thinking as *theōria* and the determination of knowing as 'theoretical' behavior occur already within the 'technical' interpretation of thinking. Such characterization is a reactive attempt to rescue thinking and preserve its autonomy over against acting and doing. Since then 'philosophy' has been in the constant predicament of having to justify its existence before the 'sciences.' It believes it can do that most effectively by elevating itself to the rank of a science. But such an effort is the abandonment of the essence of thinking. Philosophy is hounded by the fear that it loses prestige and validity if it is not a science. Not to be a science is taken as a failing that is equivalent to being unscientific. Being, as the element of thinking, is abandoned by the technical interpretation of thinking. 'Logic,' beginning with the Sophists and Plato, sanctions this explanation. Thinking is judged by a standard that does not measure up to it. Such judgment may be compared to the procedure of trying to evaluate the essence and powers of a fish by seeing how long it can live on dry land. For a long time now, all too long, thinking has been stranded on dry land. Can then the effort to return thinking to its element be called 'irrationalism'?

Surely the questions raised in your letter would have been better answered in direct conversation. In written form thinking easily loses its flexibility. But in writing it is difficult above all to retain the multidimensionality of the realm peculiar to thinking. The rigor of thinking, in contrast to that of the sciences, does not consist merely in an artificial, that is, technical-theoretical exactness of concepts. It lies in the fact that speaking remains purely in the element of Being and lets the simplicity of its manifold dimensions rule. On the other hand, written composition exerts a wholesome pressure toward deliberate linguistic formulation. Today I would like to grapple with only one of your questions. Perhaps its discussion will also shed some light on the others.

You ask: *Comment redonner un sens au mot 'Humanisme'*? [How can we restore meaning to the word 'humanism'?] This question proceeds from your intention to retain the word 'humanism.' I wonder whether that is necessary. Or is the damage caused by all such terms still not sufficiently obvious? True, '-isms' have for a long time now been suspect. But the market of public opinion continually demands new ones. We are always prepared to supply the demand. Even such names as 'logic,' 'ethics,' and 'physics' begin to flourish only when original thinking comes to an end. During the time of their greatness the Greeks thought without such headings. They did not even call thinking 'philosophy.' Thinking comes to an end when it slips out of its element. The element is what enables thinking to be a thinking. The element is what properly enables: it is the enabling [*das Vermögen*]. It embraces thinking and so brings it into its essence. Said plainly, thinking is the thinking of Being. The genitive says something twofold. Thinking is of Being inasmuch as thinking, propriated by Being, belongs to Being. At the same time thinking is of Being insofar as thinking, belonging to Being, listens to Being. As the belonging to Being that listens, thinking is what it is according to its essential origin. Thinking *is* – this says: Being has fatefully embraced its essence. To embrace a 'thing' or a 'person' in its essence means to love it, to favor it. Thought in a more original way such favoring [*Mögen*] means to bestow essence as a gift. Such favoring is the proper essence of enabling, which not only can achieve this or that but also can let something essentially unfold in its provenance, that is, let it be. It is on the 'strength' of such enabling by favoring that something is properly able to be. This enabling is what is properly 'possible' [*das 'Mögliche'*], whose essence resides in favoring. From this favoring Being enables thinking. The former makes the latter possible. Being is the enabling-favoring, the 'may be' [*das 'Mög-liche'*]. As the element, Being is the 'quiet power' of the favoring-enabling, that is, of the possible. Of course, our words *möglich* [possible] and *Möglichkeit* [possibility], under the dominance of 'logic' and 'metaphysics,' are thought solely in contrast to 'actuality'; that is, they are thought on the basis of a definite – the metaphysical – interpretation of Being as *actus* and *potentia*, a distinction identified with the one between *existentia* and *essentia*. When I speak of the 'quiet power of the possible' I do not mean the *possibile* of a merely represented *possibilitas*, nor *potentia* as the *essentia* of an *actus* of *existentia*; rather, I mean Being itself, which in its favoring presides over thinking and hence over the essence of humanity, and that means over its relation to Being. To enable something here means to preserve it in its essence, to maintain it in its element.

When thinking comes to an end by slipping out of its element it replaces this loss by procuring a validity for itself as *technē*, as an instrument of education and therefore as a classroom matter and later a cultural concern. By and by philosophy becomes a technique for explaining from highest causes. One no longer thinks; one occupies oneself with 'philosophy.' In competition with one another, such occupations publicly offer themselves as '-isms' and try to offer more than the others. The dominance of such terms is not accidental. It rests above all in the modern age upon the peculiar dictatorship of the public realm. However, so-called 'private existence' is not really essential, that is to say free, human being. It simply insists on negating the public realm. It remains an offshoot that depends upon the public and nourishes itself by a mere withdrawal from it. Hence it testifies, against its own will, to its subservience to the public realm. But because it stems from the dominance of subjectivity the public realm itself is the metaphysically conditioned establishment and authorization of the openness of individual beings in their unconditional objectification. Language thereby falls into the service of expediting communication along routes where objectification – the uniform accessibility of everything to everyone – branches out and disregards all limits. In this way language comes under the dictatorship of the public realm, which decides in advance what is intelligible and what must be rejected as unintelligible. What is said in *Being and Time* (1927), sections 27 and 35, about the 'they' in no way means to furnish an incidental contribution to sociology.[2] Just as little does the 'they' mean merely the opposite, understood in an ethical-existentiell way, of the selfhood of persons. Rather, what is said there contains a reference, thought in terms of the question of the truth of Being, to the word's primordial belongingness to Being. This relation remains concealed beneath the dominance of subjectivity that presents itself as the public realm. But if the truth of Being has become thought-provoking for thinking, then reflection on the essence of language must also attain a different rank. It can no longer be a mere philosophy of language. That is the only reason *Being and Time* (section 34) contains a reference to the essential dimension of language and touches upon the simple question as to what mode of Being language as language in any given case has.[3] The widely and rapidly spreading devastation of language not only undermines aesthetic and moral responsibility in every use of language; it arises from a threat to the essence of humanity. A merely cultivated use of language is still no proof that we have as yet escaped the danger to our essence. These days, in fact, such usage might sooner testify that we have not yet seen and cannot see the danger because we have never yet placed ourselves in view of it. Much bemoaned of late, and much too lately, the downfall of language is, however, not the grounds for, but already a consequence of, the state of affairs in which language under the dominance of the modern metaphysics of subjectivity almost irremediably falls out of its element. Language still denies us its essence: that it is the house of the truth of Being. Instead, language surrenders itself to our mere willing and trafficking as an instrument of domination over beings. Beings themselves appear as actualities in the interaction of cause and effect. We encounter beings as actualities in a calculative businesslike way, but also scientifically and by way of philosophy, with explanations and proofs. Even the assurance that something is inexplicable belongs to these explanations and proofs. With such statements we believe that we confront the mystery. As if it were already decided that the truth of Being lets itself at all be established in causes and explanatory grounds or, what comes to the same, in their incomprehensibility.

But if man is to find his way once again into the nearness of Being he must first learn to exist in the nameless. In the same way he must recognize the seductions of the public realm as well as the impotence of the private. Before he speaks man must first let himself be claimed again by Being, taking the risk that under this claim he will seldom have much to say. Only thus will the price-lessness of its essence be once more bestowed upon the word, and upon man a home for dwelling in the truth of Being.

But in the claim upon man, in the attempt to make man ready for this claim, is there not implied a concern about man? Where else does 'care' tend but in the direction of bringing man back to his essence?[4] What else does that in turn betoken but that man *(homo)* become human *(humanus)*? Thus *humanitas* really does remain the concern of such thinking. For this is humanism: meditating and caring, that man be human and not inhumane, 'inhuman,' that is, outside his essence. But in what does the humanity of man consist? It lies in his essence.

But whence and how is the essence of man determined? Marx demands that 'man's humanity' be recognized and acknowledged.[5] He finds it in 'society.' 'Social' man is for him 'natural' man. In 'society' the 'nature' of man, that is, the totality of 'natural needs' (food, clothing, reproduction, economic sufficiency) is equably secured. The Christian sees the humanity of man, the *humanitas* of *homo*, in contradistinction to *Deitas*. He is the man of the history of redemption who as a 'child of God' hears and accepts the call of the Father in Christ. Man is not of this world, since the 'world,' thought in terms of Platonic theory, is only a temporary passage to the beyond.

Humanitas, explicitly so called, was first considered and striven for in the age of the Roman Republic. *Homo humanus* was opposed to *homo barbarus*. *Homo humanus* here means the Romans, who exalted and honored Roman *virtus* through the 'embodiment' of the *paideia* [education] taken over from the Greeks. These were the Greeks of the Hellenistic age, whose culture was acquired in the schools of philosophy. It was concerned with *eruditio et institutio in bonas artes* [scholarship and training in good conduct]. *Paideia* thus understood was translated as *humanitas*. The genuine *romanitas* of *homo romanus* consisted in such *humanitas*. We encounter the first humanism in Rome: it therefore remains in essence a specifically Roman phenomenon, which emerges from the encounter of Roman civilization with the culture of late Greek civilization. The so-called Renaissance of the fourteenth and fifteenth centuries in Italy is a *renascentia romanitatis*. Because *romanitas* is what matters, it is concerned with *humanitas* and therefore with Greek *paideia*. But Greek civilization is always seen in its later form and this itself is seen from a Roman point of view. The *homo romanus* of the Renaissance also stands in opposition to *homo barbarus*. But now the in-humane is the supposed barbarism of gothic Scholasticism in the Middle Ages. Therefore a *studium humanitatis*, which in a certain way reaches back to the ancients and thus also becomes a revival of Greek civilization, always adheres to historically understood humanism. For Germans this is apparent in the humanism of the eighteenth century supported by Winckelmann, Goethe, and Schiller. On the other hand, Hölderlin does not belong to 'humanism,' precisely because he thought the destiny of man's essence in a more original way than 'humanism' could.

But if one understands humanism in general as a concern that man become free for his humanity and find his worth in it, then humanism differs according to one's conception of the 'freedom' and 'nature' of man. So too are there various paths toward the realization of such conceptions. The humanism of Marx does not need to return to antiquity any more than the humanism which Sartre conceives existentialism to be. In this broad sense Christianity too is a humanism, in that according to its teaching everything depends on man's salvation (*salus aeterna*); the history of man appears in the context of the history of redemption. However different these forms of humanism may be in purpose and in principle, in the mode and means of their respective realizations, and in the form of their teaching, they nonetheless all agree in this, that the *humanitas of homo humanus* is determined with regard to an already established interpretation of nature, history, world, and the ground of the world, that is, of beings as a whole.

Every humanism is either grounded in a metaphysics or is itself made to be the ground of one. Every determination of the essence of man that already presupposes an interpretation of beings without asking about the truth of Being, whether knowingly or not, is metaphysical. The result is that what is peculiar to all metaphysics, specifically with respect to the way the essence of man is determined, is that it is 'humanistic.' Accordingly, every humanism remains metaphysical. In defining the humanity of man humanism not only does not ask about the relation of Being to the essence of man; because of its metaphysical origin humanism even impedes the question by neither recognizing nor understanding it. On the contrary, the necessity and proper form of the question concerning the truth of Being, forgotten in and through metaphysics, can come to light only if the question 'What is metaphysics?' is posed in the midst of metaphysics' domination. Indeed every inquiry into Being, even the one into the truth of Being, must at first introduce its inquiry as a 'metaphysical' one.

The first humanism, Roman humanism, and every kind that has emerged from that time to the present, has presupposed the most universal 'essence' of man to be obvious. Man is considered to be an *animal rationale*. This definition is not simply the Latin translation of the Greek *zōon logon echon* but rather a metaphysical interpretation of it. This essential definition of man is not false. But it is conditioned by metaphysics. The essential provenance of metaphysics, and not just its limits, became questionable in *Being and Time*. What is questionable is above all commended to thinking as what is to be thought, but not at all left to the gnawing doubts of an empty skepticism.

Metaphysics does indeed represent beings in their Being, and so it thinks the Being of beings. But it does not think the difference of both.[6] Metaphysics does not ask about the truth of Being itself. Nor does it therefore ask in what way the essence of man belongs to the truth of Being. Metaphysics has not only failed up to now to ask this question, the question is inaccessible to metaphysics as such. Being is still waiting for the time when it will become thought-provoking to man. With regard to the definition of man's essence, however one may determine the *ratio* of the *animal* and the reason of the living being, whether as a 'faculty of principles' or a 'faculty of categories' or in some other way, the essence of reason is always and in each case grounded in this: for every apprehending of beings in their Being, Being itself is already illumined and propriated in its truth. So too with *animal, zōon*, an interpretation of 'life' is already posited that necessarily lies in an interpretation of beings as *zōē* and *physis*, within which what is living appears. Above and beyond everything else, however, it finally remains to ask whether the essence of man primordially and most decisively lies in the dimension of *animalitas* at all. Are we really on the right track toward the essence of man as long as we set him off as one living creature among others in contrast to plants, beasts, and God? We can proceed in that way; we can in such fashion locate man within being as one being among others. We will thereby always be able to state something correct about man. But we must be clear on this point, that when we do this we abandon man to the essential realm of *animalitas* even if we do not equate him with beasts but attribute a specific difference to him. In principle we are still thinking of *homo animalis* – even when *anima* [soul] is posited as *animus sive mens* [spirit or mind], and this in turn is later posited as subject, person, or spirit [*Geist*]. Such positing is the manner of metaphysics. But then the essence of man is too little heeded and not thought in its origin, the essential provenance that is always the essential future for historical mankind. Metaphysics thinks of man on the basis of *animalitas* and does not think in the direction of his *humanitas*.

Metaphysics closes itself to the simple essential fact that man essentially occurs only in his essence, where he is claimed by Being. Only from that claim 'has' he found that wherein his essence dwells. Only from this dwelling 'has' he 'language' as the home that preserves the ecstatic for his essence.[7] Such standing in the clearing of Being I call the ek-sistence of man. This way of Being is proper only to man. Ek-sistence so understood is not only the ground of the possibility of reason, *ratio*, but is also that in which the essence of man preserves the source that determines him.

Ek-sistence can be said only of the essence of man, that is, only of the human way 'to be.' For as far as our experience shows, only man is admitted to the destiny of ek-sistence. Therefore ek-sistence can also never be thought of as a specific kind of living creature among others – granted that man is destined to think the essence of his Being and not merely to give accounts of the nature and history of his constitution and activities. Thus even what we attribute to man as *animalitas* on the basis of the comparison with 'beasts' is itself grounded in the essence of ek-sistence. The human body is something essentially other than an animal organism. Nor is the error of biologism overcome by adjoining a soul to the human body, a mind to the soul, and the existentiell to the mind, and then louder than before singing the praises of the mind – only to let everything relapse into 'life-experience,' with a warning that thinking by its inflexible concepts disrupts the flow of life and that thought of Being distorts existence. The fact that physiology and physiological chemistry can scientifically investigate man as an organism is no proof that in this 'organic' thing, that is, in the body scientifically explained, the essence of man consists. That has as little validity as the notion that the essence of nature has been discovered in atomic energy. It could even be that nature, in the face it turns toward man's technical mastery, is simply concealing its essence. Just as little as the essence of man consists in being an animal organism can this insufficient definition of man's essence be overcome or offset by outfitting man with an immortal soul, the power of reason, or the character of a person. In each instance essence is passed over, and passed over on the basis of the same metaphysical projection.

What man is – or, as it is called in the traditional language of metaphysics, the 'essence' of man – lies in his ek-sistence. But ek-sistence thought in this way is not identical with the traditional concept of *existentia*, which means actuality in contrast to the meaning of *essentia* as possibility. In *Being and Time* (p. 42) this sentence is italicized: 'The "essence" of Dasein lies in its existence.' However, here the opposition between *existentia* and *essentia* is not under consideration, because neither of these metaphysical determinations of Being, let alone their relationship, is yet in question. Still less does the sentence contain a universal statement about *Dasein*, since the word came into fashion in the eighteenth century as a name for 'object,' intending to express the metaphysical concept of the actuality of the actual. On the contrary, the sentence says: man occurs essentially in such a way that he is the 'there' [*das 'Da'*], that is, the clearing of Being. The 'Being' of the *Da*, and only it, has the fundamental character of ek-sistence, that is, of an ecstatic inherence in the truth of Being. The ecstatic essence of man consists in ek-sistence, which is different from the metaphysically conceived *existentia*. Medieval philosophy conceives the latter as *actualitas*. Kant represents *existentia* as actuality in the sense of the objectivity of experience. Hegel defines *existentia* as the self-knowing Idea of absolute subjectivity. Nietzsche grasps *existentia* as the eternal recurrence of the same. Here it remains an open question whether through *existentia* – in these explanations of it as actuality, which at first seem quite different – the Being of a stone or even life as the Being of plants and animals is adequately thought. In any case living creatures are as they are without standing outside their Being as such and within the truth of Being, preserving in such standing the essential nature of their Being. Of all the beings that are, presumably the most difficult to think about are living creatures, because on the one hand they are in a certain way most closely akin to us, and on the other are at the same time separated from our ek-sistent essence by an abyss. However, it might also seem as though the essence of divinity is closer to us than what is so alien in other living creatures, closer, namely, in an essential distance which, however distant, is nonetheless more familiar to our ek-sistent essence than is our scarcely conceivable, abysmal bodily kinship with the beast. Such reflections cast a strange light upon the current and therefore always still premature designation of man as *animal rationale*. Because plants and animals are lodged in their respective environments but are never placed freely in the clearing of Being which alone is 'world,' they lack language. But in being denied language they are not thereby suspended worldlessly in their environment. Still, in this word 'environment' converges all that is puzzling about living creatures. In its essence, language is not the utterance of an organism; nor is it the expression of a living thing. Nor can it ever be thought in an essentially correct way in terms of its symbolic character, perhaps not even in terms of the character of signification. Language is the clearing-concealing advent of Being itself.

Ek-sistence, thought in terms of *ecstasis*, does not coincide with *existentia* in either form or content. In terms of content ek-sistence means standing out into the truth of Being. *Existentia* (*existence*) means in contrast *actualitas*, actuality as opposed to mere possibility as Idea. Ek-sistence identifies the determination of what man is in the destiny of truth. *Existentia* is the name for the realization of something that is as it appears in its Idea. The sentence 'Man ek-sists' is not an answer to the question of whether man actually is or not; rather, it responds to the question concerning man's 'essence.' We are accustomed to posing this question with equal impropriety whether we ask what man is or who he is. For in the *Who?* or the *What?* we are already on the lookout for something like a person or an object. But the personal no less than the objective misses and misconstrues the essential unfolding of ek-sistence in the history of Being. That is why the sentence cited from *Being and Time* (p. 42) is careful to enclose the word 'essence' in quotation marks. This indicates that 'essence' is now being defined from neither *esse essentiae* nor *esse existentiae* but rather from the ek-static character of Dasein. As ek-sisting, man sustains Da-sein in that he takes the *Da*, the clearing of Being, into 'care.' But Da-sein itself occurs essentially as 'thrown.' It unfolds essentially in the throw of Being as the fateful sending.

But it would be the ultimate error if one wished to explain the sentence about man's ek-sistent essence as if it were the secularized transference to human beings of a thought that Christian theology expresses about God (*Deus est suum esse* [God is His Being]); for ek-sistence is not the realization of an essence, nor does ek-sistence itself even effect and posit what is essential. If we understand what *Being and Time* calls 'projection' as a representational positing, we take it to be an achievement of subjectivity and do not think it in the only way the 'understanding of Being' in the context of the 'existential analysis' of 'being-in-the-world' can be thought – namely, as the ecstatic relation to the clearing of Being. The adequate execution and completion of this other thinking that abandons subjectivity is surely made more difficult by the fact that in the publication of *Being and Time* the third division of the first part, 'Time and Being,' was held back (cf. *Being and Time*, p. 87, above). Here everything is reversed. The division in question was held back because thinking failed in the adequate saying of this turning [*Kehre*] and did not succeed with the help of the language of metaphysics. The lecture 'On the Essence of Truth,' thought out and delivered in 1930 but not printed until 1943, provides a certain insight into the thinking of the turning from 'Being and Time' to 'Time and Being.' This turning is not a change of standpoint from *Being and Time*, but in it the thinking that was sought first arrives at the location of that dimension out of which *Being and Time* is experienced, that is to say, experienced from the fundamental experience of the oblivion of Being.

By way of contrast, Sartre expresses the basic tenet of existentialism in this way: Existence precedes essence.[8] In this statement he is taking *existentia* and *essentia* according to their metaphysical meaning, which from Plato's time on has said that *essentia* precedes *existentia*. Sartre reverses this statement. But the reversal of a metaphysical statement remains a metaphysical statement. With it he stays with metaphysics in oblivion of the truth of Being. For even if philosophy wishes to determine the relation of *essentia* and *existentia* in the sense it had in medieval controversies, in Leibniz's sense, or in some other way, it still remains to ask first of all from what destiny of Being this differentiation in Being as *esse essentiae* and *esse existentiae* comes to appear to thinking. We have yet to consider why the question about the destiny of Being was never asked and why it could never be thought. Or is the fact that this is how it is with the differentiation of *essentia* and *existentia* not at all a sign of forgetfulness of Being? We must presume that this destiny does not rest upon a mere failure of human thinking, let alone upon a lesser capacity of early Western thinking. Concealed in its essential provenance, the differentiation of *essentia* (essentiality) and *existentia* (actuality) completely dominates the destiny of Western history and of all history determined by Europe.

Sartre's key proposition about the priority of *existentia* over *essentia* does, however, justify using the name 'existentialism' as an appropriate title for a philosophy of this sort. But the basic tenet of 'existentialism' has nothing at all in common with the statement from *Being and Time* – apart from the fact that in *Being and Time* no statement about the relation of *essentia* and *existentia* can yet be expressed, since there it is still a question of preparing something precursory. As is obvious from what we have just said, that happens clumsily enough. What still today remains to be said could perhaps become an impetus for guiding the essence of man to the point where it thoughtfully attends to that dimension of the truth of Being which thoroughly governs it. But even this could take place only to the honor of Being and for the benefit of Da-sein, which man ek-sistingly sustains; not, however, for the sake of man, so that civilization and culture through man's doings might be vindicated.

But in order that we today may attain to the dimension of the truth of Being in order to ponder it, we should first of all make clear how Being concerns man and how it claims him. Such an essential experience happens to us when it dawns on us that man is in that he ek-sists. Were we now to say this in the language of the tradition, it would run: the ek-sistence of man is his substance. That is why in *Being and Time* the sentence often recurs, 'The "substance" of man is existence' (pp. 117, 212, 314). But 'substance,' thought in terms of the history of Being, is already a blanket translation of *ousia*, a word that designates the presence of what is present and at the same time, with puzzling ambiguity, usually means what is present itself. If we think the metaphysical term 'substance' in the sense already suggested in accordance with the 'phenomenological destructuring' carried out in *Being and Time* (cf. p. 63, above), then the statement 'The "substance" of man is ek-sistence' says nothing else but that the way that man in his proper essence becomes present to Being is ecstatic inherence in the truth of Being. Through this determination of the essence of man the humanistic interpretations of man as *animal rationale*, as 'person,' as spiritual-ensouled-bodily being, are not declared false and thrust aside. Rather, the sole implication is that the highest determinations of the essence of man in humanism still do not realize the proper dignity of man. To that extent the thinking in *Being and Time* is against humanism. But this opposition does not mean that such thinking aligns itself against the humane and advocates the inhuman, that it promotes the inhumane and deprecates the dignity of man. Humanism is opposed because it does not set the *human itas* of man high enough. Of course the essential worth of man does not consist in his being the substance of beings, as the 'Subject' among them, so that as the tyrant of Being he may deign to release the beingness of beings into an all too loudly bruited 'objectivity.'

Man is rather 'thrown' from Being itself into the truth of Being, so that ek-sisting in this fashion he might guard the truth of Being, in order that beings might appear in the light of Being as the beings they are. Man does not decide whether and how beings appear, whether and how God and the gods or history and nature come forward into the clearing of Being, come to presence and depart. The advent of beings lies in the destiny of Being. But for man it is ever a question of finding what is fitting in his essence that corresponds to such destiny; for in accord with this destiny man as ek-sisting has to guard the truth of Being. Man is the shepherd of Being. It is in this direction alone that *Being and Time* is thinking when ecstatic existence is experienced as 'care' (cf. section 44 C, pp. 226ff.).

Yet Being – what is Being? It is It itself. The thinking that is to come must learn to experience that and to say it. 'Being' – that is not God and not a cosmic ground. Being is farther than all beings and is yet nearer to man than every being, be it a rock, a beast, a work of art, a machine, be it an angel or God. Being is the nearest. Yet the near remains farthest from man. Man at first clings always and only to beings. But when thinking represents beings as beings it no doubt relates itself to Being. In truth, however, it always thinks only of beings as such; precisely not, and never, Being as such. The 'question of Being' always remains a question about beings. It is still not at all what its elusive name indicates: the question in the direction of Being. Philosophy, even when it becomes 'critical' through Descartes and Kant, always follows the course of metaphysical repre-sentation. It thinks from beings back to beings with a glance in passing toward Being. For every departure from beings and every return to them stands already in the light of Being.

But metaphysics recognizes the clearing of Being either solely as the view of what is present in 'outward appearance' (*idea*) or critically as what is seen as a result of categorial representation on the part of subjectivity. This means that the truth of Being as the clearing itself remains concealed for metaphysics. However, this concealment is not a defect of metaphysics but a treasure withheld from it yet held before it, the treasure of its own proper wealth. But the clearing itself is Being. Within the destiny of Being in metaphysics the clearing first affords a view by which what is present comes into touch with man, who is present to it, so that man himself can in apprehending (*noein*) first touch upon Being (*thigein*, Aristotle, *Met.* IX, 10). This view first gathers the aspect to itself. It yields to such aspects when apprehending has become a setting-forth-before-itself in the *perceptio* of the *res cogitans* taken as the *subiectum* of *certitudo*.

But how – provided we really ought to ask such a question at all – how does Being relate to ek-sistence? Being itself is the relation to the extent that It, as the location of the truth of Being amid beings, gathers to itself and embraces ek-sistence in its existential, that is, ecstatic, essence. Because man as the one who ek-sists comes to stand in this relation that Being destines for itself, in that he ecstatically sustains it, that is, in care takes it upon himself, he at first fails to recognize the nearest and attaches himself to the next nearest. He even thinks that this is the nearest. But nearer than the nearest and at the same time for ordinary thinking farther than the farthest is nearness itself: the truth of Being.

Forgetting the truth of Being in favor of the pressing throng of beings unthought in their essence is what ensnarement [*Verfallen*] means in *Being and Time*.[9] This word does not signify the Fall of Man understood in a 'moral-philosophical' and at the same time secularized way; rather, it designates an essential relationship of man to Being within Being's relation to the essence of man. Accordingly, the terms 'authenticity' and 'inauthenticity,' which are used in a provisional fashion, do not imply a moral-existentiell or an 'anthropological' distinction but rather a relation which, because it has been hitherto concealed from philosophy, has yet to be thought for the first time, an 'ecstatic' relation of the essence of man to the truth of Being. But this relation is as it is not by reason of ek-sistence; on the contrary, the essence of ek-sistence derives existentially-ecstatically from the essence of the truth of Being.

The one thing thinking would like to attain and for the first time tries to articulate in *Being and Time* is something simple. As such, Being remains mysterious, the simple nearness of an unobtrusive governance. The nearness occurs essentially as language itself. But language is not mere speech, insofar as we represent the latter at best as the unity of phoneme (or written character), melody, rhythm, and meaning (or sense). We think of the phoneme and written character as a verbal body for language, of melody and rhythm as its soul, and whatever has to do with meaning as its mind. We usually think of language as corresponding to the essence of man represented as *animal rationale*, that is, as the unity of body-soul-mind. But just as ek-sistence – and through it the relation of the truth of Being to man – remains veiled in the *humanitas* of *homo animalis*, so does the metaphysical-animal explanation of language cover up the essence of language in the history of Being. According to *this* essence, language is the house of Being, which is propriated by Being and pervaded by Being. And so it is proper to think the essence of language from its correspondence to Being and indeed as this correspondence, that is, as the home of man's essence.

But man is not only a living creature who possesses language along with other capacities. Rather, language is the house of Being in which man ek-sists by dwelling, in that he belongs to the truth of Being, guarding it.

So the point is that in the determination of the humanity of man as ek-sistence what is essential is not man but Being – as the dimension of the *ecstasis* of ek-sistence. However, the dimension is not something spatial in the familiar sense. Rather, everything spatial and all space-time occur essentially in the dimensionality that Being itself is.

Thinking attends to these simple relationships. It tries to find the right word for them within the long-traditional language and grammar of metaphysics. But does such thinking – granted that there is something in a name – still allow itself to be described as humanism? Certainly not so far as humanism thinks metaphysically. Certainly not if humanism is existentialism and is represented by what Sartre expresses: *précisément nous sommes sur un plan où il y a seulement des hommes* [We are precisely in a situation where there are only human beings].[10] Thought from *Being and Time*, this should say instead: *précisément nous sommes sur un plan où il y a principalement l'Être* [We are precisely in a situation where principally there is Being]. But where does *le plan* come from and what is it? *L'Être et le plan* are the same. In *Being and Time* (p. 212) we purposely and cautiously say, *il y a l'Être*: 'there is / it gives' ['*es gibt*'] Being. *Il y a* translates 'it gives' imprecisely. For the 'it' that here 'gives' is Being itself. The 'gives' names the essence of Being that is giving, granting its truth. The self-giving into the open, along with the open region itself, is Being itself.

At the same time 'it gives' is used preliminarily to avoid the locution 'Being is'; for 'is' is commonly said of some thing that is. We call such a thing a being. But Being 'is' precisely not 'a being.' If 'is' is spoken without a closer interpretation of Being, then Being is all too easily represented as a 'being' after the fashion of the familiar sorts of beings that act as causes and are actualized as effects. And yet Parmenides, in the early age of thinking, says, *esti gar einai*, 'for there is Being.' The primal mystery for all thinking is concealed in this phrase. Perhaps 'is' can be said only of Being in an appropriate way, so that no individual being ever properly 'is.' But because thinking should be directed only toward saying Being in its truth, instead of explaining it as a particular being in terms of beings, whether and how Being is must remain an open question for the careful attention of thinking.

The *esti gar einai* of Parmenides is still unthought today. That allows us to gauge how things stand with the progress of philosophy. When philosophy attends to its essence it does not make forward strides at all. It remains where it is in order constantly to think the Same. Progression, that is, progression forward from this place, is a mistake that follows thinking as the shadow that thinking itself casts. Because Being is still unthought, *Being and Time* too says of it, 'there is / it gives.' Yet one cannot speculate about this *il y a* precipitately and without a foothold. This 'there is / it gives' rules as the destiny of Being. Its history comes to language in the words of essential thinkers. Therefore the thinking that thinks into the truth of Being is, as thinking, historical. There is not a 'systematic' thinking and next to it an illustrative history of past opinions. Nor is there, as Hegel thought, only a systematics that can fashion the law of its thinking into the law of history and simultaneously subsume history into the system. Thought in a more primordial way, there is the history of Being to which thinking belongs as recollection of this history, propriated by it. Such recollective thought differs essentially from the subsequent presentation of history in the sense of an evanescent past. History does not take place primarily as a happening. And its happening is not evanescence. The happening of history occurs essentially as the destiny of the truth of Being and from it.[11] Being comes to destiny in that It, Being, gives itself. But thought in terms of such destiny this says: it gives itself and refuses itself simultaneously. Nonetheless, Hegel's definition of history as the development of 'Spirit' is not untrue. Neither is it partly correct and partly false. It is as true as metaphysics, which through Hegel first brings to language its essence – thought in terms of the absolute – in the system. Absolute metaphysics, with its Marxian and Nietzschean inversions, belongs to the history of the truth of Being. Whatever stems from it cannot be countered or even cast aside by refutations. It can only be taken up in such a way that its truth is more primordially sheltered in Being itself and removed from the domain of mere human opinion. All refutation in the field of essential thinking is foolish. Strife among thinkers is the 'lovers' quarrel' concerning the matter itself. It assists them mutually toward a simple belonging to the Same, from which they find what is fitting for them in the destiny of Being.

Assuming that in the future man will be able to think the truth of Being, he will think from ek-sistence. Man stands ek-sistingly in the destiny of Being. The ek-sistence of man is historical as such, but not only or primarily because so much happens to man and to things human in the course of time. Because it must think the ek-sistence of Da-sein, the thinking of *Being and Time* is essentially concerned that the historicity of Dasein be experienced.

But does not *Being and Time* say on p. 212, where the 'there is it gives' comes to language, 'Only so long as Dasein is, is there [*gibt es*] Being'? To be sure. It means that only so long as the clearing of Being propriates does Being convey itself to man. But the fact that the *Da*, the clearing as the truth of Being itself, propriates is the dispensation of Being itself. This is the destiny of the clearing. But the sentence does not mean that the Dasein of man in the traditional sense of *existentia*, and thought in modern philosophy as the actuality of the *ego cogito*, is that being through which Being is first fashioned. The sentence does not say that Being is the product of man. The 'Introduction' to *Being and Time* says simply and clearly, even in italics, 'Being' is the *transcendens* pure and simple.' Just as the openness of spatial nearness seen from the perspective of a particular thing exceeds all things near and far, so is Being essentially broader than all beings, because it is the clearing itself. For all that, Being is thought on the basis of beings, a consequence of the approach – at first unavoidable – within a metaphysics that is still dominant. Only from such a perspective does Being show itself in and as a transcending.

The introductory definition. 'Being is the *transcendens* pure and simple,' articulates in one simple sentence the way the essence of Being hitherto has illumined man. This retrospective definition of the essence of Being from the clearing of beings as such remains indispensable for the prospective approach of thinking toward the question concerning the truth of Being. In this way thinking attests to its essential unfolding as destiny. It is far from the arrogant presumption that wishes to begin anew and declares all past philosophy false. But whether the definition of Being as the *transcendens* pure and simple really does express the simple essence of the truth of Being – this and this alone is the primary question for a thinking that attempts to think the truth of Being. That is why we also say (p. 230) that how Being is *is* to be understood chiefly from its 'meaning' ['*Sinn*'], that is, from the truth of Being, Being is illumined for man in the ecstatic projection [Entwurf]. But this projection does not create Being.

Moreover, the projection is essentially a thrown projection. What throws in projection is not man but Being itself, which sends man into the ek-sistence of Da-sein that is his essence. This destiny propriates as the clearing of Being – which it is. The clearing grants nearness to Being. In this nearness, in the clearing of the *Da*, man dwells as the ek-sisting one without yet being able properly to experience and take over this dwelling. In the lecture on Hölderlin's elegy 'Homecoming' (1943) this nearness 'of' Being, which the *Da* of Dasein is, is thought on the basis of *Being and Time*; it is perceived as spoken from the minstrel's poem; from the experience of the oblivion of Being it is called the 'homeland.' The word is thought here in an essential sense, not patriotically or nationalistically, but in terms of the history of Being. The essence of the homeland, however, is also mentioned with the intention of thinking the homelessness of contemporary man from the essence of Being's history. Nietzsche was the last to experience this homelessness. From within metaphysics he was unable to find any other way out than a reversal of metaphysics. But that is the height of futility. On the other hand, when Hölderlin composes 'Homecoming' he is concerned that his 'countrymen' find their essence. He does not at all seek that essence in an egoism of his nation. He sees it rather in the context of a belongingness to the destiny of the West. But even the West is not thought regionally as the Occident in contrast to the Orient, nor merely as Europe, but rather world-historically out of nearness to the source. We have still scarcely begun to think of the mysterious relations to the East that found expression in Hölderlin's poetry.[12] 'German' is not spoken to the world so that the world might be reformed through the German essence; rather, it is spoken to the Germans so that from a fateful belongingness to the nations they might become world-historical along with them.[13] The homeland of this historical dwelling is nearness to Being.

In such nearness, if at all, a decision may be made as to whether and how God and the gods withhold their presence and the night remains, whether and how the day of the holy dawns, whether and how in the upsurgence of the holy an epiphany of God and the gods can begin anew. But the holy, which alone is the essential sphere of divinity, which in turn alone affords a dimension for the gods and for God, comes to radiate only when Being itself beforehand and after extensive preparation has been illuminated and is experienced in its truth. Only thus does the overcoming of homelessness begin from Being, a homelessness in which not only man but the essence of man stumbles aimlessly about.

Homelessness so understood consists in the abandonment of Being by beings. Homelessness is the symptom of oblivion of Being. Because of it the truth of Being remains unthought. The oblivion of Being makes itself known indirectly through the fact that man always observes and handles only beings. Even so, because man cannot avoid having some notion of Being, it is explained merely as what is 'most general' and therefore as something that encompasses beings, or as a creation of the infinite being, or as the product of a finite subject. At the same time 'Being' has long stood for 'beings' and, inversely, the latter for the former, the two of them caught in a curious and still unraveled confusion.

As the destiny that sends truth, Being remains concealed. But the world's destiny is heralded in poetry, without yet becoming manifest as the history of Being. The world-historical thinking of Hölderlin that speaks out in the poem 'Remembrance' is therefore essentially more primordial and thus more significant for the future than the mere cosmopolitanism of Goethe. For the same reason Hölderlin's relation to Greek civilization is something essentially other than humanism. When confronted with death, therefore, those young Germans who knew about Hölderlin lived and thought something other than what the public held to be the typical German attitude.

Homelessness is coming to be the destiny of the world. Hence it is necessary to think that destiny in terms of the history of Being. What Marx recognized in an essential and significant sense, though derived from Hegel, as the estrangement of man has its roots in the homelessness of modern man.[14] This homelessness is specifically evoked from the destiny of Being in the form of metaphysics, and through metaphysics is simultaneously entrenched and covered up as such. Because Marx by experiencing estrangement attains an essential dimension of history, the Marxist view of history is superior to that of other historical accounts. But since neither Husserl nor – so far as I have seen till now – Sartre recognizes the essential importance of the historical in Being, neither phenomenology nor existentialism enters that dimension within which a productive dialogue with Marxism first becomes possible.

For such dialogue it is certainly also necessary to free oneself from naive notions about materialism, as well as from the cheap refutations that are supposed to counter it. The essence of materialism does not consist in the assertion that everything is simply matter but rather in a metaphysical determination according to which every being appears as the material of labor. The modern metaphysical essence of labor is anticipated in Hegel's *Phenomenology of Spirit* as the self-establishing process of unconditioned production, which is the objectification of the actual through man experienced as subjectivity. The essence of materialism is concealed in the essence of technology, about which much has been written but little has been thought. Technology is in its essence a destiny within the history of Being and of the truth of Being, a truth that lies in oblivion. For technology does not go back to the *technē* of the Greeks in name only but derives historically and essentially from *technē* as a mode of *alētheuein*, a mode, that is, of rendering beings manifest [*Offenbarmachen*]. As a form of truth technology is grounded in the history of metaphysics, which is itself a distinctive and up to now the only perceptible phase of the history of Being. No matter which of the various positions one chooses to adopt toward the doctrines of communism and to their foundation, from the point of view of the history of Being it is certain that an elemental experience of what is world-historical speaks out in it. Whoever takes 'communism' only as a 'party' or a 'Weltanschauung' is thinking too shallowly, just as those who by the term 'Americanism' mean, and mean derogatorily, nothing more than a particular life-style. The danger into which Europe as it has hitherto existed is ever more clearly forced consists presumably in the fact above all that its thinking – once its glory – is falling behind in the essential course of a dawning world destiny which nevertheless in the basic traits of its essential provenance remains European by definition. No metaphysics, whether idealistic, materialistic, or Christian, can in accord with its essence, and surely not in its own attempts to explicate itself, 'get a hold on' this destiny yet, and that means thoughtfully to reach and gather together what in the fullest sense of Being now is.

In the face of the essential homelessness of man, man's approaching destiny reveals itself to thought on the history of Being in this, that man find his way into the truth of Being and set out on this find. Every nationalism is metaphysically an anthropologism, and as such subjectivism. Nationalism is not overcome through mere internationalism; it is rather expanded and elevated thereby into a system. Nationalism is as little brought and raised to *humanitas* by internationalism as individualism is by an ahistorical collectivism. The latter is the subjectivity of man in totality. It completes subjectivity's unconditioned self-assertion, which refuses to yield. Nor can it be even adequately experienced by a thinking that mediates in a one-sided fashion. Expelled from the truth of Being, man everywhere circles round himself as the *animal rationale*.

But the essence of man consists in his being more than merely human, if this is represented as 'being a rational creature.' 'More' must not be understood here additively, as if the traditional definition of man were indeed to remain basic, only elaborated by means of an existentiell postscript. The 'more' means: more originally and therefore more essentially in terms of his essence. But here something enigmatic manifests itself: man is in thrownness. This means that man, as the ek-sisting counter-throw [*Gegenwurf*] of Being, is more than *animal rationale* precisely to the extent that he is less bound up with man conceived from subjectivity. Man is not the lord of beings. Man is the shepherd of Being. Man loses nothing in this 'less'; rather, he gains in that he attains the truth of Being. He gains the essential poverty of the shepherd, whose dignity consists in being called by Being itself into the preservation of Being's truth. The call comes as the throw from which the thrownness of Da-sein derives. In his essential unfolding within the history of Being, man is the being whose Being as ek-sistence consists in his dwelling in the nearness of Being. Man is the neighbor of Being.

But – as you no doubt have been wanting to rejoin for quite a while now – does not such thinking think precisely the *humanitas* of *homo humanus*? Does it not think *humanitas* in a decisive sense, as no metaphysics has thought it or can think it? Is this not 'humanism' in the extreme sense? Certainly. It is a humanism that thinks the humanity of man from nearness to Being. But at the same time it is a humanism in which not man but man's historical essence is at stake in its provenance from the truth of Being. But then does not the ek-sistence of man also stand or fall in this game of stakes? Indeed it does.

In *Being and Time* . . . it is said that every question of philosophy 'recoils upon existence.' But existence here is not the actuality of the *ego cogito*. Neither is it the actuality of subjects who act with and for each other and so become who they are. 'Ek-sistence,' in fundamental contrast to every *existentia* and '*existence*,' is ecstatic dwelling in the nearness of Being. It is the guardianship, that is, the care for Being. Because there is something simple to be thought in this thinking it seems quite difficult to the representational thought that has been transmitted as philosophy. But the difficulty is not a matter of indulging in a special sort of profundity and of building complicated concepts; rather, it is concealed in the step back that lets thinking enter into a questioning that experiences – and lets the habitual opining of philosophy fall away.

It is everywhere supposed that the attempt in *Being and Time* ended in a blind alley. Let us not comment any further upon that opinion. The thinking that hazards a few steps in *Being and Time* has even today not advanced beyond that publication. But perhaps in the meantime it has in one respect come farther into its own matter. However, as long as philosophy merely busies itself with continually obstructing the possibility of admittance into the matter for thinking, i.e., into the truth of Being, it stands safely beyond any danger of shattering against the hardness of that matter. Thus to 'philosophize' about being shattered is separated by a chasm from a thinking that is shattered. If such thinking were to go fortunately for a man, no misfortune would befall him. He would receive the only gift that can come to thinking from Being.

But it is also the case that the matter of thinking is not achieved in the fact that talk about the 'truth of Being' and the 'history of Being' is set in motion. Everything depends upon this alone, that the truth of Being come to language and that thinking attain to this language. Perhaps, then, language requires much less precipitate expression than proper silence. But who of us today would want to imagine that his attempts to think are at home on the path of silence? At best, thinking could perhaps point toward the truth of Being, and indeed toward it as what is to be thought. It would thus be more easily weaned from mere supposing and opining and directed to the now rare handicraft of writing. Things that really matter, although they are not defined for all eternity, even when they come very late still come at the right time.

Whether the realm of the truth of Being is a blind alley or whether it is the free space in which freedom conserves its essence is something each one may judge after he himself has tried to go the designated way, or even better, after he has gone a better way, that is, a way befitting the question. On the penultimate page of *Being and Time* (p. 437) stand the sentences: 'The *conflict* with respect to the interpretation of Being (that is, therefore, not the interpretation of beings or of the Being of man) cannot be settled, *because it has not yet been kindled.* And in the end it is not a question of "picking a quarrel," since the kindling of the conflict does demand some preparation. To this end alone the foregoing investigation is under way.' Today after two decades these sentences still hold. Let us also in the days ahead remain as wanderers on the way into the neighborhood of Being. The question you pose helps to clarify the way.

You ask, *Comment redonner un sens au mot 'Humanisme'?* 'How can some sense be restored to the word "humanism"?' Your question not only presupposes a desire to retain the word 'humanism' but also contains an admission that this word has lost its meaning.

It has lost it through the insight that the essence of humanism is metaphysical, which now means that metaphysics not only does not pose the question concerning the truth of Being but also obstructs the question, insofar as metaphysics persists in the oblivion of Being. But the same thinking that has led us to this insight into the questionable essence of humanism has likewise compelled us to think the essence of man more primordially. With regard to this more essential *humanitas* of *homo humanus* there arises the possibility of restoring to the word 'humanism' a historical sense that is older than its oldest meaning chronologically reckoned. The restoration is not to be understood as though the word 'humanism' were wholly without meaning and a mere *flatus vocis* [empty sound]. The '*humanum*' in the word points to *humanitas*, the essence of man; the '-ism' indicates that the essence of man is meant to be taken essentially. This is the sense that the word 'humanism' has as such. To restore a sense to it can only mean to redefine the meaning of the word. That requires that we first experience the essence of man more primordially; but it also demands that we show to what extent this essence in its own way becomes fateful. The essence of man lies in ek-sistence. That is what is essentially – that is, from Being itself – at issue here, insofar as Being appropriates man as ek-sisting for guardianship over the truth of Being into this truth itself. 'Humanism' now means, in case we decide to retain the word, that the essence of man is essential for the truth of Being, specifically in such a way that what matters is not man simply as such. So we are thinking a curious kind of 'humanism.' The word results in a name that is a *lucus a non lucendo* [literally, a grove where no light penetrates].

Should we still keep the name 'humanism' for a 'humanism' that contradicts all previous humanism – although it in no way advocates the inhuman? And keep it just so that by sharing in the use of the name we might perhaps swim in the predominant currents, stifled in metaphysical subjectivism and submerged in oblivion of Being? Or should thinking, by means of open resistance to 'humanism,' risk a shock that could for the first time cause perplexity concerning the *humanitas* of *homo humanus* and its basis? In this way it could awaken a reflection – if the world-historical moment did not itself already compel such a reflection – that thinks not only about man but also about the 'nature' of man, not only about his nature but even more primordially about the dimension in which the essence of man, determined by Being itself, is at home. Should we not rather suffer a little while longer those inevitable misinterpretations to which the path of thinking in the element of Being and time has hitherto been exposed and let them slowly dissipate? These misinterpretations are natural reinterpretations of what was read, or simply mirrorings of what one believes he knows already before he reads. They all betray the same structure and the same foundation.

Because we are speaking against 'humanism' people fear a defense of the inhuman and a glorification of barbaric brutality. For what is more 'logical' than that for somebody who negates humanism nothing remains but the affirmation of inhumanity?

Because we are speaking against 'logic' people believe we are demanding that the rigor of thinking be renounced and in its place the arbitrariness of drives and feelings be installed and thus that 'irrationalism' be proclaimed as true. For what is more 'logical' than that whoever speaks against the logical is defending the alogical?

Because we are speaking against 'values' people are horrified at a philosophy that ostensibly dares to despise humanity's best qualities. For what is more 'logical' than that a thinking that denies values must necessarily pronounce everything valueless?

Because we say that the Being of man consists in 'being-in-the-world' people find that man is downgraded to a merely terrestrial being, whereupon philosophy sinks into positivism. For what is more 'logical' than that whoever asserts the worldliness of human being holds only this life as valid, denies the beyond, and renounces all 'Transcendence'?

Because we refer to the word of Nietzsche on the 'death of God' people regard such a gesture as atheism. For what is more 'logical' than that whoever has experienced the death of God is godless?

Because in all the respects mentioned we everywhere speak against all that humanity deems high and holy our philosophy teaches an irresponsible and destructive 'nihilism.' For what is more 'logical' than that whoever roundly denies what is truly in being puts himself on the side of nonbeing and thus professes the pure nothing as the meaning of reality?

What is going on here? People hear talk about 'humanism,' 'logic,' 'values,' 'world,' and 'God.' They hear something about opposition to these. They recognize and accept these things as positive. But with hearsay – in a way that is not strictly deliberate – they immediately assume that what speaks against something is automatically its negation and that this is 'negative' in the sense of destructive. And somewhere in *Being and Time* there is explicit talk of 'the phenomenological destructuring.' With the assistance of logic and *ratio* – so often invoked – people come to believe that whatever is not positive is negative and thus that it seeks to degrade reason – and therefore deserves to be branded as depravity. We are so filled with 'logic' that anything that disturbs the habitual somnolence of prevailing opinion is automatically registered as a despicable contradiction. We pitch everything that does not stay close to the familiar and beloved positive into the previously excavated pit of pure negation, which negates everything, ends in nothing, and so consummates nihilism. Following this logical course we let everything expire in a nihilism we invented for ourselves with the aid of logic.

But does the 'against' which a thinking advances against ordinary opinion necessarily point toward pure negation and the negative? This happens – and then, to be sure, happens inevitably and conclusively, that is, without a clear prospect of anything else – only when one posits in advance what is meant by the 'positive' and on this basis makes an absolute and absolutely negative decision about the range of possible opposition to it. Concealed in such a procedure is the refusal to subject to reflection this presupposed 'positive' in which one believes oneself saved, together with its position and opposition. By continually appealing to the logical one conjures up the illusion that one is entering straightforwardly into thinking when in fact one has disavowed it.

It ought to be somewhat clearer now that opposition to 'humanism' in no way implies a defense of the inhuman but rather opens other vistas.

'Logic' understands thinking to be the representation of beings in their Being, which representation proposes to itself in the generality of the concept. But how is it with meditation on Being itself, that is, with the thinking that thinks the truth of Being? This thinking alone reaches the primordial essence of *logos*, which was already obfuscated and lost in Plato and in Aristotle, the founder of 'logic.' To think against 'logic' does not mean to break a lance for the illogical but simply to trace in thought the *logos* and its essence, which appeared in the dawn of thinking, that is, to exert ourselves for the first time in preparing for such reflection. Of what value are even far-reaching systems of logic to us if, without really knowing what they are doing, they recoil before the task of simply inquiring into the essence of *logos*? If we wished to bandy about objections, which is of course fruitless, we could say with more right: irrationalism, as a denial of *ratio*, rules unnoticed and uncontested in the defense of 'logic,' which believes it can eschew meditation on *logos* and on the essence of *ratio*, which has its ground in *logos*.

To think against 'values' is not to maintain that everything interpreted as 'a value' – 'culture,' 'art,' 'science,' 'human dignity,' 'world,' and 'God' – is valueless. Rather, it is important finally to realize that precisely through the characterization of something as 'a value' what is so valued is robbed of its worth. That is to say, by the assessment of something as a value what is valued is admitted only as an object for man's estimation. But what a thing is in its Being is not exhausted by its being an object, particularly when objectivity takes the form of value. Every valuing, even where it values positively, is a subjectivizing.

It does not let beings: be. Rather, valuing lets beings: be valid – solely as the objects of its doing. The bizarre effort to prove the objectivity of values does not know what it is doing. When one proclaims 'God' the altogether 'highest value,' this is a degradation of God's essence. Here as elsewhere thinking in values is the greatest blasphemy imaginable against Being. To think against values therefore does not mean to beat the drum for the valuelessness and nullity of beings. It means rather to bring the clearing of the truth of Being before thinking, as against subjectivizing beings into mere objects.

The reference to 'being-in-the-world' as the basic trait of the *humanitas* of *homo humanus* does not assert that man is merely a 'worldly' creature understood in a Christian sense, thus a creature turned away from God and so cut loose from 'Transcendence.' What is really meant by this word would be more clearly called 'the transcendent.' The transcendent is supersensible being. This is considered the highest being in the sense of the first cause of all beings. God is thought as this first cause. However, in the name 'being-in-the-world,' 'world' does not in any way imply earthly as opposed to heavenly being, nor the 'worldly' as opposed to the 'spiritual.' For us 'world' does not at all signify beings or any realm of beings but the openness of Being. Man is, and is man, insofar as he is the ek-sisting one. He stands out into the openness of Being. Being itself, which as the throw has projected the essence of man into 'care,' is as this openness. Thrown in such fashion, man stands 'in' the openness of Being. 'World' is the clearing of Being into which man stands out on the basis of his thrown essence. 'Being-in-the-world' designates the essence of ek-sistence with regard to the cleared dimension out of which the 'ek-' of ek-sistence essentially unfolds. Thought in terms of ek-sistence, 'world' is in a certain sense precisely 'the beyond' within existence and for it. Man is never first and foremost man on the hither side of the world, as a 'subject,' whether this is taken as 'I' or 'We.' Nor is he ever simply a mere subject which always simultaneously is related to objects, so that his essence lies in the subject-object relation. Rather, before all this, man in his essence is ek-sistent into the openness of Being, into the open region that clears the 'between' within which a 'relation' of subject to object can 'be.'

The statement that the essence of man consists in being-in-the-world likewise contains no decision about whether man in a theologico-metaphysical sense is merely a this-worldly or an other-worldly creature.

With the existential determination of the essence of man, therefore, nothing is decided about the 'existence of God' or his 'non being,' no more than about the possibility or impossibility of gods. Thus it is not only rash but also an error in procedure to maintain that the interpretation of the essence of man from the relation of his essence to the truth of Being is atheism. And what is more, this arbitrary classification betrays a lack of careful reading. No one bothers to notice that in my essay 'On the Essence of Ground' the following appears: 'Through the ontological interpretation of Dasein as being-in-the-world no decision, whether positive or negative, is made concerning a possible being toward God. It is, however, the case that through an illumination of transcendence we first achieve an *adequate concept of Dasein*, with respect to which it can now be asked how the relationship of Dasein to God is ontologically ordered.'[15] If we think about this remark too quickly, as is usually the case, we will declare that such a philosophy does not decide either for or against the existence of God. It remains stalled in indifference. Thus it is unconcerned with the religious question. Such indifferentism ultimately falls prey to nihilism.

But does the foregoing observation teach indifferentism? Why then are particular words in the note italicized – and not just random ones? For no other reason than to indicate that the thinking that thinks from the question concerning the truth of Being questions more primordially than metaphysics can. Only from the truth of Being can the essence of the holy be thought. Only from the essence of the holy is the essence of divinity to be thought. Only in the light of the essence of divinity can it be thought or said what the word 'God' is to signify. Or should we not first be able to hear and understand all these words carefully if we are to be permitted as men, that is, as ek-sistent creatures, to experience a relation of God to man? How can man at the present stage of world history ask at all seriously and rigorously whether the god nears or withdraws, when he has above all neglected to think into the dimension in which alone that question can be asked? But this is the dimension of the holy, which indeed remains closed as a dimension if the open region of Being is not cleared and in its clearing is near man. Perhaps what is distinctive about this world-epoch consists in the closure of the dimension of the hale [*des Heilen*]. Perhaps that is the sole malignancy [*Unheil*].

But with this reference the thinking that points toward the truth of Being as what is to be thought has in no way decided in favor of theism. It can be theistic as little as atheistic. Not, however, because of an indifferent attitude, but out of respect for the boundaries that have been set for thinking as such, indeed set by what gives itself to thinking as what is to be thought, by the truth of Being. Insofar as thinking limits itself to its task it directs man at the present moment of the world's destiny into the primordial dimension of his historical abode. When thinking of this kind speaks the truth of Being it has entrusted itself to what is more essential than all values and all types of beings. Thinking does not overcome metaphysics by climbing still higher, surmounting it, transcending it somehow or other; thinking overcomes metaphysics by climbing back down into the nearness of the nearest. The descent, particularly where man has strayed into subjectivity, is more arduous and more dangerous than the ascent. The descent leads to the poverty of the ek-sistence of *homo humanus*. In ek-sistence the region of *homo animalis*, of metaphysics, is abandoned. The dominance of that region is the mediate and deeply rooted basis for the blindness and arbitrariness of what is called 'biologism,' but also of what is known under the heading 'pragmatism.' To think the truth of Being at the same time means to think the humanity of *homo humanus*. What counts is *humanitas* in the service of the truth of Being, but without humanism in the metaphysical sense.

But if *humanitas* must be viewed as so essential to the thinking of Being, must not 'ontology' therefore be supplemented by 'ethics'? Is not that effort entirely essential which you express in the sentence, '*Ce que je cherche à faire, depuis longtemps déjà, c'est préciser le rapport de l'ontologie avec une éthique possible*' ['What I have been trying to do for a long time now is to determine precisely the relation of ontology to a possible ethics']?

Soon after *Being and Time* appeared a young friend asked me, 'When are you going to write an ethics?' Where the essence of man is thought so essentially, i.e., solely from the question concerning the truth of Being, but still without elevating man to the center of beings, a longing necessarily awakens for a peremptory directive and for rules that say how man, experienced from ek-sistence toward Being, ought to live in a fitting manner. The desire for an ethics presses ever more ardently for fulfillment as the obvious no less than the hidden perplexity of man soars to immeasurable heights. The greatest care must be fostered upon the ethical bond at a time when technological man, delivered over to mass society, can be kept reliably on call only by gathering and ordering all his plans and activities in a way that corresponds to technology.

Who can disregard our predicament? Should we not safeguard and secure the existing bonds even if they hold human beings together ever so tenuously and merely for the present? Certainly. But does this need ever release thought from the task of thinking what still remains principally to be thought and, as Being, prior to all beings, is their guarantor and their truth? Even further, can thinking refuse to think Being after the latter has lain hidden so long in oblivion but at the same time has made itself known in the present moment of world history by the uprooting of all beings?

Before we attempt to determine more precisely the relationship between 'ontology' and 'ethics' we must ask what 'ontology' and 'ethics' themselves are. It becomes necessary to ponder whether what can be designated by both terms still remains near and proper to what is assigned to thinking, which as such has to think above all the truth of Being.

Of course if both 'ontology' and 'ethics,' along with all thinking in terms of disciplines, become untenable, and if our thinking therewith becomes more disciplined, how then do matters stand with the question about the relation between these two philosophical disciplines?

Along with 'logic' and 'physics,' 'ethics' appeared for the first time in the school of Plato. These disciplines arose at a time when thinking was becoming 'philosophy,' philosophy *epistēmē* (science), and science itself a matter for schools and academic pursuits. In the course of a philosophy so understood, science waxed and thinking waned. Thinkers prior to this period knew neither a 'logic' nor an 'ethics' nor 'physics.' Yet their thinking was neither illogical nor immoral. But they did think *physis* in a depth and breadth that no subsequent 'physics' was ever again able to attain. The tragedies of Sophocles – provided such a comparison is at all permissible – preserve the *ēthos* in their sagas more primordially than Aristotle's lectures on 'ethics.' A saying of Heraclitus which consists of only three words says something so simply that from it the essence of the *ēthos* immediately comes to light.

The saying of Heraclitus (Fragment 119) goes. *ēthos anthrōpōi daimōn*. This is usually translated, 'A man's character is his daimon.' This translation thinks in a modern way, not a Greek one. *Ēthos* means abode, dwelling place. The word names the open region in which man dwells. The open region of his abode allows what pertains to man's essence, and what in thus arriving resides in nearness to him, to appear. The abode of man contains and preserves the advent of what belongs to man in his essence. According to Heraclitus's phrase this is *daimōn*, the god. The fragment says: Man dwells, insofar as he is man, in the nearness of god. A story that Aristotle reports (*De partibus animalium*, I, 5, 645a 17ff.) agrees with this fragment of Heraclitus.

> The story is told of something Heraclitus said to some strangers who wanted to come visit him. Having arrived, they saw him warming himself at a stove. Surprised, they stood there in consternation – above all because he encouraged them, the astounded ones, and called for them to come in, with the words, 'For here too the gods are present.'

The story certainly speaks for itself, but we may stress a few aspects.

The group of foreign visitors, in their importunate curiosity about the thinker, are disappointed and perplexed by their first glimpse of his abode. They believe they should meet the thinker in circumstances which, contrary to the ordinary round of human life, everywhere bear traces of the exceptional and rare and so of the exciting. The group hopes that in their visit to the thinker they will find things that will provide material for entertaining conversation – at least for a while. The foreigners who wish to visit the thinker expect to catch sight of him perchance at that very moment when, sunk in profound meditation, he is thinking. The visitors want this 'experience' not in order to be overwhelmed by thinking but simply so they can say they saw and heard someone everybody says is a thinker.

Instead of this the sightseers find Heraclitus by a stove. That is surely a common and insignificant place. True enough, bread is baked here. But Heraclitus is not even busy baking at the stove. He stands there merely to warm himself. In this altogether everyday place he betrays the whole poverty of his life. The vision of a shivering thinker offers little of interest. At this disappointing spectacle even the curious lose their desire to come any closer. What are they supposed to do here? Such an everyday and unexciting occurrence – somebody who is chilled warming himself at a stove – anyone can find any time at home. So why look up a thinker? The visitors are on the verge of going away again. Heraclitus reads the frustrated curiosity in their faces. He knows that for the crowd the failure of an expected sensation to materialize is enough to make those who have just arrived leave. He therefore encourages them. He invites them explicitly to come in with the words, *Einai gar kai entautha theous*, 'Here too the gods come to presence.'

This phrase places the abode (*ēthos*) of the thinker and his deed in another light. Whether the visitors understood this phrase at once – or at all – and then saw everything differently in this other light the story does not say. But the story was told and has come down to us today because what it reports derives from and characterizes the atmosphere surrounding this thinker. *Kai entautha*, 'even here,' at the stove, in that ordinary place where every thing and every condition, each deed and thought is intimate and commonplace, that is, familiar [*geheuer*], 'even there' in the sphere of the familiar, *einai theous*, it is the case that 'the gods come to presence.'

Heraclitus himself says, *ēthos anthrōpōi daimōn*, 'The (familiar) abode for man is the open region for the presencing of god (the unfamiliar one).'

If the name 'ethics,' in keeping with the basic meaning of the word *ēthos*, should now say that 'ethics' ponders the abode of man, then that thinking which thinks the truth of Being as the primordial element of man, as one who ek-sists, is in itself the original ethics. However, this thinking is not ethics in the first instance, because it is ontology. For ontology always thinks solely the being (*on*) in its Being. But as long as the truth of Being is not thought all ontology remains without its foundation. Therefore the thinking that in *Being and Time* tries to advance thought in a preliminary way into the truth of Being characterizes itself as 'fundamental ontology.' [See *Being and Time*, sections 3 and 4 ...] It strives to reach back into the essential ground from which thought concerning the truth of Being emerges. By initiating another inquiry this thinking is already removed from the 'ontology' of metaphysics (even that of Kant). 'Ontology' itself, however, whether transcendental or precritical, is subject to criticism, not because it thinks the Being of beings and thereby reduces Being to a concept, but because it does not think the truth of Being and so fails to recognize that there is a thinking more rigorous than the conceptual. In the poverty of its first breakthrough, the thinking that tries to advance thought into the truth of Being brings only a small part of that wholly other dimension to language. This language even falsifies itself, for it does not yet succeed in retaining the essential help of phenomenological seeing while dispensing with the inappropriate concern with 'science' and 'research.' But in order to make the attempt at thinking recognizable and at the same time understandable for existing philosophy, it could at first be expressed only within the horizon of that existing philosophy and its use of current terms.

In the meantime I have learned to see that these very terms were bound to lead immediately and inevitably into error. For the terms and the conceptual language corresponding to them were not rethought by readers from the matter particularly to be thought; rather, the matter was conceived according to the established terminology in its customary meaning. The thinking that inquires into the truth of Being and so defines man's essential abode from Being and toward Being is neither ethics nor ontology. Thus the question about the relation of each to the other no longer has any basis in this sphere. Nonetheless, your question, thought in a more original way, retains a meaning and an essential importance.

For it must be asked: If the thinking that ponders the truth of Being defines the essence of *humanitas* as ek-sistence from the latter's belongingness to Being, then does thinking remain only a theoretical representation of Being and of man; or can we obtain from such knowledge directives that can be readily applied to our active lives?

The answer is that such thinking is neither theoretical nor practical. It comes to pass before this distinction. Such thinking is, insofar as it is, recollection of Being and nothing else. Belonging to Being, because thrown by Being into the preservation of its truth and claimed for such preservation, it thinks Being. Such thinking has no result. It has no effect. It satisfies its essence in that it is. But it is by saying its matter. Historically, only one saying [*Sage*] belongs to the matter of thinking, the one that is in each case appropriate to its matter. Its material relevance is essentially higher than the validity of the sciences, because it is freer. For it lets Being – be.

Thinking builds upon the house of Being, the house in which the jointure of Being fatefully enjoins the essence of man to dwell in the truth of Being. This dwelling is the essence of 'being-in-the-world.' The reference in *Being and Time* (p. 54) to 'being-in' as 'dwelling' is no etymological game.[16] The same reference in the 1936 essay on Hölderlin's verse, 'Full of merit, yet poetically, man dwells on this earth,' is no adornment of a thinking that rescues itself from science by means of poetry. The talk about the house of Being is no transfer of the image 'house' to Being. But one day we will, by thinking the essence of Being in a way appropriate to its matter, more readily be able to think what 'house' and 'to dwell' are.

And yet thinking never creates the house of Being. Thinking conducts historical ek-sistence, that is, the *humanitas of homo humanus*, into the realm of the upsurgence of healing [*des Heilens*].

With healing, evil appears all the more in the clearing of Being. The essence of evil does not consist in the mere baseness of human action, but rather in the malice of rage. Both of these, however, healing and the raging, can essentially occur only in Being, insofar as Being itself is what is contested. In it is concealed the essential provenance of nihilation. What nihilates illuminates itself as the negative. This can be addressed in the 'no.' The 'not' in no way arises from the no-saying of negation. Every 'no' that does not mistake itself as willful assertion of the positing power of subjectivity, but rather remains a letting-be of ek-sistence, answers to the claim of the nihilation illumined. Every 'no' is simply the affirmation of the 'not.' Every affirmation consists in acknowledgment. Acknowledgment lets that toward which it goes come toward it. It is believed that nihilation is nowhere to be found in beings themselves. This is correct as long as one seeks nihilation as some kind of being, as an existing quality in beings. But in so seeking, one is not seeking nihilation. Neither is Being any existing quality that allows itself to be fixed among beings. And yet Being is more in being than any being. Because nihilation occurs essentially in Being itself we can never discern it as a being among beings. Reference to this impossibility never in any way proves that the origin of the not is no-saying. This proof appears to carry only if one posits beings as what is objective for subjectivity. From this alternative it follows that every 'not,' because it never appears as something objective, must inevitably be the product of a subjective act. But whether no-saying first posits the 'not' as something merely thought, or whether nihilation first requires the 'no' as what is to be said in the letting-be of beings – this can never be decided at all by a subjective reflection of a thinking already posited as subjectivity. In such a reflection we have not yet reached the dimension where the question can be appropriately formulated. It remains to ask, granting that thinking belongs to ek-sistence, whether every 'yes' and 'no' are not themselves already dependent upon Being. As these dependents, they can never first posit the very thing to which they themselves belong.

Nihilation unfolds essentially in Being itself, and not at all in the existence of man – so far as this is thought as the subjectivity of the *ego cogito*. Dasein in no way nihilates as a human subject who carries out nihilation in the sense of denial; rather, Da-sein nihilates inasmuch as it belongs to the essence of Being as that essence in which man ek-sists. Being nihilates – as Being. Therefore the 'not' appears in the absolute Idealism of Hegel and Schelling as the negativity of negation in the essence of Being. But there Being is thought in the sense of absolute actuality as unconditioned will that wills itself and does so as the will of knowledge and of love. In this willing Being as will to power is still concealed. But just why the negativity of absolute subjectivity is 'dialectical,' and why nihilation comes to the fore through this dialectic but at the same time is veiled in its essence, cannot be discussed here.

The nihilating in Being is the essence of what I call the nothing. Hence, because it thinks Being, thinking thinks the nothing.

To healing Being first grants ascent into grace; to raging its compulsion to malignancy.

Only so far as man, ek-sisting into the truth of Being, belongs to Being can there come from Being itself the assignment of those directives that must become law and rule for man. In Greek, to assign is *nemein*. *Nomos* is not only law but more originally the assignment contained in the dispensation of Being. Only the assignment is capable of dispatching man into Being. Only such dispatching is capable of supporting and obligating. Otherwise all law remains merely something fabricated by human reason. More essential than instituting rules is that man find the way to his abode in the truth of Being. This abode first yields the experience of something we can hold on to. The truth of Being offers a hold for all conduct. 'Hold' in our language means protective heed. Being is the protective heed that holds man in his ek-sistent essence to the truth of such protective heed – in such a way that it houses ek-sistence in language. Thus language is at once the house of Being and the home of human beings. Only because language is the home of the essence of man can historical mankind and human beings not be at home in their language, so that for them language becomes a mere container for their sundry preoccupations.

But now in what relation does the thinking of Being stand to theoretical and practical behavior? It exceeds all contemplation because it cares for the light in which a seeing, as *theoria*, can first live and move. Thinking attends to the clearing of Being in that it puts its saying of Being into language as the home of ek-sistence. Thus thinking is a deed. But a deed that also surpasses all *praxis*. Thinking towers above action and production, not through the grandeur of its achievement and not as a consequence of its effect, but through the humbleness of its inconsequential accomplishment.

For thinking in its saying merely brings the unspoken word of Being to language.

The usage 'bring to language' employed here is now to be taken quite literally. Being comes, clearing itself, to language. It is perpetually under way to language. Such arriving in its turn brings ek-sisting thought to language in a saying. Thus language itself is raised into the clearing of Being. Language *is* only in this mysterious and yet for us always pervasive way. To the extent that language which has thus been brought fully into its essence is historical, Being is entrusted to recollection. Ek-sistence thoughtfully dwells in the house of Being. In all this it is as if nothing at all happens through thoughtful saying.

But just now an example of the inconspicuous deed of thinking manifested itself. For to the extent that we expressly think the usage 'bring to language,' which was granted to language, think only that and nothing further, to the extent that we retain this thought in the heedfulness of saying as what in the future continually has to be thought, we have brought something of the essential unfolding of Being itself to language.

What is strange in the thinking of Being is its simplicity. Precisely this keeps us from it. For we look for thinking – which has its world-historical prestige under the name 'philosophy' – in the form of the unusual, which is accessible only to initiates. At the same time we conceive of thinking on the model of scientific knowledge and its research projects. We measure deeds by the impressive and successful achievements of *praxis*. But the deed of thinking is neither theoretical nor practical, nor is it the conjunction of these two forms of behavior.

Through its simple essence, the thinking of Being makes itself unrecognizable to us. But if we become acquainted with the unusual character of the simple, then another plight immediately befalls us. The suspicion arises that such thinking of Being falls prey to arbitrariness; for it cannot cling to beings. Whence does thinking take its measure? What law governs its deed?

Here the third question of your letter must be entertained: *Comment sauver l'élément d'aventure que comporte toute recherche sans faire de la philosophie une simple aventurière?* [How can we preserve the element of adventure that all research contains without simply turning philosophy into an adventuress?] I shall mention poetry now only in passing. It is confronted by the same question, and in the same manner, as thinking. But Aristotle's words in the *Poetics*, although they have scarcely been pondered, are still valid – that poetic composition is truer than exploration of beings.

But thinking is an *adventure* not only as a search and an inquiry into the unthought. Thinking, in its essence as thinking of Being, is claimed by Being. Thinking is related to Being as what arrives (*l'avenant*[17]). Thinking as such is bound to the advent of Being, to Being as advent. Being has already been dispatched to thinking. Being *is* as the destiny of thinking. But destiny is in itself historical. Its history has already come to language in the saying of thinkers.

To bring to language ever and again this advent of Being that remains, and in its remaining waits for man, is the sole matter of thinking. For this reason essential thinkers always say the Same. But that does not mean the identical. Of course they say it only to one who undertakes to think back on them. Whenever thinking, in historical recollection, attends to the destiny of Being, it has already bound itself to what is fitting for it, in accord with its destiny. To flee into the identical is not dangerous. To risk discord in order to say the Same is the danger. Ambiguity threatens, and mere quarreling.

The fittingness of the saying of Being, as of the destiny of truth, is the first law of thinking – not the rules of logic, which can become rules only on the basis of the law of Being. To attend to the fittingness of thoughtful saying does not only imply, however, that we contemplate at every turn *what* is to be said of Being and *how* it is to be said. It is equally essential to ponder *whether* what is to be thought is to be said – to what extent, at what moment of the history of Being, in what sort of dialogue with this history, and on the basis of what claim, it ought to be said. The threefold thing mentioned in an earlier letter is determined in its cohesion by the law of the fittingness of thought on the history of Being: rigor of meditation, carefulness in saying, frugality with words.

It is time to break the habit of overestimating philosophy and of thereby asking too much of it. What is needed in the present world crisis is less philosophy, but more attentiveness in thinking; less literature, but more cultivation of the letter.

The thinking that is to come is no longer philosophy, because it thinks more originally than metaphysics – a name identical to philosophy. However, the thinking that is to come can no longer, as Hegel demanded, set aside the name 'love of wisdom' and become wisdom itself in the form of absolute knowledge. Thinking is on the descent to the poverty of its provisional essence. Thinking gathers language into simple saying. In this way language is the language of Being, as clouds are the clouds of the sky. With its saying, thinking lays inconspicuous furrows in language. They are still more inconspicuous than the furrows that the farmer, slow of step, draws through the field.

NOTES

1. This new translation of *Brief über den Humanismus* by Frank A. Capuzzi in collaboration with J. Glenn Gray appears here in its entirety. I have edited it with reference to the helpful French bilingual edition, Martin Heidegger, *Lettre sur l'humanisme*, translated by Roger Munier, revised edition (Paris: Aubier Montaigne, 1964). A previous English translation by Edgar Lohner is included in *Philosophy in*

the Twentieth Century, edited by William Barrett and Henry D. Aiken (New York: Random House, 1962), III, 271–302. The German text was first published in 1947 by A. Francke Verlag, Bern; the present translation is based on the text in Martin Heidegger, *Wegmarken* (Frankfurt am Main: Vittorio Klostermann Verlag, 1967), pp. 145–94.

2. The preparatory fundamental analysis of Dasein tries to define concrete structures of human being in its predominant state, 'average everydayness.' For the most part Dasein is absorbed in the public realm (*die öffentlichkeit*), which dictates the range of possibilities that shall obtain for it in all dimensions of its life: 'We enjoy ourselves and take our pleasures as *they* do; we read, see, and judge works of literature and art as *they* do; but we also shrink back in revulsion from the 'masses' of men just as *they* do; and are '*scandalized*' by what *they* find shocking' (*Sein und Zeit*, 1962, pp. H126–27). Heidegger argues that the public realm – the neutral, impersonal 'they' – tends to level off genuine possibilities and force individuals to keep their distance from one another and from themselves. It holds Dasein in subservience and hinders knowledge of the self and the world. It allows the life-and-death issues of existence proper to dissolve in 'chatter,' which is 'the possibility of understanding everything without prior dedication to, and appropriation of, the matter at stake' (*Sein und Zeit*, 1962, p. H169). (All references to *Being and Time* in this essay and throughout the book cite the pagination of the German edition.) – Ed.

3. In section 34 of *Being and Time* Heidegger defines the existential-ontological foundation of language as speech or talk (*die Rede*). It is as original a structure of being-in-the-world as mood or understanding, of which it is the meaningful articulation. To it belong not only speaking out and asserting but also hearing and listening, heeding and being silent and attentive. As the Greeks experienced it, Dasein is living being that speaks, not so much in producing vocal sounds as in discovering the world, and this by letting beings come to appear as they are . . . – Ed.

4. In the final chapter of division one of *Being and Time* Heidegger defines 'care' as the Being of Dasein. It is a name for the structural whole of existence in all its modes and for the broadest and most basic possibilities of discovery and disclosure of self and world. Most poignantly experienced in the phenomenon of anxiety – which is not fear of anything at hand but awareness of my being-in-the-world as such – 'care' describes the sundry ways I get involved in the issue of my birth, life, and death, whether by my projects, inclinations, insights, or illusions. 'Care' is the all-inclusive name for my concern for other people, preoccupations with things, and awareness of my proper Being. It expresses the movement of my life out of a past, into a future, through the present. In section 65 the ontological meaning of the Being of care proves to be *temporality*. – Ed.

5. The phrase *der menschliche Mensch* appears in Karl Marx, *Economic-philosophic Manuscripts of 1844*, the so-called 'Paris Manuscripts,' third MS, p. IV. Cf. *Marx-Engels-Werke* (Berlin, 1973), Ergänzungsband I, 536. This third manuscript is perhaps the best source for Marx's syncretic 'humanism,' based on man's natural, social, practical, and conscious species-existence. – Ed.

6. Cf. Martin Heidegger, *Vom Wesen des Grundes* (1929), p. 8; *Kant and the Problem of Metaphysics*, trans. Richard Taft (Bloomington: Indiana University Press, 1990), section 43; and *Being and Time*, section 44, p. 230.

7. In *Being and Time* 'ecstatic' (from the Greek *ekstasis*) means the way Dasein 'stands out' in the various moments of the temporality of care, being 'thrown' out of a past and 'projecting' itself toward a future by way of the present. The word is closely related to another Heidegger introduces now to capture the unique sense of man's Being – *ek-sistence*. This too means the way man 'stands out' into the truth of Being and so is exceptional among beings that are at hand only as things of nature or human production . . . – Ed.

8. See Jean-Paul Sartre, *L'Existentialisme est un humanisme* (Paris: Nagel, 1946), pp. 17, 21, and elsewhere. – Ed.

9. In *Being and Time* (see esp. sections 25–7, 38, and 68 C) *Verfallen*, literally a 'falling' or 'lapsing,' serves as a third constitutive moment of being-in-the-world. Dasein is potentiality for Being, directed toward a future in which it can realize its possibilities: this is its 'existentiality.' But existence is always 'thrown' out of a past that determines its trajectory: this is its 'facticity.' Meanwhile, Dasein usually busies itself in quotidian affairs, losing itself in the present, forgetting what is most its own: this is its *Verfallensein*. (The last-named is not simply a matter of 'everyday' dealings, however, since the tendency to let theoretical problems slip into the ready-made solutions of a tradition affects interpretation itself.) To forget what is most its own is what Heidegger means by *Uneigentlichkeit*, usually rendered as 'inauthenticity' but perhaps better understood as 'inappropriateness.' – Ed.

10. Heidegger cites Sartre's *L'Existentialisme est un humanisme*, p. 36. The context of Sartre's remark is as follows. He is arguing (pp. 33ff.) 'that God does not exist, and that it is necessary to draw the consequences to the end.' To those who assert that the death of God leaves traditional values and norms untouched – and humanism is one such value – Sartre rejoins 'that it is very distressing that God does not exist, because with him vanishes every possibility of finding values in some intelligible heaven; we can no longer locate an *a priori* Good since there is no infinite and perfect consciousness to think it; it is nowhere written that the Good exists, that we must be honest, that we mustn't lie, precisely because we are in a situation where there are only human beings.' – Ed.

11. See the lecture on Hölderlin's hymn, 'Wie wenn am Feiertage ...' in Martin Heidegger, *Erläuterungen zu Hölderlins Dichtung*, fourth, expanded ed. (Frankfurt am Main: V. Klostermann, 1971), p. 76.

12. Cf. 'The Ister' and 'The Journey' [Die Wanderung], third stanza and ff. [In Holderlin, *Selected Poems*, translations by Michael Hamburger (Ann Arbor: University of Michigan Press, 1966) pp. 492ff. and 392ff.]

13. Cf. Hölderlin's poem 'Remembrance' [*Andenken*] in the *Tübingen Memorial* (1943), p. 322. [Hamburger, pp. 488ff.]

14. On the notion of *Entfremdung*, estrangement or alienation, see Marx's *first* Paris MS, pp. XXIIff., *Werke*, Ergänzungsband I, 510–22. The relation of estrangement to the 'world-historical' developments that Heidegger here stresses is perhaps more clearly stated in Marx-Engels, *The German Ideology*, in *Marx-Engels Werke*, III, 34–6. – Ed.

15. Martin Heidegger, *Vom Wesen des Grundes*, p. 28 n. 1.

16. Citing an analysis of the word 'in' by Jacob Grimm, Heidegger relates 'being-in' to *innan, wohnen*, inhabit, reside, or dwell. To be *in* the world means to dwell and be at home there, i.e., to be familiar with meaningful structures that articulate people and things ... – Ed.

17. *L'avenant* (cf. the English *advenient*) is most often used as an adverbial phrase, *à l'avenant*, to be in accord, conformity, or relation to something. It is related to *l'aventure*, the arrival of some unforeseen challenge, and *l'avenir*, the future, literally, what is to come. Thinking is in relation to Being insofar as Being advenes or arrives. Being as arrival of presencing is the 'adventure' toward which Heidegger's thought is on the way. – Ed.

7

SIMONE DE BEAUVOIR
(1908–1986)

Born in Paris in January 1908, Simone de Beauvoir was the first child of Georges de Beauvoir, the descendant of a long line of Catholic landowners in the south-west, and Françoise Brasseur, whose family were bourgeois Catholics from the north-east. Georges' mother had died when he was thirteen and he later felt that many aspects of his life were thwarted; he really wanted to be an actor, but this was frowned on, so he turned to the legal profession. Her father's religious scepticism and her mother's conventional piety were two sources of tension which Simone felt in her own life and sought in many ways to overcome. From an early age she was educated at a rather second-rate convent school, the Institut Adeline-Désir; her later account of her childhood education is some-what implausible, but it definitely was conservative, upper middle-class, un-distinguished and thoroughly Catholic. Her mother took Simone and her sister Hélène to daily mass at the local church, supervised their school work and led them in nightly prayers. When the First World War ended the family found they had little money left, due to the fact that their small savings had been invested in Russian railways and mining stock.

At the age of fourteen, as de Beauvoir later confessed, her belief in the Christian God had evaporated, and within the next year she thought that she would most like to be a writer. During the school year 1917–18, she became close friends with Elisabeth Mabille, known as Zaza (Simone gave almost everyone nicknames), who for the next ten years of her own short life exercised a positive, even liberating influence on de Beauvoir. Zaza was an orthodox religious believer but she had an audacity and sarcastic outlook that made her more flirtatious than the ungainly and graceless Simone. This was to be the first of many strong long-lasting friendships with women, some of whom became her lovers, and some of whom she shared as lovers with Sartre. In 1925, having decided to become an instructor of philosophy, she moved to the Institut Sainte-Marie at Neuilly, under the direction of the fashionable and influential Madame Daniélou. About this time she became quite fond of her cousin Jacques who introduced her to drinking and smoking, fast cars and wild nights at the nightclub. She refers constantly to his presence in *Memoirs of a Dutiful Daughter*, where Jacques assumes the role of advisor, elder brother, almost-lover and confidante; she often seemed to measure her success or comprehension by Jacques' comments. De Beauvoir studied Latin and French Literature at Neuilly, mathematics at the Institut Catholique, and then philosophy at the Sorbonne, in preparation for her entrance to the Ecole Normale Supérieure. Among her other close friends at the time were Maurice Merleau-Ponty (who appears in her memoirs under the pseudonym 'Jean Pradelle'), Maurice de Gandillac and Claude Lévi-Strauss. In her examination for the *license* for philosophy at the Sorbonne, she came in second place, Simone Weil (canonised as a saint 70 years later) came in first place and Merleau-Ponty in third.

On the advice of her supervisor at the Sorbonne, the Kantian scholar Léon Brunschvicg, de Beauvoir began to prepare her dissertation on Leibniz's metaphysics of monads or 'formal atoms', an exceptionally difficult topic which she struggled with for some time. In the summer of 1929, she became acquainted with an elite clique of students at the Ecole Normale, a tight band who kept apart from everyone else and looked down with disdain on mere mortals: René Maheu, Paul Nizan and Jean-Paul Sartre.

> They had a bad reputation. It was said of them that they were unsympathetic. Violently opposed to the 'priesties' among their fellow-students, they belonged to a clique composed mainly of Alain's ex-pupils and well known for its brutality; its members threw water-bombs on distinguished students at the Normale returning home at night in evening dress ... Sartre wasn't bad to look at, but it was rumored that he was the worst of the lot, and he was even accused of drinking. (1963 [1958], pp. 309–10)

De Beauvoir still kept in almost daily contact with her older friends, but among the ones she most cared about, tragedy soon struck. After several false starts and hesitant promises, Zaza had become engaged to Merleau-Ponty, but Zaza became seriously ill (possibly meningitis) and died not long before her marriage was to take place. (See the introduction to Merleau-Ponty in Chapter 5 above.)

Although initially attracted more to René Maheu, de Beauvoir became fascinated with Sartre, the most outrageous, the most brilliant and the one who would make his mark more than any other in their little group. She was taken in as an equal partner with this trio, who referred to themselves as the Eugenes (literally 'good family'), an imaginary caste invented by the surrealist poet Jean Cocteau.

They relegated all their other fellow-students to inferior categories: among [these were] the Marrhanes who loll about in the infinite, or among the Mortimers who slop about in the blue of the heavens ... I was ranked among the 'earthy' women, the ones with a future.

These three had created their own philosophical mythology, an ancestry and taxonomy of monstrous figures born of deranged metaphysics:

> The Catobelpas, that eats its own feet; the Catoboryx, that expresses itself in borborygmic rumbles ... 'Let me tell you that all thoughts of order are unbearably sad', this was the Eugene's first lesson. He disdained science and industry and made a mock of all universal moral systems ... The Eugene tries to make his life an original work of art ... to reach a certain comprehension of the singular.

The quartet's sympathy with Nietzsche's transvaluation of all moral values, his emphasis on the unique individual and his doctrine that a free spirit creates his or her life as a work of art are readily apparent in de Beauvoir's later recollection. She drew an important philosophical lesson from these ridiculous injunctions, that

> every individual possesses his own law, which is as exacting as a categorical imperative, although not universal; one only had the right to approve or disapprove of his actions in so far as they were a reflection of this personal norm. (1963 [1958], pp. 321–2)

In the fiercely competitive final exams, Sartre came in first place (though he had failed the previous year) and de Beauvoir came in second. They promised to be faithful to one another for two years, although they were obliged to separate for the time being; Sartre had hoped to go to Japan, but instead was given a teaching post at Le Havre; de Beauvoir was posted to Marseilles. She made every effort to visit him, though they were on opposite sides of France. The Ministry of Education was surprisingly considerate since, with full knowledge of their liaison, in 1932 they changed her posting to Rouen, only an hour by train from Le Havre. From this time till his death in 1980, de Beauvoir and Sartre were an exceptional couple: never married, each had many, many affairs; often separated for long stretches they kept in constant touch, confiding the most intimate details to one another. She often, though not always, subjugated her own considerable talents and ambitions to further his career and reputation. Their relation and rapport are impossible to judge by any standard, but each encouraged the other to work as hard as they could and follow their own paths. Sartre decided to follow the path of phenomenology at this time, spending one year in Berlin, reading and studying the major works of Husserl and Heidegger.

After several halting starts over the previous few years, she now found time to write; the five short stories in *La primauté du spirituel* were composed before she was posted to the Lycée Molière in Paris in 1936, when Sartre was moved to Laon, about an hour to the north-east. In Paris, de Beauvoir and Sartre formed a little family with their close friends; over the years, other young men and women would enter this charmed circle, often as de Beauvoir's or Sartre's lovers. Things took a turn for the worse in early 1937 when de Beauvoir became seriously ill with a collapsed lung, a debility she shared at the same time with Camus' struggle with tuberculosis. She managed to revise her short stories and added another one, changing the collective title to *Quand prime le spirituel*; this change didn't impress the publishers, and both Gallimard and Grasset rejected the manuscript. She began an affair (which she would resume years later) with Sartre's protégé Jacques Bost during one of their joint summer holidays, shortly after which she began work on a novel, *L'Invitée* (translated as *She Came to Stay*.) Sartre had achieved an astonishing literary success with the publication of *The Transcendence of the Ego* (1936), *The Imagination: A Psychological Critique* (1936), *Outline for a Theory of the Emotions* (1939) and especially his ground-breaking novel *Nausea* (1938). There is no doubt that Sartre discussed most aspects of these works with de Beauvoir and that he actively sought her own informed opinions and criticisms. In any case, these events certainly provoked her enough to carry forward her own writing, but at first she had little success. One of Gallimard Press's senior readers, Brice Parain, read the first third of her novel and turned it down; it wasn't published until 1943. The Fullbrooks have argued (1994, 1998) that Sartre derived many of his central insights, especially about the other and intersubjective relations, from *She Came to Stay*, but it's not feasible to enter this controversy about literary priority here.

The Nazi occupation of Paris imposed many restrictions on the lives of writers, artists and intellectuals, as well as food and fuel shortages. De Beauvoir found that the Café Flore, which was a favourite among some German officers, had good heating and so she often did much of her reading and writing there. Like everyone else, she suffered from cold, hunger and fatigue, but as long as she didn't make any trouble for the German authorities, they left her and her friends alone. Her novel had been well received and she went immediately forward with the themes of existential freedom and communication in an important short book *Pyrrhus and Cineas* the next year (it is unfortunate that there is no English translation), another novel *Le Sang des autres*, the play *Les Bouches inutiles* and, after the liberation, her major ethical treatise, *Pour une morale de l'ambiguité* (1946). During the two years before the liberation, Simone and Sartre made new friends among an extraordinary variety of writers and artists gathered in Paris for the duration. On one very special occasion, twelve of them organized a full-scale reading of Picasso's surrealist play *Desire Caught by the Tail*.

With the publication of several important books in quick succession and the immensely influential public lecture 'Existentialism is a Humanism' Sartre had gained a worldwide audience. He was invited on a lecture tour of the United States, and began an affair with an American socialite (perhaps the only affair that annoyed de Beauvoir). Over the next four or five years, she accompanied Sartre to the United States on several return trips and began her four-year affair with the great American novelist Nelson Algren (their correspondence has recently been published under the title *That Chicago Man*). In consecutive issues of *Les Temps Modernes* she published four essays on Existentialism and Literature, essays that she regarded as important preludes to her memoirs. Before the outbreak of war, she had been contemplating a large-scale work on the nature and range of women's experience over history, their status in different cultures, myths and stories that classify their role in society, the forms of oppression that subjugate their existence, and many other significant areas of inquiry she felt had been completely overlooked by philosophers and social theorists. After the liberation she began to work in earnest on this massive project and completed it in about three years. *The Second Sex* was published in book form in 1949 and made de Beauvoir's name in her own right; it ensured her financial security, was translated into eighteen languages and sold approximately four million copies. She completed work on *The Mandarins*, perhaps her greatest work of fiction, and, despite Nelson Algren's requests not to publicise his affair with the author (even in fictional disguise), Gallimard brought it out in 1954. *The Mandarins* offered a broad and detailed panorama of intellectual life in Paris after the war; through an intricate plot that centres on an idealist newspaper editor and a woman psychiatrist, it exposed the sense of disillusion and lost dreams felt by a group of left-wing characters.

For almost twenty years, from the early 1950s till his health began to decline in the early 1970s, de Beauvoir accompanied Sartre as his permanent consort; they went to China together in 1955, to Cuba, and then Brazil in 1960, three visits to the USSR in the mid-1960s, and Israel and Egypt in 1967, where they were welcomed as celebrities by both Jews and Arabs. In 1958, she published the first in her autobiographical series, *Memoirs of a Dutiful Daughter*, followed in 1960 by *The Prime of Life*, in 1963 *The Force of Circumstance* and closing in 1972 with *All Said and Done*. Taken together, these four volumes are, without doubt, the most significant account by a single author of the intellectual, artistic and political events in France from the 1920s to the 1970s. With the second volume, Sartre becomes as much the principal character as the author herself; de Beauvoir took upon herself the role of Sartre's expositor, secretary, assistant and defender. After his death in 1980, she published an account of the day-to-day details of the last ten years of Sartre's life, thinking that everyone would want this sort of information. The great French 'national treasure' now blind and infirm, had adopted as his daughter his most recent lover, Arlette Elkaim, who thus owned the copyrights to Sartre's works. Until her death in April 1986, de Beauvoir was constantly on watch to interpret and protect her lifetime partner's lifetime work, an engaged and committed philosophical endeavour whose point of departure had been a new vision of Existential Philosophy.

De Beauvoir had committed herself to some distinctive existential theses in her own work, especially in her wartime publications, *Pyrrhus and Cineas* and *Towards a Morality of Ambiguity*. The former title was written in the form of a series of conversations (they are hardly dialogues) between Pyrrhus, a spontaneous and adventurous person, and Cineas, a wise and restrained thinker. Their conversations are conducted in an imaginary place, Candide's Garden, and circle around several themes central to the Existentialist approach: the moment or instant, the infinite, the absence of God, the human situation, social community with others, devotion to a grand project and politically engaged action. In contrast with Kantian and Hegelian universal ethics, she says:

> This effort alone to identify myself as the universal leads directly to insanity. It is impossible for me to affirm that it is universal since it is me who affirms: in affirming I make myself be; it is me who is. Just as I distinguish my pure presence in tending toward an other thing than me, I distinguish also the other toward whom I tend, by making myself as I tend toward him; my presence is. It breaks the unity and the continuity of that mass of indifference in which I pretend to be absorbed.

After criticising Spinoza and Hegel on this score, she continues:

> The human cannot be indefinitely reduced to his being, nor to an expansion to infinity; he can find repose; but because of this movement is he brought to a null part? One finds again in the order of action the same antinomy as in the order of speculation; every pause is impossible since transcendence is a perpetual passing-away; but an indefinite project is absurd since it touches on nothing. (1944, pp. 34–5)

De Beauvoir was not entirely satisfied with her arguments in these fifteen 'essays', although, in my opinion, this brief piece deserves far better treatment than it's usually accorded. She returned to many of these same issues in a more sophisticated fashion three years later in *Toward a Morality of Ambiguity*, where she develops an existential ethics that is independent of religious belief and theological speculation. This version of an existential ethics recognises not an absolute freedom, but instead a *situated freedom*, one that is circumscribed and influenced by the actions of others over whom the individual may have no control. While there are no grounds that justify any specific values or warrant their imposition on others, the concept of freedom *in a concrete situation* demands limits for morally acceptable choices. Any choice that infringes or derogates this basic dimension of freedom is morally unacceptable; whatever values we choose as individuals, we must always will our own freedom, since our freedom is a necessary precondition for any choice and action. Moreover, a similar recognition holds with respect to the freedom of others. To the extent that human existence is an ambiguous, embodied existence, human beings are always vulnerable to others. And to the extent that their activities take place in a social world, the success of their projects depends at least on the non-interference of others and often on their active assistance. Thus, to recognise this *being-for-others* is to acknowledge the extent to which one's actions are not totally within one's own power. Further, in willing one's own ends, one must will not just the non-interference of others, but also their active assistance, and hence *their* freedom as a precondition of their being able to assist you.

De Beauvoir's ethics of ambiguity are also in basic agreement with Sartre's mature ethics (his *Notebooks* were written at about the same time) in that they affirm various measures to avoid or overcome some of the processes of *alienation*. Although some degree of alienation is basic to the human condition, the alienation that results from bad faith or self-deception is not basic and should be expunged. One form which alienation takes on the social level is that of oppression of one or more groups by a dominant group. This form of oppression is open to the same existential criticisms as those directed at individuals who act in such a way that they fail to recognise and affirm their own and others' freedom. In Sartre's later works, he became more aware of the ways in which oppression denies the freedom of large numbers of people; their freedom is so seriously curtailed that it is little more than 'the ability to choose the sauce with which freedom will be devoured'. De Beauvoir saw that oppression could be so severe that its victims never become aware even minimally of themselves and their options, and as a result have no real freedom at all; the most serious widespread instance of this is the oppressed condition of women. An ethics of reciprocal freedom maintains a tension between an individual's intentions on one hand, and the consequences of actions on the other. De Beauvoir and Sartre maintained this tension by undercutting the clear separation between action and intention. To separate choice from action, she argued, leads to an abstract ethics, that of the good conscience, the idea that one can be good without changing the situation, and this is the kind of morality which they both rejected (see Bell, 1999, pp. 164–6).

PRINCIPAL WORKS

(1944) *Pyrrhus et Cineas*. Paris: Gallimard. (There is no English translation.)
(1947) *The Ethics of Ambiguity*, trans. Bernard Frechtman. New York: Citadel Press, 1970.
(1949) *The Second Sex*, trans. by H. M. Parshley. Harmondsworth: Penguin Books, 1972.
(1958) *Memoirs of a Dutiful Daughter*, trans. James Kirkup. Harmondsworth: Penguin Books, 1963.
(1960) *The Prime of Life*, trans. Peter Green. Harmondsworth: Penguin Books, 1965.
(1963) *The Force of Circumstance*, trans. Richard Howard. Harmondsworth: Penguin Books, 1965.
(1981) *Adieux: A Farewell to Sartre*. Harmondsworth: Penguin Books, 1984.

RECOMMENDED READING

Bair, Deirdre (1990) *Simone de Beauvoir: A Biography*. London: Jonathan Cape.
Bell, Linda (1999) 'Existential Ethics', in *Encyclopedia of Continental Philosophy*, ed. Simon Glendenning. Edinburgh: Edinburgh University Press, pp. 163–73.
Bergoffen, Debra (1996) *Gendered Phenomenologies, Erotic Generosities*. New York: State University of New York Press.
Francis, Claude and Gontier, Fernande (1989) *Simone de Beauvoir*. London: Mandarin Press.
Fullbrook, Kate and Fullbrook, Edward (1994) *Simone de Beauvoir and Jean-Paul Sartre*. New York: Basic Books.
Fullbrook, Kate and Fullbrook, Edward (1998) 'de Beauvoir', in *A Companion to Continental Philosophy*. eds Simon Critchley and William Schroeder. Oxford: Blackwell, pp. 269–80.
Lundgren-Gothlin, Eva (1996) *Sex and Existence: Simone de Beauvoir's 'The Second Sex'*. London: Athlone Press.
Moi, Toril (1994) *Simone de Beauvoir: The Making of an Intellectual Woman*. Oxford: Blackwell.
Simons, Margaret (ed.) (1995) *New Feminist Essays on Simone de Beauvoir*. University Park: Pennsylvania State University Press.

'AMBIGUITY AND FREEDOM' (1947)[*]

Simone de Beauvoir

'Life in itself is neither good nor evil, it is the place of good and evil, according to what you make it.'

– Montaigne.

'The continous work of our life,' says Montaigne, 'is to build death.' He quotes the Latin poets: *Prima, quae vitam dedit, hora corpsit*. And again: *Nascentes morimur*. Man knows and thinks this tragic ambivalence which the animal and the plant merely undergo. A new paradox is thereby introduced into his destiny. 'Rational animal,' 'thinking reed,' he escapes from his natural condition without, however, freeing himself from it. He is still a part of this world of which he is a consciousness. He asserts himself as a pure internality against which no external power can take hold, and he also experiences himself as a thing crushed by the dark weight of other things. At every moment he can grasp the non-temporal truth of his existence. But between the past which no longer is and the future which is not yet, this moment when he exists is nothing. This privilege, which he alone possesses, of being a sovereign and unique subject amidst a universe of objects, is what he shares with all his fellow-men. In turn an object

* From *The Ethics of Ambiguity*, trans. Bernard Frechtman. New York: Philosophical Library, 1948; Citadel Press, 1962.

for others, he is nothing more than an individual in the collectivity on which he depends.

As long as there have been men and they have lived, they have all felt this tragic ambiguity of their condition, but as long as there have been philosophers and they have thought, most of them have tried to mask it. They have striven to reduce mind to matter, or to reabsorb matter into mind, or to merge them within a single substance. Those who have accepted the dualism have established a hierarchy between body and soul which permits of considering as negligible the part of the self which cannot be saved. They have denied death, either by integrating it with life or by promising to man immortality. Or, again they have denied life, considering it as a veil of illusion beneath which is hidden the truth of Nirvana.

And the ethics which they have proposed to their disciples has always pursued the same goal. It has been a matter of eliminating the ambiguity by making oneself pure inwardness or pure externality, by escaping from the sensible world or by being engulfed in it, by yielding to eternity or enclosing oneself in the pure moment. Hegel, with more ingenuity, tried to reject none of the aspects of man's condition and to reconcile them all. According to his system, the moment is preserved in the development of time; Nature asserts itself in the face of Spirit which denies it while assuming it; the individual is again found in the collectivity within which he is lost; and each man's death is fulfilled by being canceled out into the Life of Mankind. One can thus repose in a marvelous optimism where even the bloody wars simply express the fertile restlessness of the Spirit.

At the present time there still exist many doctrines which choose to leave in the shadow certain troubling aspects of a too complex situation. But their attempt to lie to us is in vain. Cowardice doesn't pay. Those reasonable metaphysics, those consoling ethics with which they would like to entice us only accentuate the disorder from which we suffer. Men of today seem to feel more acutely than ever the paradox of their condition. They know themselves to be the supreme end to which all action should be subordinated, but the exigencies of action force them to treat one another as instruments or obstacles, as means. The more widespread their mastery of the world, the more they find themselves crushed by uncontrollable forces. Though they are masters of the atomic bomb, yet it is created only to destroy them. Each one has the incomparable taste in his mouth of his own life, and yet each feels himself more insignificant than an insect within the immense collectivity whose limits are one with the earth's. Perhaps in no other age have they manifested their grandeur more brilliantly, and in no other age has this grandeur been so horribly flouted. In spite of so many stubborn lies, at every moment, at every opportunity, the truth comes to light, the truth of life and death, of my solitude and my bond with the world, of my freedom and my servitude, of the insignificance and the sovereign importance of each man and all men. There was Stalingrad and there was Buchenwald, and neither of the two wipes out the other. Since we do not succeed in fleeing it, let us therefore try to look the truth in the face. Let us try to assume our fundamental ambiguity. It is in the knowledge of the genuine conditions of our life that we must draw our strength to live and our reason for acting.

From the very beginning, existentialism defined itself as a philosophy of ambiguity. It was by affirming the irreducible character of ambiguity that Kierkegaard opposed himself to Hegel, and it is by ambiguity that, in our own generation, Sartre, in *Being and Nothingness*, fundamentally defined man, that being whose being is not to be, that subjectivity which realizes itself only as a presence in the world, that engaged freedom, that surging of the for-oneself which is immediately given for others. But it is also claimed that existentialism is a philosophy of the absurd and of despair. It encloses man in a sterile anguish, in an empty subjectivity. It is incapable of furnishing him with any principle for making choices. Let him do as he pleases. In any case, the game is lost. Does not Sartre declare, in effect, that man is a 'useless passion,' that he tries in vain to realize the synthesis of the for-oneself and the in-oneself, to make himself God? It is true. But it is also true that the most optimistic ethics have all begun by emphasizing the element of failure involved in the condition of man; without failure, no ethics; for a being who, from the very start, would be an exact co-incidence with himself, in a perfect plenitude, the notion of having-to-be would have no meaning. One does not offer an ethics to a God. It is impossible to propose any to man if one defines him as nature, as something given. The so-called psychological or empirical ethics manage to establish themselves only by introducing surreptitiously some flaw within the man-thing which they have first defined. Hegel tells us in the last part of *The Phenomenology of Mind* that moral consciousness can exist only to the extent that there is disagreement between nature and morality. It would disappear if the ethical law became the natural law. To such an extent that by a paradoxical 'displacement,' if moral action is the absolute goal, the absolute goal is also that moral action may not be present. This means that there can be a having-to-be only for a being who, according to the existentialist definition, questions himself in his being, a being who is at a distance from himself and who has to be his being.

Well and good. But it is still necessary for the failure to be surmounted, and existentialist ontology does not allow this hope. Man's passion is useless; he has no means for becoming the being that he is not. That too is true. And it is also true that in *Being and Nothingness* Sartre has insisted above all on the abortive aspect of the human adventure. It is only in the last pages that he opens up the perspective for an ethics. However, if we reflect upon his descriptions of existence, we perceive that they are far from condemning man without recourse.

The failure described in *Being and Nothingness* is definitive, but it is also ambiguous. Man, Sartre tells us, is 'a being who *makes himself* a lack of being *in order that there might be* being.' That means, first of all, that his passion is not inflicted upon him from without. He chooses it. It is his very being and, as such, does not imply the idea of unhappiness. If this choice is considered as useless, it is because there exists no absolute value before the passion of man, outside of it, in relation to which one might distinguish the useless from the useful. The word 'useful' has not yet received a meaning on the level of description where *Being and Nothingness* is situated. It can be defined only in the human world established by man's projects and the ends he sets up. In the original helplessness from which man surges up, nothing is useful, nothing is useless. It must therefore be understood that the passion to which man has acquiesced finds no external justification. No outside appeal, no objective necessity permits of its being called useful. It *has* no reason to will itself. But this does not mean that it can not justify itself, that it can not *give itself* reasons for being that it does not *have*. And indeed Sartre tells us that man makes himself this lack of being *in order that* there might be being. The term *in order that* clearly indicates an intentionality. It is not in vain that man nullifies being. Thanks to him, being is disclosed and he desires this disclosure. There is an original type of attachment to being which is not the relationship 'wanting to be' but rather 'wanting to disclose being.' Now, here there is not failure, but rather success. This end, which man proposes to himself by making himself lack of being, is, in effect, realized by him. By uprooting himself from the world, man makes himself present to the world and makes the world present to him. I should like to be the landscape which I am contemplating, I should like this sky, this quiet water to think themselves within me, that it might be I whom they express in flesh and bone, and I remain at a distance. But it is also by this distance that the sky and the water exist before me. My contemplation is an excruciation only because it is also a joy. I can not appropriate the snow field where I slide. It remains foreign, forbidden, but I take delight in this very effort toward an impossible possession. I experience it as a triumph, not as a defeat. This means that man, in his vain attempt to *be* God, makes himself exist *as* man, and if he is satisfied with this existence, he coincides exactly with himself. It is not granted him to exist without tending toward this being which he will never be. But it is possible for him to want this tension even with the failure which it involves. His being is lack of being, but this lack has a way of being which is precisely existence. In Hegelian terms it might be said that we have here a negation of the negation by which the positive is re-established. Man makes himself a lack, but he can deny the lack as lack and affirm himself as a positive existence. He then assumes the failure. And the condemned action, insofar as it is an effort to be, finds its validity insofar as it is a manifestation of existence. However, rather than being a Hegelian act of surpassing, it is a matter of a conversion. For in Hegel the surpassed terms are preserved only as abstract moments, whereas we consider that existence still remains a negativity in the positive affirmation of itself. And it does not appear, in its turn, as the term of a further synthesis. The failure is not surpassed, but assumed. Existence asserts itself as an absolute which must seek its justification within itself and not suppress itself, even though it may be lost by preserving itself. To attain his truth, man must not attempt to dispel the ambiguity of his being but, on the contrary, accept the task of realizing it. He rejoins himself only to the extent that he agrees to remain at a distance from himself. This conversion is sharply distinguished from the Stoic conversion in that it does not claim to oppose to the sensible universe a formal freedom which is without content. To exist genuinely is not to deny this spontaneous movement of my transcendence, but only to refuse to lose myself in it. Existentialist conversion should rather be compared to Husserlian reduction: let man put his will to be 'in parentheses' and he will thereby be brought to the consciousness of his true condition. And just as phenomenological reduction prevents the errors of dogmatism by suspending all affirmation concerning the mode of reality of the external world, whose flesh and bone presence the reduction does not, however, contest, so existentialist conversion does not suppress my instincts, desires, plans, and passions. It merely prevents any possibility of failure by refusing to set up as absolutes the ends toward which my transcendence thrusts itself, and by considering them in their connection with the freedom which projects them.

The first implication of such an attitude is that the genuine man will not agree to recognize any foreign absolute. When a man projects into an ideal heaven that impossible synthesis of the for-itself and the in-itself that is called God, it is because he wishes the regard of this existing Being to change his existence into being; but if he agrees not to be in order to exist genuinely, he will abandon the dream of an inhuman objectivity. He will understand that it is not a matter of being right in the eyes of a God, but of being right in his own eyes. Renouncing the thought of seeking the guarantee for his existence outside of himself, he will also refuse to believe in unconditioned values which would set themselves up athwart his freedom like things. Value is this lacking-being of which freedom *makes itself* a lack; and it is because the latter makes itself a lack that value appears. It is desire which creates the desirable, and the project which sets up the end. It is human existence which makes values spring up in the world on the basis of which it will be able to judge the enterprise in which it will be engaged. But first it locates itself beyond any pessimism, as beyond any optimism, for the fact of its original springing forth is a pure contingency. Before existence there is no more reason to exist than not to exist. The lack of existence can not be evaluated since it is the fact on the basis of which all evaluation is defined. It can not be compared to anything for there is nothing outside of it to serve as a term of comparison. This rejection of any extrinsic justification also confirms the rejection of an original pessimism which we posited at the beginning. Since it is unjustifiable from without, to declare from without that it is unjustifiable is not to condemn it. And the truth is that outside of existence there is nobody. Man exists. For him it is not a question of wondering whether his presence in the world is useful, whether life is worth the trouble of being lived. These questions make no sense. It is a matter of knowing whether he wants to live and under what conditions.

But if man is free to define for himself the conditions of a life which is valid in his own eyes, can he not choose whatever he likes and act however he likes?

Dostoievsky asserted, 'If God does not exist, everything is permitted.' Today's believers use this formula for their own advantage. To re-establish man at the heart of his destiny is, they claim, to repudiate all ethics. However, far from God's absence authorizing all license, the contrary is the case, because man is abandoned on the earth, because his acts are definitive, absolute engagements. He bears the responsibility for a world which is not the work of a strange power, but of himself, where his defeats are inscribed, and his victories as well. A God can pardon, efface, and compensate. But if God does not exist, man's faults are inexpiable. If it is claimed that, whatever the case may be, this earthly stake has no importance, this is precisely because one invokes that inhuman objectivity which we declined at the start. One can not start by saying that our earthly destiny *has* or *has not* importance, for it depends upon us to give it importance. It is up to man to make it important to be a man, and he alone can feel his success or failure. And if it is again said that nothing forces him to try to justify his being in this way, then one is playing upon the notion of freedom in a dishonest way. The believer is also free to sin. The divine law is imposed upon him only from the moment he decides to save his soul. In the Christian religion, though one speaks very little about them today, there are also the damned. Thus, on the earthly plane, a life which does not seek to ground itself will be a pure contingency. But it is permitted to wish to give itself a meaning and a truth, and it then meets rigorous demands within its own heart.

However, even among the proponents of secular ethics, there are many who charge existentialism with offering no objective content to the moral act. It is said that this philosophy is subjective, even solipsistic. If he is once enclosed within himself, how can man get out? But there too we have a great deal of dishonesty. It is rather well known that the fact of being a subject is a universal fact and that the Cartesian *cogito* expresses both the most individual experience and the most objective truth. By affirming that the source of all values resides in the freedom of man, existentialism merely carries on the tradition of Kant, Fichte, and Hegel, who, in the words of Hegel himself, 'have taken for their point of departure the principle according to which the essence of right and duty and the essence of the thinking and willing subject are absolutely identical.' The idea that defines all humanism is that the world is not a given world, foreign to man, one to which he has to force himself to yield from without. It is the world willed by man, insofar as his will expresses his genuine reality.

Some will answer, 'All well and good. But Kant escapes solipsism because for him genuine reality is the human person insofar as it transcends its empirical embodiment and chooses to be universal.' And doubtless Hegel asserted that the 'right of individuals to their particularity is equally contained in ethical substantiality, since particularity is the extreme, phenomenal modality in which moral reality exists (*Philosophy of Right*, § 154).' But for him particularity appears only as a moment of the totality in which it must surpass itself. Whereas for existentialism, it is not impersonal universal man who is the source of values, but the plurality of concrete, particular men projecting themselves toward their ends on the basis of situations whose particularity is as radical and as irreducible as subjectivity itself. How could men, originally separated, get together?

And, indeed, we are coming to the real situation of the problem. But to state it is not to demonstrate that it can not be resolved. On the contrary, we must here again invoke the notion of Hegelian 'displacement.' There is an ethics only if there is a problem to solve. And it can be said, by inverting the preceding line of argument, that the ethics which have given solutions by effacing the fact of the separation of men are not valid precisely because there *is* this separation. An ethics of ambiguity will be one which will refuse to deny *a priori* that separate existants can, at the same time, be bound to each other, that their individual freedoms can forge laws valid for all ...

As for us, whatever the case may be, we believe in freedom. Is it true that this belief must lead us to despair? Must we grant this curious paradox: that from the moment a man recognizes himself as free, he is prohibited from wishing for anything?

On the contrary, it appears to us that by turning toward this freedom we are going to discover a principle of action whose range will be universal. The characteristic feature of all ethics is to consider human life as a game that can be won or lost and to teach man the means of winning. Now, we have seen that the original scheme of man is ambiguous: he wants to be, and to the extent that he coincides with this wish, he fails. All the plans in which this will to be is actualized are condemned; and the ends circumscribed by these plans remain mirages. Human transcendence is vainly engulfed in those miscarried attempts. But man also wills himself to be a disclosure of being, and if he coincides with this wish, he wins, for the fact is that the world becomes present by his presence in it. But the disclosure implies a perpetual tension to keep being at a certain distance, to tear oneself from the world, and to assert oneself as a freedom. To wish for the disclosure of the world and to assert oneself as freedom are one and the same movement. Freedom is the source from which all significations and all values spring. It is the original condition of all justification of existence. The man who seeks to justify his life must want freedom itself absolutely and above everything else. At the same time that it requires the realization of concrete ends, of particular projects, it requires itself universally. It is not a ready-made value which offers itself from the outside to my abstract adherence, but it appears (not on the plane of facility, but on the moral plane) as a cause of itself. It is necessarily summoned up by the values which it sets up and through which it sets itself up. It can not establish a denial of itself, for in denying itself, it would deny the possibility of any foundation. To will oneself moral and to will oneself free are one and the same decision.

It seems that the Hegelian notion of 'displacement' which we relied on a little while ago is now turning against us. There is ethics only if ethical action is not present. Now, Sartre declares that every man is free, that there is no way of his not being free. When he wants to escape his destiny, he is still freely fleeing it. Does not this presence of a so to speak natural freedom contradict the notion of ethical freedom? What meaning can there be in the words *to will oneself* free, since at the beginning we *are* free? It is contradictory to set freedom up as something conquered if at first it is something given.

This objection would mean something only if freedom were a thing or a quality naturally attached to a thing. Then, in effect, one would either have it or not have it. But the fact is that it merges with the very movement of this ambiguous reality which is called existence and which *is* only by making itself be; to such an extent that it is precisely only by having to be conquered that it gives itself. To will oneself free is to effect the transition from nature to morality by establishing a genuine freedom on the original upsurge of our existence.

Every man is originally free, in the sense that he spontaneously casts himself into the world. But if we cansider this spontaneity in its facticity, it appears to us only as a pure contingency, an upsurging as stupid as the clinamen of the Epicurean atom which turned up at any moment whatsoever from any direction whatsoever. And it was quite necessary for the atom to arrive somewhere. But its movement was not justified by this result which had not been chosen. It remained absurd. Thus, human spontaneity always projects itself toward something. The psychoanalyst discovers a meaning even in abortive acts and attacks of hysteria. But in order for this meaning to justify the transcendence which discloses it, it must itself be founded, which it will never be if I do not choose to found it myself. Now, I can evade this choice. We have said that it would be contradictory deliberately to will oneself not free. But one can choose not to will himself free. In laziness, heedlessness, capriciousness, cowardice, impatience, one contests the meaning of the project at the very moment that one defines it. The spontaneity of the subject is then merely a vain living palpitation, its movement toward the object is a flight, and itself is an absence. To convert the absence into presence, to convert my flight into will, I must assume my project positively. It is not a matter of retiring into the completely inner and, moreover, abstract movement of a given spontaneity, but of adhering to the concrete and particular movement by which this spontaneity defines itself by thrusting itself toward an end. It is through this end that it sets up that my spontaneity confirms itself by reflecting upon itself. Then, by a single movement, my will, establishing the content of the act, is legitimized by it. I realize my escape toward the other as a freedom when, assuming the presence of the object, I thereby assume myself before it as a presence. But this justification requires a constant tension. My project is never founded; it founds itself. To avoid the anguish of this permanent choice, one may attempt to flee into the object itself, to engulf one's own presence in it. In the servitude of the serious, the original spontaneity strives to deny itself. It strives in vain, and meanwhile it then fails to fulfill itself as moral freedom.

We have just described only the subjective and formal aspect of this freedom. But we also ought to ask ourselves whether one can will oneself free in any matter, whatsoever it may be. It must first be observed that this will is developed in the course of time. It is in time that the goal is pursued and that freedom confirms itself. And this assumes that it is realized as a unity in the unfolding of time. One escapes the absurdity of the clinamen only by escaping the absurdity of the pure moment. An existence would be unable to found itself if moment by moment it crumbled into nothingness. That is why no moral question presents itself to the child as long as he is still incapable of recognizing himself in the past or seeing himself in the future. It is only when the moments of his life begin to be organized into behaviour that he can decide and choose. The value of the chosen end is confirmed and, reciprocally, the genuineness of the choice is manifested concretely through patience, courage, and fidelity. If I leave behind an act which I have accomplished, it becomes a thing by falling into the past. It is no longer anything but a stupid and opaque fact. In order to prevent this metamorphosis, I must ceaselessly return to it and justify it in the unity of the project in which I am engaged. Setting up the movement of my transcendence requires that I never let it uselessly fall back upon itself, that I prolong it indefinitely. Thus I can not genuinely desire an end today without desiring it through my whole existence, insofar as it is the future of this present moment and insofar as it is the surpassed past of days to come. To will is to engage myself to persevere in my will. This does not mean that I ought not aim at any limited end. I may desire absolutely and forever a revelation of a moment. This means that the value of this provisional end will be confirmed indefinitely. But this living confirmation can not be merely contemplative and verbal. It is carried out in an act. The goal toward which I surpass myself must appear to me as a point of departure toward a new act of surpassing. Thus, a creative freedom develops happily without ever congealing into unjustified facticity. The creator leans upon anterior creations in order to create the possibility of new creations. His present project embraces the past and places confidence in the freedom to come, a confidence which is never disappointed. It discloses being at the end of a further disclosure. At each moment freedom is confirmed through all creation.

However, man does not create the world. He succeeds in disclosing it only through the resistance which the world opposes to him. The will is defined only by raising obstacles, and by the contingency of facticity certain obstacles let themselves be conquered, and others do not. This is what Descartes expressed when he said that the freedom of man is infinite, but his power is limited. How can the presence of these limits be reconciled with the idea of a freedom confirmimg itself as a unity and an indefinite movement?

In the face of an obstacle which it is impossible to overcome, stubbornness is stupid. If I persist in beating my fist against a stone wall, my freedom exhausts itself in this useless gesture without succeeding in giving itself a content. It debases itself in a vain contingency. Yet, there is hardly a sadder virtue than resignation. It transforms into phantoms and contingent reveries projects which had at the beginning been set up as will and freedom. A young man has hoped for a happy or useful or glorious life. If the man he has become looks upon these miscarried attempts of his adolescence with disillusioned indifference, there they are, forever frozen in the dead past. When an effort fails, one declares bitterly that he has lost time and wasted his powers. The failure condemns that whole part of ourselves which we had engaged in the effort. It was to escape this dilemma that the Stoics preached indifference. We could indeed assert our freedom against all constraint if we agreed to renounce the particularity of our projects. If a door refuses to open, let us accept not opening it and there we are free. But by doing that, one manages only to save an abstract notion of freedom. It is emptied of all content and all truth. The power of man ceases to be limited because it is annulled. It is the particularity of the project which determines the limitation of the power, but it is also what gives the project its content and permits it to be set up. There are people who are filled with such horror at the idea of a defeat that they keep themselves from ever doing anything. But no one would dream of considering this gloomy passivity as the triumph of freedom.

The truth is that in order for my freedom not to risk coming to grief against the obstacle which its very engagement has raised, in order that it might still pursue its movement in the face of the failure, it must, by giving itself a particular content, aim by means of it at an end which is nothing else but precisely the free movement of existence. Popular opinion is quite right in admiring a man who, having been ruined or having suffered an accident, knows how to gain the upper hand, that is, renew his engagement in the world, thereby strongly asserting the independence of freedom in relation to thing. Thus, when the sick Van Gogh calmly accepted the prospect of a future in which he would be unable to paint any more, there was no sterile resignation. For him painting was a personal way of life and of communication with others which in another form could be continued even in an asylum. The past will be integrated and freedom will be confirmed in a renunciation of this kind. It will be lived in both heartbreak and joy. In heartbreak, because the project is then robbed of its particularity – it sacrifices its flesh and blood. But in joy, since at the moment one releases his hold, he again finds his hands free and ready to stretch out toward a new future. But this act of passing beyond is conceivable only if what the content has in view is not to bar up the future, but, on the contrary, to plan new possibilities. This brings us back by another route to what we had already indicated. My freedom must not seek to trap being but to disclose it. The disclosure is the transition from being to existence. The goal which my freedom aims at is conquering existence across the always inadequate density of being.

However, such salvation is only possible if, despite obstacles and failures, a man preserves the disposal of his future, if the situation opens up more possibilities to him. In case his transcendence is cut off from his goal or there is no longer any hold on objects which might give it a valid content, his spontaneity is dissipated without founding anything. Then he may not justify his existence positively and he feels its contingency with wretched disgust. There is no more obnoxious way to punish a man than to force him to perform acts which make no sense to him, as when one empties and fills the same ditch indefinitely, when one makes soldiers who are being punished march up and down, or when one forces a schoolboy to copy lines. Revolts broke out in Italy in September 1946 because the unemployed were set to breaking pebbles which served no purpose whatever. As is well known, this was also the weakness which ruined the national workshops in 1848. This mystification of useless effort is more intolerable than fatigue. Life imprisonment is the most horrible of punishments because it preserves existence in its pure facticity but forbids it all legitimation. A freedom can not will itself without willing itself as an indefinite movement. It must absolutely reject the constraints which arrest its drive toward itself. This rejection takes on a positive aspect when the constraint is natural. One rejects the illness by curing it. But it again assumes the negative aspect of revolt when the oppressor is a human freedom. One can not deny being: the in-itself is, and negation has no hold over this being, this pure positivity; one does not escape this fullness: a destroyed house *is* a ruin; a broken chain *is* scrap iron: one attains only signification and, through it, the for-itself which is projected there; the for-itself carries nothingness in its heart and can be annihilated, whether in the very upsurge of its existence or through the world in which it exists. The prison is repudiated as such when the prisoner escapes. But revolt, insofar as it is pure negative movement, remains abstract. It is fulfilled as freedom only by returning to the positive, that is, by giving itself a content through action, escape, political struggle, revolution. Human transcendence then seeks, with the destruction of the given situation, the whole future which will flow from its victory. It resumes its indefinite rapport with itself. There are limited situations where this return to the positive is impossible, where the future is radically blocked off. Revolt can then be achieved only in the definitive rejection of the imposed situation, in suicide.

It can be seen that, on the one hand, freedom can always save itself, for it is realized as a disclosure of existence through its very failures, and it can again confirm itself by a death freely chosen. But, on the other hand, the situations which it discloses through its project toward itself do not appear as equivalents. It regards as privileged situations those which permit it to realize itself as indefinite movement; that is, it wishes to pass beyond everything which limits its power; and yet, this power is always limited. Thus, just as life is identified with the will-to-live, freedom always appears as a movement of liberation. It is only by prolonging itself through the freedom of others that it manages to surpass death itself and to realize itself as an indefinite unity. Later on we shall see what problems such a relationship raises. For the time being it is enough for us to have established the fact that the words 'to will oneself free' have a positive and concrete meaning. If man wishes to save his existence, as only he himself can do, his original spontaneity must be raised to the height of moral freedom by taking itself as an end through the disclosure of a particular content.

But a new question is immediately raised. If man has one and only one way to save his existence, how can he choose not to choose it in all cases? How is a bad willing possible? We meet with this problem in all ethics, since it is precisely the possibility of a perverted willing which gives a meaning to the idea of virtue. We know the answer of Socrates, of Plato, of Spinoza: 'No one is willfully bad.' And if Good is a transcendent thing which is more or less foreign to man, one imagines that the mistake can be explained by error. But if one grants that the moral world is the world genuinely willed by man, all possibility of error is eliminated. Moreover, in Kantian ethics, which is at the origin of all ethics of autonomy, it is very difficult to account for an evil will. As the choice of his character which the subject makes is achieved in the intelligible world by a purely rational will, one can not understand how the latter expressly rejects the law which it gives to itself. But this is because Kantism defined man as a pure positivity, and it therefore recognized no other possibility in him than coincidence with himself. We, too, define morality by this adhesion to the self; and this is why we say that man can not positively decide between the negation and the assumption of his freedom, for as soon as he decides, he assumes it. He can not positively will not to be free for such a willing would be self-destructive. Only, unlike Kant, we do not see man as being essentially a positive will. On the contrary, he is first defined as a negativity. He is first at a distance from himself. He can coincide with himself only by agreeing never to rejoin himself. There is within him a perpetual playing with the negative, and he thereby escapes himself, he escapes his freedom. And it is precisely because an evil will is here possible that the words 'to will oneself free' have a meaning. Therefore, not only do we assert that the existentialist doctrine permits the elaboration of an ethics, but it even appears to us as the only philosophy in which an ethics has its place. For, in a metaphysics of transcendence, in the classical sense of the term, evil is reduced to error; and in humanistic philosophies it is impossible to account for it, man being defined as complete in a complete world. Existentialism alone gives – like religions – a real role to evil, and it is this, perhaps, which make its judgments so gloomy. Men do not like to feel themselves in danger. Yet, it is because there are real dangers, real failures and real earthly damnation that words like victory, wisdom, or joy have meaning. Nothing is decided in advance, and it is because man has something to lose and because he can lose that he can also win.

Therefore, in the very condition of man there enters the possibility of not fulfilling this condition. In order to fulfill it he must assume himself as a being who 'makes himself a lack of being so that there might be being.' But the trick of dishonesty permits stopping at any moment whatsoever. One may hesitate to make oneself a lack of being, one may withdraw before existence, or one may falsely assert oneself as being, or assert oneself as nothingness. One may realize his freedom only as an abstract independence, or, on the contrary, reject with despair the distance which separates us from being. All errors are possible since man is a negativity, and they are motivated by the anguish he feels in the face of his freedom. Concretely, men slide incoherently from one attitude to another. We shall limit ourselves to describing in their abstract form those which we have just indicated ...

... The ambiguity of freedom, which very often is occupied only in fleeing from itself, introduces a difficult equivocation into relationships with each individual taken one by one. Just what is meant by the expression 'to love others'? What is meant by taking them as ends? In any event, it is evident that we are not going to decide to fulfill the will of every man. There are cases where a man positively wants evil, that is, the enslavement of other men, and he must then be fought. It also happens that, without harming anyone, he flees from his own freedom, seeking passionately and alone to attain the being which constantly eludes him. If he asks for our help, are we to give it to him? We blame a man who helps a drug addict intoxicate himself or a desperate man commit suicide, for we think that rash behavior of this sort is an attempt of the individual against his own freedom; he must be made aware of his error and put in the presence of the real demands of his freedom. Well and good. But what if he persists? Must we then use violence? There again the serious man busies himself dodging the problem; the values of life, of health, and of moral conformism being set up, one does not hesitate to impose them on others. But we know that this pharisaism can cause the worst disasters: lacking drugs, the addict may kill himself. It is no more necessary to serve an abstract ethics obstinately than to yield without due consideration to impulses of pity or generosity; violence is justified only if it opens concrete possibilities to the freedom which I am trying to save; by practising it I am willy-nilly assuming an engagement in relation to others and to myself; a man whom I snatch from the death which he had chosen has the right to come and ask me for means and reasons for living; the tyranny practised against an invalid can be justified only by his getting better; whatever the purity of the intention which animates me, any dictatorship is a fault for which I have to get myself pardoned. Besides, I am in no position to make decisions of this sort indiscriminately; the example of the unknown person who throws himself in to the Seine and whom I hesitate whether or not to fish out is quite abstract; in the absence of a concrete bond with this desperate person my choice will never be anything but a contingent facticity. If I find myself in a position to do violence to a child, or to a melancholic, sick, or distraught person the reason is that I also find myself charged with his upbringing, his happiness, and his health: I am a parent, a teacher, a nurse, a doctor, or a friend ... So, by a tacit agreement, by the very fact that I am solicited, the strictness of my decision is accepted or even desired; the more seriously I accept my responsibilities, the more justified it is. That is why love authorizes severities which are not granted to indifference. What makes the problem so complex is that, on the one hand, one must not make himself an accomplice of that flight from freedom that is found in heedlessness, caprice, mania, and passion, and that, on the other hand, it is the abortive movement of man toward being which is his very existence, it is through the failure which he has assumed that he asserts himself as a freedom. To want to prohibit a man from error is to forbid him to fulfill his own existence, it is to deprive him of life. At the beginning of Claudel's *The Satin Shoe*, the husband of Dona Prouheze, the Judge, the Just, as the author regards him, explains that every plant needs a gardener in order to grow and that he is the one whom heaven has destined for his young wife; beside the fact that we are shocked by the arrogance of such a thought (for how does he know that he is this enlightened gardener? Isn't he merely a jealous husband?) this likening of a soul to a plant is not acceptable; for, as Kant would say, the value of an act lies not in its *conformity* to an external model, but in its internal truth. We object to the inquisitors who want to create faith and virtue from without; we object to all forms of fascism which seek to fashion the happiness of man from without; and also the paternalism which thinks that it has done something for man by prohibiting him from certain possibilities of temptation, whereas what is necessary is to give him reasons for resisting it.

Thus, violence is not immediately justified when it opposes willful acts which one considers perverted; it becomes inadmissible if it uses the pretext of ignorance to deny a freedom which, as we have seen, can be practised within ignorance itself. Let the 'enlightened elites' strive to change the situation of the child, the illiterate, the primitive crushed beneath his superstitions; that is one of their most urgent tasks; but in this very effort they must respect a freedom which, like theirs, is absolute. They are always opposed, for example, to the extension of universal suffrage by adducing the incompetence of the masses, of women, of the natives in the colonies; but this forgetting that man always has to decide by himself in the darkness, that he must want beyond what he knows. If infinite knowledge were necessary (even supposing that it were conceivable), then the colonial administrator himself would not have the right to freedom; he is much further from perfect knowledge than the most backward savage is from him. Actually, to vote is not to govern; and to govern is not merely to maneuver; there is an ambiguity today, and particularly in France, because we think that we are not the master of our destiny; we no longer hope to help make history, we are resigned to submitting to it; all that our internal politics does is reflect the play of external forces, no party hopes to determine the fate of the country but merely to foresee the future which is being prepared in the world by foreign powers and to use, as best we can, the bit of indetermination which still escapes their foresight. Drawn along by this tactical realism, the citizens themselves no longer consider the vote as the assertion of their will but as a maneuver, whether one adheres completely to the maneuvering of a party or whether one invents his own strategy; the electors consider themselves not as men who are consulted about a particular point but as forces which are numbered and which are ordered about with a view to distant ends. And that is probably why the French, who formerly were so eager to declare their opinions, take no further interest in an act which has become a disheartening strategy. So, the fact is that if it is necessary not to vote but to measure the weight of one's vote, this calculation requires such extensive information and such a sureness of foresight that only a specialized technician can have the boldness to express an opinion. But that is one of the abuses whereby the whole meaning of democracy is lost; the logical conclusion of this would be to suppress the vote. The vote should really be the expression of a concrete will, the choice of a representative capable of defending, within the general frame-work of the country and the world, the particular interests of his electors. The ignorant and the outcast also has interests to defend; he alone is 'competent' to decide upon his hopes and his trust. By a sophism which leans upon the dishonesty of the serious, one does not merely argue about his formal impo-tence to choose, but one draws arguments from the content of his choice. I recall, among others, the naivete of a right-thinking young girl who said, 'The vote for women is all well and good in principle, only, if women get the vote, they'll all vote red.' With like impudence it is almost unanimously stated today in France that if the natives of the French Union were given the rights of self-determination, they would live quietly in their villages without doing anything, which would be harmful to the higher interests of the Economy. And doubtless the state of stagnation in which they choose to live is not that which a man can wish for another man; it is desirable to open new possibilities to the indolent negroes so that the interests of the Economy may one day merge with theirs. But for the time being, they are left to vegetate in the sort of situation where their freedom can merely be negative: the best thing they can desire is not to tire themselves, not to suffer, and not to work; and even this freedom is denied them. It is the most consummate and inacceptable form of oppression.

However, the 'enlightened elite' objects, one does not let a child dispose of himself, one does not permit him to vote. This is another sophism. To the extent that woman or the happy or resigned slave lives in the infantile world of ready-made values, calling them 'an eternal child' or 'a grown-up child' has some meaning, but the analogy is only partial. Childhood is a particular sort of situation: it is a natural situation whose limits are not created by other men and which is thereby not comparable to a situation of oppression; it is a situation which is common to all men and which is temporary for all; therefore, it does not represent a limit which cuts off the individual from his possibilities, but, on the contrary, the moment of a development in which new possibilities are won. The child is ignorant because he has not yet had the time to acquire knowledge, not because this time has been refused him. To treat him as a child is not to bar him from the future but to open it to him; he needs to be taken in hand, he invites authority, it is the form which the resistance of facticity, through which all liberation is brought about, takes for him. And on the other hand, even in this situation the child has a right to his freedom and must be respected as a human person. What gives *Emile* its value is the brilliance with which Rousseau asserts this principle. There is a very annoying naturalistic optimism in *Emile*; in the rearing of the child, as in any relationship with others, the ambiguity of freedom implies the outrage of violence; in a sense, all education is a failure. But Rousseau is right in refusing to allow childhood to be oppressed. And in practice raising a child as one cultivates a plant which one does not consult about its needs is very different from considering it as a freedom to whom the future must be opened.

Thus, we can set up point number one: the good of an individual or a group of individuals requires that it be taken as an absolute end of our action; but we are not authorized to decide upon this end *a priori*. The fact is that no behavior is ever authorized to begin with, and one of the concrete consequences of existentialist ethics is the rejection of all the previous justifications which might be drawn from the civilization, the age, and the culture; it is the rejection of every principle of authority. To put it positively, the precept will be to treat the other (to the extent that he is the only one concerned, which is the moment that we are considering at present) as a freedom so that his end may be freedom; in using this conducting-wire one will have to incur the risk, in each case, of inventing an original solution. Out of disappointment in love a young girl takes an overdose of pheno-barbital; in the morning friends find her dying, they call a doctor, she is saved; later on she becomes a happy mother of a family; her friends were right in considering her suicide as a hasty and heedless act and in putting her into a position to reject it or return to it freely. But in asylums one sees melancholic patients who have tried to commit suicide twenty times, who devote their freedom to seeking the means of escaping their jailers and of putting an end to their intolerable anguish; the doctor who gives them a friendly pat on the shoulder is their tyrant and their torturer. A friend who is intoxicated by alcohol or drugs asks me for money so that he can go and buy the poison that is necessary to him; I urge him to get cured, I take him to a doctor, I try to help him live; insofar as there is a chance of my being successful, I am acting correctly in refusing him the sum he asks for. But if circumstances prohibit me from doing anything to change the situation in which he is struggling, all I can do is give in; a deprivation of a few hours will do nothing but exasperate his torments uselessly; and he may have recourse to extreme means to get what I do not give him. That is also the problem touched on by Ibsen in *The Wild Duck*. An individual lives in a situation of falsehood; the falsehood is violence, tyranny: shall I tell the truth in order to free the victim? It would first be necessary to create a situation of such a kind that the truth might be bearable and that, though losing his illusions, the deluded individual might again find about him reasons for hoping. What makes the problem more complex is that the freedom of one man almost always concerns that of other individuals. Here is a married couple who persist in living in a hovel; if one does not succeed in giving them the desire to live in a more healthful dwelling, they must be allowed to follow their preferences; but the situation changes if they have children; the freedom of the parents would be the ruin of their sons, and as freedom and the future are on the side of the latter, these are the ones who must first be taken into account. The Other is multiple, and on the basis of this new questions arise.

One might first wonder for whom we are seeking freedom and happiness. When raised in this way, the problem is abstract; the answer will, therefore, be arbitrary, and the arbitrary always involves outrage. It is not entirely the fault of the district social-worker if she is apt to be odious; because, her money and time being limited, she hesitates before distributing it to this one or that one, she appears to others as a pure externality, a blind facticity. Contrary to the formal strictness of Kantianism for whom the more abstract the act is the more virtuous it is, generosity seems to us to be better grounded and therefore more valid the less distinction there is between the other and ourself and the more we fulfill ourself in taking the other as an end. That is what happens if I am engaged in relation to others. The Stoics impugned the ties of family, friendship, and nationality so that they recognized only the universal form of man. But man is man only through situations whose particularity is precisely a universal fact. There are men who expect help from certain men and not from others, and these expectations define privileged lines of action. It is fitting that the negro fight for the negro, the Jew for the Jew, the proletarian for the proletarian, and the Spaniard in Spain. But the assertion of these particular solidarities must not contradict the will for universal solidarity and each finite undertaking must also be open on the totality of men.

But it is then that we find in concrete form the conflicts which we have described abstractly; for the cause of freedom can triumph only through particular sacrifices. And certainly there are hierarchies among the goods desired by men: one will not hesitate to sacrifice the comfort, luxury, and leisure of certain men to assure the liberation of certain others; but when it is a question of choosing among freedoms, how shall we decide? ...

... It is incumbent upon ethics not to follow the line of least resistance; an act which is not destined, but rather quite freely consented to; it must make itself effective so that what was at first facility may become difficult. For want of internal criticism, this is the role that an opposition must take upon itself. There are two types of opposition. The first is a rejection of the very ends set up by a regime: it is the opposition of anti-fascism to fascism, of fascism to socialism. In the second type, the oppositionist accepts the objective goal but criticizes the subjective movement which aims at it; he may not even wish for a change of power, but he deems it necessary to bring into play a contestation which will make the subjective appear as such. Thereby he exacts a perpetual contestation of the means by the end and of the end by the means. He must be careful himself not to ruin, by the means which he employs, the end he is aiming at, and above all not to pass into the service of the oppositionists of the first type. But, delicate as it may be, his role is, neverthless, necessary. Indeed, on the one hand, it would be absurd to oppose a liberating action with the pretext that it implies crime and tyranny; for without crime and tyranny there could be no liberation of man; one can not escape that dialectic which goes from freedom to freedom through dictatorship and oppression. But, on the other hand, he would be guilty of allowing the liberating movement to harden into a moment which is acceptable only if it passes into its opposite; tyranny and crime must be kept from triumphantly establishing themselves in the world; the conquest of freedom is their only justification, and the assertion of freedom against them must therefore be kept alive.

8

JEAN-PAUL SARTRE
(1905–1980)

Perhaps more than any other writer discussed in this text, the prodigious achievements of Jean-Paul Sartre defined the shape and scope of Existential Philosophy in the twentieth century. It would be entirely unfeasible in a brief outline such as this to provide anything more than an informed glance at one dimension of his voluminous writings in nearly every field of French letters. Iris Murdoch gave this sharp precis of Sartre the thinker, artist and activist:

> So versatile, so committed, so serious, industrious, courageous, learned, talented, clever, [he] certainly lived his own time to the full, and, whatever the fate of his general theories, must survive as one of its most persistent and interesting critics. (Murdoch, 1998)

His life as a writer was a writerly life (in Roland Barthes' phrase); in his 'memoirs' *The Words* (1964), every aspect of books and the life of words is made into the source of his own life. His father, Jean-Baptiste, was the son of a medical doctor and his mother, Anne-Marie Schweitzer, was the youngest of four children of a German teacher from Alsace (later annexed by the Germans), whose brother was the great medical missionary, Albert Schweitzer. Sartre's father died when he was still an infant, an event which instilled a feeling of permanent absence in Sartre's later life.

> If he had lived, my father would have lain down on me and crushed me ...
> I left behind me a dead young man who did not have time to be my father

and who could, today, be my son ... Even today, I am amazed how little I know about him. Yet he loved, he wanted to live and he saw himself dying; that is enough to make up a whole man. (1964, p. 15)

Sartre was born in June 1905 in the house in Meudon in which his mother's parents lived; until he was six, he and his mother lived with her parents, completely dependent on them. Anne-Marie was treated like an older child by her own parents, to such an extent that, in his memoirs (our only source for this information), the little boy thought that she was, in some strange way, his sister. In his appearance and behavior Sartre's grandfather was an autocrat, the sole being in charge of their large household, issuing edicts and decrees like an Old Testament patriarch. Although his wife's family was Catholic, Karl Schweitzer was Protestant and fiercely anti-Prussian, sentiments which baffled the young boy, even then making every effort to understand everything. Eventually Anne-Marie persuaded the government to award her a widow's pension, Grandpa Karl retired, and the whole family moved to Paris, where the same family arrangement continued. In Paris, Karl Schweitzer founded a modern language institute (something like the Berlitz School) and had high hopes for a literary future for his grandson. In his memoirs, Sartre recounts the amusing details of how his mother succeeded in partly steering his interests away from French *belles-lettres* and toward illustrated comic books and silent films.

His grandfather bullied the headmaster of the Lycée Montaigne into putting Jean-Paul in an advanced class for the gifted or talented students, but the boy did poorly and was placed in a more normal classroom. He was not allowed to play with other children and instead spent more and more time with his 'little friends', the characters in his story books. After trying one or two other primary schools, he was enrolled in the prestigious Lycée Henri IV, perhaps the best school of its kind in France at the time, where one of his teachers was the philosopher Alain. In 1916, Sartre met Paul Nizan, who until his premature death in May 1940 was to be one of Sartre's closest friends and confidantes. The next year, his mother married Joseph Mancy, who had been a fellow student with her in college, and the couple moved to La Rochelle where Sartre's stepfather had been appointed manager in a shipyard. After several awkward and somewhat unhappy years there, he returned to the Lycée Henri IV as an enrolled boarder, renewing his close association with Paul Nizan. In 1922, Sartre and Nizan transferred to the Lycée Louis-le-Grand which had an excellent reputation for preparing its pupils for entry to the elite Ecole Normale Supérieure (ENS).

Sartre later said that he spent five happy and exciting years at the ENS where he and Nizan and three others, all ex-pupils of Alain, formed an elite little group. Simone de Beauvoir was allowed to join this clique, though she did not take part in their elaborate pranks, nor approve of their offensive behaviour (see the introduction to de Beauvoir in Chapter 7 above). Sartre didn't attend the classes he had enrolled for, but instead took an interest in pathology and psychology; he experimented with some rather half-baked essays and reviews which did not bode well. Oscar Levi sarcastically comments on Sartre's written work at this time:

> His virtuosic fluency on the basis of half-digested ideas and an inadequate foundation in factual knowledge was allowed to develop without the inhibitions which rigorous research and criticism would have imposed, but at least Sartre was surrounded for the moment by his intellectual peers, a situation he would not willingly allow to recur in later life, unless his peers were also his juniors. (Levi, 1992, p. 538)

On his first attempt at the competitive examination, his good friend Raymond Aron came first while Sartre himself failed. On his second attempt the next year, Sartre passed the aggregation in philosophy with flying colours; he came first and de Beauvoir second. In 1930, Karl Schweitzer died and left his grandson 80,000 francs, which Sartre managed to get through in two or three years since he detested bank accounts, savings and thrift. Sartre had made several attempts to write sketches for novels and stories but, even though Paul Nizan and André Malraux scouted around on his behalf, he couldn't find a publisher. One novelette, called 'Defeat', was based on Nietzsche's doctrine of the will to power and an essay, 'The Legend of Truth', was published in the monthly literary review *Bifur*.

Among his close friends, Paul Nizan had already moved on, spending the winter of 1926–7 in Aden (Saudia Arabia) and joining the Communist Party. Raymond Aron had gone to Germany to study philosophy and it was on Aron's return to Paris in the Spring of 1933 that Sartre was alerted to Husserl's teaching in phenomenology (see the first section of the Introduction in this book). He and de Beauvoir had come to an arrangement that suited them both – not to marry, to allow each other independence and to share their adventures. De Beauvoir was posted to a school in Marseilles and Sartre to a school in Le Havre. She made more of an effort to visit him than he did to visit her, but they were often together. The Ministry of Education was aware of their liaison, and in 1932 they changed her posting to Rouen, only an hour by train from Le Havre. About this time he began work on the novel which would eventually become the landmark existentialist document *Nausea*. He spent the Easter school holidays in England, and though he liked Canterbury Cathedral, he refused to enter the Oxford colleges, which he thought to be snobbish, and instead preferred the London slums. In autumn 1933 he went to the French Institute in Berlin, taking the chance to study Husserl's and Heidegger's works, as well as Kafka's novels. The impact of the phenomenological approach on his thinking was profound, for it offered him an exact and open-ended method for bringing together many of his prior interests in the 'nature' of human being, consciousness, psychological schemas, and the process of imaginative recreation. Sartre was working at an incredible pace, switching back and forth between several works in progress, a compulsion for literary production which he was to carry through his entire life. In order to counteract his fits of depression he took larger and larger doses of sedatives; in February 1935, in pursuit of his ongoing study of images, he took mescalin, an unfortunate choice, since it took him six months to 'come down'. But his immense appetite for scholarly work paid off: in 1936 *The Transcendence of the Ego* appeared in *Recherches Philosophiques*, edited by Jean Wahl (Gabriel Marcel's close associate), Alcan published the first part of his phenomenological study *The Imagination*, and the *Nouvelle Revue Française* printed one of his short stories.

Sartre had built up an amazing repertoire of material which, with the furor caused by the appearance of *Nausea* in 1938, publishers were eager to seize on. In 1939 Hermann published his *Outline for a Theory of the Emotions*, and the next year Gallimard published the second part of his study on the imagination, called *The Imaginary* (the English translation misleadingly titles this second book *The Imagination*, like the first). In this same two-year period, a collection of five short stories came out, as well as eight articles on a variety of topics. But all of these works were eclipsed in 1943 by the publication of his masterpiece *Being and Nothingness: An Essay on Phenomenological Ontology*. In the Introduction and Book Two, Chapter One Sartre built on his previous work in *The Transcendence of the Ego*, where he rejected Husserl's concept of transcendental consciousness. Sartre argued that Husserl's insistence on the phenomenological reduction left only 'a little residue', the subjective remainder of the process of bracketing the world's being. Such an ego, he said, is the subject that cannot be an object, and instead became a thing-in-itself, unknowable to any being, including oneself. In its place, Sartre spoke in favour of consciousness as 'a pure spontaneous upsurge' that required no ego behind the scenes to hold everything together. In this short work, he concluded that the transcendental ego itself must be transcended, that is, shown to be superfluous, and the empirical, everyday ego resuscitated. He prefigured his later work in several ways, for example by claiming that the 'natural attitude' is one of flight from the freedom to perform the reduction towards refuge in the empirical ego whose basic role is to mask from consciousness its own spontaneity.

The two halves of his study on the imagination comprise a critique of previous psychological theories of the imaginative power of consciousness, and a radically new theory based on an explicitly phenomenological description of the cognitive acts and 'objects' of the imagination. The imagination is a specific mode of conscious thought, and as such, it intends its 'objects' but in a special fashion, namely as absent, non-existent and unreal 'objects'. Previous psychological theories of the *imagination* treated the 'objects' of their studies as 'images', the inner icons of some exterior object, and succumbed to a picture of the mind as an inner theatre with a built-in 'observer', the ego. In the second half, Sartre proposes an investigation of the *imaginary* (hence the different title), that is, the imaging process of consciousness, which he argued should be conceived as a manner of being-in-the-world (Heidegger's term). Through intentional analysis of the imaging act and its 'object' one sees that the imaginary process *derealises* the perceptual or remembered 'object' by taking psychical material to serve as an *analogue* for the imagined 'object'. Sartre's early efforts here to explore the ways in which representative analogues figure in artistic production are integral to his later existential biographies of the 'lords of the imaginary', Jean Genet, Baudelaire, Flaubert and Mallarmé.

His work on a new theory of the prereflective, empirical ego, the imaginary as a specialised form of conscious recreation and the emotions as bodily modes of conduct towards things are, to some degree, preliminary studies for his land-mark work, *Being and Nothingness*. This massive text cannot be adequately summarised in this context, except to provide some flavour of its highlights. The Introduction is called 'The Pursuit of Being' and here Sartre declares that the being which pursues the question or the meaning of Being is a *conscious* being. His distinctly existential approach, one that sharply separates his orientation from that of other phenomenological studies, is clearly indicated when he states that conscious being is superfluous (*de trop*). This means 'that consciousness absolutely cannot derive being from anything, either from another being, or from a possibility, or from a necessary law. Uncreated, without reason for being, without any connection with another being, being-in-itself is *de trop* for eternity' (1956 [1943], p. xlii).

Part One is devoted to the problem of nothingness and the origin of negation, of which there are three sorts. First, the irruption or seepage of nothingness through the experience of an absence or *negatité*, for instance the concrete experience of someone's not being there. Second, the fact that there is *nothing* which can account for a person's being conscious of a world; one is suspended over an abyss since the emphasis is on 'nothing' in the statement 'there is nothing which separates my existence from non-existence'. And third, the insight that the world is just as it is and *not otherwise*; no further reflection can render the fact that the world exists into something rational. Sartre refers to the unique being which characterises consciousness as *for-itself* and the inert, passive, non-conscious state of things as *in-itself*. So the question then becomes what is it about being that might generate nothingness? The being-in-itself of objects can hardly be expected to play this role, since the being of objects is full and positive. Whatever turns out to be responsible for this generation of nothingness must show (in Peter Caws' phrase) 'suicidal tendencies', since the negation of being must involve to some degree its own annihilation. Can some being be found which carries within itself the seeds of its own annihila-tion? Sartre's obvious answer is that human beings alone have this 'power'; it is the power they have of *changing their relationship* to that kind of being. We can refuse to accept things as they are, we can reject things as having no value, and so forth; in this fashion, we put up some kind of buffer of nothingness between ourselves and the world. The for-itself can 'secrete a nothingness which isolates it from all other beings'; this isolation is a means of detaching human being from the causal chain of natural events, and this power is what Sartre calls *freedom*.

The primary function of Sartrean freedom is to repudiate the causal influence of one's own past, to negate all those things which might determine the self one way rather than another; it is within your freedom to *put out of play* all those factors which would have given you good 'cause' to do just this *and not otherwise*.

The whole of Part Two is concerned with the notion of presence to itself as the law of being-for-itself, this self-presence has three important aspects. The first is that conscious being is *translucent*, that is conscious of itself as a conscious being. There is no feature of human thought or conduct that is opaque or hidden from conscious awareness. Second, being-for-itself is *undetermined*, that is it does not already have, nor can it acquire, a fixed 'nature' or essence. Conscious being can be situated only by being conscious of its own situation, and its only essence is an essence which it is conscious of having. Third, being-for-itself has the power of *withdrawal* or detachment from itself; what is central to human reality is not its involvement in the world and its own activities, but its capacity to step back, to witness itself and the world. Part Three focuses on being-for-others and the structures of intersubjectivity through the modes of embodied being, specifically the forms of concrete relations with others, such as sexuality, indifference and hatred. Part Four focuses on the conditions for human freedom in action, the concrete situations that realise this freedom, and the hope which psychoanalysis extends to reveal the manner in which conscious beings occlude or cover over their authentic selves.

After the liberation Sartre picked up his breakneck pace; in less than four years he produced more than forty pieces of work, including the manuscript for *Cahiers pour une morale*, which on its own was longer than *Being and Nothingness*. One of his colleagues joked that the mastermind behind all this was 'Sartre and his five brains', but Sartre himself thought of his overall workplace as the 'engine room'. Annie Cohen-Solal gives us a vivid picture of Sartre's activities at this time:

> The engine room is of course the central chamber of this formidable system, a hidden place, a secret, intimate, extremely sophisticated environment ... Watching over the whole [is] the master, the engineer, constantly on the lookout ... a genius and a madman, drunk on the vapors and infernal heat, pushing all the machines to the utmost, particularly his own – coffee to stay awake, orthedrine pills to keep the speed up, whiskey to relax – a strong, stocky, energetic, witty, stimulating forty-year-old man, an indefatigable drinker, smoker, and good-timer. (Solal, 1988, p. 281)

It is beyond the scope of this preamble to trace any of Sartre's main works in his later period from 1950 to 1980, but some indication should be given of efforts which Sartre expended to further stabilise or make coherent the Existentialist themes first broached in *Being and Nothingness*. On the final pages of that text he raises several interlinked questions which have been thrown up by difficulties and seeming contradictions in his prior analysis of the ethical foundations of existential freedom; his final words are that he will devote 'a future work' to the answers to these questions. This future work, the *Notebooks for an Ethics*, reached enormous proportions, but Sartre became dissatisfied for various reasons and abandoned the manuscript. Until its first publication in 1983, three years after the author's death, many commentators on Sartre's work and Existentialist ethical theories assumed that it had not even been *written*, and found fault with Sartre for loose ends and false steps that he had himself already taken into account.

Sartre's novel *Nausea* had been accused of an anti-humanist sentiment, and by now the author had contended with dozens of scurrilous attacks and ill-informed misinterpretations. In October 1945 at the Salle de Centraux in Paris, Sartre delivered a public lecture called 'Existentialism is a Humanism'; it was *the* cultural event of the year – fistfights broke out with near riots on the streets, while reporters and radio crews relayed the news of this philosophical lightning strike. This lecture was perhaps the defining moment for Existentialism in the general public's awareness (see Solal, 1988, pp. 249–53). Heidegger's long response to the printed version of this lecture, invited by an intermediary, appeared in 1947 as the 'Letter on Humanism'. Among his many other replies to challenges, Sartre felt that he had to respond to Heidegger's 'On the Essence of Truth' which had just appeared in French translation. Sartre's extended essay 'Truth and Existence' was written in the over-heated, over-worked year of 1948, but wasn't released in print for another forty years. In his Introduction to the English translation of that text, Ronald Aronson succinctly captures the scope of Sartre's later work by relating it to some of the central issues of *Notebooks for an Ethics* and 'Truth and Existence'. Sartre's outpouring of books on many different fronts had several thematically connected goals.

> He sought to intervene politically on behalf of a radical conception of freedom; to work out the consequences for ... an ontology on which it was based; to connect his idea of freedom, and himself as its author, with history and society both as conceptions and as realities; to demand other intellectuals' political commitment; to explore the theme itself of commit-ment (and its evasion). It was a coherent, if complex project, unfolding on numerous fronts, characterized by its intellectual and political bite, its energy and ambition, its synthesizing power, and its extraordinary self-confidence. (Aronson, in Sartre, 1948, p. xi)

In October 1964 Sartre created yet another scandal when he refused to accept the Nobel Prize for literature, 'for personal and for objective reasons', as he said at the time. The personal reason he cited was that 'the writer must refuse to let himself be transformed by institutions', even if they are honorable; and the 'objective' reason was that he considered the Nobel Prize to be a bourgeois award reserved for Western bloc writers alone. Until his death in 1980 Sartre continued to run face to face with controversy, scandal and triumph; whether you loved him or hated him, no one could be indifferent to his life and work. His funeral was organised by a tight band of his close friends but it was attended by at least 50,000 people who lined the streets of Paris for one last look at their 'national treasure'. His funeral

> was modest and noble, sober and out of control. Sartre was going away, provoking by his departure one of the most unusual demonstrations of intellectual power in the late 20th century. The lonely little man, isolated, anarchist, the childless father entered that day the realm of legend. (Solal, 1988, p. 524)

PRINCIPAL WORKS

(1936) *The Transcendence of the Ego*, trans. Forrest Williams and Robert Kirkpatrick. New York: Noonday Press, 1962.

(1936) *Imagination, a Psychological Critique*, trans. Forrest Williams. Ann Arbor: University of Michigan Press, 1962.

(1938) *Nausea*, trans. Lloyd Alexander. New York: New Directions, 1949; trans. Robert Baldick. Harmondsworth: Penguin Books, 1965.

(1939) *The Emotions: Outline of a Theory*, trans. Bernard Frechtman. New York: Philosophical Library, 1948; *Sketch for a Theory of the Emotions*, trans. Philip Mairet. London: Methuen, 1962.

(1940) *The Imaginary*, trans. by Bernard Frechtman as *The Psychology of the Imagination*. New York: Philosophical Library, 1948.

(1943) *Being and Nothingness*, trans. Hazel E. Barnes. New York: Philosophical Library, 1956.

(1946) *Existentialism is a Humanism*, trans. Bernard Frechtman. New York: Philosophical Library, 1947, 1957; trans. by Philip Mairet as *Existentialism and Humanism*. London: Methuen, 1957.

(1948) *Notebooks for an Ethics*, trans. David Pellauer. Chicago: University of Chicago Press, 1992.

(1948) *What is Literature?*, trans. Bernard Frechtman. New York: Philosophical Library, 1949, 1965.

(1948) *Truth and Existence*, trans. Adrian van den Hoven. Chicago: University of Chicago Press, 1992.

(1964) *The Words*, trans. Irene Clephane. Harmondsworth: Penguin Books, 1964.

RECOMMENDED READING

Aronson, Ronald (1980) *Jean-Paul Sartre: Philosophy in the World*. London: New Left Books.

Aronson, Ronald (1987) *Sartre's Second Critique*. Chicago: University of Chicago Press.

Barnes, Hazel E. (1973) *Sartre*. New York: J. B. Lippincott.

Busch, Thomas W. (1990) *The Power of Consciousness and the Force of Circumstances in Sartre's Philosophy*. Bloomington: Indiana State University Press.

Catalano, J. (1974) *A Commentary on Sartre's 'Being and Nothingness'*. New York: Harper & Row.

Caws, Peter (1979) *Sartre*, Arguments of the Philosophers Series. London: Routledge & Kegan Paul.

Cohen-Solal, Annie (1988) *Sartre: A Life*, trans. anon. London: Heinemann.

Dilman, Ilham (1993) *Existentialist Critiques of Cartesianism*. London: Macmillan.

Fell, Joseph (1979) *Heidegger and Sartre: An Essay on Being and Place*. New York: Columbia University Press.

Flynn, Thomas (1994) 'Philosophy of Existence 2: Sartre', in Richard Kearney (ed.), *Twentieth-Century Continental Philosophy*. London and New York: Routledge.

Grene, Marjorie (1973) *Sartre*. New York: New Viewpoints.

Howells, Christina (1988) *Sartre: The Necessity of Freedom*. Cambridge: Cambridge University Press.

Howells, Christina (ed.) (1992) *Cambridge Companion to Sartre*. Cambridge: Cambridge University Press.

LaCapra, Dominic (1979) *A Preface to Sartre*. London: Methuen.

Levi, Oscar (ed.) (1992) *Twentieth Century French Writers*. London: St Martin's Press, pp. 582–95.

Murdoch, Iris (1998) Essay on 'Sartre', in *Existentialists and Mystics*, intro. by George Steiner. Harmondsworth: Penguin Books.

Schroeder, William (1984) *Sartre and His Predecessors*. London: Routledge & Kegan Paul.

Silverman, Hugh and Elliston, Fred (eds) (1980) *Jean-Paul Sartre: Contemporary Approaches*. Pittsburgh: Duquesne University Press.

Wilcocks, R. (ed.) (1988) *Critical Essays on Jean-Paul Sartre*. Boston: G. K. Hall.

'A NEW, AUTHENTIC WAY OF BEING ONESELF' (1948)[*]

Jean-Paul Sartre

A new, '*authentic*,' way of being oneself and for oneself, which transcends the dialectic of sincerity and bad faith. This way of being has four terms this time: reflected (reflection/reflecting), reflective (reflected/reflecting).

A thematic grasping of freedom, of gratuity, of unjustifiability.

A new relation of man to his project: he is both inside and outside.

I am going to examine these three characteristics in succession. We shall see that they entail a modification of my project.

1) Concerning the new way that man has of existing his existence. In truth, the answer can already be found underlying the dialectic of bad faith.[1] Since sincerity and bad faith were set side-by-side in order to examine being and nonbeing, it goes without saying that authenticity lies in unveiling being through the mode of nonbeing. If it is false that I am courageous and false that I am not so, we have to make our concepts more subtle to the point that I can grasp myself in terms of my original tension: I *am not* courageous since I project being so; in other words, since my project gets carried out as a kind of negativity in relation to a sort of original cowardice. But neither am I a coward

---

* From *Notebooks for an Ethics*, trans. David Pellauer. Chicago: University of Chicago Press, 1992.

for this quality would imply some thesis about being. Rather it is a question of a sort of original dispersion, a kind of waxlike flexibility depending on circumstances, a docile imitation of others, in such a way as to prolong almost hypothetically those forms of behavior sketched out by the situation: these skis start off, I follow behind, etc. In this sense, courage is a substituting of a spirit of experimentation for a spirit of observation. Courage is leaning forward and going along with his skis, cowardice is the form of behavior appropriate to the spirit of observation. So it is false to see some given quality here, since it has to be continually modified. In this sense, *no one* is courageous, but it is equally false to see here the product of some contingency: Koestler showing the torture victim who keeps silent because the water makes him choke just at the moment he was going to talk.[2] This contingency can aid him only given the project of being courageous. Except that the project *of being* courageous is itself formal and abstract since it does not take into consideration any particular circumstances. What is more, it is itself a kind of mystification since the *quality* of being courageous can be conferred upon one only by others in light of certain forms of behavior; in the end, it is a project of bad faith since one acts in this way in order to confer on oneself the being or quality of an in-itself-for-itself. In a word, it is a matter of acting in such and such a way, in circumstances that cannot be defined in advance, so that Others will hang an *objective* label on you that you will then internalize in the form of an element of your psyche or as an in-itself-for-itself.

Therefore there is an original form of alienation in the effort to be courageous, just as in the 'sincere' confession 'I am not courageous.' In reality I fled, in certain circumstances, I did not talk despite the torture, but in fleeing it seemed to me that, in other almost similar circumstances, I would not have fled and that those who were able to keep silent say that in slightly different circumstances they would have talked.

In other words, in authenticity, not only do I reduce the internalized objective quality to a sequence of behavior, I also discover that I *am not* any one of these behaviors, or rather that I am and am not. Lord Jim does not recognize himself in his act and yet he limits himself by this very act.[3] It would be absurd to limit him to this act, yet he is nothing other than this act of flight at the moment when he flees. What we call sincerity consists in taking up this act and in judging it as an other would judge it: I am a coward. But in fact this sincerity is a kind of lying for it surpasses the true which is the pure and simple assumption of one's act. I must, if I take flight, assume my flight and also at the same time accept that characteristic of 'cowardliness' that comes to me from the other, almost like a destiny. This cowardliness is a situation that besieges me. However there is also a bad faith resignation, and, fundamentally, a search for an excuse to put behind my act as though it were a quality.

Authenticity therefore leads to renouncing every project of being courageous (cowardly), noble (vile), etc. Because they are not realizable and because they all lead in any case to alienation. Authenticity reveals that the only meaningful project is that of *doing* (not that of being) and that the project to do something cannot itself be universal without falling into what is abstract (for example, the project to *do good*, always to tell the truth, etc., etc.). The one meaningful project is that of acting on a concrete situation and modifying it in some way. This project implies secondary forms of behavior: it may imply not fleeing, or cutting one's wrists and not talking. Yet if the goal sought is *to be* courageous, the apparent and concrete end becomes a pretext for mystification.

In reality, what is necessary has *to be done*. Hence one has to choose, from two equally efficacious ways, the easiest one, the one that allows you to conserve your strength. If one does choose the more difficult path, it is because, in a roundabout way, he wants to be. So, originally, authenticity consists in refusing any quest for being, because I am always *nothing*.

The same thing applies to feelings and to beliefs. Elsewhere I have noted that I *believe* means both: I am persuaded of it – and – I simply believe it. I believe in Pierre's friendship. This means, at the same time, that 'I would rather be cut to pieces than to think that he is not my friend' and that 'I am not certain of his friendship.' Hence if I solemnly tell him, 'I believe in your friendship,' I immediately give rise to the counterposition in myself, 'I am not sure.' Here sincerity turns into bad faith because it is going to neglect that quiet voice that says: 'I really only believe it,' just as the physicist neglects what comes after the decimal point, because I like Pierre and I want him to confer my belief on me in return as a Being. I want to become in his eyes (to reassure him if he is upset, to regain his friendship if he is disloyal) the-one-who-believes-in-his-friendship.

Yet authenticity would be to maintain the tension by positing that to believe is to believe that one believes and that this is only belief, it is also not to believe. Then faith becomes an act of willing and acting at the same time that it is aware of its limits. Believing becomes choosing to believe and knowing that this believing is limited, that is, that Pierre's friendship is a matter of probability. With this, *believing* it ceases to be a right (you misled me, me who *believed* in your friendship) and becomes an undertaking.

As in every other instance, this undertaking presupposes *time*, that is, it clearly surpasses my obvious current possibilities, therefore I put off until that time when my life will be over the final decision on this point. In other words, I know that to believe is also not to believe; what is more, I do not know whether I believe in the limited sense that I have just defined, yet I do want to believe. Better yet – authenticity would be complete – I do not want to believe: I want to build this friendship in a movement of temporalization wherein each of my acts will model itself on one of Pierre's acts and vice versa, where an intuitive certitude will correspond to each particular time of this undertaking. This is not nominalism. It is not at all a question of reducing our friendship to a succession of instants, but rather of considering its unifying theme as an intentional choice *to do something* (to make a friendship) and, from this perspective, to allow each moment its concrete development.

The same thing applies to feelings. Thus we see the psyche dissolve: it will remain, on the one hand, the transparent world of *Erlebnisse* and, on the other, the set of information (to be taken up) about the nature of my being-for-others. Thus, even while taking up my cowardice as my destiny in the world, I merely would like to be the one who realizes this particular work. As regards feelings, as we have seen, they reduce to undertakings; hate and love are oaths. But because I grasp myself in freedom, they will always preserve a problematic aspect. Therefore the nature of any feeling changes absolutely. It is not some reality underlying my being, nor is it merely something *experienced*. Even to experience it is to call it into question. It is part of its nature to be called into question in that very consciousness that experiences it, to be affirmed within this interrogation.

It is not a question simply of having an experience at each instant like the woman who says, 'today I love you less than I did yesterday.' On the contrary, this type of examination presupposes that one believes in the being of the feeling, and to decide to experience it in each instant through some alleged sincerity is to decide to not love without reservation, it is to decide to decide at every instant whether one loves, which is already not to love, not to see that to love and to will to love are one and the same. Yet if on the other hand one is persuaded that to love and to will to love are one and the same, then along with this the feeling is problematic in its very nature. For if to will to love were the whole of this feeling, it would be a matter of a purely abstract decision, whereas if loving were everything, it would be an unnamed purely passive experience. But through this twofold characteristic of love there is a reciprocal contestation: to love is never just to love since it is also to will to love, and willing to love is never pure willing to love since it is to love in spite of oneself, to allow oneself to be overcome by one's love.

And since the feeling is upheld in its being by choice, the oath that structures it stops short of the future and has to be renewed. (Proust has well described the horror felt by those who while in love do not want to think that this love might end.) So in love itself, at its heart, there will be, if it is authentic, this being or not being, and thus a fundamental anxiety that this love might not be. And just as love is willed at the same time that it is felt, this anxiety too must be willed in authenticity as our only defense against the future. Not that our future freedom comes to us like a thief who will destroy everything, but rather that we shall be for this freedom whatever form the past will take, whose meaning it will decide upon. So we discover a new tension at the heart of our authenticity: that of being a living absolute that nothing can change during the time that we live and that of being irremediably and necessarily a future past about which a freedom that will be both new and yet me will decide.

Thus the past is a future state defenseless against the decrees of a freedom that slips into the heart of the absolute present. And authenticity must precisely lay claim to live this very situation: this will be love as *tension*. There will no longer be love/psyche but just this lived calling into question of self by self in an undertaking centered on the external. There still remain intentions as such taken as choices (whether original or not): *am* I at least this: a man who *wants* to resist torture to save his comrades, who *wants* to believe in Pierre's friendship, who *wants* to love Anny.[4]

But first of all wanting is not being. And precisely if I want being it is because I am not it. Therefore to *want* to be is both, in one way, to be (to will to the point of not talking, is not to talk) and, in another way, not to be (I will against the continual solicitations that risk making me a man who does talk). To want to be, to will to be is precisely to be in question in his being, to be clear what I am (in the mode of not being it) by means of what I am not (in the mode of having to be it). So authenticity would rather see the will as a calling into question at the heart of the existing being than as that rigid blade one would like to define it as being.

Moreover, an intention does not decipher itself when it occurs. Not that it is incapable of being translucent to reflection, but because it is abstract. Originally, the intention to realize a work is the scantiest kind. It lacks any common measure with the realized work (which presupposes a perpetual problem of means and a perpetual enriching by way of the world).

Finally, the original intention does not include the decision to *refuse* these or those means, to prefer failure to using those means, for the excellent reason that the historical context has not yet been given and does not include these means; nor does it include that difficult invention that will give rise to this or that difficulty, because the difficulty is not even there. Thus the total intention coincides absolutely with the total work and it is the total work that reveals the total intention. As a result, authenticity will grasp the intention as an open-ended project, a certain shifting relation to the world, in which only the scantiest and most abstract structures can stay unchanged.

This does not indicate, on the contrary, that the For-itself has to choose to define itself through the caprice of the instant (for the caprice of the instant is a caprice only in appearance; it gets its capricious form from a background of some constant choice), but only that the For-itself must itself describe itself in terms of perspective, and as a direction, and even more so by what it *does* than by what it wills. What allows it to be unveiled is the factory that it builds or the hospital that it founds, not its will to do the good or to take care of its neighbors. What will define its love is the concrete sacrifice that it makes today, not what it thinks or feels. Hence the authentic For-itself, refusing being and the Psyche, unveils itself to itself both in the immediacy of its perpetual calling into question (*Erlebnis*) and in the reflective description of its concrete undertaking, insofar as it unveils itself to this For-itself in the world. At this level its future is the future of this factory, this hospital, the future of its political program. The *Me* is an abusive intermediary: the *eidos* my work refers to, whose future prefigures my future, and the ipseity of calling things into question must take its place.

However, this shifting ensemble of perpetually calling things into question and of perpetually surpassing them can be revealed only to a reflection that *does not will* Being but rather existence, for reflection is not contemplative: it is either accessory or purifying reflection. In either case it is a project. What therefore can the project of a reflection that refuses to look for Being be? It can only be a question of a radical decision for autonomy. The whole system for recovering accessory reflection has appeared, in effect, as a noematic projection of the self as the Other and finally as a form of heteronomy. The decision of pure reflection is both negative and positive at the same time: as negative, it renounces the attempt at a synthetic unification of the self by the self, which leads necessarily to realizing this unification outside itself and to sacrificing lived consciousness to the noema; as positive, it understands that the unity of existence cannot be of the same type as that synthetic unification that crushes the reflected into the reflecting, but rather must be of a new type which is an *accord with oneself*.

If, indeed, the passage to reflection does not realize a unity of being of the For-itself and instead opens a new abyss within consciousness, it does realize another kind of unity: for through reflection existence appears to itself in the form of a theme and a question. It does not identify itself with itself, but it maintains itself since immediately the problem arises of knowing whether it will continue or stop (both in terms of its modalities – will I give up this project – and as a nonsubstantial absolute – suicide).

Reflection therefore is in no way contemplative, it is itself a project. It is a project issuing from a nonreflective project and a decision to suspend or to pursue this project. With this, the existent in effect renounces being as in-itself-for-itself, that is, as the cause of itself (given the hypothesis that the cause would come before the self, that is, that it will maintain itself *a priori*), yet it does maintain itself by itself *a posteriori* insofar as it has accepted calling itself into question as existing and has *replied* to this question by the decision to go on. But precisely to acquire this autonomy and this regaining of contingency, the existent must first accept and take up its mode of being, which is precisely the mode of diasporic being.[5] More exactly, the assumption of this mode of being is, radically, one with the regaining of the self on the basis of contingency.

In sum, the existent is a project, and reflection is the project of taking up this project. Naturally, it is in the mode of being and not being that the process unfolds, for reflection is and is not the reflected upon. But what really matters is that reflection is not contemplation. It is a form of willing. If the project is not recaptured contemplatively, at least it is recaptured *practically*. Reflection makes this project one's *own*, not through identification or appropriation but by consent and forming a covenant. In other words, conversion consists in renouncing the category of *appropriation*, which can govern only those relations of the For-itself with things, in order to introduce into the internal relation of the Person the relation of *solidarity*, which will subsequently be modified into solidarity with others. By refusing to possess the reflected, conversion unveils the unappropriable aspect of the reflected-upon *Erlebnis*. But at the same time it realizes a type of unity peculiar to the existent, which is an *ethical* unity brought about by calling things into question and a contractual agreement with oneself.

In other words, unity is never given, it is never an aspect of *being*. Unity is willed. Sincerity is excluded therefore because it bears on what I *am*. Authenticity has to do with what I will. Sincerity presents itself as contemplation and an announcement of what I am. Pure, authentic reflection is a willing of what I will. It is the refusal to define myself by what I am (Ego) but instead by what I will (that is, by my very undertaking, not insofar as it appears to others – objective – but insofar as it turns its subjective face toward me). Is this what differentiates engineers and other 'serious' types, who consider their undertaking directly with the eyes of others, that is, in terms of objectivity? That one ought *also* to take up the objectivity of the work is what we shall see later.

So the grasping of the authentic self is not based on being, it is a willing directed to a willing: it is a project that loses itself in order to save itself, that takes a reflective distance on itself as a quasi object in order *also* to be able to will itself in terms of quasi objectivity. And the will centered on the reflected upon will does not dwell upon this fact (which would be to cut it off and fix it as an *hexis*). As we have noted to the contrary, an intention properly surpasses itself and enriches itself through an act: reflective willing *wills* what is reflected upon. But it does not will it as accessory reflection does, which *does not* call into question the reflected-upon project. It calls the project into question before willing it. It examines this project in order to decide whether it may not destroy itself in becoming an object for itself. With this, we shall see below, it radically changes its relation to Being, for it does not originally grasp this relation as inspired by transcendent values (the spirit of seriousness) or by the Ego (alienation), but precisely it is present to itself as a free project upon which depend all values as well as the Ego. This is why it wills being without complicity inasmuch as it is a free, autonomous choice, for it is as such that it will also be able to challenge Being.

We must not, however, imagine reflection as operating on the reflected like seeing operates on what is seen. Reflection *does not see* what is reflected upon and does not will to see it. Yet since it issues from the reflected-upon, it is the reflected-upon itself that decomposes and sets itself at a distance from itself, and by this very fact modifies itself, since there it is, not just a *choice* of some maxim but a choice of itself inasmuch as it is a choice of A. (It can also be a rejection of itself, otherwise it would not be a choice, but we shall discuss below the reasons that may lead reflection to make a rejection.) Therefore it is not a matter of introducing some 'impartial spectator' that would once again alienate the project. It is the project as project that agrees to lose itself in order to appear as summoned before itself. It is a project that wills to exist as a calling into question of itself by itself. And with this it becomes for itself a totality. The project conscious *of* itself as project, that is, wanting itself, represents a whole that recaptures itself in the existential dimension of a *choice*.

I noted at the beginning that every project summoned to appear before reflection is changed because one would like to do it for the Me. Thus the Me appears as a bloody idol that feeds on all its projects. But this is because we were on the ground of accessory reflection. The Me being suppressed by pure reflection, the project stops being related to anything other than its goal. Therefore it preserves that immediacy that it has in the unreflected, because it itself mediates itself. In this immediacy I see that poor fellow who is thirsty, I give him water because water immediately appears as desirable for him. In accessory reflection, I give him water because my Me is one that does good. However in pure reflection the project of giving water is limited to discovering itself as itself in its ipseity, that is, the consciousness of water as desirable thematizes itself. In this sense, the water does not pass over to the inessential, rather the project of giving water calls itself into question before itself. The water remains the essential, but instead of being the immediately essential – that is, unveiling itself as desirable to a project that forgets itself – it remains the essential as the meaning and the qualification of my project.

In a word: the immediate is contingent, mediation by the Me leads to alienation; the mediation of the project by itself leaves its autonomy to the project and its essentialness to the sought-for goal. The For-itself always wills the end for itself, but it is conscious of itself as willing this end. There is a double dimension: 1st, the water is desirable (it continues to affirm the reflected by its initial, unaltered intention). 2d, The For-itself is through its project an unveiling of the water as desirable. Subjectivity appears as an unveiling act. Existential vertigo: the project appears to reflection in its absolute gratuity. But since reflection *wills* it, it is recaptured. Except it is recaptured as absolute and a totality without ceasing to be gratuitous.

It is this double simultaneous aspect of the human project, gratuitous at its core and consecrated by a reflective reprise, that makes it into *authentic existence*. The active discovery (unveiling/assumption, discovery/founding) of the pure field of existence has indeed initially to grasp its perfect *gratuity*. The contingency of its upsurge prevents us from reattaching it to some necessity, and the disappearance of the Me (the pure subject of rights because it is pure alienation. The Me is homogeneous with the He: Gide's unjustified astonishment at the native speaking about him in the third person.[6] Koestler and Uncle Arthur. A Right is the other's demand internalized into the Me) entails the disappearance of Right. Hence the For-itself appears in its absolute unjustifiability and its relationship to the universe is altered. It has no right, even mystical, that its project must succeed, it is *de trop* in relation to the social world and to the world in general, the universe can get along without it. Its success or absolute failure is within the order of probability. It can demand nothing of others nor of the world, not even respect for its freedom.

Yet at the same time it does not take refuge as the Stoic does in the *ta eph umin*, in pure, formal freedom. Its existence does try to define itself by definition as an *ouk eph umin*, since it is fixed on an undertaking that it has no right to demand the success of, nor any guarantee concerning it, and which makes it depend on the world as whole. Therefore it inserts itself into an undertaking that to succeed presupposes some favorable aspect or at least some constant aspect of the universe, which is not given absolutely. There is a consent to chance. The For-itself wagers, takes a risk, it assumes its possible loss in its very act.

But, at the same time, it is gratuitous, it is assumed gratuitousness. But assumed *by itself alone*. This reflective doubling assumes this gratuitousness. Through this reflexivity, I consent to be a man, that is, in order to commit myself to an adventure has that as much chance of finishing badly, I transform my contingency into a *Passion*.

As for my undertaking, I justify it for myself by the single fact that I call it into question. I grasp it in its contingency but also as an unsurpassable, insurmountable absolute, which draws its absolute character from its being willed as it wills itself.

Thus, I can as well say no one will ever bear witness for me and that I am my own witness. It is me, which nothing justifies, who justifies myself inwardly. Subjective absolute as justification, pure contingency viewed from the outside. I can never persuade Others of my objective necessity, and suddenly it will no longer have any place whatsoever; but, caught up in pure gratuitousness, my accord with myself confers subjective necessity on me.

Therefore we arrive at the type of intuition that will unveil authentic existence: an absolute contingency that has only itself to justify itself by assuming itself and that can assume itself only within itself without the project justified inwardly ever being able on this basis to justify itself to others in its subjectivity (we shall see that there can be a justification by others of my undertaking as an object if they take it up) and that justifies itself only by risking losing itself. But that all at once constitutes itself in a risk and in anxiety (who am I to justify myself) as *pure autonomy*. I have no right whatsoever to will what I will, and what I will confers no right upon me, yet I am justified in willing it because I will to will what I will.

Someone may object that reflection is not the final instance, that it implies a reflection upon this reflection, at least as a possibility. This is true, but this possibility, even though it always exists, takes nothing from reflection's aspect of being a final instance, for if all impure reflection can be challenged in its very being – because it can be the object of a pure reflection – pure reflection can be the object only of a pure reflection (for an accessory reflection cannot stem from a nonaccessory reflection – otherwise what would it be accessory to?). So (pure) reflection on (pure) reflection is just a doublet that adds nothing to the primitive phenomenon.

2) At this level the radical transformation of the reflected-upon project takes place. For reflection being an unveiling of freedom, the project is always to *will being*, but to will it not as upholding the For-itself, but as upheld by it. There is a conversion from the project to-be-for-itself-in-itself and appropriation or identification to a project of unveiling and creation.

To compare unveiling and the project of being *Causa Sui*. In the *Causa Sui* the for-itself as nihilation gives itself being, that is, transforms itself into an

In-itself-For-itself. What lies *behind* the *Causa Sui* (in the psychoanalytic sense) is the project of the For-itself that feels itself to be *Nothing* and wills to give itself *Being*. But Being can not come from Existence, that is excluded. In unveiling, on the contrary, Being and the For-itself are already given and Being as a whole is given to the For-itself as *world*. Yet certain regions of Being are given (implicitly) in a confused manner. What *there* is behind these trees, I do not know. Therefore I intend it through an empty intention that will seek it out in its indifference of exteriority, that is, in the state as close as possible to the pure In-itself. Thus the world is crisscrossed with regions of Being that do exist for me but merely in terms of their pure, abstract exteriority as In-itself.

If I unveil Being, this operation is like the symbol and the indication of two impossible operations: the first one would be the opposite of the *Causa Sui*: the In-itself giving itself the For-itself in order to recapture itself rather than lose itself. For this is the incurable deficiency of Being of the In-itself seen by the For-itself. If it does not regain itself, Being just has Being *for nothing*. The contingency that defines pure Being has its roots in the fact of being for Nothing and for No One. Even were it to be the necessary product of Being, we could say nothing other than it *Is*[7] and that, in being for nothing, its Being is fulfilled in Non-Being. All the categories of unveiling being that we know, in effect, disappear: the relation to self and to others, unifiability, coefficient of adversity, instrumentality, signifiability. Being is in no way more graspable *for the Other* than we are. Yet, on the other hand, not belonging to itself or being for itself, it escapes itself by dint of *being itself*; its existence is a lost generosity by dint of not being anyone. This is why Heidegger is correct to use Night as the symbol of pure Being.[8] All of Being is there but enmeshed in a total undifferentiatedness. So Being is at the same time *not being*, which is to say, being-in-order-to-be-lost-in-nothingness.

The For-itself, on the contrary, in nihilating itself regains itself; because it makes a dimension of Nothingness appear in itself, it can be For-itself. If we accept the *myth* of a *conatus* of Being toward its fulfillment – that is, for Being to be to itself – we will say that it wins the For-itself, even in losing its Being. Whence the opposite myth of the *Causa Sui*: it is not the For-itself that gives rise to Being, it is Being that, in wanting to recapture itself, loses its Being. Hence in a world where *there is* Being, its undifferentiated regions make an appeal to the For-itself. In the world, Being is an appeal.

Naturally, it is the For-itself that constitutes itself for itself as an appeal of Being. But this appeal is no less the expression of the structural relation of the For-itself to the In-itself. In a world *where there is* Being, some regions of Being are such that there is and there is not Being in these regions, so that *what there is* is always conditioned, surrounded, visited, supported by a *there is not* that tends to fall back into *Nothingness* (into that particular nothingness that is what pure Being opens upon). The For-itself as pure presence to itself of *Nothing* (Nothing so long as there is not consciousness *of* the transcendent One) does not justify itself and exists only inasmuch as it reveals itself to itself as consciousness *of* this or that. Hence the hidden, the undifferentiated, the distant *intended* by its pure, empty intention appears to it as its future as existing. It is the appeal of Being (that the For-itself should become more and more conscious of Being).

At the same time, the For-itself becomes conscious of itself as destined to bring it about *that there be* more and more Being, that is, as destined to *manifest* Being. From the fact that the For-itself exists only as unveiling Being and that Being cannot Be without some nothingness that it *is for*, the Existence of the For-itself gives Being a meaning, which is To-Be-in-order-to-manifest-itself.

If the For-itself really does will to lose itself, that is, not be tempted to recapture itself as Being, not consider itself as its own end in the form of the Me/ thing, then its task appears to it: through it Being is saved from Nothingness, Being manifests itself: the For-itself springs up so that Being may become Truth. In this way, the For-itself has a task of quasi creation since it extirpates from the shadows of undifferentiatedness what in essence always falls back into them. The For-itself is the pure clarity of Being. It saves Being, which, in effect, will never be For-itself but rather *for* an existent that is for-itself. In any case, recovery takes place, since the For-itself is for-itself in recovering Being. In other words, the relation: there is Being for a For-itself, is an absolute. The For-itself is not Being, Being is not the For-itself, but Being is for – the For-itself that is – for-itself.

This relation, if it is grasped in its purity following conversion, is neither appropriation nor identification. Being is other than the For-itself and unveils itself as irreducibly other. And the For-itself grasps itself in this unveiling as irreducibly *in exile* in relation to Being. This is a relation for which there are no terms but which is originally *ecstatic*. The For-itself loses itself as self in order to cooperate with what Being should be; it intends to be nothing other than that across which Being manifests itself; and at the same time, it is the foundation and has consciousness of being, either nonthetically or reflectively, in that by it Being comes into the world.

Hence freedom is founding; through it, the world exists; if it nihilates itself, Being is opened to Nothingness. And every possibility of freedom (technological, artistic, etc.) being *at the same time* an unveiling of Being, the For-itself reaches itself as the infinite possibility of infinitely manifesting Being. For it is not in passive contemplation that the For-itself makes the most being appear, but on the contrary through the multiple facets of action (Saint-Exupéry). Here *joy* comes from this curious reality: in creating (governing) the airplane one unveils an aspect of Being that was but was not (since it was for no one, it was in absolute undifferentiation).

To unveil is *to create what is*. These are the limits of Man: the God that he conceives would create what is not. But then it is impossible that he should be able to project his creation outside his subjectivity. Man in creating what is preserves all Being's transcendence, but at the same time he makes it *appear* upon the foundation of freedom. However the relation is not of Being to an absolute and universal consciousness that would be coextensive with it by the contemporaneous infinity of its points of view.

Here there is a tendency we must be careful about: the illusion of being everything. I am inclined, seeing the sea from the shore, to believe that I unveil the *whole* sea. I thereby cover over my anxiety about being just one point of view. I take what I pull from the shadows as a symbol of what remains there in the shadows and, denying my historicity, each time that I unveil *a* being, I pretend that it counts for the *whole* of being. But this is wrong. I unveil *a* being against the background of undifferentiation. And this unveiling does not keep it from falling back into the shadows. I have not assimilated this reef to some great universal consciousness in seeing it; I have manifested it for a historical, mortal, forgetful subjectivity. I move on, the reef will remain there.

So the world as universe has the derisory fate of manifesting itself *by way of* a particular consciousness and above all *to* a particular consciousness. All its 'there is'-ness hangs on my finitude. Therefore there is a perpetual temptation to consider this unveiling activity as a form of *vanity* because it is contingent, finite, ephemeral, and subjective. To which we must respond that, in the first place, the For-itself is led in this way to unveil for others, with others, in the service of others. We shall come back to this. But at this moment we are considering the For-itself in its solitude. We said that this regret at not being a universal consciousness is derisory. For precisely it is not the absence of a point of view that will make this unveiling absolute but the reflective reprise at the very heart of the subject. I said above: I have no right to will what I will, but I am justified in willing it because I will to will what I will. This is what has to be applied here. An absolute contingency has only itself to justify itself, but with this it confers absolute justification on itself within its contingency. So when by my reflective look I approve of myself for unveiling this being and I will myself in unveiling it, then because I do unveil this being I reach myself as an absolute and in attaining myself as absolute I confer on this unveiling here and now an absolute character.

So the rock or the sea is *from this point of view* for an Absolute; its being is justified by the single fact that I justify my own, it passes over to the absolute by my free acceptance of contingency and finitude, and joy comes from the fact that I reach myself in the depths of myself as ipseity assuming its finitude in the very moment when I confer its Being-for on Being, that is, its absolute Being. I shall say later how this creative assumption of Being and of myself must necessarily be fulfilled in a relation to Others.

The For-itself is God in that if it decides that Being has a meaning, Being will have a meaning *for the For-itself*. But since the For-itself is an absolute/subject, it is absolutely certain that Being will have a meaning. Principle: the absolute is subject because only (thetic or nonthetic) recovery prevents Being from opening itself to Nothingness. In other words, either Nothingness is *in* Being (existence – absolute/subject) or Being collapses into an external Nothingness (In-itself). Being nihilates itself in itself or outside itself. Consequence: the modes of existence of the absolute/subject are themselves absolutes because the absolute/subject is entirely in its modes. Conclusion: if the In-itself has a meaning for the Absolute/subject, this meaning, absolutely experienced, is absolute. Ethics, in liberating the For-itself from alienation (which makes it something *inessential*), renders its *absolute* existence to consciousness.

What prevents us from grasping the clarity of this argument is that God has not gone away. He is always in consciousnesses – it is God's point of view that one envisages when one thinks that our grasping of Being remains relative to our finitude. If God does not exist, we have to decide by ourselves on the meaning of Being.

But precisely because 'making there be Being' and 'giving a meaning to Being' are one and the same thing, it is not in contemplation that Being will be unveiled as having a meaning: it is in effort so that man has a meaning, that is, in action.

To act is to posit that the goal is realizable, that is, that it will be inscribed in the world. Therefore upheld by Being. To act is to posit that Being has a meaning: through the instrumentality of action, Being unveils itself as endowed with meaning. If action is successful, the meaning is inscribed. And fundamentally one acts *so that* Being has a meaning. This is the goal of every goal. To act and to succeed at one's act would be to prove both that Being has a meaning and that man has a meaning. To act and to fail is to prove that the meaning of Being is to make human life impossible. Here the poet intervenes.[9] So to make there be Being is to integrate the maximum of being in an attempt to make the meaning of human life appear. Action is revealing/unifying. But precisely because consciousness is from some point of view, because there is a necessity that it be a contingent point of view, Being has to be unveiled from *my* point of view. This indicates that I must renounce that perpetual tendency to slide back and forth between my point of view and the reality of universal eyeglasses, or rather the absence of any point of view.

That Arab who is passing along the road is half concealed from me by the iron bar of my balcony.[10] One will easily recognize in himself the tendency I am describing and which I say we have to divest ourselves of: to set aside the bars by thinking them gone and to attempt to see the Arab as he is: that is, to constitute an abstraction which, by the way, is not well founded since fundamentally it is to replace a point of view that is mine with one that is more *convenient* that I do not have. This is the purpose of classical art (I have shown elsewhere how sculpture falls into this illusion).[11]

Another type of abstraction (Barrès)[12] will be to perceive things in terms of values and to leave aside everything in one's perception that does not correspond to these values (dirtiness, disorder, ignoble objects, etc.). Culture appears here as a perpetual effort to redress perception on the basis of nobility. Which is necessarily to constitute a *lesser* perception. If cooking odors or worse float around a monument, this humiliated beauty is precisely the unveiled meaning of Being, and it would not be fitting to impoverish it. This unveiling has to occur through an assumption of oneself as a point of view, which implies an unveiling of the *totality of being*. There is no poor perception, there are only impoverished perceptions. This unveiling is the unveiling of the *concrete*, it occurs by staking a claim to itself as a point of view. This unveiling takes place in terms of the single purpose of unveiling the *maximum of being* by being oneself as much as possible (not as Me but in terms of ipseity). And since this unveiling is articulated in terms of that action that is creation, one sees that it occurs as *surpassing toward*. Contemplation limits its goal to this unveiling, it suppresses transcendence. But concrete unveiling takes place marginally in and through such surpassing. The creation of what is is variable, dependent even within this creation on what is not. y(unveiling) = f(of its)(creation).

If Saint-Exupéry sees the mountains from his airplane as he does, it is *first of all* because he is piloting the plane and these mountains appear to him as means and as danger in that surpassing them brings him toward his goal (to land in Morocco).[13] *Next*, he does not seek to substitute for these mountains as he sees them the mountains as they are (that is, as they are from a more familiar point of view, whether more convenient or deliberately chosen). Therefore he resolutely claims his point of view in his contingency as creator of what is. This is what the mountains *are*. Undoubtedly they are other things as well (for the shepherd, for the mountain climber, etc.), but these points of view cannot be rendered equivalent to one another in terms of some abstract logic.

In reality as lived, my action suddenly makes the being of the mountains unfold, like a flower that blossoms, and I want this being with the very movement that brings it about that I choose myself. In the same way, it undoubtedly makes sense that I struggle, in the name of my concrete project, against anxiety, dejection, laziness, despair, depersonalization, psychasthenia, etc. Yet I must not, for all that, refuse them as themselves unveiling. Being-in-the-world-with-others has as one of its consequences that each immanent determination is an absolute unveiling of the transcendent. Laziness just like depersonalization reveals useful information to me about man's condition in the world among men, and I have to take account of these unveilings when I organize (see below) the total unveiling of the world.

Ethical rationalism is correct to reject internal dispositions when they are pitfalls for action; it is wrong to consider them as moods, that is, as purely subjective agitations that procure only illusions about Being. Everything is *true*. An upset woman doubts her husband's love – because to the extent that love is doubtful, her husband *does not love her* in those moments when he most loves her, because to believe is to believe and not to believe, etc. Another person, dejected and despairing, feels crushed by the world. Because Being is *crushing* for the For-itself, even when the For-itself seems to succeed in its project; a person who cannot make up his mind no longer knows what it means to want something – because a human goal, however absolute it may be when it is willed, is absurd *before* and *after*.

So it makes sense both to will and not to will one's moods. To repress them is not to take account of them all the while giving them the most extreme importance. To assume them as an unveiling of Being and surpass them toward a concrete chosen goal. That upset woman who doubts her husband is authentic if she refuses to 'take account' of this doubt in the sense that doing so might lead to irretrievable acts or words and if, at the same time, she discovers in and through her mood an aspect of love that she will integrate into her total experience. Man, existent, 'revealed/revealing,' is a perpetual revelation.

And if one assumes the gratuity and the contingency of one's point of view, this comes down to assuming one's historicity. I am within 'the course of the world' and I contribute to its happening. I may practically do everything I can so that this war can be avoided, but if it does break out I *have to live it through*. I do not change my point of view concerning it, I persist in condemning it, perhaps I even decide in the midst of this war to carry on an antimilitaristic propaganda campaign; but, even so, I have to live it out as if it were me who had decided it should happen. I reject it and assume it exactly as in the case of my moods. It is an opportunity for unveiling the world. At the very moment that I condemn it, or repress it, I have to allow it its maximum unveiling of being. My refusal must not be a *flight*, I must not refuse to live it, to try not to take account of it, to repress its joys, its experiences. Rather, on the contrary, push them to the absolute. From this point of view, the man who has chosen to unveil things, considers everything that happens to him *as an opportunity*, in that what happens to him permits him to unveil even more (even the risk of death). And with this, assuming even his *date* in its contingency, he considers as *his own* the historical perspective in which he is placed. This is what I need now to make sense of.

Whatever I do, in effect, my historical presence calls into question the 'course of the world' and a refusal to call it into question is still a calling into question and an invented answer. My concrete situation is defined as a particular point of view on my historical situation. 'I-am-in' History and every one of my acts will provoke a modification of the course of the world or on the contrary will express this course. In this sense, everything I do from dawn to dusk (from my manner of washing myself to my way of reading or of looking at things) will be significant for a future historian, even if I should be lost in the mass of humanity and my memories preserved only by accident.

From this fact, my future outlines itself in terms of the society that surrounds me and reciprocally the future of this society is what makes it my future. I share the ignorance of my era and I struggle against its superstitions. But the most solidly established ones are precisely those I do not fight against. I may well struggle today against a half-dead Christianity, but not on the contrary against some sociological or biological assumption upon which I base my struggle. To want to reach the eternal by passing over this ignorance, these superstitions, these complicities, this social structure that makes me a member of one class or another, and these events that my inertia gambles on or that my action brings about, is to deny that consciousness has a point of view, to deny that contingency is an ontological necessity.

Ordinarily we are well aware of our biological contingency. We rebel, on the contrary, against our historical contingency. We are quite willing to be astonished that we have *just* five senses; we do not reflect enough on the fact that Pascal was unaware of Carnot's principle, Marxism, or psychoanalysis, and that he thought *with the means at hand*, and above all that *we* think with the means at hand. What we have here is the same abstraction as when we suppress the bars of the balcony in order to see the Arab better. We try to place ourselves within universality, that is, within the total absence of a point of view or within God's point of view.

And no doubt a universal does exist. But it itself is lived out historically: in principle and in terms of abstraction, all Mathematical possibilities are given at once and to infinity. In fact, in each era they pose concrete problems. We can not see how non-Euclidean mathematics could have been conceived in the 17th century. Hegel resolved the difficulty by placing himself at the end of History. But History not being finished, I can assume my contingency and make it the absolute that I defined above only by assuming it within History. And this is precisely what is called historizing oneself.[14x]

So I historize myself in laying claim to myself as the free consciousness of an epoch in a situation within that epoch, having its future in the future of this epoch, and being able to manifest *just* this epoch, not being able to surpass it except by assuming it, and knowing that even this surpassing of my epoch belongs to this epoch and contributes to its taking place. Hence my epoch is mine – in assuming it, I assume myself; I see no task for myself except *in* this epoch and in relation to it. This does not mean that I can have nothing to do with the great transcendent things that surpass it (a party, a political end, the conservation of an institution, of a culture), but it is a question of conserving or developing them *with the means at hand* and of assuring their passage from one epoch to another.

So, before manifesting my epoch to itself, before changing it into itself and for itself, I am nothing other than its pure mediation. Except this mediation being consciousness (of) self and assuming itself saves the epoch and makes it pass over to the absolute. This is what allows us to resolve the following antinomy: it is said that great men express their epoch and that they surpass it. The truth is: I can *express* my epoch only in surpassing it (to express is already to surpass the given – and furthermore expression is marginal. One expresses in a surpassing meant to change) but this surpassing is itself part of this epoch – through me my epoch surpasses itself and contains its own surpassing. For my epoch, being a detotalized totality of transcendences, is itself a transcendence.

It is because the individual genius has been seen as a kind of transcendence by considering his epoch as given and as immanence that it has been believed that they *surpassed* it. In reality, they do surpass a given, but wherever they surpass something they bring their epoch along with them like a banner. An epoch is neither finite nor infinite, it is indefinite, or, if one prefers, it is finite but not limited. Therefore, to will myself is to will *my* epoch. I cannot will to suppress War. The conditions for such a thing are not given and, moreover, the freedom of my descendants may bring it back again. But I can will to suppress *this* war. And I can will it in the name of the same principles that make pacifists want to suppress war in general. I can want *my time* to be one where a certain imminent war was avoided.

So [I] must in no way reject anything that happens (even if I have tried with all my might to avoid it), instead I have to claim it as my own and make it pass over to the absolute. Marx saw this well: a war is neither praiseworthy nor condemnable in itself, we have to see whether, in the historical circumstances, it serves the interests of the proletariat.

This means that there is no *a priori* principle of ethical universality in whose name we can judge any event of an epoch (which would be to introduce the judgment of the past or of the future), rather I am here so my epoch may judge itself through me in terms of its own principles and so that it may determine itself to exist according to them. For an epoch *is nothing if no one thinks about it*, it is at the heart of every thought that it attains itself. So it has a thousand absolute facets but is never the *unity* (detotalized totality) of these facets, even though in each of them it is unified. And each of them, as thinking and changing this epoch, is *outside of it* as what upholds it within the absolute – and when thought and unified as one epoch by another they are *within it*.

Each facet, therefore, will attain absolute authenticity if it realizes the tension of thinking its epoch as the absolute that attains itself can think it and itself think itself (the passage to the objective) in that epoch as others think it. Two distinct operations but ones that we must always have simultaneously present in our minds (we shall return to this, it is the problem of the passage from the act to the objective).

In sum, my epoch is me. I am that being immanent to it by which it transcends itself toward its salvation. I have to assume it as I assume myself and make it pass over to the absolute in attaining myself as absolute. In this way I manifest Being by way of my moods and my epoch in and through a project that saves and founds this epoch. It is in historizing myself that I assume myself as absolute (in taking up my gratuitousness for my own account) and it is in historizing myself that I manifest and unveil the concrete maximum of being (the being already revealed by my epoch and the revealing/revealed being of this epoch *on* Being).

3) Authenticity at this level is a double source of joy: through the transformation of gratuity into absolute freedom – through the contact with the being of the phenomenon.

α) Gratuitousness and joy. Consciousness is gratuitous because it is not its own foundation and because it is contingent (a point of view) by necessity. There is a contradiction in a consciousness without a point of view because the infinity of points of view exclude each other and cannot be all supported at once within one and the same consciousness. And if we admit that this consciousness grasps Being and not appearances, it is at least excluded from these appearances and realizes in turn a point of view. Hegel's self-conscious spirit may be able to integrate Stoicism but not the Stoic. Thus consciousness, if it stops deploring its underlying structure, will be able to attain its necessity within its gratuitousness. It is not necessary that it should exist, but it is necessary that this not be necessary; it is not necessary that it should have just this point of view, but it is necessary that it have some point of view and that this point of view not be necessary. So the consciousness of its gratuitousness will encompass any consciousness of the necessity of this gratuitousness.

Consciousness that is able to grasp the necessity of this gratuitousness can and must love this gratuitousness as an *a priori* condition of its existence and of the salvation of being. A consciousness without a point of view, not being able to be anything other than every realized possible-point-of-view, would therefore be *without possibles*. Being without possibles, it would be pure necessity and consequently without freedom. No action would be *possible* for it, since it would be consciousness of everything. Hence the contingency of consciousness thrown into the midst of Being is a condition of its freedom.

In a word, a consciousness is necessarily finite and free; free because it is finite. In its contingent finitude, therefore, consciousness is able to grasp the necessary condition of its freedom and its existence; it cannot refuse it without refusing itself. But since in assuming its contingency, consciousness, on the contrary, alleges its faith in this contingency and upholds it with its freedom, free consciousness that assumes itself attains – and produces by attaining – the point of view where freedom, contingency, and necessity intersect. My contingency is necessary to my freedom, but my freedom assumes my contingency. In a word, my freedom takes into itself and founds the necessary condition of its existence. My freedom gives the dimension of freedom to what was necessity, and contingency gives the dimension of necessity to what was undetermined freedom. I assume these eyes, these senses, this head, this body because through them I am free, I assume my liberating ignorance.

At the same time, this body and this ignorance and this perpetual risk of death *are for* my freedom. My freedom is their end. But, with this, my freedom also has a face: it is this outline of action in the universe, therefore this body, this ignorance, this risk. But at the same time my contingency existing for itself in the transparency of an absolute reflexive choice shifts to the absolute. Contingency is transformed into autonomy. I was contingent because I could not derive any necessity from myself. But, if, precisely, I were to derive from some necessity, I could not assume myself for I would be rigorously defined by this very necessity. My being would therefore be relative to this necessity (even if it were 'internal,' which in fact means nothing). However, precisely because I am gratuitous, I can assume myself, that is, not *found* this gratuity which will always remain what it is, but rather *to take it up* as mine. That is, consider myself perpetually for myself *as an accident*.

Children do this more or less spontaneously when, for example, they suddenly rejoice in thinking: what good luck I have to be French, to be a boy, to belong to this family. However this assumption remains caught up in inauthenticity, because it is subsequent to *a posteriori* motives: the family is prosperous, united, indulgent, France had won the war of '14–'18, etc.

For it is the very contingency of our appearing in the world that we have to consider as an accident. Bataille says: the craziest of accidents.[15] But it is inauthentic as well because this *is not* an *a priori* and so to speak mathematical accident. An accident for whom? Stemming from what? Rather it is *a posteriori* through my assuming it, and my coming back from my free project to my contingency alone is what makes possible my having to consider my contingency as an accident. An accident because my project illuminates it and gives it value as what has allowed this project. We have to love having been able not to be; being *de trop*, etc. Only in this way can the *new* come into the world. Better: only in this way can there be a world.

So what Pascal calls the misery and greatness of man appears as more closely bound together than the Christian may think and in an opposite sense as well.[16] For Pascal, greatness is given first, which is participation in God or the point of view without a point of view. Then comes the fall which is a fall into a body and the contingent limitation of having a point of view, and this fall is historization (sin). As for the greatness of man, it stems from the fact that he still possesses within himself traces of his participation in the divine omniscience and because it has been promised that he can return to it.

For the authentic man, on the contrary, man's greatness (I am using Pascal's terms but giving them a purely subjective sense. Man is neither great nor miserable since he is not so for any witness. Yet within the concrete whole that makes up a society and in relation to certain norms, *a* man is great or miserable) derives necessarily from his misery or contingency. Because he is a point of view, finitude, contingency, ignorance, he makes there be a world, that is, he can take on all at once the responsibility for himself and for the universe. And the universal itself or essence, as I have shown (B & N)[17] can appear only by starting from the limitation of some point of view. The universal or the possibility of perpetually surpassing my finitude.

Thus the authentic man perpetually surpasses the temptation Bataille has described for us: *to be* everything. Within the world of alienation, the fact of *having* a me entails, in effect, the desire that this Me should be everything. However, the relation of the For-itself to everything is different if the Me falls away. Henceforth it is: to exist as someone for whom *there is* everything. Instead of there being a fall, there is a surpassing. And the relation to contingency is similarly inverted: in being taken up it becomes *gratuitousness*, that is, the perpetual outbreak of the free decision *that there is* a world.

β) This consciousness of gratuitousness (or of generosity as the original structure of authentic existence) is indissolubly linked to the consciousness of Being as a fixed explosion. The myth of God was tranquilizing. The whole world was *seen*. We have all, at first, defended this mythic tranquilizing, whose original necessity is obvious: someone took it upon himself to draw the world out of blind Being; so long as I look at this sea, I make it be that *there is* this sea. But subsequently there continues *to be* this sea, that is, its cold, obscure Being is reheated and upheld within the world by God's looking at it. So I have no more to do than to make there be a 'let there be' within a world that is already a 'there is.' My look looks within God's look, I never see anything more than the *already seen*. In this way, I am, on the one hand, tranquilized, but, on the other hand, I fall into the inessential. God's look falls on the flowers like that of the master in Mallarmé's *Toast funèbre*.[18] And the best I can do is to see a part of what God sees *for his glory*.

The presupposition of realism is that God exists and sees. But if God disappears, the *things seen* disappear along with him (I am not yet taking up what is seen by the Other). Being remains. However its tendency to persevere in its Being turns into a tendency to open itself to Nothingness. Being remains what it *is*, that is, compact cohesion, total adhesion to itself, absolute contingency. But at the same time, since it *no longer is for*, at the same time that it is, it is not. (The myth of Jupiter as the arranger of *chaos*. This chaos is Being without any *there is*.) In this way, man finds himself the heir of the mission of the dead God: to draw Being from its perpetual collapse into the absolute indistinctness of night. An infinite mission.

When Pascal writes: the eternal silence of these infinite spaces terrifies me, he speaks as an unbeliever, not as a believer.[19] For if God exists, there is no silence, there is a harmony of the spheres. But if God does not exist, then, yes, this silence is terrifying, for it is neither the nothingness of being nor Being illuminated by a look. It is the appeal of Being to man; and already Pascal takes himself to be a passion caught up *alone* into these spaces in order to integrate them into the world.

Consequently *to see* is to pull Being back from its collapsing. And as soon as it is revealed, Being springs into this unveiling with all the reaffirmation of its Being. Perception is the upsurge of Being, the fixed, dizzying explosion of Being into the 'there is,' and this is originally for the For-itself *enjoyment*. Indeed, it is in *its* perception that Being perpetually blossoms forth, it is to *its* look that this dizzying and unmoving setting up of the Whole takes place.

And no doubt the For-itself only grasps phenomena, but the being of these phenomena are entirely given to it (at the same time as this being is entirely transcendent). Its presence to Being unveils Being to the For-itself as a gift rigorously correlative with Being's generosity to it. Being is not in-itself and for-itself as in the Hegelian consciousness – it is in-itself and for the For-itself. This means that it is totally *itself*, without any parts, any facets, separated from me only by what Mallarmé calls the *lacuna*.[20]

However this lacuna is once again the For-itself. Being is separated from the For-itself only by the For-itself and the For-itself is itself its own separation from Being, and through the assumption of this separation it draws Being from the night and makes it *appear* within the Absolute. It accepts not being the In-itself so that the in-itself should appear in its total majesty. Thus its passion is enjoyment since by its renouncement of Being, Being is entirely *for it*, totally given within its perceptual field, making its absolute objectivity explode into the region of its subjectivity. The enjoyment here is to be Being by going to the farthest point of 'not being it.' That *is* – there is *nothing but* Being since outside of Being I am nothing but an absolute consent that Being be. That is and that is (in the mode of the 'there is') *through me*. I give way so that that *should be*, I am an exile so that Being which is *to be for*, so that the movement of this foliage should be saved, exists absolutely. From this moment on, making there be Being becomes the mission, the passion of the For-itself, it perpetually turns around in order to avoid the collapse of Being behind its back, it continually goes on, it is *called* everywhere, Being appears to it as to Ponge, as to Gide, a perpetual effort at expression that can only exist through its mediation.[21]

Gide, *Journal* [volume 1: 1889–1913], 299: 'Before the expectant beauty of crude nature, my liberated brain became more excited than before the work of art.'

Through me, Being exists for the absolute and this absolute is me. Through me permanence, eternity (atemporality), right fit, absolute immanence, purity (to be what one is) enter into the absolute and this absolute is me.

Here for the first time intervenes the true relation between things and the authentic man (which we shall rediscover in his relation to his work and to Others), which is neither identification nor appropriation: to lose oneself so that some reality may be. Mallarmé well understood this: to take part overlooked, unknown in the crowd, at some anonymous performance of his work. There is a *taste* for Being.

We also need to comprehend clearly what is meant by 'making it be that there be being.' This is not just to manifest pure Being, *it is to make pure Being* appear within a world, to *put it into relation*. I have already discussed this topic, I showed that the For-itself *adds* nothing, it limits itself to perceiving within the unity of a world that which by itself tends to fall back into to the exteriority of indifference.[22] So through the For-itself Being comes to the world. The For-itself *is Relatedness*.[23] There is a relation [only] because the For-itself is a relation to itself and relates to Being through its ontological structure.[24]

There are therefore two ways of losing myself: one is to want to grasp myself in the manner of realism (which is the ontology of the spirit of seriousness) as being aware of and thereby confirming this relation, which is given in the nature of things. Then consciousness becomes the inessential. What is more, it is nothing more than a passive luminosity. Inessential passivity relative to absolute Being, submitting to the relation without being it, the For-itself is no longer that by which Being comes to the world, since the world is given without it. Therefore it is unable to assume itself as absolute since the absolute lies outside it.

The other way of losing myself is to conceive of myself as creating the relation without myself being this relation (Kant).[25] In this case, the relation is not the

For-itself itself, it emanates from the For-itself and falls outside it. The For-itself remains a Being, one that produces relations. What it lacks is being a relation to itself within the absolute. No doubt it does constitute itself as a set of relations in unifying itself as the world, but then it appears to itself as an already constituted relation or nature (which is what I call the region of the Psyche) and as purely relative, not as being its own relation to itself and to the world.

At the same time, it is the world that becomes the inessential, since it is no longer anything more than the noematic correlate of a unifying operation. We lose the joy of unveiling *what is*. A joy that cannot subsist unless what *is* is in the absolute and unless its discovery is absolutely valid. Thus, in realism, consciousness loses all joy by becoming pure contemplative passivity, epiphenomenal – in idealism, it loses all joy because it and the world appear as pure relativity. The element common to both of them is that the relation affirmed by consciousness is given outside it (either by God, or by a transcendental activity that makes consciousness possible, but which is not it).

Led on by the notion of *relation* connoted by the idea of relativity, they have seen that without a doubt there are two terms relative to each other united by a relation at the heart of this relation – because this relation comes from the outside, but not that *the Relation* inasmuch as it springs forth from itself toward the world is necessarily an Absolute; that is, the For-itself itself. For the relation is precisely the unity of this duality, something that cannot come to the world except through a being that is for itself a duality in this unity (which presupposes an intimate negation of each term by the other, a repulsion in the attraction).

So the unveiling of Being is a contact of two absolutes where each one is centered on the other. Consciousness could not exist without Being and it is immediately a double relation: it makes itself into a relation to itself as itself being the not-being of *this* being and it is a relation of internal negation (as not-being-this-being) with Being. So it is through an internal negation *of* Being that consciousness wells up as absolute, and reciprocally Being is absolutely in the world because consciousness being the absolute as a relation, all relations set up are relations within the absolute. In this way, the world that appears to me is the source of my joy in that I discover myself as absolute in discovering it as absolute. It is a system of relations because I am the relation and these relations come absolutely to Being through my absolute upsurge.

However, at the same time that I add nothing and Being appears to me as it *is*, I discover myself as absolute in and through the unveiling of the absoluteness of Being. I have the *absolute existence* of being the authentic discovery of an absoluteness of Being: this absoluteness comes toward me from Being. And Being has an absolute *truth* because I am the absoluteness of the relation. Thus when the form of Being symbolizes pure Being apart from any relations (the sand, the sea, the night), I particularly grasp myself as drawing my absoluteness from it (at the limit we have realism). In the face of pure, eternal, undifferentiated Being, I grasp myself as a pure, almost inessential unveiling, subordinated to Being, and my consciousness is essential only to the extent that the inessential is essential to the essential. The pure joy of the passion and the gratuitousness and the radical placing into question of the For-itself in the face of Being.

And since Being is only Being and I am nothing other than not-being-Being, Being and Nothingness pass back and forth into one another and Absoluteness is Nothingness passing into Being or Being passing into Nothingness, pure temporalization as temporalization of the consciousness of the Eternal. Either the passage of the Eternal to the purely temporal (it is the Eternal grasped in terms of pure succession), or the passage of pure Time to the Eternal (temporalization is a pure successive grasping of the Eternal).

On the other hand, when the object through its variety necessitates a continuous deepening of relationships (a complex yet harmonious landscape), I grasp myself as that through which the relation comes to Being, without this relation thereby ceasing to be an absolute structure of worldly Being (since I am myself absolute), and without this relation ceasing to be a pure revelation of *what is* (since I add nothing to Being).

Thus Being becomes what it is through being placed absolutely in relation with what already was. And this placing into relation is not my whim or an activity analogous to that of Stoic causality which does not implicate the agent. This relation is *me*, it is my type of existence. I am not first and then subsequently placed in relation, rather I well up as a being placed in relation to Being. So this unveiling is neither subjective nor objective. It is an absolute upsurge of absolute Being into the absoluteness of subjectivity. I can never find this subjectivity if I look for it, for it is *nothing*. Everything I can see and touch is Being in its absolute transcendence – and I can nowhere grasp Being as it is since *there is* being *only* through being set into a relation, I am everywhere as a relation. And Being returns back to me what I am, for, since I am the Relation, the more the world is multiple the more the me who loses myself so that this multiplicity exists, I am rich.

Thereby we rediscover, although in terms of the humility of finitude, the ecstasis of divine Creation. The hitch in the idea of divine creation is that the *perfect* God, creating the best of all *possible* worlds and peopling it with imperfect creatures in his image, creates something *beneath himself*. Valéry saw this clearly: creation, taken in this sense (A creates B, B < A), has to be a *defect*.[26] And indeed this is how we do understand it psychologically when we reproach an artist for creating something beneath his ability (facility). At the same time, the antinomy of divine Creation is: if Being is given, there is no creation, and if it emanates from God, we shall never get beyond subjectivity. Instead man creates the World (an infinitely complex reality) above-himself or rather – since this notion of superiority makes little sense here – he *surpasses himself* through this creation and he is this very surpassing, he is nothing other than this absolute nihilating of himself so that the world may exist. He has the joy of being consciousness of being and, at the same time, of not being his creation. It is the fact that *Being already is* that confers its transcendence upon it, it is the fact that for man there is Being that makes the world a creation. As pure subjectivity creation would not lead to joy, nor would it do so as pure objectivity. This joy comes from finding oneself on the outside when one has lost oneself on the inside. The world is me in the dimension of the Not-me.

However negativity cannot be overcome and it is not a question here of dreaming about assimilating this Not-me as in Hegel or Fichte.[27] No digestion:[28] it is me but always in another dimension of Being, always *other than myself*. We thereby rediscover the characteristics of the work of Art since in this *too* there must be some 'matter to shape' that lends its Being (otherwise it would remain subjective and a dream); therefore the transcendent is *given* and, consequently, if the work appears outside of me once made, it is because I have worked on Being.

So originally man is generosity, his springing up is the creation of the world. He is not initially in order next to create (as God currently is represented), rather in his very being he is the world's creation. And when he assumes himself through reflection, he makes this very creation a required and an accepted absolute. Everything takes place as though he had said: 'I choose to lose myself so that the world can exist, I chose to be nothing more than the absolute meaning of Being, I choose to be *nothing* so that the world can be everything, and in this way, since I am the Relation and the Creation in my being, I choose to be what I am. I do not have to give myself the mission of bringing it about that there be Being – I am that mission. Simply stated, this mission can turn back on itself and give itself its being within the absolute – in this way it upholds itself by itself and the pure gratuitousness of its mission and its creation are transformed into absolute freedom.'

4) However, within the world there are men and other living beings. I do not wish to demonstrate yet how I can organize *my* creation in theirs and *give* it to them. We shall come back to this later. But before even considering them as revealing looks, I want to show them as revealed creatures. For one of the structures of *Mitsein* is to reveal the Other in the world. In the Hell of passions (described in B & N), this revelation of the other is conceived of as a pure surpassing.[29] And the other thereby grasped as transcended transcendence, as a fragile body in the universe is immediately disarmed. I surpass his ends with my own, therefore they are nothing other than givens, I transform his freedom into a given quality, I can do violence to him.

We shall see below how all this may be transformed through conversion. But what I want to note here is that within this hell there is already generosity and creation. For in springing up within the world I give other For-itselves a new dimension of being. Being is within the world. The existent is-in-the-world. But this being-in-the-world is a surpassed being-within-the-world. Except this surpassed being-within-the-world is *for me* only as being-in-the-world, I grasp my body as a taste of my *Erlebnisse*, I do not grasp my being laid siege to by objects except as a situation to surpass. Being alone can reveal to me that dimension of Being that is my surpassed Being, but Being is not consciousness, it is the pure indifference of Being, it crushes me with no consciousness of my fragility. Thus through the Other I am enriched in a new dimension of Being: through the Other I come to exist in the dimension of Being, through the Other I become an object.

And this is in no way a fall or a threat *in itself*.[30] This comes about only if the Other refuses to see a freedom in me *too*. But if, on the contrary, he makes me exist as an existing freedom as well as a *Being/object*, if he makes this autonomous moment exist and thematizes this contingency that I perpetually surpass, he enriches the world and me, he *gives a meaning* to my existence *in addition* to the subjective meaning I myself give it, he brings to light the *pathetic* aspect of the human condition, a pathos I cannot grasp myself, since I am perpetually the negation through my action of this pathos.

In other words, the other makes *there be* a within-the-worldness to being-in-the-world. He does not invent this 'within-the-worldness'; were I alone in the world, an avalanche of boulders could crush me (except that I would only grasp this avalanche as an *accident to be avoided*); he unveils it, he thematizes my fragility. If therefore I am conscious of this, a new category of the unveiling of being intervenes: in authenticity I choose to unveil the Other. I *too* am going to create men in the world.

Let us be careful to grasp just what this means. Note, first of all, that this cannot be (although we shall discuss this further below) except on the foundation of the recognition of the Other as absolute freedom. But how can one unveil the Other as freedom? One can no doubt – and this comes first – grasp the Other as a look. But this disquieting, undifferentiated, and intermittent freedom is not the freedom of *this* Other; it is the intuition of *another* freedom in general. In fact, freedom that is nothing other than the free project of some undertaking does not unveil itself *to itself* except in and through this undertaking. If therefore its structure implies that it is always *concrete* and defined by its goal, we do not grasp the freedom of others except through its goal. But there are different ways of grasping the goal: if I simply transcend it on the way toward my own goal, it becomes a *thing*. It is absurd and contingent. But the contemplation of the work of art allows us to grasp how I can apprehend the Other's goal: the work of art presents itself to me as an absolute end, a demand, a call. It addresses itself to my pure freedom and in this way reveals to me the pure freedom of the Other.

If therefore I grasp the work of the other (it doesn't really matter whether it is a work of art) as an absolute demand requiring my approbation and my agreement, I grasp the man in the process of making it as freedom. Naturally, this freedom in the Other *must* not deny itself (which is most often the case), but we do not have to deal here yet with the way in which we have to grasp the freedom of someone who denies his freedom. We will assume – since we are within the city of ends – that the Other has chosen a goal that confirms his freedom. In this case, therefore, we grasp the man in terms of his future (commencing with the perception 'it is like this') and this future appears to our own freedom as an unconditional end *for it*. On the basis of this organized grasping of an activity and an end that illuminates it (I look at the speaker, he belongs to my party, I approve of what he is saying), I come back to the man in the process of acting and I grasp him as *within the world*: which is to say that all at once on the basis of an absolute goal (an absolute relation to *subjectivity*), I suddenly discover the total contingency, the absolute fragility, the finitude, and the mortality of the one who is proposing this goal to himself. With this I unveil the being-within-the-world of the one who through his freedom is surpassing the world and demanding that I surpass it.

This finitude must not incite me to *contest* this goal since, 1st, this goal imposes itself *unconditionally* and as coming first (the personality of the artist must not incite me to contest the work. If Gide is *miserly*, this is not a reason for contesting the calls for generosity that his work may contain). It is the goal that defines the man, not the man who defines the goal. 2d, it is finitude (which I know through my own conversion and through everything that precedes it) that is a necessary condition for the inventing of an unconditional goal. In quite the opposite sense, therefore, I must unconditionally accept this finitude, this contingency, and this fragility.

Yet it is no less true that I *reveal* it. Here we are able to understand what *loving* signifies in its authentic sense. I love if I *create* the contingent finitude of the Other as being-within-the-world in assuming my own subjective finitude and in *willing* this subjective finitude, and if through the same movement that makes me assume my finitude/subject, I assume his finitude/object as being the necessary condition for the free goal that it projects and that it presents to me as an unconditional end. Through me *there is* a vulnerability of the Other, but I will this vulnerability since he surpasses it and it has to be there so that he can surpass it. Thus one will love the gauntness, the nervousness of this politician or that doctor, who pushes aside and overcomes this thin, nervous body and *forgets* it. For it is made to be forgotten by him (and for rediscovering itself transposed into his work) yet, on the contrary, to be thematized or objectified by me. This vulnerability, this finitude *is the body*. The body for others. To unveil the other in his being-within-the-world is to love him in his body.

What does this mean? By illuminating the world from my point of view, which is finite, I illuminate a related set of objects some of which stand in an internal relation to the Other whom I see, whereas the remainder are merely externally and indifferently related to him (owing to the fact that he is finite). These latter objects do not exist for him, since he is unaware of them, but from the very fact that he exists for me at the same time they do, I constitute a supplementary layer of existence for the For-itself: that of existing in relation to certain objects in terms of the *nur verweilen bei*, being-alongside-of, contiguity. And from this point of view, he is constituted for me in the mode of the *being* of *Being*, for, in effect, this road he turns his back to, or those scientific laws he is unaware of, are things he has a certain way of not being without thereby *having* not to be them. He *is* not, he is never just being when I consider him in himself, but he has a 'not being' that is precisely the not being of Being (when it reveals itself in the *there is*).

In this sense, he is determined in his being by the set of negative relations I establish between him and the world. Without me the unperceived, the un-modified would collapse into pure exteriority *for him*. The unperceived cannot determine his finitude, which would be pure *existence*, that is, freely assumed by him. His limits would be internal ones, in the sense that it would never be possible to say whether his finitude was something chosen or submitted to. But through my presence his finitude receives a *being*.

For example: to see a man *from the rear* is to see him in terms of what he does not see, it is to constitute him on the basis of what he is unaware of, to foresee what he cannot foresee, and to foresee him in terms of what he cannot foresee about himself. To see the rock that he does not see rolling toward him is precisely to unveil his being-within-the-world in terms of this rock as a permanent, given, and *received* possibility of no longer being there. It is to grasp this man as dependent in his being on the whole order of the universe.

This man whom I see, on the other hand, is not merely some pure relation of contiguity. In other words, if he has the not-being of the being of the *there is*, it is no longer so easy to grasp him in his *being*. For as soon as I try to know what this object *is* that is not the rock or the surrounding sands, his being escapes me. I grasp him at present in terms of his relation to the world he is illuminating: he fishes, swims, dances, hikes. And I am obliged to grasp him in terms of his undertaking, that is, in terms of what is not, in terms of that whose virtual existence exists as a virtuality only through him. Hence I find myself in the following odd situation. Each one of his gestures is a surpassing of his being and he never hands over his being to me except by way of this double malady of Being: his movement and his project. Yet at each moment I *catch a glimpse* of the *being* of this existent *underlying* its very existence, like a town shimmering in the rain. I catch sight of the perpetual relation of the soles of his feet to the ground, of his body to his weight, I catch sight of the *features of his look across* his physiognomy and his look, I grasp the spot on his shoulder.

Consider this dancer, at first she is the *dance*, yet the trembling of her breasts is not the dance, it is a kind of inertia. This runner *is sweating*. Beneath her project I catch sight of an order of life and beneath this order of life I catch a glimpse of the order of Being, without ever *reaching* it. In this way, then, I reveal a quite unusual type of object: the pink of these cheeks, the shine in these eyes, the curve of this nose which are part of the *there is* only by way of me. Yes, they do represent quite well the *being of* that woman as a taken for granted deter-mination. But I never see them except in relation to what she *makes of them*.

And in the end this only appears to me as a limit. A limit that the other cannot surpass but which I cannot really *grasp*. The being of this mouth or nose for me is that the other *could not have any other*, even though she surpasses them by the interplay of her physiognomy; that is, they are in relation to her temporality in the relation of the exteriority of indifference: within the perpetually changing unity of a man I see unchanging elements or ones that change independently (a cold. He is talking politics, telling about his projects, and his nose is running) or, if you will, in relation to the end projected by the man and grasped by me, there are structures of his being which are in a state of indifference. And these structures are not yet *pure Being* for they can be *lived* (illness, etc.: the typical example, cancer), but their relation to his project is one of *external* negation, which means that they are *something like pure being* in relation to his project and, consequently, to his body inasmuch as his body is *man*.

In this way we bring to light the one relation of pure Being to man in the *there is: destruction*. The relation for which man is the origin is surpassing his own being and Being in general insofar as his being is amidst Being. However with man's worlding pro-ject, a change in Being introduces a relation whose fundamental origin is man, but that, on the basis of the absolute Relation, stems from Being. The one relation that can come from Being is the introduction of a mass of exteriority of indifference into a project, which breaks apart its unity. This is what, according to human nomenclature, is called destruction. The basis of this destruction is the impenetrability of Being. The one relation possible between two impenetrable things is contiguity, and if two impenetrable things clash into each other, one of them has to disappear (in fact there are combinations of impenetrability, grasped on the human scale, that clash into each other). Therefore I grasp and unveil the destructibility of the Other by unveiling that beyond the relation of unveiling and surpassing, which is the human relation of man to things, there is a permanent relation of the exteriority of indifference of Being to man and even within man. But this relation has to unveil itself through the being for which and by which the relation exists. Therefore it is me who unveils/creates the *fragility* of the other.

So the finitude that comes from me to the other is that he is, in relation to what is not illuminated by his project, like the being that *is not* another being (he has the not-being of being), and his fragility is that in surpassing the being that he has to be, he does not surpass *all* the being he is. There is within him being in relation to which he stands in the exteriority of indifference – within the being he is as having to be it, *there is* being that he is without having to be it (he *is* dolichocephalic).

But, what is more, without for all that ceasing to affirm totally his fundamental project, my place in the world can reveal to me that by this or that secondary project that man is in the process of destroying this project and perhaps every possibility of a project. I affirm that comrade in the battle whom I see from afar crawl toward the enemy, I fight as he does, his project is mine. But I *see* that he is going to fall right into a trap. The origin of his behavior is his ignorance and I am similarly ignorant about what concerns me. But this ignorance, which *is* nothing when I am caught up in my action, I unveil in terms of the other. Result: I reveal his project as self-destructing. His goal: to get close to the enemy without getting killed is contested by the means he is using: crawling across this field which I know is mined. He will be killed before he gets anywhere near the enemy. It is not *chance* that will kill him but his own combination of means. In order to avoid the enemy's fire (and save his life) he is going right at that boulder, behind which, I know, there is a mine. So his act is constituted with a signification that he *gives it*, on the basis of one that I give it in terms of the world. And since the result – death – comes at the end of a long intelligible accumulation of ends and means: he *hits* the mine, he tries to conceal himself in order to get there safely, he is being careful in order to avoid the bullet that might only have wounded him, and thereby saved his life – the final end, his death, is given as the outcome of a *project*. And this project (which is an odd combination of human finality and the disposition of Being) comes down to the *true* future prepared in ignorance at every moment of the action, this project has the outward aspect of finality but within the externality of indifference, since it is the disposition of Being that articulates it. It is like an illusion of a project within the dimension of Being, a stonelike finality (likes those faces we think we see in the rocks).

We give it the name *fatum*, adversity, etc.: evil power. In fact it comes from the man himself. But in unveiling it (I alone can unveil it. He, if he should escape, will only see an *accident*, and his point of view is just as correct as mine, and just as incomplete), I consider it as a counterproject neutralizing the Other's project. With this, the Other's project becomes epiphenomenal, a recoil of transcendence having transcended and neutralized it, it hardly differs from the movement of a rolling stone except through a vain claim which will be that unhappy fellow's loss. This project thereby becomes *being* to the very extent that Being in-itself (the mine) reveals itself as a project. At the limit we have Laius and Oedipus: a negation of every project since any means will lead to the same result.

At this moment the project appears as determined in man by Being. The project is constituted in terms of Being. The bottom of the whole affair is that the man is indeed the artisan responsible for his death in acting *against* his ignorance. He can not do otherwise. From the inside, it is a risk, it is the very heart of his project and his freedom. From the outside, if his ignorance is not what it seems, it is *madness*. That is, every project is revealed to the Other in terms of its perpetual possibility of becoming a thing/project, provoking totally undetermined events in relation to the conscious undertaking, which lies, *at least*, in the externality of indifference in relation to its consequences.

Or, to put it differently, my act gets detached from my will and my choice. Cutting down this side street so as to avoid Z, I run into him. The explanation of this fact will not take account of my will. I ran into Z because I took this street and Z was out walking along it this morning (which I did not know). My act becomes purely blind behavior; it has become Being and my consciousness and will are like epiphenomena.

Our earlier example was a case of extremes. The Other was ignorant of what was happening as he ran to his end and I knew that he was unaware of what was happening. But all behavior involves risks, it always has an aspect of *thingness* for me, even when it is lived out with the greatest freedom (the acceptance of this risk).

So, beyond finitude and fragility, I unveil *ignorance*, that is, the aspect by which any project to surpass the universe is negated in its surpassing and falls back into absurd immanence, imitating blind instinct (a necessary structure of *every* project or the permanent possibility of failure). But this ignorance not being lived in the first place, it comes to the man through me. Contingency, finitude, fragility, ignorance are all ways of being its being that I unveil in the existent as such.

An existent is perpetually threatened by Being; his ambiguity comes from the fact that he *is* the being he has to be. If I surpass his fundamental project with my own, nothing more is required to oppress him. But if his fundamental project is an absolute and unconditioned demand on me, then, coming back to these characteristics, I grasp them in their concrete unveiling as indispensable conditions of this project. The other is pure surpassing *for himself*, the world is the surpassed; through me, as the witness who creates and witnesses the Other, there are surpassings of the world within the world; the world recaptures these surpassings in the form of the future that comes to it: *there is* a future of the world – and this future is the one by whose perspective I order my projects.

So in unveiling men, I unveil the future of Being. An absolute future which is not for all that the one I give it. What is more, originally Being has *futures* (a plurality). So the unveiling of others is the unveiling of the adventure of Being as objective temporalization. (Each concrete time is a temporalization that temporalizes itself. The *given* temporality is just the noematic unification of many temporalities. It is *no one's* temporality. It becomes *alienation* because *my* temporality becomes, *in* the given temporality, social and alienated by it; I perceive my own time on the basis of others' times. Belongs above.)

I am the one through whom the being of the existent is revealed. And since this *being* is the express condition for the surpassing that I affirm, I come back to this being in order to assume it. To the degree that I throw myself into the surpassing of Being by the Other, as *also* being my future, I initially find it somewhat difficult to come back to this Being of the Other which seems to me, at first glance, more like a contingent hindrance to the realization of the affirmed project.

For example, the Other's state of health, if it is unstable, has to appear to me initially as a coefficient of adversity. And it is precisely (except in the case in point) pure contingency for me, since it is a determination of revealed being about which I can do nothing. Hence the unveiling of the health of a doctor, a political leader, an artist who has undertaken a long-term work is immediately grasped as fragility and making a difference to the project. The stone in Cromwell's bladder appears to his partisans as an external condition imposed on a project which he affirms. The Puritan accepts with one and the same movement the project and the resistances in the world illuminated by his project. He accepts as a chosen adversity which *must be conquered* the resistance of the barely converted population, the political programs of other countries, etc. But he is not *at first* able to accept that adversity that seizes man from behind, which can be illuminated by no look but his own. Yet if he has made the conversion to authenticity and if he does not have the spirit of seriousness, he conceives that the value of his goal stems precisely from the fact that it is posited through the surpassing of *this* body and that it was just this body that was required so that freedom could consume it and surpass it toward a project that is both the assuming of *this* body and its negation.

Thus, through me, the project itself comes to have an outside; it is limited like a *being;* it is both the effort to suppress contingency in one region of the world (illumination, organization of this world) and caught up again by contingency, forsaken, lost. Exposed to a double failure: the one that comes to it *head on* from the world and the one that grabs it from *behind* through the fragility of the body.

And since I grasp it in terms of my own temporality, it appears as *a struggle against the clock.* Within my own temporality I make there be an objective signifying temporality of the Other and this temporality is pathetic because it is a struggle against *fragility.* In other words, there is an inside and an outside to this temporality. Its inside is the signifying calculation of time by the Other: he takes everything into account – the time that a law allows for itself to be accepted, the concomitant actions of foreign governments, etc. Yet this temporality also has an outside: the time, for example, that brings (within the perspective of my own temporality) the leprosy that sets the leprous king outside the battle.

But if I have comprehended what a man is and brought about my conversion, I do not just wish that my project should be realized, I wish that it be so by way of this man, that is, through contingency and fragility. My task *for me* therefore is, since I unveil the being of the project and of the existent, to take this being for an end and to surpass this being of the project by taking it up and surpassing it to the very extent that there is a being. So the being of the Other is *my affair.*

But, furthermore, if I want the project to be realized by a man, this is because I want it to be a victory over fragility. So I assume this fragility. It becomes *precious.* In the terms of classical ethics, I will say that it has a value. It is both the original tool and the necessary obstacle. And it is in terms of this double point of view that I value it. What is more, it is what makes the project something finite. Precisely to the extent that I have, in attaining myself through conversion, refused the abstract in order to will the concrete, that is, the maximum of being, I value it in that it makes this project a concrete and particular existence, much richer than any merely abstract dogma. This project that the authentic man of action pursues is never 'the good of humanity,' but rather in such and such particular circumstances, with such and such means, at such and such historical conjuncture, the liberation or the development of such and such concrete group.

And for *me* who is a witness of the Other, the maximum of concreteness is given by the fact that it is just this particular man, with just this past and just this body, who undertakes this liberation, with the knowledge that it is through the surpassing of this body alone that this project can be. So this body, this face, this finitude come to be for me, who grasps them in terms of this project, like the replica of this project in Being; I rediscover in them the project as finitude and fragility, as the pure possibility of failure, and as the inexhaustible infinitude of being, I grasp the infinity of freedom (which is its unpredictability) in the infinity of their being. The infinity of points of view that I can assume on this body, on this face are the symbol of the fact that the Other's freedom is always beyond what he is, or, to put it another way, my perpetual possibility of deepening this Being that allows itself to be glimpsed under this freedom symbolizes with [*sic*] the perpetual possibility of freedom to deepen the given and to surpass it.[31]

Freedom per se is not lovable for it is nothing more than negation and productivity. Nor is pure Being any more *lovable* in its total exteriority of indifference. But the Other's body is lovable insofar as it is freedom in the dimension of Being. And loving here signifies something wholly other than the desire to appropriate. It is first of all an unveiling/creator: here too, in pure generosity, I assume myself as losing myself so that the fragility and finitude of the Other exist absolutely as revealed within the world. Through me, the Other's *qualities* appear, which can only exist *for me* and through my own upsurge. For example, the other *becomes* witty if I exist. He cannot be witty for himself. To be witty is to reveal a certain new, unexpected, humorous aspect of the world, filled with insight. But the one who *reveals* this aspect grasps only the *aspect*, he makes fun of the world. It is the world that suddenly turns toward him with this humorous depth. If I intervene, he is the one who will reveal this aspect of the world to me; he will become *for me* the subjectivity who guided my apprehension of the world, etc. In this way I am conscious of being at the same time a creator and an unveiling of pure Being.

And as with regard to pure Being, I rejoice that the Other should become what he is through my passion. Yet I do not limit myself to conferring another dimension of being on him. I also make myself the guardian of his finitude. In my freedom his finitude finds safety: I am the one who watches his back and who deflects from his back the danger he cannot see (without my turning away from my own ends – otherwise we would have a sacrifice and negation of man in me). He exists for me in secret, hidden from himself, since he will never fully reach himself; yet I never want this existence except to protect its finitude and so that it may all the more surely surpass itself.

At the same time, I *marvel*, coming back from the goal to the fragile being, that this could have come from that and it is the project that I admire in its finitude. I am in on the secret of the secret weakness and contingency of the project that I approve, and I support this weakness against the world; I assume it, I take it up in approving of it; I do not stop defending it and deepening it; I reintegrate it into the human by surpassing it in turn toward the same end. Thanks to me, the exploitation of that instrument that is the Other's body is carried on even further. Indeed, through me this surpassing gets partly fixed in Being and I resurpass this fixed surpassing toward the same goal.

Here is an original structure of authentic love (we shall have to describe many other such structures): to unveil the Other's being-within-the-world, to take up this unveiling, and to set this Being within the absolute; to *rejoice* in it without appropriating it; to give it safety in terms of my freedom, and to surpass it only in the direction of the Other's ends.

5) However the unveiling of Being is, as I have said, a dependent structure. I unveil Being in and through my project of *creating* Being. For every project of an action is a project of creation. Through conversion we grasp ourselves and accept ourselves as unjustifiable. At the same time, we grasp the freedom in us and we establish a new relation of the For-itself to its project (outside/inside).

Indeed, reflection (whether accessory or nonaccessory) grasps man at the heart of his project and as a project. It grasps man *in action*. And action is originally *creation*. The three directions in which man manifests himself in his humanity: affirmation, action, creation, are really one. Man is/creator. Alienation conceals his character of being a creator from him. Which is easy to understand.

In a wholly superficial fashion we can distinguish the following types of action: the action of producing and distributing goods, political action, religious action, social action, ethical action, aesthetic action. In all these domains alienation has played itself out in such a way that most of the time the action appears as *inessential*. It is repetition, or a fully determined phenomenon, or the mere accomplishing of an already existing task, at least as required, or conservation. What is more, the action effaces itself in favor of its goal. If, indeed, the goal is given as *already given*, the action becomes totally inessential. It is demanded by the end. And if, for another thing, freedom is marked by determinism, the action is squeezed between an already given goal and a succession of being that constitutes it itself as a being. Finally, if one has defined creation as the production of being-in-itself, following the model of divine creation, it becomes clear that man does not create: he discovers or rediscovers.

Marx has written concerning the work of production: 'The worker puts his life into the object; then it no longer belongs to him but to the object. The greater this activity, the poorer the worker. What the product of his work is, he is not. The greater this product is, the smaller he is himself. The *externalization* of the worker in his product means not only that his work becomes an object, an *external* existence, but also that it exists *outside him* independently, alien, an autonomous power, opposed to him. The life he has given to the object confronts him as hostile and alien.'[32]

The product of repetition *already exists*. It is a matter of indefinitely reproducing it. And to the extent that the machine is interposed between the worker and the object, the work appears as some pure functioning of an already existing machine that need only be set in motion. On the other hand, machines, products, shifts, pay scales, etc. being *already arranged* when the worker is old enough to join the factory, the *work* appears as a concrete and essential reality, while each worker is inessential and replaceable. The work becomes a world (the 'world of work') with its laws and its own ways of doing things where the worker comes in as a purely inessential means.

The *reality* of work implies the nonreality of the worker; the reality of *production* implies the unreality of the producer. This is how the worker grasps himself and is grasped by other classes, as just contributing to *maintaining* this already existing dynamic form called work, where the object is mechanically produced like a physical effect by a physical agent. The action, moreover, being collective (work on an assembly line, for example), the worker never rediscovers his part in the creation of the object produced. It always seems to him that object is already given to him and that he is limited to finishing it, to polishing it up – which is easily likened to *returning it to its original status*. The object appears as having an essence that precedes its existence and the worker is limited on his part to making it conform just a bit more to this essence.

In this sense creation can hardly be distinguished from *repair* work. In both cases, an object conceived of as already existing is given as having to be made more in conformity with its essence. And it hardly matters then whether the essence might have been perfectly represented by *another* object fabricated earlier or by *this very object* at some earlier time. The object itself appears, moreover, as already represented by the requirement of some *need*. And since this need is give as natural (hunger, for example, as an expression of our *nature* as a species), the object itself (food production, for example) appears as natural.

For the worker there is a way of representing himself as a mediation between Nature and Nature. Those middle classes for whom work is essentially *repair* work have no sense of the creative value of their activity. They are intermediaries. And the product, being already finished, has only to be *distributed*.

It has been said (Burckhardt) that the Arabs (*The Thousand and One Nights*) have no sense of play, the Koran having pointed them toward the discovery of hidden treasures.[33] But it is not the Koran that is responsible. This is simply the mythical expression of a society of merchants. The merchant *finds* in some distant land an already manufactured object. The inhabitants of this land are unaware of the value that this product might have in another land. They let him have it for a song. If we carry the ignorance of the owner and the value of the object which he is unaware of to the extreme, we have the cave (the image of the home of this blind man) and its hidden treasure.

To bring back the manufactured object is then just a work of defense against its being worn out and against whatever dangers are involved. Space appears here as a homogeneous and neutral setting and, just as movement conceived of as the relocating of this object in this space is forgotten, so the work of the merchant is forgotten. He has created nothing; he merely transported something and relocation amounts to nothing. The most one might conceive of here is a magical theory of the natural place. The object will be in its 'right place,' there where it will be most appreciated (that is, bring the most money).[34]

The storekeeper today participates in the same myths. If he considers himself to be indispensable to society, it is insofar as he appears as a switching yard in the circulation of merchandise or, to put it differently, as the traffic cop who directs this circulation. He exchanges already manufactured products for already minted pieces of gold. He stands on the level of pure quantity, which is a *nothing* (a relation without any relations). As for his goal, it is just accumulation (getting rich). As for his relation to others, it is governed by destruction rather than by construction. He perpetually provides goods to be destroyed. Around this society are its *defenders*, whose primary role is to *preserve* it: the military who *destroy* in order to preserve; the medical doctor who returns to good form the woman who returns her home to good form, the government that *administers* things.

All these individuals as consumers carry out a destructive activity on given objects as already existing and as capable of being replaced at will (one goes to the merchant who keeps them *in stock*). A meal and pleasure are given as destructive activities. A holiday is a collective destruction of goods. They are replaced, without a doubt, but it is always *others* that replace them. The peasant, being close to life, is conscious of soliciting and protecting a natural development, whence the sexual myths of fertility. So production is not aware of itself, it is destruction and conservation that are conscious.

Mental activities are equally alienated. Religion is prayer, sacrifice, and giving (of existing objects); it is also contemplation, that is, passivity, which may extend as far as quietism; it is purification (that is, preservation, conservation, and destruction); it is a struggle against Evil, that is, once again destruction; and, finally, it proclaims that all Being comes from God. Man by himself and without grace is nothingness, only capable of error and wrongdoing. His freedom is to adhere to what is. The ethical life is ruled by the spirit of seriousness: values exist. There is an ethical order to be realized, but this order is already given; ethics is a form of Manicheanism: Good (God) already exists, but passions and failings conceal it. The ethical life is therefore a struggle against Evil that is constantly being reborn. The Good is the partial destruction of Evil. It suffices to *do* what one *sees* (*meliora video proboque, deteriora sequor*).[35] Here again man is a kind of mediation. He is just the go-between between Good and the world.

Then there is art. But precisely in a society of this kind, art grasps itself as a form of imitation. The picture imitates a model. Therefore it has an inessential existence in relation to created being. It merely sets forth what *is*. It is contemplative. And at this level of art we can make sense of Pascal's saying: 'Why pay attention to an object one is not concerned about in its reality?'[36]

Thus *creation* is strictly limited in everyday life to certain activities: the engineer, the artisan, the artist (despite the reservations given above). Furthermore, *theory* will limit practice. The engineer 'obeying Nature' does not have an ideology likely to make him realize his creative power. Liquid air *was already there* latently in nature. He awakens things rather than creating them. And an architect, at least so long as he does not impose his style, indefinitely recommences the existing model by repeating it. Society as a whole is suspicious about *creation*. For it quickly appears as an overturning and negation of what is. The new is not *requested*; needs are defined within the framework of the society that satisfies them. To refuse the Apocalypse and the will to remain *in equilibrium* within some institutional framework are one and the same thing. And analytical reason, considering the *new* as scandalous, undertakes (Bergson) to reduce it to what is old. Science *discovers* and reduces what it discovers to what has been already discovered. Every ideology (the homogeneity of space and time, the reducibility of phenomena, determinism) undertakes to destroy the very idea of creation. Current forms of psychology (behaviorism, psychoanalysis) have no way of explaining or describing inventiveness. They have even gotten rid of the idea. Bourgeois wisdom has invented *experience*, which allows it to control the new with the old. Cf. Gide and the lessons of History – *Journal*, p. 284.[37]

As a result, man's consciousness of himself is alienated, it is the consciousness of an existent who springs up in a world that is to be preserved, cleansed, contemplated. Action slides over the surface of things. At most it can come close to something that had not existed until that moment. It *combines* things, but the elements so joined together preserve their independence. Thanks to all this man justifies himself through the world. He is inessential and the world is essential. Man is essential only in that he is indispensable, in his very inessentialness, to the universe. He is its gardener. With this we have the Greek distinction between *praxis* and *poiesis*. A nonaccessory reflection will quickly demonstrate the fundamental identity of action and creation and, with this, manifest its freedom to the For-itself.

In alienated action one acts in order to be or one acts in order to have. In other words, doing something is a means and is wiped out at the end of the operation since it is *pure existence*. I act in order *to be* – I do this act in order to be courageous. Not, by the way, in order *to create* myself as courageous but rather to make manifest that I am so. Indeed, since the *quality* of being courageous comes to me through the Other and is *affirmed* by the Other and is conferred on me by the Other as retrospectively temporally permanent – 'Peter *is* courageous' – through the Other my act of courage is destined to confer on me in being the quality of being courageous. Then I internalize this quality and allow it to affect my 'me' which appears to me as *always-already-having-been-courageous*, and the act itself, on the one hand, is cut off from any concrete project, and, on the other hand, appears as the manifestation of an essence. Thus it loses all its novelty. It is just the consequence or manifestation of an essence. But, what is more, this way of taking the act removes every possibility for man to satisfy himself because he can never *play out* his courage, exist [as] his courage. Having been unveiled *by the Other*, this courage is an object of enjoyment only through the Other. For the For-itself, it is a purely formal and transcendent quality that will never *be given as his own to his consciousness*. So the state of someone who relates his acts to his Me is one of perpetual dissatisfaction.

When I act in order *to have*, there is not much difference. Here again the operation is inessential. The goal is appropriation, that is, the assimilation to Me of objects that will thereby become visible qualities. These objects are ready-made. They conform to a fixed essence within the tranquillity of the In-itself, but at the same time they are identified with Me; they are the Me in the dimension of Being, but, here again, there is dissatisfaction since consciousness will be consciousness *of* these objects and not consciousness/object. The In-itself-for-itself is lacking. Or rather one relates together the Me (which is a noema) and the object, but their relation falls outside of consciousness, it is magical and mysterious, it alienates consciousness. Consciousness looks for its Me among things without finding it there, it seeks to grasp the contribution of these things to its Me (the point of view of property) without being able to discover it there, and it is constantly referred from one term to the other.

The disappearance of the Me leads to the vanishing of the illusion that one can exist in oneself in repose. One grasps the pure field of existence as a finite movement of escape outward and one then sees that the movement of the For-itself is to announce what is through what is not yet and to modify the aspect of the world as a function of what is not. So whatever the For-itself may do, whatever action it may undertake, it produces modifications in the world in terms of a future that is *something other* than given Being.

But, what is more, these modifications must necessarily be grasped *from the point of view of the concrete or the maximum of being* as an appearance of a new *being*. If I pick up and transport an object from one room to another, the abstract and analytic point of view that overlooks the change will reduce this action to one of pure relocation, everything else remaining the same; that is, it will assimilate the *Umwelt* to a homogeneous and unvarying space and the moved object will appear as identical with itself. Action so conceived by a witness will therefore not be considered *productive*. But it is precisely because one began by totally denying *the concrete*; one set oneself outside the world, considered as the unity of the infinity of relations of Being, in order to consider abstract beings that have the variety and plurality of things in the world and the exteriority of indifference of Being *outside* of any relationship.

However if we return to the concrete world and the decision to unveil Being in terms of the concreteness of our point of view – that is, in terms of its maximum of being – it is self-evident that the organization of the human world is changed just as much by a mere relocating as by any rearrangement, as is well known to housewives who move a cabinet to different corners of a room in order to see 'where it fits best.' The idea that moving something is not productive holds only if we dehumanize the world (which will only have the result of producing in the realm of the imaginary another equally human world).

Still in a world provided with meanings and where every object is what it is in relation to everything else, moving something will be a *qualitative* change. In the hodological space that is our space, whether we wish it or not, an object's place is a *potentiality:* through its place it receives the force of the poles of this hodological space (an object from Swann's side is not the same if it is shifted over to the Guermantes')[38] and it will alter the human meaning of the objects around it. It will not stand out against the same background, therefore it will not have *the same nature;* it will not be lighted in the same way, etc.

We must presuppose a substantial and unchanging *quid* [something] *underlying* its appearance if we are to consider these modifications in potentiality as unstable accidents. But even if we do adopt this idea, these accidents at least will have an absolute being *as accidents.* Consider a cabinet totally unchanged in its *essence as a cabinet*, we still have to admit that the reflection of the carpet in its glass doors has a being as a reflection and that it is *new.* And it would serve no purpose to reduce this reflection to a set of physical phenomena, for it is true that physics has an absolute truth for the consciousness that unveils the world of science from a certain attitude, but this absolute world in no way changes that other absolute that is the world of perception and of *praxis.* And if one does abstract from the being of the reflection, one does so precisely by placing oneself in that inauthentic and serious point of view we condemned above (which classifies things as different kinds of being according to a system of *a priori* values and which overlooks some of them as a result of these values).

What is more, this being/reflection or any other 'accident' does not just appear fortuitously; on the contrary, it was precisely the object of some project. It was to obtain this red reflection, not yet existing, that one moved the cabinet to that place, this is what is drawn from Nothingness to Being, this is what was the end, the theme, and the unity of the action of moving it. The classic contestation of appropriation by appropriation (I liked this object before I acquired it, I don't like it any more) unveils the creation underlying acquisition: by acquiring the object, by bringing it home, I change it and I change its surroundings. The relations it has to its new setting are new. By claiming to possess what already is, I create what is not.

The illusion of possessive consciousness (which would change one into King Midas) is that it would like to assimilate Being without changing it, whereas it transforms everything it touches. A property owner, therefore, has an internal contradiction within himself: he creates in order to possess, but to possess is to possess what *is*, so he denies his creation in affirming his possessing. He has to blind himself to his creative power and not take into account the external changes he produces. Authentic consciousness, on the contrary, grasps itself in its deepest structure as creative. It makes there be a world in its very springing forth, it cannot see without unveiling, and, as we have seen, to unveil is to create what is.

The very structure of the most conservative project is creation – for to conserve is to prolong in existence an institution or an object in conditions that are not easily compatible with the project, the institution, or the object. Therefore it means giving a new meaning to the institution that one preserves, perpetually modifying it and perpetually reinventing it, so as to adapt it to the flow of the world, inventing ever new justifications for it against ever new attacks, etc. Even my body, in the contingency of its motoricity, is a creator or at least it throws us into creation since it perpetually modifies our relation to the world that we have to unveil.

Thus authenticity will unveil to us that we are condemned to create and that at the same time we have to be this creation to which we are condemned. The very structure of freedom imposes this upon us: if freedom is defined in an act as its aspect of being a *first beginning*, it goes without saying that the free act is creation since through it something *begins* which was not.

NOTES

1. Cf. *Being and Nothingness*, Part I, chap. 3. – Ed.
2. Arthur Koestler, *Arrival and Departure* (New York: Macmillan, 1948), p. 100. The French translation of this novel, *Croisade sans croix*, appeared in 1947 (Paris: Calmann-Lévy).
3. Joseph Conrad, *Lord Jim* (New York: Random House, 1931).
4. See Sartre's discussion of the affective aspects of the imaginary life in terms of 'my love for Annie or my indignation against Peter,' in *The Psychology of Imagination*, p. 202.
5. Cf. *Being and Nothingness*, pp. 136, 201.
6. In 'Youth,' a *feuilleton* first published in 1931 in the *Nouvelle Revue Française* and reprinted in *Autumn Leaves*, trans. Elsi Pell (New York: Philosophical Library, 1950), pp. 12–31, Gide recounts his encounter with a local laborer and exconvict, Mulot, during the period when Gide, as the major local land owner, was mayor of the commune of La Roque in Calvados. 'Of all the people in my commune, Mulot was the only one who did not speak to me in the third person' (p. 26).
7. Cf. *Being and Nothingness*, pp. lxv–lxvii.
8. Does Sartre mean Hegel's reference in the Preface to his *Phenomenology of Spirit* to the night 'in which, as the saying goes, all cows are black' (p. 9)?
9. In the first section of the *Notebooks* Sartre wrote concerning poetry as the love of failure. – Ed.
10. Sartre traveled in Algeria with Simone de Beauvoir during August 1948 (*Oeuvres romanesques*, p. lxvii).
11. Cf. 'N-Dimensional Sculpture,' in *The Writings of Jean-Paul Sartre*, volume 2: *Selected Prose*, ed. Michel Contat and Michel Ryblaka, trans. Richard McCleary (Evanston: Northwestern University Press, 1974), pp. 165–71. This essay first appeared in the catalog for a 1947 exhibition of sculptures by David Hare at the Maeght Gallery.
12. Maurice Barrès (1862–1923), an antirepublican and strongly nationalistic French writer, elected to the Académie Française in 1906. He was elected deputy from Nancy in 1889 and then from Paris (1906–23).
13. 'There is a peak ahead, still distant. The pilot will not reach it before another hour of flight in the night . . . ' Antoine de Saint-Exupéry, *Wind, Sand, and Stars*, trans. Lewis Galantière (New York: Reynal & Hitchcock, 1939), p. 33.
14. In their translation of *Being and Time*, Macquarrie and Robinson create the verb 'to historize' to translate Heidegger's use of the German verb *geschehen*, in order to

mark its kinship with the noun *Geschichte*, i.e., history as it actually happens, not as it is recounted by historians, which is *Historie*. Cf. ibid., pp. 30 n. 1 and 41 n. 1. Henri Corbin did the same for his 1937 French translation of Heidegger's 'What is Metaphysics,' reprinted in Martin Heidegger, *Questions I* (Paris: Gallimard, 1968). Cf. ibid., p. 18.

15. Georges Bataille's *Sur Nietzsche* (Paris: Gallimard, 1945), reprinted in volume 4 of his *Oeuvres Complètes* (Paris: Gallimard, 1973), is subtitled: 'Volonté de chance.' It includes an appendix entitled 'Réponse à Jean-Paul Sartre' (ibid., pp. 195–202) directed against Sartre's critique of *Inner Experience*. Cf. also Bataille, 'Un Nouveau Mystique,' pp. 146, 148, 155.

16. 'Man's greatness comes from knowing he is wretched' (Pascal, *Pensées*, p. 59).

17. 'But human reality can make being appear as an organized totality in the world only by surpassing being. All determination for Heidegger is surpassing since it supposes a withdrawal from a particular point of view' (*Being and Nothingness*, p. 17).

18. 'The Master, with his eyes profound bent low,/ appeased, as he went, the troubled marvel of eden / whose final shudder, in his voice only, wakens / for the Rose and the Lily the mystery of a name.' Stephane Mallarmé, *Toast funèbre*, in *Selected Poems*, trans. C. F. MacIntyre (Berkeley: University of California Press, 1971), p. 61.

19. 'The eternal silence of these infinite spaces fills me with dread' (Pascal, *Pensées*, p. 95).

20. 'They [the Mob] play the game without rules and for useless stakes; they force Our Lady and Patron Saint to reveal Her dehiscence, Her lacuna, Her misunderstanding of special dreams which contribute to the common measure of all things.' Mallarmé, 'Mystery in Literature,' in *Selected Prose*, p. 30.

21. Francis Ponge, (1899–1988), French poet. Cf. 'L'Homme et les choses,' in Jean-Paul Sartre, *Situations, I* (Paris: Gallimard, 1947), pp. 226–70.

22. Cf. *Being and Nothingness*, Part II, chap. 3. – Ed.

23. 'A Human Being is spirit. But what is spirit? Spirit is the self. But what is the self? The self is a relation that relates itself to itself or is the relation's relating itself to itself in the relation; the self is not the relation but is the relation's relating itself to itself.' Soren Kierkegaard, *The Sickness Unto Death: A Christian Psychological Exposition for Upbuilding and Awakening*, ed. and trans. Howard V. Hong and Edna H. Hong (Princeton: Princeton University Press, 1980), p. 13.

24. 'The "I" is the *content* of the connection and the connecting itself. Opposed to an other, the "I" is its own self, and at the same time it overarches this other which, for the "I," is equally only the "I" itself' (Hegel, *Phenomenology of Spirit*, p. 104, quoted by Hyppolite, *Genesis and Structure*, p. 158).

25. Cf. *Being and Nothingness*, pp. 216–18.

26. Paul Valéry (1871–1945), French poet, essayist, and critic.

27. Johann Gottlieb Fichte (1762–1814), German Idealist philosopher.

28. Jean-Paul Sartre, 'Intentionality: A Fundamental Idea of Husserl's Intentionality,' trans. Joseph P. Fell, *Journal of the British Society for Phenomenology* 1:2 (May 197): 4–5. Cf. *Being and Nothingness*, p. 187.

29. Sartre's examples in *Being and Nothingness* include indifference, desire, hate, sadism, and masochism. 'Thus the masochist ultimately treats the Other as an object and transcends him toward his own objectivity' (ibid., p. 379).

30. Cp. *Being and Nothingness*, p. 263: 'My original fall is the existence of the other.'

31. In the French text the editor suggests dropping the 'with' in this sentence.

32. Marx, 'Economic and Philosophic Manuscripts (1844),' in *Writings of the Young Marx on Philosophy and Society*, p. 290.

33. Jacob Burckhardt (1818–1897), art and cultural historian best known for his *The Civilization of the Renaissance in Italy* (1878). 'It is certain that the Mohammedan peoples would have preceded it in that path if, at the very beginning, the Koran had not protected Islamism by forbidding gaming, and if it had not directed the imagination of Muslims toward the *discovery of hidden treasures* (Burckhardt:

The Renaissance, Vol. II, pp. 193–4).' Quoted in *The Journals of André Gide*, volume 1, pp. 308–9, and again in volume 2: *1914–1927*, trans. Justin O'Brien (New York: Alfred A. Knopf, 1948), p. 375.

34. 'Right place' is in English in the French text.

35. 'I see the better and approve it, but I follow the worse.' Ovid, *Metamorphoses*, vii, 20.

36. 'How vain painting is, exciting admiration by its resemblance to things of which we do not admire the originals!' (Pascal, *Pensées*, p. 38).

37. 'Thinking over the weak arguments that Madeline opposes to Valéry, I have come to believe that nothing so confirmed Valéry's opinion as the comparative study he was led to make, for his speech welcoming Marshal Pétain into the Academy, of the contrasting strategy of Foch and Pétain the former relying precisely on the teaching of history, the other refusing to take account of earlier experience and judging, with superior wisdom, that it can be of no value in the face of necessarily new conditions. It is to that consideration of the past that we owe our most ruinous errors in the 'last war'; it was that clinging to the so-called lessons of history that made the machine-guns be set up to the rear, which monstrously sacrificed our infantry by hurling it forward in the conviction, 'based on experience,' that the dash of the first offensive belonged to the infantry alone, etc. The best lesson that Madeline might have gathered from history is just that the past cannot throw light on the future and that, in order to face up to new events, it is better to have a mind blind to tradition than dazzled by its false brilliance.' *The Journals of André Gide*, volume 3: *1928–1939*, trans. Justin O'Brien (New York: Alfred A. Knopf, 1949).

38. Sartre is referring to two major sections of Marcel Proust's *Remembrance of Things Past*, which in French are 'Du Côté de chez Swann' and 'Le Côté de Guermantes.' Cf. *Being and Nothingness*, p. 279.

INDEX

Main entries for authors are in **bold**.
There are no entries to the Principal Works or Suggested Readings.